P9-DTP-034

The Write Start with Readings

SENTENCES TO PARAGRAPHS

Second Edition

ANNOTATED INSTRUCTOR'S EDITION

Lawrence Checkett

St. Charles Community College

Gayle Feng-Checkett

St. Charles Community College

PEARSON

Longman

New York   San Francisco   Boston
London   Toronto   Sydney   Tokyo   Singapore   Madrid
Mexico City   Munich   Paris   Cape Town   Hong Kong   Montreal

To the best teachers
we've ever had . . . our parents.

Vice President and Editor-in-Chief: Joe Terry
Senior Acquisitions Editor: Steven Rigolosi
Senior Marketing Manager: Melanie Craig
Supplements Editor: Donna Campion
Media Supplements Editor: Nancy Garcia
Production Manager: Ellen MacElree
Project Coordination, Text Design, and Electronic Page Makeup: Nesbitt Graphics, Inc.
Cover Design Manager: Wendy Ann Fredericks
Cover Designer: Joe DePinho
Cover Photo: Copyright © Bob Challinor/Alamy
Photo Researcher: Photosearch, Inc.
Manufacturing Manager: Dennis J. Para
Printer and Binder: Quebecor World-Taunton
Cover Printer: Coral Graphic Services

For permission to use copyrighted material, grateful acknowledgment is made to the copyright holders on pp. 472–473, which are hereby made part of this copyright page.

Library of Congress Cataloging-in-Publication Data

Checkett, Lawrence
    The write start with readings : sentences to paragraphs / Lawrence Checkett, Gayle
Feng-Checkett.—2nd ed.
        p. cm
    Includes index.
    ISBN 0-321-10381-5 (student ed.)—ISBN 0-321-10380-7 (instructor's ed.)
    1. English language—Paragraphs. 2. English language—Sentences. 3. English
language—Rhetoric. 4. College readers. 5. Report writing. I. Feng-Checkett, Gayle. II.
Title.

PE1439.C48 2003
808'.0427—dc21

                                                            2003047417

Copyright © 2004 by Pearson Education, Inc.

All rights reserved. No part of this publication may be reproduced, stored in a retrieval system, or transmitted, in any form or by any means, electronic, mechanical, photocopying, recording, or otherwise, without the prior written permission of the publisher. Printed in the United States.

Please visit our Web site at http://www.ablongman.com/checkett

ISBN 0-321-10381-5 (Student Edition)
ISBN 0-321-10380-7 (Instructor's Edition)

1 2 3 4 5 6 7 8 9 10—WCT—06 05 04 03

DETAILED CONTENTS

Page 4

Page 4

PART 2

Writing Effective Paragraphs   127

Page 154

Page 171

Page 173

Page 228

Page 216

Readings   407

PREFACE

We are very pleased at how well the first edition of *The Write Start with Readings: Sentences to Paragraphs,* and its companion title, *The Write Start with Readings: Paragraphs to Essays,* have been received. Dozens of schools from across the country have adopted *The Write Start* as their developmental writing text. In this second edition we have made improvements, while retaining the basic strengths of the first edition. Developmental writing teachers who used the first edition were unanimously positive in their comments. They praised the text's organization, which combines grammar instruction and writing instruction from the start; the varied and focused practices and writing assignments, which allow students of various backgrounds, including English as a second language students, to write about topics of interest to them; The Writer's Resources, which provide additional grammar instruction and practice for those who need it; and the book's design, which is attractive, simple, and functional. Such praise from fellow developmental writing teachers is both gratifying and energizing. They have made our commitment to the teaching of writing even more steadfast and resolute. In this regard, we have taken the suggestions of our colleagues across the country and have added to and refined the contents and organization of the second edition of *The Write Start with Readings: Sentences to Paragraphs.*

What's New in the Second Edition

We have kept the first edition's basic approach and have added new features to make the text more flexible, clear, and useful.

▼ *New Editing Practice Exercises.* We have added a substantial number of editing practice exercises, in paragraph form, to Chapters 3–12. These give students the realistic experience of correcting grammatical errors embedded in paragraph-length prose.

▼ *New Topic Bank and Photo Exercises.* The old "Other Paragraph Topics" has been changed to "Topic Bank" and repositioned at the end of each chapter following the "Chapter Review." In addition, chapter opening photographs have been added to Chapters 13 through 22. The photograph at the beginning of each chapter is tied to a Topic Bank writing suggestion, and can serve as the topic of a student paragraph. This organization helps to unify the chapter's instruction and bring a sense of completeness to the chapter's content.

▼ *New Content.* An expanded discussion of the thesis sentence and introductory paragraph has been added to Chapter 22 to round out the instruction on the essay.

▼ *New Readings.* To better facilitate instruction and generate student interest, many readings have been replaced in the Additional Readings section. Also, student essays are now grouped with professional essays and clustered by mode of development for easier identification and understanding.

▼ *New Writer's Resources Exercises for Native and ESL Students.* In order to provide additional practice in grammar for native and nonnative students alike, additional exercises have been provided in each of the sections of The Writer's Resources.

▼ *New Practice Exercise Titles.* Practice exercises have been given titles to better clarify the focus of each exercise.

Overview

Unlike most texts for developing writers, *The Write Start* begins with sentence formation, moves to paragraph organization, and ends with one chapter on the full essay. While this is one suggestion for a course outline, the chapters are self-contained units allowing for flexibility of design depending on the instructor's own needs and that of the class. Within the text, references are made to other chapters and to The Writer's Resources section when appropriate.

Organization of the Text

To the Student: Chapters 1 and 2

This section introduces developing writers to the importance of writing well. It stresses the idea that writing is difficult but, like other life skills, it can be mastered with the proper attitude, information, and hard work.

Writing Effective Sentences: Chapters 3 to 12

This section helps developing writers understand the fundamentals of good sentence building and establishes the importance of sentence variety in writing. Ten different sentence types are each given their own chapter. Each chapter contains examples to illustrate instruction. Multiple practice sets allow for the transference of specific skill-building ideas into clear, concise, and complete sentences.

Writing Effective Paragraphs: Chapters 13 to 21

This section teaches developing writers how to organize and construct body paragraphs in a variety of rhetorical modes. The chapters incorporate both professional and student paragraph models, as well as technique questions that focus on the elements necessary for effective paragraphs. Specific detail and sentence variety are an integral part of each paragraph chapter.

Writing Effective Essays: Chapter 22

The final product of most writing programs—developmental programs included—is the essay. For instructors who wish to include the essay in their courses, Chapter 22 introduces developing writers to the process of constructing a clear, concise essay. Using the skills learned in preceding sections on sentence variety and paragraph development, the demands of the essay are taught: writing the introductory paragraph, organizing and developing support in the body paragraphs, and coming to a conclusion that is appropriate for the essay's approach.

The Writer's Resources

The Writer's Resources are more than a listing of tables on parts of speech. Rather, to keep the instructional chapters "clean" so that students remain focused on the specific topic under discussion, The Writer's Resources section is a veritable warehouse of information on parts of speech, usage, punctuation, mechanics, and spelling. Examples and exercises accompany the material for illustration, clarification, and additional practice. References to The Writer's Resources are made in the text chapters where appropriate. Material helpful to English as a Second Language students is included in The Writer's Resources and appears in a special section of the accompanying Instructor's Manual.

Additional Readings and Read All About It

An exciting feature of *The Write Start* is that most professional paragraph examples excerpted in the text can be found in full—with accompanying apparatus—in the Readings section. Instructors have the flexibility of showing their students the full context of specific paragraphs and how they are integrated into the whole essay. This feature is invaluable in showing student writers how developing specific subtopics works in developing the major topic. The essays were chosen to serve as models for the modes being taught in the text.

Answer Section

At the end of *The Write Start,* an answer key contains one half of the answers to the in-text Practice exercises. This approach allows for ultimate flexibility: Students can check half their answers to gauge their development, and instructors can use the remaining questions for homework or in-class work. (A complete answer key is included in the Annotated Instructor's Edition.)

Special Features of *The Write Start*

The features embedded in *The Write Start* make it an invaluable tool for both instructors and students.

▼ *Clarity and Simplicity.* Writing, mechanics, and grammar instruction are taught as quickly and simply as possible without losing core content, focusing on valuable insights and meaningful suggestions. Key terms and concepts are boldfaced and defined in each chapter as they are introduced, with ample examples for clarification. Key terms and definitions are repeated in the glossary.

▼ *Things You Need to Know.* In anticipation of instructors choosing to teach Chapters 3 to 12 in a different order than they appear in the book, prerequisites are mentioned at the beginning of certain chapters. These prerequisites, labeled "You Need to Know," direct instructors and students to specific information in preceding chapters that is necessary for a clearer understanding of the material under discussion. In other words, visiting the prerequisite material first will make the current chapter material easier to understand.

▼ *Student Writing. The Write Start* gives equal weight to professional and student writing. While professional writing models often are engaging and prove that good writers actually do use the techniques and processes taught in writing classes, developing writers sometimes view professional writing with suspicion. They simply don't believe that they will ever approach that level of expertise. *The Write Start* uses equal amounts of student-generated and professional writing to make an important point: that developing writers use the same rules, processes, and techniques as their professional counterparts.

▼ *End-of-Chapter Reviews.* The highlighted reviews help developing writers identify and remember key terms and concepts that are to be utilized in writing, revising, and editing.

▼ *English as a Second Language Instruction.* Material aimed at students for whom English is not the first language is embedded throughout the text, but it is not labeled as such. In other words, *The Write Start* uses current ESL research and pedagogy to reach all developing writers, while not singling out specific ESL "problems." In addition, The Writer's Resources includes specific lists, charts, and exercises for ESL-specific concerns, such as verb form/tense, phrasal verbs, irregular verbs, articles, and idiomatic prepositional phrases. Finally, The Writer's Resources section offers ESL icons to point out the basic material most needed by ESL students.

▼ *Vocabulary.* Most developmental writing textbooks have vocabulary lists following the readings. In *The Write Start,* each essay is prefaced by a list of challenging words found in the essay. Readers are asked to look up the definitions of these words prior to reading the essay so that they can focus more easily on the essay's content.

▼ *Ample Grammar and Writing Practice.* Brief segments of instruction are immediately followed by Practice exercises that reinforce the concepts taught. Topic Bank writing suggestions and Writing Opportunities based on photographs give students both verbal and visual subject matter for their paragraphs and essays.

▼ *Reading and Analyzing to Improve Writing Skill.* Throughout Parts 2, 3, and the Readings, students are given "real" paragraphs and essays to read. By answering the questions following each reading, students learn the techniques that other writers use to communicate effectively.

The Write Start Series

More and more two- and four-year colleges are identifying levels of developmental writing students and are instituting developmental writing course sequences. *The Write Start* is a two-book series whose aim is to answer this need. While the content of the two books is complementary for sequenced instruction, each book can be used effectively as a stand-alone text for different levels of instruction. The series is designed for students with a variety of skill levels and for students with a variety of challenges in learning Standard English. *The Write Start with Readings: Sentences to Paragraphs* focuses primarily on sentence variety and paragraph development, with essay writing as the concluding section. *The Write Start with Readings: Paragraphs to Essays* begins with a review of paragraph construction in the rhetorical modes and moves to the thorough development of longer essays in the rhetorical modes, followed by a review of sentence grammar and variety. Both books share the same features, pedagogy, and easy-to-read format.

The Teaching and Learning Package

Each component of the teaching and learning package has been crafted to ensure that the course is rewarding for both instructors and students.

The **Annotated Instructor's Edition** is a replica of the student text, but includes all answers printed directly on the fill-in lines provided in the text. 0-321-10380-7

The **Instructor's Manual with Transparency Masters** provides information on the following: *Using the Text, Syllabus Preparation, Answer Keys, Student and Professional Reading Selections, Thesis Sentences, Outlining, Proofreading Check-*

lists, Peer Editing, English as a Second Language/English as a Foreign Language (ESL/EFL), Diagnostic Pre-Test, and *Transparency Masters.* 0-321-10384-X

The **Test Bank** provides a wealth of printed quizzes and additional practice exercises for each chapter in the text. The test bank is formatted in a way that simplifies copying and distribution. 0-321-10383-1

In addition, an **Electronic Test Bank for Writing** is also available. This electronic test bank features more than 5,000 questions in all areas of writing, from grammar to paragraphing, through essay writing, research, and documentation. With this easy-to-use CD-ROM, instructors simply choose questions from the electronic test bank, then print out the completed test for distribution. 0-321-08117-X. Also available in printed format. 0-321-08486-1

For additional exercises, summaries, and interactive activities, be sure to visit our **Companion Website,** written by Jo Ann Yaworski, at **http://www .ablongman.com/checkett.** The *Write Start Online* provides a wealth of resources, including gradable quizzes, e-mail capabilities, and Web Resources. Stop by for a visit!

The Longman Developmental English Package

In addition to the book-specific supplements discussed above, many other skills-based supplements are available for both instructors and students. All of these supplements are available either free or at greatly reduced prices.

For Additional Reading and Reference

The Dictionary Deal. Two dictionaries can be shrinkwrapped with this text at a nominal fee. *The New American Webster Handy College Dictionary* is a paperback reference text with more than 100,000 entries. *Merriam Webster's Collegiate Dictionary,* tenth edition, is a hardback reference with a citation file of more than 14.5 million examples of English words drawn from actual use. For more information on how to shrinkwrap a dictionary with your text, please contact your Longman sales representative.

Penguin Academics: *Twenty-Five Great Essays, Fifty Great Essays,* **and** *One Hundred Great Essays,* **edited by Robert DiYanni.** These alphabetically organized essay collections are published as part of the "Penguin Academics" series of low-cost, high-quality offerings intended for use in introductory college courses. All essays were selected for their teachability, both as models for writing and for their usefulness as springboards for student writing. For more information on how to shrinkwrap one of these anthologies with your text, please contact your Longman sales consultant.

100 Things to Write About. This 100-page book contains 100 individual assignments for writing on a variety of topics and in a wide range of formats, from expressive to analytical writing. Ask your Longman sales representative for a sample copy. 0-673-98239-4

Newsweek **Alliance.** Instructors may choose to shrinkwrap a 12-week subscription to *Newsweek* with any Longman text. The price of the subscription is 59 cents per issue (a total of $7.08 for the subscription). Available with the subscription is a free "Interactive Guide to *Newsweek*"—a workbook for students who are using the text. In addition, *Newsweek* provides a wide variety of instructor supplements free to teachers, including maps, Skills Builders, and weekly quizzes. For more information on the *Newsweek* program, please contact your Longman sales representative.

Electronic and Online Offerings

[NEW] The Longman Writer's Warehouse. This innovative and exciting on-line supplement is the perfect accompaniment to any developmental writing course. Created by developmental English instructors, *The Writer's Warehouse* covers every part of the writing process. Also included are journaling capabilities, multimedia activities, diagnostic tests, an interactive handbook, and a complete instructor's manual. *The Writer's Warehouse* requires no space on your school's server; rather, students complete and store their work on the Longman server, and are able to access it, revise it, and continue working at any time. For more details about how to shrinkwrap a free subscription to *The Writer's Warehouse* with this text, please consult your Longman sales representative. For a free guided tour of the site, visit **http://longmanwriterswarehouse.com.**

For Instructors

Competency Profile Test Bank, Second Edition. This series of 60 objective tests covers ten general areas of English competency, including fragments; comma splices and run-ons; pronouns; commas; and capitalization. Each test is available in remedial, standard, and advanced versions. Available as reproducible sheets or in computerized versions. Free to instructors. Paper version: 0-321-02224-6.

Diagnostic and Editing Tests and Exercises, Sixth Edition. This collection of diagnostic tests helps instructors assess students' competence in Standard Written English to determine placement or to gauge progress. Available as reproducible sheets or in computerized versions, and free to instructors. Paper: 0-321-19647-3. CD-ROM: 0-321-19645-7.

ESL Worksheets, Third Edition. These reproducible worksheets provide ESL students with extra practice in areas they find the most troublesome. A diagnostic test and post-test are provided, along with answer keys and suggested topics for writing. Free to adopters. 0-321-07765-2

Longman Editing Exercises. 54 pages of paragraph editing exercises give students extra practice using grammar skills in the context of longer passages. Free when packaged with any Longman title. 0-205-31792-8 Answer key: 0-205-31797-9

80 Practices. A collection of reproducible, ten-item exercises that provide additional practices for specific grammatical usage problems, such as comma splices, capitalization, and pronouns. Includes an answer key, and free to adopters. 0-673-53422-7

CLAST Test Package, Fourth Edition. These two 40-item objective tests evaluate students' readiness for the CLAST exams. Strategies for teaching CLAST preparedness are included. Free with any Longman English title. Reproducible sheets: 0-321-01950-4

TASP Test Package, Third Edition. These 12 practice pre-tests and post-tests assess the same reading and writing skills covered in the TASP examination. Free with any Longman English title. Reproducible sheets: 0-321-01959-8

For Students

Researching Online, **Fifth Edition.** A perfect companion for a new age, this indispensable new supplement helps students navigate the Internet. Adapted from *Teaching Online,* the instructor's Internet guide, *Researching Online* speaks directly to students, giving them detailed, step-by-step instructions for performing electronic searches. Available free when shrinkwrapped with this text. 0-321-09277-5

A Guide for Peer Response, **Second Edition.** This guide offers students forms for peer critiques, including general guidelines and specific forms for different stages in the writing process. Also appropriate for freshman-level course. Free to adopters. 0-321-01948-2

The Longman Student Planner. This daily planner for students includes daily, weekly, and monthly calendars, as well as class schedules and a mini-almanac of useful information. It is the perfect accompaniment to a Longman reading or study skills textbook, and is available free to students when shrinkwrapped with this text. 0-321-04573-4

The Longman Writer's Journal. This journal for writers, free with any Longman English text, offers students a place to think, write, and react. For an examination copy, contact your Longman sales consultant. 0-321-08639-2

[NEW] The Longman Writer's Portfolio. This unique supplement provides students with a space to plan, think about, and present their work. The portfolio includes an assessing/organizing area (including a grammar diagnostic test, a spelling quiz, and project planning worksheets), a before and during writing area (including peer review sheets, editing checklists, writing self-evaluations, and a personal editing profile), and an after-writing area (including a progress chart, a final table of contents, and a final assessment). Ask your Longman sales representative for ISBN 0-321-10765-9.

State-Specific Supplements

[FOR FLORIDA ADOPTIONS] *Thinking Through the Test,* **by D.J. Henry.** This special workbook, prepared specially for students in Florida, offers ample skill and practice exercises to help students prep for the Florida State Exit Exam. To shrinkwrap this workbook free with your textbook, please contact your Longman sales representative. Available in two versions: with answers and without answers. Also available: Two laminated grids (one for reading, one for writing) that can serve as handy references for students preparing for the Florida State Exit Exam.

[FOR NEW YORK ADOPTIONS] Preparing for the CUNY-ACT Reading and Writing Test, edited by Patricia Licklider. This booklet, prepared by reading and writing faculty from across the CUNY system, is designed to help students prepare for the CUNY-ACT exit test. It includes test-taking tips, reading passages, typical exam questions, and sample writing prompts to help students become familiar with each portion of the text.

[FOR TEXAS ADOPTIONS] *The Longman TASP Study Guide,* **by Jeanette Harris.** Created specifically for students in Texas, this study guide includes straightforward explanations and numerous practice exercises to help students prepare for the reading and writing sections of the Texas Academic Skills Program Test. To shrinkwrap this workbook free with your textbook, please contact your Longman sales representative.

Acknowledgments

We would like to thank everyone who has helped us write and publish *The Write Start.* As always, acquisitions editor Steve Rigolosi's vision continues to inspire us to make the text better. Our developmental editor, Marion Castellucci, helped us capture the essence of a multiplicity of subjects and present them in interesting and challenging ways. Our students contributed paragraphs and essays to the text and demonstrated through their own writing that our techniques work, while challenging us to keep improving them. And finally, many thanks to the devoted English instructors around the country who reviewed our text and made valuable suggestions for improvement, in both the first and second editions:

David Auchter, San Jacinto College
Linda Austin, Glendale Community College
Sandra Barnhill, South Plains College
Roy L. Bond, Richland College
Martha D. Bone, Maysville Community College
Charlotte M. Calobrisi, Northern Virginia Community College
Rick Casper, Prestonburg Community College
Marianne Dzik, Illinois Valley Community College
Tim Florschuetz, Mesa Community College
Bernard J. Gallagher, Louisiana State University, Alexandria
Carlotta Hill, Oklahoma City Community College
Anne P. Hutzel, Asheville Buncombe Technical Community College
Timothy J. Jones, University of Oklahoma
Patsy Krech, University of Memphis
Samantha Leass, Prairie View A&M University
Irma Luna, San Antonio College
P. Wesley Lundburg, Fergus Falls Community College
Julia L. McGregor, Inver Hills Community College
Raymond Mort, Oakland Community College
Paul E. Preston, LACCD
Linda Rollins, Motlow State Community College
Athene Sallee, Forsyth Technical Community College
Phil Skerry, Lakeland Community College
Dorothy E. Terry, Prairie View A&M University
John Thornburg, San Jacinto College—Central
Suzanne Weisar, San Jacinto College—South
Paul L. Wolford, Walters State Community College

Lawrence Checkett
Gayle Feng-Checkett

To the Student: Getting Started

In the following chapters, you will learn why writing is important at home, school, and work. You will learn that writing, like driving a car, hitting a ball, or preparing a nutritious meal, is a learned skill. You also will learn about two common problems associated with poor writing skills: unclear meaning and the negative perception that others might have of you. As you read through these chapters, you will learn that writing is a skill that will help you throughout your life.

Copyright © 2004 by Pearson Education, Inc.

1 The Importance of Writing

The first question most students ask when starting to read a book on writing is "Why is writing that important?" The simple answer is that being able to write well and express yourself will help you throughout the rest of your life. Consider the three situations in which you'll find yourself most often: school, work, and home.

▼ For school, you will be called on to write essays, reports, analyses, and research papers to show what you've learned.

▼ For work, you'll be asked to write memos, business letters, and reports to communicate clearly with co-workers, your boss, and even employees at other companies. Moreover, before getting that job, you'll need to write résumés and cover letters to your prospective employers.

▼ For personal business, you will need to write notes, letters, and e-mail to everyone from your children's teachers to local politicians and even your family and friends.

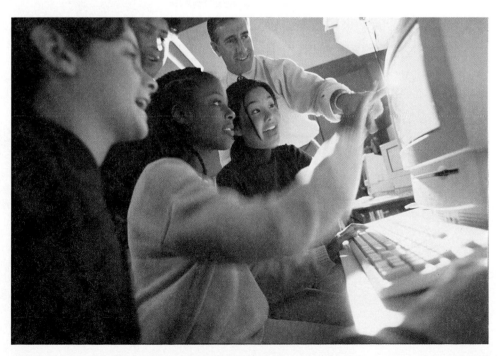

Copyright © 2004 by Pearson Education, Inc.

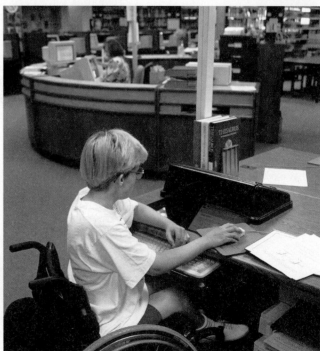

Whatever form your writing takes, and wherever you use it, you must learn to write well. Your writing for school, work, or personal business will have to express your ideas clearly. Organizing and developing your writing to achieve this clarity is one of the most important skills you can learn.

The key words in the previous paragraph are "learn" and "skills." No one is born with good writing skills. Just as you must learn how to keyboard, balance a checkbook, or cook a simple meal, you also must learn how to write well.

How do you learn to write well? You learn how to write well in the same way you develop any other skill. Consider some of your other talents:

▼ Are you a good free-throw shooter in basketball?
▼ Are you a whiz at setting up a new program on a computer?
▼ Can you make a loaf of French bread from scratch?

Why are you so successful at a particular skill? Why does it seem so easy? Is the answer "a little hard work and practice"? If so, then why should learning how to write well be any different? Remember, writing is a skill just like any other skill. If you make a commitment to learn the skill of writing, you will learn how to write and do it well.

Avoiding the Two Major Problems of Poor Writing

There are two obvious problems arising from a poor piece of writing. The first problem is one of understanding. For example, what do the following sentences mean?

1. The chef, made primarily of noodles, served the fettuccine Alfredo to his customers.
2. The truck hit the wall, and it was damaged.
3. Throwing confetti, the parade floats moved slowly down the boulevard.

Can you understand these sentences? In the first sentence, the fettuccine Alfredo is made of noodles, not the chef. In the second sentence, the pronoun "it" does not refer clearly to either truck or wall, so the reader cannot know which of the two was damaged. In the third sentence, the confetti was thrown by revelers (not mentioned), not by the parade floats.

In each of these sentences, the meaning is confused and unclear because of poor writing, but the problems are not that difficult to correct. A bit of rearranging or the addition of a key word should do the trick:

1. The chef served fettuccine Alfredo, made primarily of noodles, to his customers.
2. The truck hit the wall, and the wall was damaged.
3. The revelers on the floats threw confetti as the parade floats moved slowly down the boulevard.

The second problem arising from poor writing is one of perception. When people read writing that is difficult to understand or that contains punctuation errors, poorly constructed sentences, and misspelled words, they think less of the writer. They think that the writer is either not very intelligent or at least careless (for not proofreading the writing for errors), or possibly both. When the people making such assessments are bosses, professors, school principals, co-workers, human resource managers, and admission directors, the consequences can be devastating.

Poor writing can lead to not being admitted to college or to a failing grade on an assignment. It can mean not getting the job interview, or receiving a poor performance review. It can be the reason an issue is not taken seriously by your local city council, or your children are not getting the help they need at school. Learning to write well can help open those same doors that now seem closed.

Copyright © 2004 by Pearson Education, Inc.

Writing as a Life Skill

If you don't believe that writing well is a necessary "life skill," look in the classified ad section of your local newspaper and count how many help-wanted ads have a phrase in them that states "good communication skills necessary." You might be surprised at the number of jobs that require good writing skills, including those in which you thought writing wasn't even necessary.

Talk to people who have applied for jobs or applied to a variety of colleges, and ask them if the application asked them for a writing sample. You will find that most job and college applications do, and the reason should be no surprise. Your writing demonstrates to the reader how well you think, organize information, analyze, and communicate your thoughts to others—all skills necessary for success in school, work, or your personal business.

Writing well is a learned skill. Like any other skill, it takes a certain amount of commitment, practice, and hard work. In not too many weeks, however, if you keep at it, you can learn how to improve your writing substantially. For a few weeks' investment in time and energy, you can enjoy a lifetime of success in school, work, and your personal business.

Visit *The Write Start* Online!

For additional practice with the materials found in this chapter, visit our Website at:

http://www.ablongman.com/checkett

The Website also features additional readings, quizzes, writing activities, and Internet links, as well as a bulletin board and interactive chat.

For More Practice with Your Grammar and Writing Skills
Visit The Longman Writer's Warehouse

For further multimedia exercises and activities designed to improve your reading, thinking, writing, and grammar skills, visit The Longman Writer's Warehouse on the Web. The Writer's Warehouse offers an interactive handbook, an online journal, a bulletin board, and extensive coverage of the writing process. To take a tour, go to

http://longmanwriterswarehouse.com

Copyright © 2004 by Pearson Education, Inc.

2 Elements of Good Writing

W hat does it take to write well? Like many students, you might find that writing assignments are time-consuming, difficult, and no fun at all. If so, you're not alone. Many writers, including well-known professionals, find that writing is a chore. A good number of writers, though, find writing to be a joy, and by mastering some of the basic elements of good writing, perhaps you can too.

Good Writing: Four Misconceptions

There are four basic misconceptions about good writing that can make it seem like a chore:

▼ Good writing has to be complicated.
▼ Good writing has to be long.
▼ Good writing means writing just like you talk.
▼ Good writing means good ideas—punctuation is of secondary importance.

In reality, the first two of these misconceptions are often misunderstood, while the last two are simply wrong. After all, the whole point of writing is to get information across clearly and concisely to someone else.

Good Writing Doesn't Have to Be Complicated

When people say "complicated," what they really mean is "developed." Keep your writing as simple as possible without leaving out any important information, and make certain you explain each idea fully. Concentrate on details that clearly express the main idea, not on words that the reader has to run to a dictionary to look up.

> **Complicated/Unclear**
>
> Televised educational programming should facilitate the pedagogical manifestations embedded in the internalized psyche of the community's concern for children's edification in discrete categories.

It would take 20 minutes using a dictionary and a thesaurus to figure out the meaning of this sentence.

> **Developed/Clear**
>
> Children's educational television shows, such as *Sesame Street, Reading Rainbow,* and *Mister Rogers,* should reflect parents' concerns in regard to math, reading, and writing. The instruction should reflect the proper age and level of children's development.

Notice how simple the language is, yet the meaning is clear.

Good Writing Doesn't Have to Be Long

Some assignments dictate length by their very nature. For example, a research paper on the causes of World War II would necessarily be long. However, in most cases, short and simple writing is better. Most people in the business world and academia do not have unlimited time to read incoming communications. They want information that is clear and as short as possible without leaving out any important facts or ideas. However, you don't want your writing to be so brief that it becomes monotonous, immature, and uninformative.

> **Too Short**
>
> Tom is a Democrat. Yuri is a Republican. Yasheef is an Independent. Tom voted. Yuri voted. Yasheef voted. Senator Brown was reelected.

Here, the sing-song rhythm of the sentences is immature, and the information is insufficient. For example, is Senator Brown a Democrat, a Republican, or an Independent?

> **Too Long**
>
> Tom, a Democrat, likes chocolate ice-cream and riding his bicycle in the countryside on weekends, while Yuri, a Republican, enjoys reading science articles and owns a two-story brick house. Furthermore, Yasheef, an Independent, has a red convertible and started his own business two years ago. Tom, Yuri, and Yasheef all voted in last Tuesday's election. Because it was a bright, sunny day and the forecast predicted a continuation of good weather, many other people came out to vote, as well. Most of the voters in the district—a full 62 percent—were Democrats, while 34 percent were Republican and 4 percent were Independent. Senator Brown, a Democrat, received the most votes and was reelected.

Here, the inference is clear that Senator Brown was reelected because Democrats were the majority of voters in the district and the good weather boosted the voter turnout, but the sentences are too long and meandering. Also, most of the information has nothing to do with the topic.

> **Clear/Concise**
>
> Tom, a Democrat like the majority of voters in the district, voted along with Yuri, a Republican, and Yasheef, an Independent. Many other voters turned out because of the good weather. Later that evening, it was announced that the Democratic incumbent, Senator Brown, was reelected.

Here, all the necessary information is present, using clear, simplified language.

Good Writing Is More Formal than Talking

Writing, with the possible exception of short notes and memos to family members, friends, and co-workers, is more formal than talking. When you talk, you use slang, intonation, facial expressions, and other body language to get your point across. As a result, the exact words you use can be informal or imprecise, and your audience will still understand you. With writing, though, words are all you have to get your point across, so those words need to be more precise and more formal. Therefore, word choice, sentence structure, and paragraph organization become more important. In business and academia, do not use slang and confusing expressions that do not mean what their individual words suggest.

> **Slang**
>
> John F. Kennedy was a *cool* president, and he never *disrespected* his *posse*.
>
> **Appropriate Language**
>
> John F. Kennedy was *an effective* president, and he never *showed disrespect for his supporters.*
>
> **Confusing Expression**
>
> After the receiver dropped the pass, the coach *had a cow.*
>
> **Appropriate Language**
>
> After the receiver dropped the pass, the coach *became angry.*

The purpose of good writing is to get across information to someone in a clear and concise manner. Slang and confusing expressions are unacceptable in formal writing for several reasons.

Slang and confusing expressions are often used by a select group of people, usually belonging to a particular social group, profession, age group, or culture. The meaning of slang and confusing expressions is usually understood only by the select group. Also, slang and confusing expressions do not have an exact meaning, making it difficult for the reader to understand the intended meaning. You might use a word or an expression to mean one thing, while your reader might interpret it to mean something else. When someone says, "That song is bad," to one group, "bad" might mean "awful," while to another group, it might mean "good." A good example is the expression "The man was so angry, he had a cow." To a foreigner or to a person outside of the group familiar with its actual meaning, "having a cow"

Copyright © 2004 by Pearson Education, Inc.

would certainly be confusing; the reader would have no way to figure out the cause and effect relationship between a man being angry and his having a cow.

When you write, try to use exact language that is easy to understand and clarifies ideas, not confuses them. Omit slang and confusing expressions, and use precise language to get your points across.

Good Writing Needs Proper Punctuation

Proper punctuation is essential to attain clear meaning. Punctuation has two prime functions: First, it divides information into smaller groups, making it easier for the reader to understand; and second, it creates rhythm so that the sentences flow easily together.

By way of comparison, think of punctuation as having a similar function in writing as traffic signals do on the road. Traffic signals keep the traffic (like words in writing) moving with a coordinated ease. The signals also divide traffic into smaller, more manageable groups to regulate flow and allow everyone to travel at a reasonable rate. For instance, you might think of a period as a red light (full stop), a semicolon as a flashing red light (a full stop but not quite as long as a nonflashing red light), and a comma as a flashing yellow light (a slowing down but not a full stop).

Without Punctuation

The secretary having finished at least for the day her stack of communications was then confronted with another set of demands without help from an assistant it would take her at least another four hours consequently she called with permission from her boss a temporary employment agency.

This sentence is difficult to follow, and finding a place to take a breath is almost impossible.

With Punctuation

The secretary, having finished at least for the day her stack of communications, was then confronted with another set of demands. Without help from an assistant, it would take her at least another four hours; consequently, she called, with permission from her boss, a temporary employment agency.

Notice how the punctuation helps to clarify the content by breaking the information into smaller units. Punctuation also helps to create rhythm in the writing by making the reader slow down and pause at certain places.

The Computer, Writing, and You

Now that you're in college, many instructors will expect you to use a computer on which to do your writing. Some courses will require you to submit your papers and essays on a disk or even to send them electronically to a folder for the instructor's or your classmates' comments. But don't panic. If your instructor doesn't spend time in class teaching you how to accomplish this, your school probably has an instructional center where tutors can instruct you individually or in special classes. In a few short weeks, you'll become comfortable with using the computer to help you with all your writing assignments.

Although you may have heard a few horror stories about students losing entire papers because of a computer crash or a file being destroyed by an Internet virus, millions of students just like you are discovering how computers can help them write their papers more efficiently, more accurately, and more professionally.

Computers can help you with a multitude of tasks that are necessary to complete a variety of writing assignments. You can use a computer to help you during all phases of the writing process.

Writing
▼ Brainstorming
▼ Freewriting
▼ Rough drafts (save multiple drafts for comparison)
▼ Inserting and/or deleting sentences (also helps you achieve sentence variety)
▼ Moving paragraphs (to help you organize and develop your ideas)
▼ Thesaurus (to help you find synonyms and antonyms)
▼ Spellchecker
▼ Grammar checker
▼ Format (italics, boldface, font size, highlighting, and many other features)

Research
▼ Use the Internet and World Wide Web to find information.
▼ Access online library catalogs and databases.
▼ Write to others about your assignment using e-mail.
▼ Talk live in "chat" rooms.
▼ Exchange files and folders.
▼ Post assignments to class archives and forums.

Using a computer to write can offer many advantages when working on your assignments. As you gain experience, you will learn to access information more quickly, focus your research, organize your ideas and communicate a developed point of view, and produce a professional looking final draft. The new tools available to writers today can make many writing tasks and processes easier and quicker to accomplish.

CHAPTER REVIEW

▼ *Good writing doesn't have to be complicated.* Good writing must be developed, but it isn't necessarily complicated. Keep writing as simple as possible without leaving out any important information.
▼ *Good writing doesn't have to be long.* While some specific assignments demand length, for most writing, short and simple is better. Most people don't have unlimited time to read incoming communications, so keep your writing short and to the point.
▼ *Good writing is more formal than talking.* When writing, don't use slang or confusing expressions that might get in the way of clear understanding. In writing, word choice, sentence structure, and paragraph organization are of utmost importance.

Copyright © 2004 by Pearson Education, Inc.

▼ *Good writing is a combination of content and proper punctuation.* Proper punctuation is essential to attain clear meaning. Punctuation divides information into smaller groups, making it easier for the reader to understand. It also creates rhythm so that the sentences flow easily together.

We hope the examples you've been shown have erased some misconceptions about the writing process. Yes, writing can be difficult—but don't get discouraged—we're just getting started. The instructional chapters of this book have been designed to give you information and present techniques in a clear and concise manner so that your writing experience will be as productive as possible.

You don't have to be a professional to write well. This book also shares with you the thoughts and styles of many student writers just like you. The finished student writings that you will read are the product of the instructional chapters that went into the making of this book. These students were just like you when they began, and with work and dedication, you will be writing just like them in a relatively short time. There is a voice within you that is waiting to be discovered and developed. Let's go!

Visit *The Write Start* Online!

For additional practice with the materials found in this chapter, visit our Website at:

http://www.ablongman.com/checkett

The Website also features additional readings, quizzes, writing activities, and Internet links, as well as a bulletin board and interactive chat.

For More Practice with Your Grammar and Writing Skills
Visit The Longman Writer's Warehouse

For further multimedia exercises and activities designed to improve your reading, thinking, writing, and grammar skills, visit The Longman Writer's Warehouse on the Web. The Writer's Warehouse offers an interactive handbook, an online journal, a bulletin board, and extensive coverage of the writing process. To take a tour, go to

http://longmanwriterswarehouse.com

PART 1

Writing Effective Sentences

In the following chapters, you will learn the basic rules of grammar and the basic sentence types. You also will learn the technique known as "sentence combining" that allows writers to create a more interesting and mature style of writing. Almost every aspect of your life at home, school, and work demands longer pieces of writing (memos, letters, reports, essays, research papers) with which to communicate to family, friends, teachers, and colleagues. All of these forms of writing are created using the grammar rules that make up standard English. Without these rules, neither sentence variety nor longer pieces of writing would be possible.

Copyright © 2004 by Pearson Education, Inc.

Copyright © 2004 by Pearson Education, Inc.

3

The Simple Sentence and the Independent Clause

The sentence is the building block of all writing. Paragraphs, memos, letters, reports, and even essays and books are constructed from sentences. But what are sentences built out of? A properly constructed sentence must have a **subject,** a **verb,** and sufficient meaning.

In this chapter, we will practice identifying subjects and verbs in **simple sentences.** A simple sentence has one subject and one verb. This is also called an **independent clause.** Sentences can have more than one subject and one verb, as we will see in the next chapter.

The Subject

The subject of a sentence is usually a noun (John, car, politics) or a pronoun (I, you, he, she, it, we, they). It is usually located near the beginning of a sentence.

Nouns

A **noun** names persons, places, and things. Nouns either can be *common* (not capitalized) or *proper* (always capitalized). Notice that common nouns name general persons, places, and things while proper nouns name particular persons, places, and things.

Common Nouns	Proper Nouns
(general)	(particular)
city	Los Angeles
boy	Peter
photocopier	Xerox

The subject nouns in the following examples are *italicized*.

Examples of Subject Nouns
Proper Noun/Person: *Fred* drove to the store.
Common Noun/Person: The *manager* counted the day's receipts.
Proper Noun/Place: *New York* is a city with many tall buildings.

> Common Noun/Place: The *countryside* was very open but very quiet.
> Proper Noun/Thing: The *Washington Monument* was circled by tourists.
> Common Noun/Thing: The large *table* was filled with birthday gifts.

Pronouns

Pronouns are used to take the place of nouns.

Commonly Used Pronouns

I	we	me	it
you	they	this	that
everyone	something	nobody	which

For a complete list of pronouns, see The Writer's Resources, Grammar, Pronouns (page 312).

Subject pronouns in the following examples are *italicized*.

Examples of Subject Pronouns

I am a mechanic.

You should go to the job fair next week.

He will never graduate because he has poor study habits.

She uses positive imaging when shooting free throws.

It is a large, white, furry, carnivorous bear living near the North Pole.

We can fulfill our destiny as a nation if we work together.

They should invest in mutual funds for their baby's future college education.

Using Pronouns to Eliminate Repetition

When we want to avoid using the same noun too many times, we use a pronoun to reduce repetition.

In the following sentence, the repetition of the nouns "children," "soda," and "potato chips," makes the sentence sound awkward and almost like it was written for a very young child's reader.

> The children wanted to have a party, but the children did not have enough soda and potato chips. The children ran to the store and bought more soda and potato chips.

In the next sentence, noun repetition is eliminated by substituting pronouns for nouns. The pronoun substitutions are *italicized*.

> The children wanted to have a party, but *they* did not have enough soda and potato chips. *They* ran to the store and bought *them*.

Once the main nouns have been established, we can use pronouns to eliminate repetition. However, overuse of pronouns can lead to the common problem called *pronoun reference error.* A pronoun reference error occurs when the pronoun that is replacing a noun does not clearly refer to that noun.

> **Example**
> The truck ran into the light pole, and *it* was damaged.

Which noun, "truck" or "light pole," does the pronoun "it" refer to? There is no way for the reader to understand which reference the writer meant. Always be sure that when you substitute a pronoun for a noun, the pronoun refers clearly to that noun.

Identifying Subjects

The subject identifies *who* or *what* is *doing something* or *being something.*

> **Examples**
> *Teachers educate students.* In this sentence, "Teachers" is the subject noun doing an activity—educating students.
> *Teachers are educators.* In this sentence, "Teachers" is the subject, but now it is not doing an action or activity. Rather, the "state of being" or "state of existence" of teachers is being explained.

▼
PRACTICE 1 **Identifying Subjects**

Underline the subject in each of the following sentences.

Example: <u>Heathrow Airport</u> was crowded with vacationers returning home.

1. The <u>airliner</u> was flying the "red eye" from London to New York.

2. A thick <u>fog</u> had settled over New York's JFK airport.

3. The runway <u>lights</u> flashed blue and yellow.

4. The <u>jet</u> circled JFK for over an hour.

5. The <u>air traffic controller</u> gave the pilot landing clearance.

6. The <u>pilot</u> landed the aircraft successfully.

7. <u>Passengers</u> emptied into the large terminal.

8. <u>Flight attendants</u> helped children and senior citizens.

9. <u>Signs</u> written in many languages helped passengers find their way.

10. <u>Luggage</u> was picked up from the baggage carousel.

Copyright © 2004 by Pearson Education, Inc.

▼
PRACTICE 2   **Identifying Subjects**

Underline the subject in each of the following sentences.

1. <u>Frank Lloyd Wright</u> wanted to study architecture at the University of Wisconsin.

2. <u>It</u> did not offer architecture courses.

3. <u>Civil engineering</u> became his major area of study.

4. The <u>Adler and Sullivan Company</u> hired him as a designer.

5. <u>"Organic architecture"</u> was a style he created.

6. This <u>philosophy</u> held that a building should develop out of its natural surroundings.

7. <u>He</u> created many wonderful buildings using this idea.

8. The <u>carport</u> was one of his inventions.

9. <u>Air conditioning</u> was first used in a Frank Lloyd Wright building.

10. <u>Frank Lloyd Wright</u> became a pioneer in modern architecture.

▼
PRACTICE 3   **Identifying Subjects**

Underline the subject(s) in each of the following sentences.

1. The <u>Yukon Territory</u> is located in northwestern Canada.

2. The vast <u>area</u> (186,300 sq mi) is bordered by Alaska and British Columbia.

3. Its mineral <u>wealth</u> and scenic <u>vistas</u> are two of its main attractions.

4. The <u>name</u> Yukon is taken from an Indian expression meaning "great river."

5. High <u>plateaus</u> occupy most of the south and central portions of the territory.

6. The <u>St. Elias Mountains</u> separate the Yukon from the Pacific Ocean.

7. <u>Forests</u> cover about 40 percent of the total land area.

8. <u>White spruce</u> is the most common species of tree.

9. A subarctic <u>climate</u> prevails with severe winters and hot summers.

10. The annual <u>precipitation</u> ranges from 9 to 13 inches.

Copyright © 2004 by Pearson Education, Inc.

PRACTICE 4	Supplying Subjects

Answers will vary.

Supply a person, place, thing, or pronoun for the subject in the following sentences.

1. _____ called to his friend Oscar to see if he wanted to go for a

walk.

2. The _____ sped down the road at breakneck speed.

3. _____ enjoyed going to the movies every Saturday.

4. Three _____ landed on the deck of the aircraft carrier.

5. _____ sparkled in the clear, evening sky.

6. The thick, wool _____ kept the camper warm while she slept.

7. Many _____ visit the Grand Canyon every year.

8. _____ read many books every summer.

9. _____ listened to rock, jazz, and classical music.

10. _____ is a popular Italian pasta dish.

PRACTICE 5	Writing Sentences

Answers will vary.

Write a sentence using the subject provided.

1. Tornado— _____

_____

2. Cab driver— _____

_____

3. Actors— _____

_____

4. Apartment— _____

_____

5. Detective— _____

_____

6. Table— _____

_____

7. Grapefruit— _____

_____

8. Motorcycle— _____

_____

9. Movie— _____

_____

10. DVD player— _____

_____

Subjects and Prepositional Phrases

There is an old saying in writing: all subjects are nouns, but not all nouns are subjects. When looking for subjects, you might be confused by the noun in a prepositional phrase.

A **prepositional phrase** is a group of words containing a preposition, such as *in, of, on,* or *to,* and a noun as its object.

Preposition	+	Object	=	Prepositional Phrase
in	+	a minute	=	in a minute
of	+	the nation	=	of the nation
on	+	the roof	=	on the roof
to	+	the moon	=	to the moon

Many sentences contain prepositional phrases at or near the beginning where the subject noun is located. It is sometimes confusing to figure out which of the two nouns is the subject. The object noun of a preposition is never the subject.

In the morning, coffee is my favorite beverage.
      ↑   ↑
    noun   noun

Two nouns side-by-side in front of the verb can be confusing. One method of identifying the subject noun is to cross out the prepositional phrase (and the noun in it); the noun that remains is the subject.

~~In the morning~~, coffee is my favorite beverage.

Once "in the morning" is crossed out, the noun "coffee" is easily identified as the subject.

Learn to recognize prepositions so that you can eliminate their object nouns as possible subjects.

Here is a list of commonly used prepositions you should become familiar with:

Commonly Used Prepositions

about	beside	off
above	between	on
across	by	over
after	during	through
against	except	to
along	for	toward
among	from	under
around	in	until
at	into	up
before	like	with
behind	of	without

For a complete list of prepositions, see The Writer's Resources, Grammar, Additional Practice with Prepositions (page 356).

▼ **PRACTICE 6**   **Identifying Subjects and Prepositional Phrases**

In each of the following sentences, cross out the prepositional phrases. Then, underline the subjects.

Example: ~~At the zoo~~, most <u>animals</u> are still kept ~~in cages~~.

  1. ~~In the wind~~, <u>kites</u> are unpredictable.

  2. The <u>carton</u> ~~of oranges~~ floated ~~in the water~~.

  3. <u>Bill</u> was safe ~~in the space under the bridge~~.

  4. ~~Between the two hills~~, the <u>houses</u> are made ~~from cedar logs~~.

  5. The <u>microwave</u> ~~on the counter in the kitchen~~ was very clean.

  6. ~~During the week~~ and ~~on the weekend~~, <u>homework</u> is a constant activity.

  7. ~~Except on casual day~~, the <u>workers</u> always wore suits ~~to the office~~.

  8. ~~Over the river~~ and ~~through the woods~~, the <u>wolf</u> raced ~~to Grandmother's house~~.

  9. The <u>couple</u> arrived ~~at the wedding reception without a gift~~.

  10. <u>Three</u> ~~of the guitarists~~ are alternative musicians.

Copyright © 2004 by Pearson Education, Inc.

▼ **PRACTICE 7** **Identifying Subjects and Prepositional Phrases**

In each of the following sentences, cross out the prepositional phrases. Then, underline the subjects.

1. ~~In a presidential election~~, the <u>challenger</u> has to choose a running mate.

2. ~~Until the process ends~~, the party's <u>campaigning</u> cannot start.

3. ~~At the beginning of the process~~, many <u>candidates</u> are considered.

4. ~~Before the interviews~~, the candidates' party <u>credentials</u> are inspected.

5. ~~After the elimination of some candidates~~, a short <u>list</u> is assembled.

6. ~~From the short list~~, <u>interviews</u> are scheduled.

7. ~~Without the interview process~~, the final <u>choice</u> cannot be made.

8. ~~During the interview~~, the <u>candidate</u> must clarify specific positions.

9. ~~By the end of the process~~, the <u>challenger</u> can make a clear choice ~~for the party~~.

10. ~~Behind each political partnership~~, a <u>lot</u> ~~of work~~ has to be done.

▼ **PRACTICE 8** **Identifying Subjects and Prepositional Phrases**

In each of the following sentences, cross out the prepositional phrases. Then, underline the subjects.

1. ~~In the plane~~, the tour <u>passengers</u> slept lightly.

2. The rocking <u>motion</u> ~~of the plane~~ was somewhat disturbing.

3. <u>Many</u> ~~of the passengers~~ slept ~~with a pillow under their heads~~.

4. ~~Outside the cabin~~, the <u>stars</u> shone like small fireflies ~~in the dark~~.

5. <u>There</u> was a hushed silence ~~inside the cabin~~.

6. ~~In most cases~~, smaller <u>children</u> slept ~~on their parent's laps~~.

7. The <u>people</u> ~~with older children~~ were free to roll ~~over on their sides~~ if they wanted to.

8. ~~After the flight landed~~, the <u>passengers</u> walked ~~to the baggage carousel~~.

9. ~~On the waiting ramp~~, the <u>passengers</u> were required to show tickets ~~to the skycaps~~.

10. ~~During the trip to the hotel~~, their <u>bags</u> were carried ~~on the top of the bus~~.

The Verb

As a developing writer, you should become familiar with three types of verbs: *action verbs, linking verbs,* and *helping verbs.*

Action Verbs

Action verbs describe an activity the subject is performing:

Commonly Used Action Verbs		
arrive	soar	eat
study	run	smile
speak	construct	race
climb	called	leave

Examples

The mailman *arrives* with a package.
The dog *races* the squirrel to the tree.
The eagle *soars* high above the cliffs.
The defense lawyer *speaks* with a Southern drawl.

▼ **PRACTICE 9**   **Identifying Action Verbs**

Underline the action verb in each of the following sentences. To help you find the action verb, circle the subject. Cross out any prepositional phrases.

Example: On average, (Tiger Woods) hits a golf ball over 290 yards off the tee.

1. As a young child, (he) learned the proper mechanics of the swing.

2. His (father) guided his golf instruction.

3. The (youngster) progressed rapidly as a golfer.

4. (He) garnered three Junior Amateur championships in a row.

5. Without hesitation, (Woods) won three straight Amateur championships.

6. On the professional tour, (Tiger) arrived at the Masters tournament as a tour rookie.

7. (He) regularly launched 300-yard drives on the longer holes.

8. His (length) off the tee catapulted him to victory again.

Copyright © 2004 by Pearson Education, Inc.

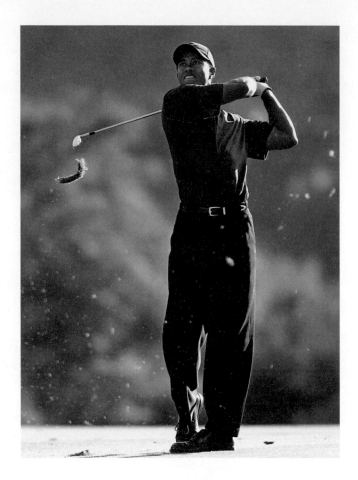

9. (Tiger) stunned the golfing world ~~with his outstanding and exciting play~~.

10. (Woods) earned ~~over a million dollars~~ his first full year ~~on the professional~~

~~tour~~.

Underline the action verb in each of the following sentences. To help you find the action verb, circle the subject. Cross out any prepositional phrases.

1. A (letter) arrived ~~at Marjorie's apartment~~.

2. (She) opened the letter ~~on the kitchen table~~.

3. A handwritten (note) fell ~~from the envelope~~.

4. (She) unfolded the piece ~~of paper~~.

5. ~~For no apparent reason,~~ (she) read the message out loud.

6. (Tears) ~~of happiness~~ flowed ~~from her eyes~~.

7. A major (airline) had selected her name ~~from a list of contest entrants~~.

8. After calming down, (Marjorie) called her mother and father on the phone.

9. (She) told them the happy news.

10. (She) had won round trip tickets for four to London.

▼ **PRACTICE 11**   **Identifying Action Verbs**

Underline the action verb in each of the following sentences. To help you find the action verb, circle the subject. Cross out any prepositional phrases.

1. Most (people) participate in outdoor activities.

2. One (person) scuba dives in the Caribbean.

3. (Another) skis in the mountains of Colorado.

4. (People) on both Florida coasts fish for trophy marlin and swordfish.

5. A (group) from Vermont searches for rare birds in the deep forests.

6. ("Spelunkers") crawl through narrow caves.

7. (Missourians) ride bikes on the scenic Katy Trail.

8. (Individuals) connected with ropes climb the faces of steep cliffs.

9. (Others) leap from bridges with bungee cords attached to their ankles.

10. Small (groups) in military garb play "paintball" in the woods.

▼ **PRACTICE 12**   **Writing Sentences**

Answers will vary.

Write a sentence using the action verb provided.

1. Starts— _____

_____

2. Jumps— _____

_____

3. Study— _____

_____

4. Bake— _____

_____

Copyright © 2004 by Pearson Education, Inc.

5. Swerves— _____

_____

6. Builds— _____

_____

7. Travels— _____

_____

8. Speaks— _____

_____

9. Looks— _____

_____

10. Crashes— _____

_____

Linking Verbs

Linking verbs indicate a condition or state of being. The linking verb connects the subject with a word or phrase identifying or describing something about the subject:

Commonly Used Linking Verbs		
act	feel	look
appear	grow	seem
be (am, is, are, was, were, have been)	become	taste

Examples

Dr. Smith _is_ a surgeon.

The wool sweater _feels_ rough.

The desert sand _becomes_ cool in the evening.

Aretha _appears_ tired and sluggish.

PRACTICE 13   Identifying Linking Verbs

There is a linking verb in each of the following sentences. To help identify the linking verb, circle the subject, and draw a line to the word or words that describe the subject. Then, circle that word or group of words. Finally, underline the linking verb between the two circles.

Examples: The (building) is a [skyscraper].

The (player) seems [nervous].

(Nurses) are [intelligent and caring].

1. The (concert) was very [exciting].

2. The (foyer) looked (buffed and polished) from floor to ceiling.

3. The (hall) felt [cold and stuffy].

4. (People) in the audience seemed [nervous].

5. (Members) of the orchestra were [relaxed].

6. The symphony (orchestra) sounded [confident and well-rehearsed].

7. The (cookies) served during intermission smelled [heavenly].

8. The (music) remained (controlled) throughout the evening.

9. The (conductor) appeared (pleased) with the orchestra members' effort.

10. At the concert's end, the (applause) became (louder) with each bow.

▼
PRACTICE 14   Identifying Linking Verbs

There is a linking verb in each of the following sentences. To help identify the linking verb, circle the subject, and draw a line to the word or words describing the subject. Then, circle that word or group of words. Finally, underline the linking verb between the two circles.

1. My (life) was not [wonderful].

2. (I) appeared (surly and cantankerous) to my friends.

3. My family said (I) looked [depressed].

4. My (job) became [boring and uninteresting].

5. Even (food) smelled [dull and tasteless].

6. (I) had become [lazy and indifferent].

7. (I) felt (disassociated) from my true self.

8. These unproductive (states of mind) were not [acceptable].

9. (I) turned to a counselor [for help].

10. After many months, the (therapy) seems [to be helping].

Copyright © 2004 by Pearson Education, Inc.

▼ PRACTICE 15   Writing Sentences

Answers will vary.

Write a sentence using the linking verb provided.

1. Was— _____

_____

2. Seem— _____

_____

3. Is— _____

_____

4. Feel— _____

_____

5. Become— _____

_____

6. Am— _____

_____

7. Appear— _____

_____

8. Were— _____

_____

9. Have been— _____

_____

10. Are— _____

_____

Helping Verbs

Helping verbs combine with a main verb to form a group of words called a *verb phrase*. The helping verb gives the main verb a specific time reference or meaning.

Commonly Used Helping Verbs		
can	could	may
might	must	shall
should	will	would
forms of the irregular verbs *be, do,* and *have*		

For a list of irregular verbs, see The Writer's Resources, Grammar, Irregular Verbs (pages 326–330).

Examples

The manager *can* fire employees if they break regulations.
Keeping a diary *might* help you better understand yourself.
Studying *will* enhance your grade point average.
A positive attitude *should* make your day more enjoyable.

▼ **PRACTICE 16**   Identifying Helping Verbs and Verb Phrases

There is a helping verb and a main verb in each of the following sentences. To help identify the helping verb, circle the subject. Then, cross out any prepositional phrases. Finally, underline the entire verb phrase.

Example: Studies ~~of all ages~~ indicate that (exercising) can help overall mental and physical health ~~for most people~~.

1. (People) ~~of all ages~~ should exercise.

2. However, (exercising) must be done ~~on a regular basis~~.

3. (Working out) three times a week can create a more healthy person.

4. ~~On the other hand~~, (exercising) too much may be detrimental ~~to your health~~.

5. An effective (workout) must include exercises ~~for both muscles and the cardiovascular system~~.

6. (Lifting weights) should be accompanied ~~by an aerobic exercise~~.

7. Some experts think (walking) might be ~~as beneficial as jogging~~.

8. (Mental health) also will be stimulated ~~by physical exercise~~.

9. Good (mental health) could facilitate success ~~in other areas of your life~~.

10. Regular (exercising) would lower health-related costs nationally.

Copyright © 2004 by Pearson Education, Inc.

| ▼ **PRACTICE 17** | **Identifying Helping Verbs and Verb Phrases** |

There is a helping verb and a main verb in each of the following sentences. To help identify the helping verb, circle the subject. Then, cross out any prepositional phrases. Finally, underline the entire verb phrase.

1. How <u>do</u> (you) <u>start</u> a hobby?

2. First, (you) <u>can buy</u> a hobby magazine and learn the varieties ~~of hobbies~~ ~~available~~.

3. Then, (you) <u>should ask</u> your friends and neighbors what hobbies they have.

4. (You) <u>will need</u> to figure out how much time and money you have to invest ~~in the hobby~~.

5. (Budgeting) <u>may help</u> you narrow your choices.

6. ~~Of course,~~ (you) <u>must ask</u> ~~for advice at a hobby shop~~ near you.

7. (This) <u>could put</u> you ~~in touch with other enthusiasts~~ interested ~~in the same hobby as you~~.

8. A (hobby club) <u>will be</u> an invaluable resource ~~for furthering your enjoyment~~.

9. (Being a member) ~~of a club~~ also <u>might get</u> you discounts ~~on materials and publications~~.

10. Also, other (members) <u>would assist</u> you with difficult aspects ~~of your hobby~~.

| ▼ **PRACTICE 18** | **Writing Sentences** |

Answers will vary.

Write a sentence using the helping verb provided. You also will have to choose a main verb to combine with the helping verb as you create each sentence.

Examples: Can—I <u>can</u> *ride* a unicycle for five minutes before losing my balance.
　　　　　　　　↑　　↑
　　　　　　helping main
　　　　　　　verb　verb

1. Could— _____

　_____

2. May— _____

　_____

3. Can— _____

　_____

4. Might— _____

_____

5. Must— _____

_____

Verb Tense (Time)

In writing, time is called *tense*. Because tense is shown primarily through the *verb*, time is more accurately called **verb tense.** It is important to know whether an action or linking verb is in the past, present, or future tense. After all, you would certainly react differently if something had already happened, was happening at present, or was not going to happen until later. This section deals with the simplest forms of past, present, and future verb tense in regard to the action and linking verbs we have already studied.

For additional information regarding verb tense, see The Writer's Resources, Grammar, Verbs (page 324).

Examples of Simple Past, Present, and Future Verb Tense	
Past	I <u>talked</u> yesterday.
	I <u>worked</u> last Saturday.
	He <u>talked</u> for two hours.
	He <u>worked</u> last summer.
Present	I <u>talk</u> now.
	I <u>work</u> all the time.
	She <u>talks</u> in her sleep.
	She <u>works</u> at Benny's.
Future	I <u>will talk</u> later.
	I <u>will work</u> tomorrow.
	They <u>will talk</u> next Monday.
	They <u>will work</u> after dinner.

For a complete list of tenses, see The Writer's Resources, Grammar, Verbs (page 326).

Examples

Past Tense Linking Verb: Juan *was* a student at USC last year.

Present Tense Linking Verb: Juan *is* a student at USC this year.

Future Tense Linking Verb: Juan *will be* a student at USC next year.

Past Tense Action Verb: Amy *skated* yesterday.

Present Tense Action Verb: Amy *skates* today.

Future Tense Action Verb: Amy *will skate* tomorrow.

Copyright © 2004 by Pearson Education, Inc.

Complete the following sentences by filling in the blank spaces with the past tense form, the present tense form, and the future tense form of the verb provided.

1. Verb: practice

   Past Tense: The girls' soccer team __**practiced**__ for the tournament.

   Present Tense: The girls' soccer team __**practices**__ for the tournament.

   Future Tense: The girls' soccer team __**will practice**__ for the tournament.

2. Verb: dance

   Past Tense: The ballerina __**danced**__ *Swan Lake* for the first time.

   Present Tense: The ballerina __**dances**__ *Swan Lake* for the first time.

   Future Tense: The ballerina __**will dance**__ *Swan Lake* for the first time.

3. Verb: cook

   Past Tense: I __**cooked**__ seafood gumbo for my guests.

   Present Tense: I __**cook**__ seafood gumbo for my guests.

   Future Tense: I __**will cook**__ seafood gumbo for my guests.

4. Verb: play

   Past Tense: Jasmine __**played**__ the guitar for her boyfriend.

   Present Tense: Jasmine __**plays**__ the guitar for her boyfriend.

   Future Tense: Jasmine __**will play**__ the guitar for her boyfriend.

5. Verb: clean

   Past Tense: Melvin __**cleaned**__ his school locker.

   Present Tense: Melvin __**cleans**__ his school locker.

   Future Tense: Melvin __**will clean**__ his school locker.

Complete the following sentences by filling in the blank spaces with the past tense form, the present tense form, and the future tense form of the verb provided.

1. Verb: corner

Past Tense: The dog ___**cornered**___ the cat in the alley.

Present Tense: The dog ___**corners**___ the cat in the alley.

Future Tense: The dog ___**will corner**___ the cat in the alley.

2. Verb: assume

Past Tense: The professor ___**assumed**___ the students had read the chapter.

Present Tense: The professor ___**assumes**___ the students had read the chapter.

Future Tense: The professor ___**will assume**___ the students had read the chapter.

3. Verb: consume

Past Tense: The crocodile ___**consumed**___ a large portion of meat for its daily meal.

Present Tense: The crocodile ___**consumes**___ a large portion of meat for its daily meal.

Future Tense: The crocodile ___**will consume**___ a large portion of meat for its daily meal.

4. Verb: type

Past Tense: The secretary ___**typed**___ a letter for the Vice President.

Present Tense: The secretary ___**types**___ a letter for the Vice President.

Future Tense: The secretary ___**will type**___ a letter for the Vice President.

5. Verb: camp

Past Tense: The scientist ___**camped**___ deep in the Amazon rain forest.

Present Tense: The scientist ___**camps**___ deep in the Amazon rain forest.

Future Tense: The scientist ___**will camp**___ deep in the Amazon rain forest.

Copyright © 2004 by Pearson Education, Inc.

▼ **PRACTICE 21**   **Using Verb Tenses**

Complete the following sentences by filling in the blank spaces with the past tense form, the present tense form, and the future tense form of the verb provided.

1. Verb: trust

Past Tense: The employees ____trusted____ their boss.

Present Tense: The employees ____trust____ their boss.

Future Tense: The employees ____will trust____ their boss.

2. Verb: coordinate

Past Tense: The manager ____coordinated____ all cleaning responsibilities.

Present Tense: The manager ____coordinates____ all cleaning responsibilities.

Future Tense: The manager ____will coordinate____ all cleaning responsibilities.

3. Verb: exercise

Past Tense: Felicia ____exercised____ every morning at 4 a.m.

Present Tense: Felicia ____exercises____ every morning at 4 a.m.

Future Tense: Felicia ____will exercise____ every morning at 4 a.m.

4. Verb: juggle

Past Tense: The executive ____juggled____ a long list of activities.

Present Tense: The executive ____juggles____ a long list of activities.

Future Tense: The executive ____will juggle____ a long list of activities.

5. Verb: jump

Past Tense: The kangaroo ____jumped____ over the fence guarding the field.

Present Tense: The kangaroo ____jumps____ over the fence guarding the field.

Future Tense: The kangaroo ____will jump____ over the fence guarding the field.

▼ **PRACTICE 22**   **Using Verb Tenses**

Answers will vary.

Supply a present, past, or future tense verb in the space provided in each of the following sentences. In the parentheses, identify the tense for the verb you wrote.

Example: The eagle glides (present tense) over the river searching for salmon.

1. The girls _____ (_____) on the freshly mowed lawn.

2. The space shuttle _____ (_____) into the sky over

Florida.

3. The college student _____ (_____) for the History 101 final exam.

4. The cyclist _____ (_____) toward the finish line.

5. The kittens _____ (_____) together in the warmth of the sunbeam.

6. All 100 senators _____ (_____) the healthcare legislation.

7. Jennifer _____ (_____) the customer choose the correct pair of glasses.

8. The judge _____ (_____) the gavel on her desk to restore order.

9. José _____ (_____) three dozen fajitas for the party.

10. The choir _____ (_____) the gospel song with feeling and emotion.

▼ **PRACTICE 23**   **Using Verb Tenses**

Answers will vary.

Supply a present, past, or future tense verb in the space provided in each of the following sentences. In the parentheses, identify the tense for the verb you wrote.

1. The skater _____ (_____) on the frozen pond.

2. Kitaro _____ (_____) the chemistry exam.

3. Tina _____ (_____) lifting weights during gym class.

4. The bird _____ (_____) its feathers after a dip in the bird bath.

5. The engine _____ (_____) as the dragster reached the start line.

6. The senator _____ (_____) at the fund raiser banquet.

7. Icebergs _____ (_____) as they float aimlessly in the ocean.

Copyright © 2004 by Pearson Education, Inc.

8. The grasshopper _____ (_____) in the field of golden

corn.

9. The severe storms _____ (_____) across the Midwest.

10. Donny _____ (_____) while riding the roller coaster.

Compound Subjects

To this point, we have been using single subjects and single verbs. However, compound subjects and compound verbs also can be used in simple sentences. First, we explore compound subjects. A **compound subject** consists of two or more nouns or pronouns connected by *and, or, either/or,* or *neither/nor.* Some special relationships exist between certain compound subjects and their verb complements. For a discussion with exercises, see The Writer's Resources, Grammar, Subject/Verb Agreement and Compound Subject/Verb Agreement on pages 339–340.

> **Examples**
>
> *Bill and Raul* drove to the cineplex.
>
> *Either you or I* will have to pick Melanie up at the train station.
>
> *Neither Venice nor Rome* is ignored by tourists.

Compound subjects can be separated by other words, but they are still considered one subject as long as they are doing the same action or being the same thing.

> **Examples**
>
> *Charles* the dentist, *Clyde* the doctor, and *Phyliss* the chiropractor met for dinner.
>
> In this sentence, Charles, Clyde, and Phyliss are having dinner together.
>
> Large, powerful *St. Bernards*, sleek, fast *Russian greyhounds*, and small, aggressive *English terriers* are popular pets around the world.
>
> In this sentence, the various types of dogs share a common experience.

PRACTICE 24   Identifying Compound Subjects

Underline the compound subjects in the following sentences. To help you identify the subjects, cross out any prepositional phrases you find, and circle the verb.

1. The child's ears and nose (looked) just like its mother's.

2. Neither my golf coach nor my swimming coach (was) ever a professional.

3. Jupiter, Mars, and Venus (are) planets ~~in our solar system~~.

4. ~~After the dance~~, Joan and Jillian (drove) ~~to a private party~~.

5. The antique sofa, the art deco clock, and the abstract painting (were sold) ~~at auction~~.

6. ~~At Chicago's Navy Pier~~, Fred and Dianna (bought) three sweaters and a necklace.

7. The slithery snake, the prickly hedgehog, and the colorful parrot (are) the most popular animals ~~at the children's zoo~~.

8. ~~In the middle of the room~~, the food, the drinks, and the cake (covered) the table.

9. *Hamlet* and *Macbeth* (are) two ~~of Shakespeare's~~ most famous plays.

10. Either the cat or dog (knocked) the lamp and vase ~~onto the floor~~.

▼ **PRACTICE 25**   **Identifying Compound Subjects**

Underline the compound subjects in the following sentences. To help you identify the subjects, cross out any prepositional phrases you find, and circle the verb.

1. ~~For their new business venture~~, Jamal and Nerita (purchased) two computers.

2. Brad Pitt, Harrison Ford, and Tom Cruise (are) popular movie stars.

3. ~~At the auto show~~, neither Mick, Tina, nor Jacki (bought) a car.

4. The lawn mower, the edger, and the cultivator (sat) unused ~~in the garage~~.

5. *His* and *Hers* (are) popular monograms ~~on bath towels~~.

6. Either you or I (will have to make) dinner ~~for the cub scouts~~.

7. Chrysler, General Motors, and Ford (are known) ~~as the "Big Three" auto makers~~.

8. ~~In the middle of the night~~, snoring, cat calls, and crying infants (can reduce) sleep.

Copyright © 2004 by Pearson Education, Inc.

9. The <u>yellow finch</u>, the aptly named <u>red-breasted grosbeak</u>, and the <u>red-winged blackbird</u> (are) favorite subjects ~~for bird watching clubs~~.

10. <u>Nike</u>, <u>Adidas</u>, and <u>Reebok</u> (are) best-selling athletic shoes.

Compound Verbs

Like subjects, verbs also can be compound. A **compound verb** consists of more than one verb. With few exceptions, compound verbs are almost always connected by the conjunction *and*.

> **Examples**
> Janet *laughed and cried* during the movie.
> The horse *ran and jumped* as part of the rodeo contest.
> Paris *dazzles and excites* visiting tourists.

In the sentences above, notice that the subject is not repeated in front of the second verb. We do not write: *Paris dazzles* and *Paris excites* visiting tourists. Writing "Paris" twice is unnecessarily repetitive, and it makes the rhythm of the sentence choppy and awkward.

▾ **PRACTICE 26** **Identifying Compound Verbs**

Underline the compound verbs in the following sentences.

1. The horse <u>trotted and galloped</u> around the track.

2. The mechanic <u>tuned</u> the engine and <u>lubricated</u> the chassis of the car.

3. The audience <u>laughed and cried</u> at the actor's performance.

4. The broker <u>bought and sold</u> the investor's energy stocks.

5. The motel room <u>was clean and smelled</u> of lilacs and roses.

6. A fax machine <u>can save</u> money <u>and hasten</u> communications.

7. In New York City, skateboarders <u>ride</u> on subways and <u>skate</u> in parking garages.

8. Ramon <u>caught and cleaned</u> a bucketful of fish.

9. The legislature <u>argued and voted</u> on fifty-three bills this current session.

10. The police <u>chased and arrested</u> the bank robber.

▼ **PRACTICE 27** | **Identifying Compound Verbs**

Underline the compound verbs in the following sentences.

1. Lightning cracked and popped in the darkened sky.

2. In the auditorium, students clapped their hands and stomped their feet.

3. The two elk rivals snorted and brandished their antlers at one another.

4. The old fire engine jiggled and rattled down the cobblestone street.

5. A distant waterfall roared and thundered across the plain.

6. After the huge meal, the diners moaned and groaned.

7. The truck skidded, jackknifed, and crashed into the barrier.

8. Seabirds fly, dive, swim, and float while searching for food.

9. The bull lowered its head, scraped its hooves, and charged the matador.

10. The dancers twirled and leaped in time with the music.

▼ **PRACTICE 28** | **Writing Sentences with Compound Subjects and Verbs**

Answers will vary.

Write sentences for the following compound subjects and verbs. Provide compound subjects for the compound verbs listed and compound verbs for the compound subjects when given.

Examples: Bill/Ted—Bill and Ted laughed and cried during the movie.

Dribbled/Shot—Jill and Teiko dribbled and shot during the game.

1. Flight attendant/Passenger _____

_____

2. Swam/Lifted Weights _____

_____

3. Truck/Car _____

_____

4. Shivered/Trembled _____

_____

5. Ira/Sheila _____

_____

Copyright © 2004 by Pearson Education, Inc.

6. Camped/Hiked _____

_____

7. Flower/Tree _____

_____

8. Ate/Drank _____

_____

9. Teacher/Student _____

_____

10. Stumbled/Fell _____

_____

Correcting Sentence Fragments

A simple sentence consists of a single **independent clause.** An independent clause is a series of words with a subject, verb, and complete meaning. This means that the independent clause can stand on its own as a simple sentence. When you are writing sentences, be certain that each independent clause has a subject and a verb and complete meaning. If the subject, verb, or complete meaning is missing from the independent clause, then a sentence fragment error has occurred.

> **Examples of Sentence Fragments**
>
> **1.** Kicked the football. (no subject—who or what kicked the football?)
>
> To correct, add a subject:
> The <u>football player</u> kicked the football.
>
> **2.** The chef the fettuccine Alfredo. (no verb—what did the chef do in relation to the fettuccine Alfredo?)
>
> To correct, add a verb:
> The chef <u>prepared</u> the fettuccine Alfredo.
>
> **3.** The announcement of the new dress code caused all the employees. (insufficient meaning—what did the dress code cause the employees to do?)
>
> To correct, add additional information to create complete meaning:
> The announcement of the new dress code caused all the employees <u>to buy uniforms</u>.

▼
PRACTICE 29   **Correcting Sentence Fragments**

Answers will vary.   Correct and rewrite the following sentence fragments using the three techniques listed above.

1. Marathon runners, training for the Olympics, as many as 100 miles every week.

   _____

2. Build nests and lay eggs.

   _____

3. It was time for the archeologists.

   _____

4. Cooks in a short amount of time.

   _____

5. The man wearing the red vest.

   _____

6. The gigantic iceberg a hole in _Titanic_'s hull.

   _____

7. George a computer at a discount store to save money.

   _____

8. Can earn money by investing in mutual funds.

   _____

9. Broken racket strings was the reason for her.

   _____

10. Spilled the platter of ravioli on her Aunt Vidalia's new dress.

    _____

Copyright © 2004 by Pearson Education, Inc.

▼
PRACTICE 30   **Correcting Sentence Fragments**

Answers will vary.

Correct and rewrite the following sentence fragments using the three techniques listed above.

1. Ate the delicious apple strudel for dessert.

   _____

2. Ramon 14 hours a day to save enough tuition money for school.

   _____

3. The rugby team rode a bus for 14 hours in order.

_____

4. A chipped tooth caused the movie star to.

_____

5. The wine steward the list of the restaurant's entire stock.

_____

6. Measured the foundation before pouring the concrete.

_____

7. The entered the dark cave looking for a place to sleep.

_____

8. The baker sifted the flour before.

_____

9. The security guard to the third floor to make certain the doors were locked.

_____

10. The cleaned all the desks, mopped the floors, and emptied the wastebaskets.

_____

▼ PRACTICE 31   Editing Proper and Common Nouns and Pronoun References

In the following paragraph, underline once all proper nouns that are not capitalized, and underline twice all common nouns that are capitalized. Then, correct any capitalization errors that you have marked. Next, draw a line through all pronouns that do not clearly refer to a specific noun or nouns. If the reference is not clear, make the necessary changes. Finally, write your correctly edited paragraph on the lines provided.

Mike could have been a better Student. He was a senior at martin luther king High School and planned to go to college after Graduation. His work wasn't always done on time, and sometimes he forgot it altogether. Mike didn't always study, and he partied too much. It was the reason for his poor grades. Mike always seemed to know where and when good parties were going to happen. He always brought popular goodies to the parties, so he

was always welcome. His favorite party snacks were <u>hostess ding dongs</u> and

They were s
wild turkey bourbon. ~~It was~~ a big hit. One weekend, Mike was killed when
        ^   ^

the <u>ford mustang</u> ~~Mike~~ was driving smashed into a <u>dodge caravan</u>. His blood-

alcohol level was above the <u>Legal Amount</u>, and he had been driving over the

          they both were   s
speed limit. The police said ~~it was the~~ reason for the crash. Mike had
              ^   ^

become a victim of his own drunk driving.

    Mike could have been a better student. He was a senior at Martin Luther

King High School and planned to go to college after graduation. His work

wasn't always done on time, and sometimes he forgot it altogether. Mike

didn't always study, and he partied too much. These were the reasons for

his poor grades. Mike always seemed to know where and when good

parties were going to happen. He always brought popular goodies to the

parties, so he was always welcome. His favorite party snacks were Hostess

Ding Dongs and Wild Turkey bourbon. They were big hits. One weekend,

Mike was killed when the Ford Mustang he was driving smashed into a

Dodge Caravan. His blood-alcohol level was above the legal amount, and

he had been driving over the speed limit. The police said they both were

reasons for the crash. Mike had become a victim of his own drunk driving.

Copyright © 2004 by Pearson Education, Inc.

▼ **PRACTICE 32**   **Editing Subjects and Prepositional Phrases**

Nouns in prepositional phrases are often mistaken for the subject of the sentence. In the following paragraph, draw a line through the prepositional phrases, and underline the subject nouns. Punctuate the sentences correctly, and rewrite the paragraph on the lines provided.

    ~~During a tornado~~ <u>wind</u> and <u>lightning</u> cause most destruction. ~~In high~~

~~winds~~ <u>buildings</u> can be destroyed. As it passes a <u>tornado</u> causes a sudden

drop ~~in air pressure on the outside of the building.~~ ~~Inside the building~~ <u>air</u>

cannot escape fast enough to equalize the pressure ~~on the walls and roof.~~

Before the high winds tornadoes also create lightning. Along with the wind lightning can cause additional death and destruction. In a storm lightning can strike buildings, trees, and power lines. Without electricity, fires can rage out of control.

During a tornado, wind and lightning cause most destruction. In high winds, buildings can be destroyed. As it passes, a tornado causes a sudden drop in air pressure on the outside of the building. Inside the building, air cannot escape fast enough to equalize the pressure on the walls and roof. Before the high winds, tornadoes also create lightning. Along with the wind, lightning can cause additional death and destruction. In a storm, lightning can strike buildings, trees, and power lines. Without electricity, fires can rage out of control.

▼ PRACTICE 33   Editing Sentence Fragments

In the following paragraph, identify and underline sentence fragments. Then correct the sentence fragments and rewrite the paragraph on the lines provided.

Young children have difficulty adjusting to new environments. Moving to a different community. And living in a new house. Lead to more uncertainty. Unfamiliar bedrooms and neighbors. Often cause crying and real and imagined illness. Going to a new school also can be stressful. Because of the pressure of new friends and fitting in. Meeting new friends and being accepted by them can be a challenge. Comparing new friends to old friends can definitely. A reason for feeling abandoned and alone. However, taking part in activities with new acquaintances can help relieve stress and the uncertainty of new experiences.

Young children have difficulty adjusting to new environments. Moving to a different community and living in a new house lead to more uncertainty. Unfamiliar bedrooms and neighbors often cause crying and real and

imagined illness. Going to a new school also can be stressful because of

the pressure of new friends and fitting in. Meeting new friends and being

accepted by them can be a challenge. Comparing new friends to old

friends can definitely be a reason for feeling abandoned and alone.

However, taking part in activities with new acquaintances can help relieve

stress and the uncertainty of new experiences.

CHAPTER REVIEW

▼ A simple sentence contains a subject and verb, and has sufficient meaning. This also is the definition of an independent clause.

▼ The subject of a sentence is usually a noun or a pronoun. Nouns name persons, places, and things. Nouns can be common (general) or proper (particular). Proper nouns are always capitalized.

▼ Pronouns are used to replace nouns in order to avoid repetition.

▼ Subject nouns often are confused with the nouns in prepositional phrases.

▼ To help identify the subject in a sentence, cross out prepositional phrases.

▼ There are three types of verbs you should become familiar with: action verbs, linking verbs, and helping verbs.

▼ Action verbs describe what the subject is doing.

▼ Linking verbs connect the subject with an idea that describes the subject.

▼ Helping verbs combine with a main verb to form a group of words called a verb phrase.

▼ The helping verb gives the main verb a specific time reference or meaning.

▼ In writing, time is called *tense*. Because tense is shown primarily through the verb, time is more accurately called *verb tense*. The three simplest forms of verb tense are past, present, and future.

▼ Subjects can be compound. A *compound subject* consists of two or more nouns or pronouns connected by *and, or, either/or,* or *neither/nor.*

▼ Verbs can be compound. A *compound verb* consists of more than one verb. With few exceptions, compound verbs are connected by the conjunction *and.*

▼ Sentence fragments occur when the subject, verb, or sufficient meaning are missing from the sentence. Correct by adding a subject, a verb, or adding additional information to create sufficient meaning.

Copyright © 2004 by Pearson Education, Inc.

Visit *The Write Start* Online!

For additional practice with the materials found in this chapter, visit our Website at:

http://www.ablongman.com/checkett

The Website also features additional readings, quizzes, writing activities, and Internet links, as well as a bulletin board and interactive chat.

For More Practice with Your Grammar and Writing Skills
Visit The Longman Writer's Warehouse

For further multimedia exercises and activities designed to improve your reading, thinking, writing, and grammar skills, visit The Longman Writer's Warehouse on the Web. The Writer's Warehouse offers an interactive handbook, an online journal, a bulletin board, and extensive coverage of the writing process. To take a tour, go to

http://longmanwriterswarehouse.com

Copyright © 2004 by Pearson Education, Inc.

4

Linking Independent Clauses Using the Comma and Coordinators

You Need to Know

Before reading this chapter, you need to know the following about simple sentences:

- A simple sentence contains a subject, verb, and has sufficient meaning.
- A simple sentence contains one independent clause.
- Action verbs describe what the subject is doing.
- Linking verbs connect the subject with an idea that describes the subject.
- Helping verbs combine with the main verb and give the main verb time reference or meaning.
- Verbs express tense (time)—past, present, or future.
- Subjects and verbs can be compound.

Students needing help with these concepts should review Chapter 3.

Coordinating Conjunctions

Simple sentences are the basis for most writing; however, writing only with simple sentences can lead to dull writing, and complex ideas often need a more complex sentence format for developed expression. For the sake of variety and more complex ideas, a writer connects one simple sentence to another simple sentence by **using a comma (,)** and one of the following **coordinating conjunctions: B**ut, **O**r, **Y**et, **F**or, **A**nd, **N**or, **S**o. We remember the coordinating conjunctions by **BOYFANS** (taken from the first letter of each word). The BOYFANS conjunctions link simple sentences together to create *compound sentences*. Therefore, a **compound sentence** consists of two simple sentences (two independent clauses) linked together with a coordinating conjunction and a comma. We will learn about forming compound sentences using the BOYFANS conjunctions in this chapter. (There are other methods of forming compound sentences: using a semicolon, and using a semicolon and adverbial conjunction. These will be discussed in Chapters 5 and 6.)

The list below explains the meaning of each of the coordinating conjunctions in BOYFANS. They are not interchangeable. Note that the comma is placed before each coordinating conjunction to signal the start of the second complete sentence.

Using Coordinating Conjunctions

But—Use to connect two simple sentences that have contrasting meanings:

*Jawan hit the ball, **but** Christie caught the ball.*

Or—Use to combine two simple sentences that involve a choice:

*Christie could have thrown the ball to Jose, **or** she could have thrown it to home plate.*

Yet—Use to combine two simple sentences that have contrasting meanings:

*Jawan hit the ball, **yet** Christie caught the ball.*

For—Use to combine two simple sentences that involve a reason:

*Malik tried to score from second base, **for** there were already two outs.*

And—Use to combine two simple sentences that involve adding one idea to another:

*Jason hit the ball, **and** Latoya caught the ball.*

Nor—Use when the first simple sentence is in the negative and you want to combine it with another simple sentence:

*Mark does not like striking out, **nor** does Hakeem like sliding into a base.*

So—Use to combine two simple sentences that show a result:

*Isabel scored a run, **so** her team won the game.*

Instead of expressing ideas using all simple sentences, like this:

> Jawan hit the ball. Christie caught the ball. Christie could throw the ball to first base. She could throw the ball to third. Pang ran quickly to third base. Chinua tagged him out.

We can add variety and connect ideas, like this:

> Jawan hit the ball, **but** Christie caught the ball. Christie could throw the ball to first base, **or** she could throw the ball to third. Pang ran quickly to third base, **yet** Chinua tagged him out.

Notice that the coordinating conjunctions not only combine the shorter sentences into longer, more rhythmical ones, but they also help connect two different ideas, making them easier for the reader to understand.

Copyright © 2004 by Pearson Education, Inc.
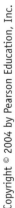

PRACTICE 1   Using Coordinating Conjunctions

Practice *coordinating* using *conjunctions*. Combine the following pairs of simple sentences by using a comma and the BOYFANS in the parentheses ( ).

1. (but) Jawan hit the ball. Christie caught the ball.

Jawan hit the ball, but Christie caught the ball.

2. (or) Christie could throw the ball to first base. She could throw the ball to third.

Christie could throw the ball to first base, or she could throw the ball

to third.

3. (yet) Pang ran quickly to third base. Chinua tagged him out.

Pang ran quickly to third base, yet Chinua tagged him out.

4. (for) Jefferson struck out three times. The pitcher threw a wicked curve-ball.

Jefferson struck out three times, for the pitcher threw a wicked curve-

ball.

5. (and) Tom singled four times. Angie hit two home runs.

Tom singled four times, and Angie hit two home runs.

6. (nor) Yoshi did not have a base on balls. Sarita did not bunt during the game.

Yoshi did not have a base on balls, nor did Sarita bunt during the game.

7. (so) Joe caused three errors. The other team scored five runs.

Joe caused three errors, so the other team scored five runs.

PRACTICE 2   Using Coordinating Conjunctions

Combine some more simple sentences, but this time you choose which BOYFANS you think works the best. Try not to use the same coordinating conjunction twice. Choose from the list:

But Or Yet For And Nor So

Examples: Mel wanted to go hiking. Shonda wanted to read a book.

Mel wanted to go hiking, but Shonda wanted to read a book.

1. Some friends wanted to go to the park. __, and__ Others wanted to go to the zoo.

2. Bicycling is good exercise. __, so__ Try to ride at least three times each week.

3. Salads are not only great tasting. __, but__ They are also healthy.

4. Morning is the best time to exercise. __, for__ There is less heat and humidity.

5. Genetics does not guarantee good health. __, so__ Eating only fruit is not the solution.

6. Fish is very tasty. __, yet__ Too much sauce can mask its taste.

7. Broccoli is a tasty and nutritious choice. __, or__ Asparagus also is a good choice.

PRACTICE 3	Using Coordinating Conjunctions

Answers will vary.

Try some more. Choose a different BOYFANS for each sentence, and remember to place a comma before each coordinating conjunction.

Examples: Flowers are very beautiful. Buying them can be expensive.

Flowers are very beautiful, but buying them can be expensive.

1. Jets travel to Chicago. Trains travel there, as well.

_____

2. Reading a book can be exciting. Listening to music can be soothing.

_____

3. Good grades are important. Study hard and do all homework.

_____

4. The car did not get good gas mileage. It did not ride smoothly either.

_____

5. John did not like the restaurant. He continued eating there.

_____

6. Jenny enjoyed hiking. The woods were both beautiful and quiet.

_____

7. Snakes can make interesting pets. They can be dangerous.

_____

PRACTICE 4   Combining Simple Sentences

Answers will vary.

Combine the following ten simple sentences. You can try different combinations in the spaces between the sentences. Write your finished effort on the blank lines provided below the sentences. You should finish with five combined sentences instead of ten single sentences.

The camping trip was exciting.

The trip to the national forest took 13 hours.

Everyone was tired but happy when they arrived.

The tents were easy to set up.

They had running water and electricity.

Dave did not bring mosquito repellant.

Juan did not bring extra blankets.

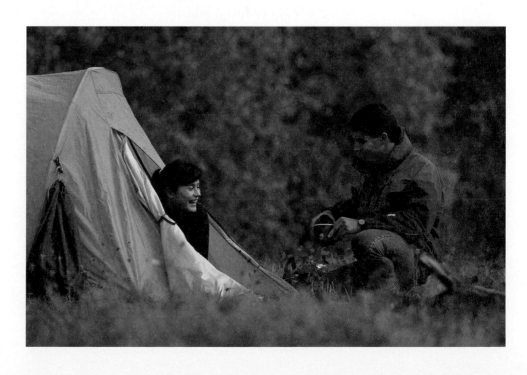

Copyright © 2004 by Pearson Education, Inc.

Everyone was hungry.

Pilar went to gather firewood.

The full moon emerged from the clouds later that evening.

Write your finished combined sentences below:

1. _____

2. _____

3. _____

4. _____

5. _____

▼
PRACTICE 5　　　**Combining Simple Sentences**

Answers will vary.　　Try combining pairs of sentences with a variety of coordinating conjunctions. You can use the spaces between the sentences to try different BOYFANS. Write your finished sentences on the blank lines provided below the sentences. You should finish with seven combined sentences instead of 14 single sentences.

Maurice loved to fish.

He went to the lake as often as possible.

His girlfriend Liz did not like to fish.

She did find riding in the boat fun.

They both liked camping.

It was restful sitting around the campfire.

Liz enjoyed cooking the fish.

She took responsibility for packing the cooking equipment.

Cleaning fish was not her favorite activity.

She did not like the taste.

Sometimes Liz would sit in the boat and read.

She would also apply lotion and try tanning in the afternoon sun.

The ride back home was long.

Both Maurice and Liz could not wait to return.

Write your finished combined sentences below:

1. _____

2. _____

3. _____

4. _____

5. _____

6. _____

7. _____

Correcting Run-on and Comma Splice Sentences

Now that you have practiced combining simple sentences to create compound sentences, there are two pitfalls you should avoid: run-on sentences and comma splice sentences.

Copyright © 2004 by Pearson Education, Inc.

Run-on

A **run-on sentence** commonly occurs when two independent clauses (complete ideas) are combined without a comma and a coordinating conjunction.

> **Example**
>
> Joan rides the subway to work the bus is too slow.
>
> This sentence announces two complete ideas:
>
> *Joan rides the subway to work—the bus is too slow.*

Here are two methods to correct a run-on sentence:

1. Create two separate sentences.

> Joan rides the subway to work. The bus is too slow.

2. Use a comma and a coordinating conjunction (**b**ut, **o**r, **y**et, **f**or, **a**nd, **n**or, **s**o) to link the two ideas together to create a correctly punctuated compound sentence.

> Joan rides the subway to work, **for** the bus is too slow.

Comma Splice

A **comma splice** sentence occurs when two independent clauses are joined with a comma but without a coordinating conjunction.

> **Example**
>
> Brian plays the cello, David plays the piano.
>
> This sentence announces two complete ideas joined (or spliced together—hence the name comma splice) by only a comma.
>
> *Brian plays the cello, David plays the piano.*

Correct the comma splice by adding a coordinating conjunction <u>after</u> the comma to create a correctly punctuated compound sentence.

> Brian plays the cello, **and** David plays the piano.

▼ **PRACTICE 6**   **Correcting Run-on and Comma Splice Errors**

Sentence corrections will vary.

Most of the following sentences contain run-on or comma splice errors. If you find a correct sentence, write **C** in the left-hand column. If the sentence contains a run-on or comma splice error, write either **RO** or **CS.** Then, correct the error using any of the techniques you have learned. Use all methods at least once.

Example: __RO__ The space shuttle program has been very expensive it has also been very successful.

The space shuttle program has been very expensive, but it has also been very successful. (coordinating conjunction added)

1. __CS__ The shuttle is designed to carry large payloads, there are accommodations for up to seven crew members.

_____

2. __CS__ The orbiter stage of the spacecraft has a lifetime of 100 missions, the winged orbiter can make unpowered landings on its return to earth.

_____

3. __C__ The shuttle is very flexible, for it can deploy and retrieve satellites.

_____

4. __RO__ Its supporters saw it as a step to space exploration they passed legislation to fund the project.

_____

5. __RO__ The first test flight occurred in 1981 various design problems surfaced.

_____

6. __CS__ The first operational flight happened in 1982, two communication satellites were placed in orbit.

_____

7. __C__ The seventh mission was memorable, for its crew included the first U.S. female astronaut, Sally K. Ride.

_____

8. __RO__ The program had many successes the program was in some trouble.

_____

9. __CS__ The shuttle program has been lagging in its commercial plan, the military began absorbing most of the payload launches.

_____

10. __RO__ Despite some setbacks, the U.S. government has not given up on the space shuttle program the program is still being funded.

_____

Copyright © 2004 by Pearson Education, Inc.

| PRACTICE 7 | Correcting Run-on and Comma Splice Errors |

Sentence corrections will vary.

Most of the following sentences contain run-on or comma splice errors. If you find a correct sentence, write **C** in the left-hand column. If the sentence contains a run-on or comma splice error, write either **RO** or **CS.** Then, correct the error using any of the techniques you have learned. Use all methods at least once.

1. __RO__ The sun dominates our solar system its huge mass produces enormous gravitational force.

_____

2. __RO__ Electromagnetic energy radiates from the sun's surface the energy supports all life on earth.

_____

3. __CS__ The sun is actually quite close to the earth, stellar phenomena can be studied in great detail.

_____

4. __C__ Many ancient cultures worshiped the sun, and others recognized its importance in the cycle of life.

_____

5. __RO__ Studying the sun has helped develop calendars solstices, equinoxes, and eclipses have also been studied for their own importance.

_____

6. __CS__ In 1611, Galileo used a telescope to discover dark spots on the sun's surface, Chinese astronomers reported sunspots in 200 B.C.

_____

7. __C__ The discovery of sunspots changed science's view of the sun, for the sun finally was seen as a dynamic, evolving body.

_____

8. __CS__ Progress in understanding the sun has continued, new scientific instruments have allowed new advances in observation.

_____

9. __CS__ The coronagraph permits study of the solar corona without the assistance of an eclipse, the magnetograph measures magnetic-field strength over the solar surface.

_____

10. __**RO**__ Interest in the sun has facilitated the discovery of new space instruments space telescopes and spectrographs sensitive to ultraviolet radiation revolutionized the study of the sun and outer space.

▼ **PRACTICE 8**   **Editing to Combine Sentences with Coordinating Conjunctions**

Answers will vary; sample answer given.

In the following paragraph, use coordinating conjunctions to reduce this eight-sentence paragraph to one containing only five sentences. Rewrite the finished paragraph on the lines provided.

While shopping at a successful department store, customers generally are offered products at a reduced price. Shoppers typically are offered items clearly marked with price tags. This allows customers to rapidly choose the merchandise that gives them the best value. A successful store honors its own coupons. It also accepts other department stores' advertised prices and coupons. Clearly marked prices and accepting all coupons ensure that the buyer will have a rewarding shopping experience. No matter which store it is, such policies offer shoppers an opportunity to receive the best possible price. Consumers have the convenience of shopping at one store instead of having to go to two or three.

While shopping at a successful department store, customers generally are offered products at a reduced price. Shoppers typically are offered items clearly marked with price tags, so this allows customers to rapidly choose the merchandise that gives them the best value. A successful store honors its own coupons, but it also accepts other department stores' advertised prices and coupons. Clearly marked prices and accepting all coupons ensure that the buyer will have a rewarding shopping experience, and no matter which store it is, such policies offer shoppers an opportunity receive the best possible price. Consumers have the convenience of shopping at one store instead of having to go to two or three.

Copyright © 2004 by Pearson Education, Inc.

PRACTICE 9   Editing to Combine Sentences with Coordinating Conjunctions

Answers will vary; sample answer given.

In the following paragraph, use coordinating conjunctions to reduce this eight-sentence paragraph to one containing only five sentences. Rewrite the finished paragraph on the lines provided.

When television was invented, most people soon forgot about listening to the radio. Only the older generation continued to listen. Television, at first, was produced in black and white and had little in the way of programming. Later, television expanded its programming both day and night. Black and white gave way to color. Years later, cable television was invented. Viewers could choose from more than 150 channels. Some people believe that television is better now than even during the 1950s, its "Golden Age."

When television was invented, most people soon forgot about listening to the radio. Only the older generation continued to listen, for television, at first, was produced in black and white and had little in the way of programming. Later, television expanded its programming both day and night, and black and white gave way to color. Years later, cable television was invented, so viewers could choose from more than 150 channels. Some people believe that television is better now than even during the 1950s, its "Golden Age."

PRACTICE 10   Editing to Correct Run-on and Comma Splice Errors

Answers will vary; sample answer given.

In the following paragraph, correct any run-on or comma splice errors you find. Rewrite the corrected paragraph on the lines provided.

Charleston and Gettysburg vary greatly in cultural attractions but both have a rich military history. Gettysburg's main attraction is based mostly on the great Civil War battle of the same name, many large monuments are located in the field where particular high points of the battle occurred. Also, a vast graveyard contains the bodies of thousands of unknown soldiers. On the other hand, Charleston possesses an equally famous Civil War monument for Fort Sumter is located at the mouth of Charleston's harbor. Tourists must

ride a ferry to the island fort and there they find a five-story museum filled

with national treasures. Because of their historical significance, both cities

make wonderful vacation stops.

Charleston and Gettysburg vary greatly in cultural attractions, but both

have a rich military history. Gettysburg's main attraction is based mostly on

the great Civil War battle of the same name; many large monuments are

located in the field where particular high points of the battle occurred.

Also, a vast graveyard contains the bodies of thousands of unknown

soldiers. On the other hand, Charleston possesses an equally famous Civil

War monument, for Fort Sumter is located at the mouth of Charleston's

harbor. Tourists must ride a ferry to the island fort, and there they find a

five-story museum filled with national treasures. Because of their historical

significance, both cities make wonderful vacation stops.

▼ **PRACTICE 11**   **Editing to Correct Run-on and Comma Splice Errors**

**Answers will vary;
sample answer given.**

In the following paragraph, correct any run-on or comma splice errors you
find. Rewrite the corrected paragraph on the lines provided.

Aerobics are programs of physical exercise, they help people improve

their level of fitness. An aerobic exercise program helps in weight reduction

and it helps lower the percentage of body fat. Aerobic exercise, sometimes

called *group fitness* or *group exercise*, enhances flexibility but it also increas-

es energy levels. Aerobics has other health benefits, it helps decrease blood

pressure and cholesterol levels. As always, contact a doctor before starting

any exercise program.

Aerobics are programs of physical exercise, so they help people

improve their level of fitness. An aerobic exercise program helps in weight

reduction, and it helps lower the percentage of body fat. Aerobic exercise,

Copyright © 2004 by Pearson Education, Inc.

sometimes called *group fitness* or *group exercise,* enhances flexibility, but
it also increases energy levels. Aerobics has other health benefits; it helps
decrease blood pressure and cholesterol levels. As always, contact a
doctor before starting any exercise program.

CHAPTER REVIEW

▼ Use coordinating conjunctions to combine simple sentences to create compound sentences. Remember the coordinating conjunctions by recalling BOYFANS—**B**ut, **O**r, **Y**et, **F**or, **A**nd, **N**or, **S**o.

▼ Each BOYFANS has its own meaning. They are not interchangeable.

But—use when contrasting meaning.

Or—use when there is a choice.

Yet—use when contrasting meaning.

For—use when there is a reason.

And—use when adding one idea to another.

Nor—use when the first simple sentence is in the negative.

So—use when a result is shown.

▼ Always place a comma before a coordinating conjunction when combining two simple sentences.

▼ Combining sentences helps connect ideas, adds sentence variety, and creates rhythm, which are important factors in making communications easier for the reader to understand.

▼ Correct run-on errors by either of two methods:

1. Create two separate sentences.
2. Add a comma and a coordinating conjunction to link the two independent clauses.

▼ Correct comma splice errors by adding a coordinating conjunction after the comma found between the two independent clauses.

Visit *The Write Start* Online!

For additional practice with the materials found in this chapter, visit our Website at:

http://www.ablongman.com/checkett

The Website also features additional readings, quizzes, writing activities, and Internet links, as well as a bulletin board and interactive chat.

For More Practice with Your Grammar and Writing Skills
Visit The Longman Writer's Warehouse

For further multimedia exercises and activities designed to improve your reading, thinking, writing, and grammar skills, visit The Longman Writer's Warehouse on the Web. The Writer's Warehouse offers an interactive handbook, an online journal, a bulletin board, and extensive coverage of the writing process. To take a tour, go to

http://longmanwriterswarehouse.com

Copyright © 2004 by Pearson Education, Inc.

5

Combining Independent Clauses Using the Semicolon

You Need to Know

In Chapter 4, you learned to link independent clauses (simple sentences) together to form compound sentences by using a comma with a coordinating conjunction. If you do not understand the relationship between independent clauses, simple sentences, coordinating conjunctions, and compound sentences, you should review Chapter 4.

Another method that a writer uses to combine simple sentences or independent clauses to create compound sentences is to use a **semicolon (;).** Keep in mind that a semicolon isn't a substitute for a comma; it's a substitute for a comma and a coordinating conjunction. Therefore, when using a semicolon, do not use a coordinating conjunction or a comma with it. Also, remember that the first word following the semicolon is *not* capitalized.

Proper Use

The anaconda is the world's largest snake; it can grow to 30 feet or more in length. ("size" is the relating idea)

Proper Use

The nurse measured the patient's blood pressure; she also took a blood sample. ("blood" is the relating idea)

Proper Use

The submarine dove to a depth of 300 fathoms; it hovered silently at that depth for two hours. ("depth" is the relating idea)

Do not combine sentences/independent clauses with a semicolon if the ideas are not closely related.

> **Improper Use**
>
> The bear rummaged through the camp food supply; some people believe in angels. (no relating idea)
>
> **Improper Use**
>
> Japan consists of four large islands; solar panels can generate electricity. (no relating idea)
>
> **Improper Use**
>
> Sundials are practical and decorative; snorkeling is a popular vacation pastime. (no relating idea)

When there is no relating idea between two simple sentences (independent clauses), as is the case in the three preceding examples, we cannot use a semicolon to combine them. Instead, we merely separate the two sentences with a period.

> **Examples**
>
> The bear rummaged through the camp food supply. Some people believe in angels.
>
> Japan consists of four large islands. Solar panels can generate electricity.
>
> Sundials are practical and decorative. Snorkeling is a popular vacation pastime.

The semicolon is used sparingly and only to connect very closely related ideas. The semicolon can add sentence variety to your writing, but don't overuse it.

▼ PRACTICE 1   Combining Sentences with Semicolons

The following ten simple sentences describe a medical operation. Because all the sentences deal with a common theme, we can combine some of them using semicolons. Choose those pairs of sentences that have a related idea and combine them with a semicolon. Leave the unrelated sentences as single simple sentences. Remember that the first word in the independent clause after the semicolon is not capitalized. Write your finished sentences, both those you combined and those you did not, on the lines following the list of original sentences.

The surgical team prepared the operating room for the procedure.

The surgeon dressed in a green surgical gown.

She wore a protective cap covering her hair.

Bach's *Toccata and Fugue in D Minor* was piped into the operating room during the operation.

It helped to maintain a relaxed atmosphere during the delicate procedure.

Copyright © 2004 by Pearson Education, Inc.

The operation was a success.

The patient experienced a quick recovery.

He was back at work in less than two weeks.

His insurance paid for the operation.

His family was happy to have him healthy again.

The surgical team prepared the operating room for the procedure.

The surgeon dressed in a green surgical gown; she wore a protective cap

covering her hair.

Bach's *Toccata and Fugue in D Minor* was piped into the operating room

during the operation; it helped to maintain a relaxed atmosphere during

the delicate procedure.

The operation was a success.

The patient experienced a quick recovery; he was back at work in less than

two weeks.

His insurance paid for the operation.

His family was happy to have him healthy again.

▼ PRACTICE 2	Writing Compound Sentences with Semicolons

Answers will vary.

Create compound sentences by adding a semicolon and an independent clause to the independent clauses below. Be certain that the independent clause you add has a relating idea that makes connecting the two ideas appropriate.

Example: The manager trained the crew each Friday _____

The manager trained the crew each Friday; the training was important.

1. The bakery held a sale once a week _____

_____

2. The passenger passed through the metal detector _____

_____

3. The books were arranged neatly on the shelves _____

_____

4. Simone waxed the china cabinet _____

_____

5. A strange noise came from the attic _____

_____

6. A flock of geese flew over the field _____

_____

7. Ari seemed perplexed by the math problem _____

_____

8. The driver applied the car's emergency brake _____

_____

9. *Gunsmoke* was a popular television western for decades _____

_____

10. The bells in the town hall steeple chimed every evening _____

_____

▼
| PRACTICE 3 | Writing Compound Sentences with Semicolons |

Answers will vary.

For each of the following topics, create a compound sentence by supplying two independent clauses combined with a semicolon. Write your finished sentences on the lines provided below the list of topics.

A favorite pet	A thoughtful gift
An exciting event	An enjoyable hobby/pastime
A memorable person	A disturbing dream
A meaningful place	A rewarding job
A fantastic meal	A fantastic vacation/trip

1. _____

_____

2. _____

_____

3. _____

_____

Copyright © 2004 by Pearson Education, Inc.

4. _____

_____

5. _____

_____

6. _____

_____

7. _____

_____

8. _____

_____

9. _____

_____

10. _____

_____

▼ PRACTICE 4　　Editing to Combine Sentences with Semicolons

Answers will vary; sample answer given.

In the following paragraph, use semicolons to reduce this nine-sentence paragraph to one containing only seven sentences. Remember, only combine sentences with a semicolon if the ideas in the two sentences are closely related. Rewrite your paragraph on the lines below.

To potential owners, any pet with the label "exotic" signals poor health and enormous veterinarian bills. However, a cockatiel is a good choice as the family pet. Cockatiels, while exotic looking, are rather hearty and can live 15 years or more. Most cockatiels are gray with white patches on their wings. They also have colorful crests that point straight toward the sky. A Pearl Lutino is a more exotic looking cockatiel. Its feathers are mostly yellow and white, with gray stripes running down long, elegant tail feathers. Big, perfectly round tufts that look like fuzzy peaches grow over the cockatiel's ears. Cockatiels are fairly small, usually measuring only 12 to 14 inches and weighing only 2 to 4 ounces.

To potential owners, any pet with the label "exotic" signals poor health and enormous veterinarian bills. However, a cockatiel is a good choice as the family pet. Cockatiels, while exotic looking, are rather hearty and can live 15 years or more. Most cockatiels are gray with white patches on their wings; they also have colorful crests that point straight toward the sky. A Pearl Lutino is a more exotic looking cockatiel. Its feathers are mostly yellow and white, with gray stripes running down long, elegant tail feathers; big, perfectly round tufts that look like fuzzy peaches grow over the cockatiel's ears. Cockatiels are fairly small, usually measuring only 12 to 14 inches and weighing only 2 to 4 ounces.

▼ PRACTICE 5   Editing to Combine Sentences with Semicolons

Answers will vary; sample answer given.

In the following paragraph, use semicolons to reduce this ten-sentence paragraph to one containing only eight sentences. Remember, only combine sentences with a semicolon if the ideas in the two sentences are closely related. Rewrite your paragraph on the lines below.

In general, cockatiels are friendly and sociable. They love to ride around on the shoulder of their owners, as if they were being chauffeured. An occasional nip on the ear is their way of showing the chauffeur appreciation for the ride. Cockatiels like to be included in all family gatherings. The most loving and affectionate cockatiels are those that are hand fed as chicks. In addition to being affectionate, cockatiels are intelligent and amusing. They are capable of whistling tunes and learning to perform a variety of tricks. Mimicry and playful interaction are further behaviors that make these birds fascinating. Like most birds, cockatiels love to have their heads scratched behind their long crest feathers. If a family chooses a cockatiel as its pet, the rewards will be well worth the effort to train and care for the bird.

In general, cockatiels are friendly and sociable; they love to ride around on the shoulder of their owners, as if they were being chauffeured. An

Copyright © 2004 by Pearson Education, Inc.

occasional nip on the ear is their way of showing the chauffeur

appreciation for the ride. Cockatiels like to be included in all family

gatherings. The most loving and affectionate cockatiels are those that are

hand fed as chicks. In addition to being affectionate, cockatiels are

intelligent and amusing; they are capable of whistling tunes and learning

to perform a variety of tricks. Mimicry and playful interaction are further

behaviors that make these birds fascinating. Like most birds, cockatiels

love to have their heads scratched behind their long crest feathers. If a

family chooses a cockatiel as its pet, the rewards will be well worth the

effort to train and care for the bird.

CHAPTER REVIEW

▼ Combine simple sentences or independent clauses with a semicolon.
▼ Make sure the sentences or independent clauses have a related idea.
▼ Do not use a coordinating conjunction (BOYFANS) with the semicolon.
▼ The word following the semicolon is not capitalized.

Visit *The Write Start* Online!

For additional practice with the materials found in this chapter, visit our Website at:

http://www.ablongman.com/checkett

The Website also features additional readings, quizzes, writing activities, and Internet links, as well as a bulletin board and interactive chat.

**For More Practice with Your Grammar and Writing Skills
Visit The Longman Writer's Warehouse**

For further multimedia exercises and activities designed to improve your reading, thinking, writing, and grammar skills, visit The Longman Writer's Warehouse on the Web. The Writer's Warehouse offers an interactive handbook, an online journal, a bulletin board, and extensive coverage of the writing process. To take a tour, go to

http://longmanwriterswarehouse.com

Copyright © 2004 by Pearson Education, Inc.

6

Combining Independent Clauses Using the Adverbial Conjunction

In Chapter 4, you learned to combine independent clauses and simple sentences by using a comma and a coordinating conjunction; in Chapter 5, you learned to do so using just a semicolon. These techniques allow you to create sentence variety and rhythm, and to establish connections between ideas.

You can add more variety to your writing by combining independent clauses and simple sentences with the use of **adverbial conjunctions.** Adverbial conjunctions are joining words that help you move from one idea to the next by linking ideas even more forcefully.

Commonly Used Adverbial Conjunctions and Their Meanings

Adverbial Conjunction	Meaning	Adverbial Conjunction	Meaning
accordingly	since, so	*however*	by contrast, in spite of
additionally	in addition	*incidentally*	by the way
also	in addition	*indeed*	in fact, undoubtedly
anyway	nevertheless, whatever	*likewise*	in the same way, similarly
besides	also, in addition	*meanwhile*	the time between events
certainly	inescapable, sure	*moreover*	in addition, more, plus
consequently	as a result of	*nevertheless*	but, despite, in spite of, still
finally	at the end	*next*	after, afterward, since
furthermore	in addition	*nonetheless*	however, nevertheless
hence	for this reason, from now	*now*	at present, immediately

(continued)

Adverbial Conjunction	Meaning	Adverbial Conjunction	Meaning
otherwise	under other circumstances	*thereafter*	from then on
similarly	as, as if, like	*therefore*	as a result, on account of
still	as before, now, yet	*thus*	as a result, in this way
then	at that time, next in time	*undoubtedly*	certainly, indeed, truly

Notice that some, but not all, adverbial conjunctions have similar meanings and can be used interchangeably. Also, notice that when using adverbial conjunctions, you must precede them with a semicolon and follow them with a comma.

Examples

The team practiced in the morning; furthermore, they practiced again in the evening.

Aunt Louisa stopped at the bakery; meanwhile, her niece waited in the car.

▼ PRACTICE 1   Using Adverbial Conjunctions

Answers will vary.

Add the adverbial conjunction that best expresses the appropriate relationship between the pairs of independent clauses that follow. Also, be sure to use correct punctuation. Do not use the same adverbial conjunction twice.

Example: Sheila hit the ball; however, she was thrown out at first base.

1. The CAT scan discovered a tumor _____ it turned out to be benign.

2. Wrestling at the high school or college level is physically demanding _____ staying in shape is a necessity.

3. Jackie did not like writing essays _____ she worked hard and received an "A" in the class.

4. The dentist warned my children to floss after every meal _____ cavities and gum disease would surely develop over the next few years.

5. The vacationers didn't like the tour guide's itinerary _____ they rented a car, bought a guide book, and went their own way.

6. The crew chief made out the weekly shift schedule _____ she

hired three evening workers.

7. The assistant unloaded the cases of soda _____ his boss settled

the account with the café's owner.

▼ **PRACTICE 2**   **Using Adverbial Conjunctions**

Answers will vary.

Read the following five independent clauses carefully. In the spaces provided, add an adverbial conjunction and an appropriately related second independent clause. Be sure that the second independent clause in each of the five resulting compound sentences clearly relates to the first, and that you use the correct adverbial conjunction to show this relationship. Also, be sure to use correct punctuation. Don't use the same adverbial conjunction more than once.

Example: The falling leaves covered the ground _____

_____.

The falling leaves covered the ground; **consequently,** the golfers had a difficult time finding their golf balls.

1. The volunteer dug the irrigation ditch for the village _____

_____

2. A puppy is cute and cuddly _____

_____

3. Speedboats are fast and exciting _____

_____

4. My boyfriend does not enjoy the ballet _____

_____

5. Purchasing a computer is important _____

_____

▼ **PRACTICE 3**   **Writing Compound Sentences with Adverbial Conjunctions**

Answers will vary.

Write five compound sentences, each having two related independent clauses. Use a different adverbial conjunction in each sentence to clarify the relationship existing between the two clauses. Do not use the same adverbial conjunction twice.

Copyright © 2004 by Pearson Education, Inc.

1. _____
   _____

2. _____
   _____

3. _____
   _____

4. _____
   _____

5. _____
   _____

▼ **PRACTICE 4**   **Editing to Combine Sentences with Adverbial Conjunctions**

Answers will vary; sample answer given.

In the following paragraph, use adverbial conjunctions to reduce this twelve-sentence paragraph to one containing only nine sentences. Remember, use a semicolon before the conjunction and a comma afterward. Also, choose the adverbial conjunction that best describes the relationship between the sentences. Rewrite your paragraph on the lines below.

During my high school career, I made a point of becoming involved. I was in many different activities, from volunteer clubs to sports. I believe that this really helped me. I made friends with classmates whom I might never have gotten to know if it weren't for the volleyball team or Kiwanis club. I learned to work with others. I also am very proud of what I achieved through my activities. I learned valuable life lessons, such as forming friendships, the importance of teamwork, and pride in a job well done. Many students go into high school as shy, timid mice. They graduate as big, roaring bears. Participating in extracurricular activities helps this process take place. It gives students self-confidence which, in turn, helps them throughout their entire lives. The activities students participate in, and the knowledge they acquire, will stay with them forever.

During my high school career, I made a point of becoming involved; **accordingly,** I was in many different activities, from volunteer clubs to sports. I believe that this really helped me. I made friends with classmates whom I might never have gotten to know if it weren't for the volleyball team or Kiwanis club. I learned to work with others. I also am very proud of what I achieved through my activities. I learned valuable life lessons, such as forming friendships, the importance of teamwork, and pride in a job well done. Many students go into high school as shy, timid mice; **however,** they graduate as big, roaring bears. Participating in extracurricular activities helps this process take place; **consequently,** it gives students self-confidence which, in turn, helps them throughout their entire lives. The activities students participate in, and the knowledge they acquire, will stay with them forever.

▼ **PRACTICE 5**   **Editing to Combine Sentences with Adverbial Conjunctions**

Answers will vary; sample answer given.

In the following paragraph, use adverbial conjunctions to reduce this twelve-sentence paragraph to one containing only nine sentences. Remember, use a semicolon before the conjunction and a comma afterward. Also, choose the adverbial conjunction that best describes the relationship between the sentences. Rewrite your paragraph on the lines below.

Many of the activities I participated in during high school involved teamwork. For example, in volleyball, the team must have a plan in order to defeat the opponent. The front line players and the back line players must coordinate their movements. Defensive and offensive strategies can shift from one second to the next depending on where the ball is hit and how the other team is positioning its players. The players have to make secret signals to one another in order to act together. Another activity I was involved with in high school took us into the city to winterize houses belonging to people who couldn't afford to do it themselves. We put plastic over the windowpanes. The plastic sheets were large and difficult to hold steady in the

Copyright © 2004 by Pearson Education, Inc.

wind. The hammers were heavy and awkward to use. It took three-person teams to finish each window. The job would have been impossible if we didn't work together. I learned how important teamwork is in everyday life.

Many of the activities I participated in during high school involved teamwork. For example, in volleyball, the team must have a plan in order to defeat the opponent; therefore, the front line players and the back line players must coordinate their movements. Defensive and offensive strategies can shift from one second to the next depending on where the ball is hit and how the other team is positioning its players; consequently, the players have to make secret signals to one another in order to act together. Another activity I was involved with in high school took us into the city to winterize houses belonging to people who couldn't afford to do it themselves. We put plastic over the windowpanes. The plastic sheets were large and difficult to hold steady in the wind; similarly, the hammers were heavy and awkward to use. It took three-person teams to finish each window. The job would have been impossible if we didn't work together. I learned how important teamwork is in everyday life.

CHAPTER REVIEW

▼ Combine simple sentences or independent clauses using an adverbial conjunction. Remember to precede the adverbial conjunction with a semicolon and follow it with a comma.
▼ The word following the comma is not capitalized.
▼ Make certain the adverbial conjunction you choose clarifies the nature of the relationship between the two independent clauses or simple sentences.

Putting It All Together

Linking two independent clauses or simple sentences by using a semicolon is the least emphatic link because it merely shows that the two ideas are related somehow.

> **Example**
>
> Glenn's favorite pastime is listening to music; he doesn't play an instrument.

Using a comma and a coordinating conjunction is a more emphatic link because the choice of BOYFANS provides a clue as to the nature of the relationship.

> **Example**
>
> Glenn's favorite pastime is listening to music, but he doesn't play an instrument.

The adverbial conjunction, however, provides the most explicit and forceful link because the choice of adverbial conjunction tells you the nature of the relationship and also adds some perceived importance because of the dramatic pause.

> **Example**
>
> Glenn's favorite hobby is listening to music; however, he doesn't play an instrument.

▼ PRACTICE 6   Combining Sentences

Answers will vary.

Combine the following pairs of independent clauses using one of the three methods you have learned in Chapters 4, 5, and 6: a semicolon, a coordinating conjunction (BOYFANS) preceded by a comma, or an adverbial conjunction preceded by a semicolon and followed by a comma. Place your choices in the spaces provided.

1. Abstract art form has little direct reference to external or perceived reality _____ it is normally synonymous with various types of twentieth century avant-garde art.

2. The term *abstract* also refers to images that have been abstracted or derived from nature _____ the images have been considerably altered or have been simplified to their basic geometric or biomorphic forms.

3. The term *nonobjective* has been abandoned by most critics _____ now they have supplanted it with the term *abstract*.

4. Abstract expressionism appeared in the mid-twentieth century _____ it was primarily concerned with expression through line and color.

Copyright © 2004 by Pearson Education, Inc.

5. The artist was interested in expressing emotional reaction to the world _____ objective experiences and situations were seen as less interesting.

6. The movement was part of the organic, emotional, expressionistic approach to art _____ it was developed to contrast with the geometrically structural, rationalistic approach of the cubists.

7. The roots of abstract expressionism can be found in the works of Kandinsky, Ernst, Duchamp, Chagall, and Tanguy _____ they inspired a blossoming of abstract expressionism among American painters in the 1950s.

8. The abstract movement centered in New York City _____ this core of American painters was dubbed the New York School.

9. The New York School included many now-famous artists _____ Pollock, de Kooning, Kline, and Rothko were the most famous American artists.

10. Abstract expressionism also flourished in Europe _____ the Tachism School emphasized patches of color while the Art Informal School rejected formal structure.

PRACTICE 7   Combining Sentences

Answers will vary.

Combine the following pairs of independent clauses using one of the three methods you learned in Chapters 4, 5, and 6: a semicolon, a coordinating conjunction (BOYFANS) preceded by a comma, or an adverbial conjunction preceded by a semicolon and followed with a comma. Place your choices in the spaces provided.

1. The moon is a natural satellite of the earth _____ the name *moon* is sometimes applied to the satellites of other planets in the solar system.

2. The moon's diameter is about 2160 miles _____ while this is a large distance, it is only about one-fourth that of earth.

3. The moon's volume is about one-fiftieth that of earth _____ the mass of the earth is 81 times greater than the mass of the moon.

4. The moon has no free water and no atmosphere _____ no weather exists to change its surface topography.

5. The moon orbits the earth at an average distance of 238,000 miles _____ it completes one revolution around the earth every 27 days, 7 hours, 43 minutes, and 11.5 seconds.

6. At any one time, an observer can see only 50 percent of the moon's entire surface _____ an additional 9 percent can be seen around the apparent edge because of the relative motion called *libration.*

7. Libration is caused by slightly different angles of view from the earth _____ different relative positions of the moon influence our "true" perception of it.

8. The moon shows progressively different phases as it moves along its orbit _____ half the moon is always in sunlight, just as half the earth has day while the other half has night.

9. In the phase called the *new moon,* the face is completely in shadow _____ about a week later, the moon is in first quarter, resembling a luminous half-circle.

10. Another week later, the full moon shows its fully lighted surface _____ a week afterward, in its last quarter, the moon appears as a half-circle once again.

Copyright © 2004 by Pearson Education, Inc.

PRACTICE 8   Editing to Combine Sentences

Choose three pairs of sentences in the following paragraph and combine them by using all three of the methods you learned in Chapters 4, 5, and 6: a semicolon, a coordinating conjunction (BOYFANS) preceded by a comma, and an adverbial conjunction preceded by a semicolon and followed with a comma. Do not use the same method more than once. Write your completed paragraph on the lines provided below.

The late November clouds gathered slowly throughout the day, forming a thick, gray blanket by the time the evening sky had darkened. The winter blizzard came to the farm during the night like a stealthy coyote sneaking up on an unsuspecting hen house. In the corners of the intersecting fences, the snowflakes waltzed in circles like miniature tornadoes. They changed speed and direction depending on the wind gusts. The snow banked high against the fence posts and rails also affected the little whirlwinds of ice and snow. Rising and falling silently, the snow swirls were silhouetted against the hazy aura of the moon straining to be seen through the overcast sky. The night grew like a black tide on the ocean. The snow stopped. The air sparkled with shimmering dust-like flakes kicked by imperceptible puffs of wind. The chilled air made the snow's surface crisp and brittle. Soon, hard rubber tires would crunch the snow into stiff, well-formed patterns.

Answers will vary, but each method should be used once to combine a pair of sentences.

Visit *The Write Start* Online!

For additional practice with the materials found in this chapter, visit our Website at:

http://www.ablongman.com/checkett

The Website also features additional readings, quizzes, writing activities, and Internet links, as well as a bulletin board and interactive chat.

For More Practice with Your Grammar and Writing Skills Visit The Longman Writer's Warehouse

For further multimedia exercises and activities designed to improve your reading, thinking, writing, and grammar skills, visit The Longman Writer's Warehouse on the Web. The Writer's Warehouse offers an interactive handbook, an online journal, a bulletin board, and extensive coverage of the writing process. To take a tour, go to

http://longmanwriterswarehouse.com

Copyright © 2004 by Pearson Education, Inc.

7 Adding a List

So far, you have been combining independent clauses and simple sentences to add sentence variety and rhythm, and to connect related ideas. Sometimes a simple sentence or a combination of two simple sentences isn't sufficient to express your thoughts as a writer. Often, you will need to add information to clarify or expand on your ideas. Another way to add variety to your writing is to use **lists**—items in a series. Not only can lists vary your writing, they also can add necessary information to explain, clarify, or illustrate one of your ideas.

> **Example**
>
> Charles went to the mall to shop.

This sentence does not clarify what it was that Charles bought.

> **Example**
>
> Charles went to the mall and purchased a <u>CD, a shirt, and sunglasses.</u>
>
>   ↑
>
>   the list

By using a list, what Charles bought at the mall is illustrated.

A **series** can consist of single words (nouns, adjectives, verbs, adverbs) or prepositional phrases.

> **Examples**
>
> The pizza was topped with <u>cheese, sausage, green onions, and mushrooms.</u> (nouns)
>
> The <u>large, powerful, and majestic</u> lion sleeps 16 hours a day. (adjectives)
>
> The athlete <u>walks, jogs, runs, and sprints</u> during practice. (verbs)
>
> The sea otter swims <u>swiftly, smoothly, and playfully.</u> (adverbs)
>
> The cruise ship offers extravagant meals <u>in the morning, in the afternoon, in the evening, and after midnight.</u> (prepositional phrases beginning with *in* and *after*)

For definitions and examples of adjectives and adverbs, see The Writer's Resources, Grammar, Adjectives, Adverbs (pages 343, 345).

Punctuating and Placing the List

The list can be added at the beginning, middle, or end of the sentence.

> **Examples**
>
> *Beginning*: Cheese, wine, and fruit were served at the picnic.
> *Middle*: The hosts served cheese, wine, and fruit at the picnic.
> *End*: The food served at the picnic included cheese, wine, and fruit.

Notice the use of commas in our examples. In lists with three or more items, you need to separate each item from the other items with a comma. In lists with only two items, you do not need to use a comma. Instead, you can separate the two items with the word *and*.

> **Examples**
>
> *Two-item series*: The taxicab stopped and started. (no commas)
> *Three-or-more-item series*: The taxicab stopped, started, and sped away.

▼ **PRACTICE 1**   **Identifying and Punctuating Series**

Underline the series in each sentence, and punctuate it correctly. If you think the sentence is correct, write a **C** in front of the sentence's number.

Example: The Super Bowl Football game included four touchdown passes, three extra-points failing, and a parachutist landing at midfield.

1. They ordered steak, potatoes, and asparagus at dinner.

2. The three cats hid under the table, in the closet, and in the basement during the thunderstorm.

C 3. The weather consisted of rain and sleet.

4. King Albert, Queen Lucinda, and Prince Arn rode inside a golden carriage.

5. The garden consisted of tulips, crocuses, and jonquils during the three months of spring.

6. The groups of high school seniors, corporate executives, and international chefs toured Rome for three days.

7. The fog blanketed the fields in the morning, during the afternoon, and after dark.

Copyright © 2004 by Pearson Education, Inc.

C **8.** Talent and poise are ingredients for a successful career in business.

9. The orchestra's <u>violins,cellos,and violas</u> answered the woodwinds during the second movement.

10. The trapeze artist <u>soared over the crowd,performed a loop,and swung upside down.</u>

▼ **PRACTICE 2**   **Writing and Punctuating Series**

Answers will vary.

Add a list to complete each of the following incomplete sentences. Punctuate correctly.

1. _____

_____ made the workers thirsty.

2. The dolphins _____

_____

3. The hosts and their guest followed dinner _____

_____

4. The entire choir _____

_____ prior to the concert.

5. Justin's favorite rides at the amusement park were _____

_____

6. The carpenter _____

_____ to complete the project.

7. The cowboy won the rodeo by _____

_____

8. The chef prepared _____

_____ for his customers.

9. _____

_____ made the farmer successful.

10. The early morning hours are the teacher's favorite time for _____

_____

Copyright © 2004 by Pearson Education, Inc.

▼ **PRACTICE 3**   **Writing Sentences with Series**

Answers will vary.   Write three different sentences, each containing three or more items in a list. Place the list at the beginning of one sentence, in the middle of one sentence, and at the end of one sentence. Punctuate each sentence correctly.

1. _____

   _____

2. _____

   _____

3. _____

   _____

Parallelism in a Series

As we have seen, lists can be made up of nouns, adjectives, verbs, adverbs, and phrases. Any items work well in the list *as long as every item in the list is the same type of word or phrase.* This is known as **parallelism.**

Mixing different categories of words or phrases in the same list makes the sentence hard to read and understand.

> **Example**
> The birds are finches, under a tree, and yellow.

In this example, a noun, a prepositional phrase, and an adjective have been mixed inappropriately as the items in the list. See how confusing this sentence is. It also sounds choppy. Additionally, the reader might be confused as to which item is yellow—the finch or the tree. Parallel lists read smoothly and rhythmically, and they clarify content.

> **Examples**
>
> At the supermarket, Sarina purchased <u>bread, butter, and milk</u>. (nouns)
>
> The garden was <u>colorful, fragrant, and beautiful</u>. (adjectives)
>
> Frank <u>swims, bicycles, and runs</u> every day for triathlon practice. (verbs)
>
> The gymnast vaulted <u>athletically, aggressively, and purposefully</u>. (adverbs)
>
> Chin looked for the passport <u>in the dresser, on the counter, and under the newspaper</u>. (prepositional phrases, beginning with *in, on,* and *under*)

▼ **PRACTICE 4**   **Writing Lists with Parallel Items**

Answers will vary.

Add a three-item list to complete each of the sentences below. Be certain that each list is parallel and achieves clear content and consistent rhythm.
Make one list each of nouns, adjectives, verbs, adverbs, and phrases.

1. My favorite music groups are _____, _____, and _____.

2. The ice-cream sundae was _____, _____, and _____.

3. When Shaunista was a teenager, she would hide her diary _____, _____, and _____.

4. The air show audience was fascinated by the experimental airplane's _____, _____, and _____ shape.

5. The space shuttle roared _____, _____, and _____ into the clouds over the Kennedy Space Center.

▼ **PRACTICE 5**   **Writing Sentences with Lists**

Answers will vary.

For each of the topics listed below, write a sentence that includes a list. Be certain that each list is parallel. Make one list each of nouns, adjectives, verbs, adverbs, and phrases. Punctuate correctly.

1. Library— _____

2. Weather— _____

_____

3. Car— _____

_____

4. Dating— _____

_____

5. Sky-diving— _____

_____

▼ **PRACTICE 6**   **Editing Series**

Answers will vary; sample answer given.

Edit the following paragraph, combining sentences (2), (3), (4), and (5) into one sentence. Do so by reducing sentences (3), (4), and (5) to a list and adding the list to sentence (2). Remember, your finished series should exhibit parallelism. Rewrite the paragraph on the lines below.

(1)Although most dogs are simply family pets, there is a class of dogs that earn their keep in more ways than one. (2)Working dogs serve humans daily through a variety of avenues. (3)They help blind persons. (4)They use their sense of smell to find illegal narcotics. (5)They also help ranchers control herds of livestock. (6)From the earliest recorded history, dogs have helped people survive by providing numerous services.

Although most dogs are simply family pets, there is a class of dogs that earn their keep in more ways than one. Working dogs serve humans daily through a variety of avenues, such as guiding the blind, assisting narcotics agents, and helping ranchers. From the earliest recorded history, dogs have helped people survive by providing numerous services.

▼ **PRACTICE 7**   **Editing Series**

Answers will vary; sample answer given.

Edit the following paragraph, combining sentences (3), (4), (5), and (6) into one sentence. Do so by reducing sentences (4), (5), and (6) to a list and adding the list to sentence (3). Remember, your finished series should exhibit parallelism. Rewrite the paragraph on the lines below.

Copyright © 2004 by Pearson Education, Inc.

(1)Oldies music stations play songs from the 50s, 60s, and 70s. (2)This music is a great hit with "baby boomers" and anyone else who used to listen to it. (3)These stations focus on playing music by the most popular performers. (4)They play tunes by the Beatles. (5)They play songs by Elvis. (6)They also play hits by the Supremes. (7)Even though music and the music industry have changed over the decades, stations that play oldies from the 50s, 60s, and 70s are still popular in the new millennium.

Oldies music stations play songs from the 50s, 60s, and 70s. This music is a great hit with "baby boomers" and anyone else who used to listen to it. These stations focus on playing music by the most popular performers, such as the Beatles, Elvis, and the Supremes. Even though music and the music industry have changed over the decades, stations that play oldies from the 50s, 60s, and 70s are still popular in the new millennium.

CHAPTER REVIEW

▼ A list of words and phrases can be added to a sentence to explain, clarify, or illustrate a basic idea.

▼ In a two-item list, the word *and* separates the items in the list, and no comma is used.

▼ In a three-item list, the items in the list are separated by a comma.

▼ The list can be added at the beginning, middle, or end of the sentence.

▼ Categories of words (nouns, adjectives, verbs, adverbs) and different kinds of phrases should not be mixed in a list. Items in a list must be parallel for clear meaning and consistent rhythm.

Visit *The Write Start* Online!

For additional practice with the materials found in this chapter, visit our Website at:

http://www.ablongman.com/checkett

The Website also features additional readings, quizzes, writing activities, and Internet links, as well as a bulletin board and interactive chat.

For More Practice with Your Grammar and Writing Skills Visit The Longman Writer's Warehouse

For further multimedia exercises and activities designed to improve your reading, thinking, writing, and grammar skills, visit The Longman Writer's Warehouse on the Web. The Writer's Warehouse offers an interactive handbook, an online journal, a bulletin board, and extensive coverage of the writing process. To take a tour, go to

http://longmanwriterswarehouse.com

Copyright © 2004 by Pearson Education, Inc.

8 Adding a Colon for Variety

To add sentence variety and to emphasize particular information, you can use a colon. A colon looks like one period above another period (:). Use a colon to do the following:

▼ To introduce a list
▼ When telling time
▼ For the salutation of a business letter
▼ To separate the title and subtitle of a book or movie

1. Use a colon after an independent clause to introduce a list.

> **Examples**
>
> Preparing a soufflé requires four ingredients: milk, eggs, butter, and cheese.
>
> The pharmacy technician ordered the items sold most often: aspirin, gauze, bandages, and antacid.

Note: Do not use a colon before a list if the list immediately follows a verb or a preposition.

> **Examples**
>
> The most popular condiments are: catsup, mustard, and mayonnaise. (omit colon after verb)
>
> You will find the cats hiding under: the house, the porch, the tool shed. (omit colon after preposition)

It is best only to use a colon after an independent clause.

> **Examples**
>
> The following are the most popular condiments: catsup, mustard, and mayonnaise.
>
> The cats were found in the following places: under the house, under the porch, and under the tool shed.

2. Use a colon when telling time.

> **Examples**
> The train arrived at 4:15 P.M.
> My 2:30 P.M. doctor's appointment was changed to 5:00 P.M.

3. Use a colon for the salutation of a business letter.

> **Examples**
> Dear Mrs. Hilliard:
> To Whom It May Concern:
> Sirs:

4. Use a colon to separate the titles and subtitles of books or movies.

> **Examples**
> *Accounting in Context: A Business Handbook*
> *Writing Made Easy: A Plain Language Rhetoric*
> *Washington: The First Leader of the Nation*
> *Star Wars: Attack of the Clones*

▼ PRACTICE 1   Using Colons

Add colons to introduce lists, to tell time, and to separate titles and subtitles of books or movies in the following sentences.

1. The teacher taught using a variety of methods: lecturing, using an overhead projector, and assigning in-class group projects.

2. Jerry enjoyed many activities while vacationing: boating, fishing, and hiking.

3. The Concorde jetliner left Paris at 6:05 P.M. instead of its scheduled time of 5:50 P.M.

4. The librarian reshelved the book left on her desk: *Retire Early: How to Make Money in Real Estate Foreclosures.*

5. The two movies had different start times: *The Front* at 4:40 P.M., and *Lord of the Rings: The Two Towers* at 4:55 P.M.

6. The office workers ate lunch in a variety of places: in the employee lounge, on the roof, and out by the lake.

Copyright © 2004 by Pearson Education, Inc.

7. Sheila enjoyed reading the new book about food shopping: *Using Coupons:*
   Free Meals for Your Family.

8. Joaquin used three types of peppers to add color to his special salsa: red,
   yellow, and green.

9. HOMES is a mnemonic device to help people remember the names of the
   five Great Lakes: Huron, Ontario, Michigan, Erie, and Superior.

10. The children enjoyed the party because of the food: hot dogs, hamburgers,
    and chips.

▼ **PRACTICE 2**   **Correcting Colon Errors**

Correct the colon errors in the following sentences. You will have to rewrite
some of the sentences to do so. Write the revised sentences on the lines
provided.

1. The two falcons: found a tree, gathered twigs, and built a nest.

   The two falcons found a tree, gathered twigs, and built a nest.

   _____

2. My bus left the station at 515, instead of 615 as written in the schedule.

   My bus left the station at 5:15, instead of 6:15 as written

   in the schedule.

3. The surgical team had a good reputation because: they were up on the

   latest techniques and had worked together for four years.

   The surgical team had a good reputation because they were up on

   the latest techniques and had worked together for four years.

4. The Liberian flag is: red, white, and blue.

   The Liberian flag is red, white, and blue.

   _____

5. The movie was titled *Strangers The Story of a Mother and a Daughter.*

   The movie was titled *Strangers: The Story of a Mother and a Daughter.*

   _____

6. The man's hidden desires turned out to be: baseball, baseball, and baseball.

   The man's hidden desires turned out to be baseball, baseball,

   and baseball.

7. The plane: could not take off: the engine wasn't powerful enough to handle the load.

   The plane could not take off; the engine wasn't powerful enough

   to handle the load.

8. The book was titled *Towards Better Scoring on the SAT An Exercise Booklet.*

   The book was titled *Towards Better Scoring on the SAT:*

   An Exercise Booklet.

9. Amelia was in a hurry because her date was at 700 P.M., and it was already 645 P.M.

   Amelia was in a hurry because her date was at 7:00 P.M., and it was

   already 6:45 P.M.

10. The children's favorite schoolyard activities were: riding the merry-go-round, climbing the jungle-gym, and playing hopscotch.

    The children's favorite schoolyard activities were riding the

    merry-go-round, climbing the jungle gym, and playing hopscotch.

▼ **PRACTICE 3**   **Writing Sentences with Colons**

Answers will vary.

Write three sentences using the colon to introduce a list, to include a time, and to illustrate a book or movie title and subtitle.

1. _____

   _____

2. _____

   _____

3. _____

   _____

Copyright © 2004 by Pearson Education, Inc.

▼ **PRACTICE 4**   Editing for Colons

Edit the following paragraph, adding colons where appropriate.

Movies are popular because of two factors : actors and genres. Star-power can almost guarantee that a movie will make money. There are a handful of stars in this category : Denzel Washington, Julia Roberts, and Tom Hanks. If tickets for movies starring one of these actors go on sale at 2 : 00 P.M., the "Sold Out" sign usually lights up by 4 : 00 P.M. Fantasy-action movies are some of the most popular movies currently running. Some of the largest grossing movies in history belong to this genre : *Star Wars* : *The Return of the Jedi, Lord of the Rings* : *The Fellowship of the Ring*, and *Harry Potter* : *The Sorceror's Stone*, to name a few. If movie producers can combine a popular star with a popular genre, a box-office bonanza is almost a sure thing.

▼ **PRACTICE 5**   Editing for Colons

Edit the following letter, adding colons where appropriate.

Dear Ms. Morgan :

Thank you for your recent inquiry concerning what to expect here at Middletown University during your first year as a student. As you know, there are certain personal traits that will stand you in good order both at school and your future place of employment : financial responsibility, time management, and cooperation. Working to help with expenses teaches the value of money and what it represents in terms of goods and services. Time management is an important skill to learn. For instance, in her best selling business book, *Time Management* : *Workplace Wizardry*, author Meghan Brooks suggests that you should never get out of bed later than 6 : 00 A.M. By 7 : 00 A.M. you should have your daily schedule complete. Doing this will keep you organized and focused on each task. Cooperation, of course, will help you enormously while you are attending Middletown. You will be working and interacting with a wide array of individuals: administrators, staff, faculty, and other students. I hope this letter helps answer your concerns. Please do not hesitate to contact me during my office hours 3:00 P.M., Wednesdays, and 10:00 A.M. Thursdays.

Sincerely yours,

Ronald Blevins, Dean

Arts & Humanities Division

CHAPTER REVIEW

▼ Use a colon after an independent clause to introduce a list.
▼ Do not use a colon before a list if the list immediately follows a verb or a preposition.
▼ Use a colon when telling time.
▼ Use a colon for the salutation of a business letter.
▼ Use a colon to separate the title and subtitle of a book or movie.

Visit *The Write Start* Online!

For additional practice with the materials found in this chapter, visit our Website at:

http://www.ablongman.com/checkett

The Website also features additional readings, quizzes, writing activities, and Internet links, as well as a bulletin board and interactive chat.

For More Practice with Your Grammar and Writing Skills
Visit The Longman Writer's Warehouse

For further multimedia exercises and activities designed to improve your reading, thinking, writing, and grammar skills, visit The Longman Writer's Warehouse on the Web. The Writer's Warehouse offers an interactive handbook, an online journal, a bulletin board, and extensive coverage of the writing process. To take a tour, go to

http://longmanwriterswarehouse.com

Copyright © 2004 by Pearson Education, Inc.

Introductory Phrase Variety

The introductory phrase is used best when it contains information that helps explain or clarify the subject or the main idea in the independent clause. This information can help define the "who, what, where, when, why, and how" of the main idea.

Examples

Who
Being *Chuck Norris*, he could do his own martial arts stunts for the show.

As *King of England*, Henry the Eighth had the power to create his own church.

What
Snow day after *snow day*, school was closed for an entire week.

Large and *sturdy*, four garbage bags were used to haul out all the trash.

Where
In *India*, people use tusked elephants like we use forklift trucks.

At the *Smithsonian Institute*, historical artifacts are on display.

When
In the *spring*, crocuses and tulips bloom even when there is still snow.

Each *morning*, the newspaper was flung into the bushes near the porch.

Why
With *little fuel* in the tank, the barbeque grill wouldn't ignite.

Because of the *hurricane threat*, all boats were moored in the harbor.

How
By *twisting* his body to the left, the electrician squeezed through the shaft.

After *adjusting the carburetor*, the driver won the next heat.

▼ **PRACTICE 3**   **Writing Introductory Phrases**

Answers will vary.

Add an introductory phrase, or phrases, to each independent clause in the following sentences. Punctuate correctly. In the parentheses provided after each sentence, indicate how the introductory phrase helps to explain or clarify the independent clause by writing in the appropriate label: **who, what, where, when, why,** or **how.**

Example: _____ the contestants could not answer.

<u>After the buzzer sounded</u>, the contestants could not answer. (Why)

1. _____ the plane returned to the airport.

(   )

2. _____ fishing became a favorite pastime.
(   )

3. _____ the clouds darkened and the rain came pounding down on the village. (   )

4. _____ the two teams shook hands and went to the locker room. (   )

5. _____ losing to her opponent was especially painful. (   )

6. _____ Denise decided the Mediterranean cruise was much too expensive. (   )

7. _____ they needed to buy extra ice and fans.
(   )

8. _____ Lonnie jumped right back up into the saddle. (   )

9. _____ three hundred geese landed on the small pond. (   )

10. _____ all three intersections were blocked by the train. (   )

Special effects, properties, and relationships that exist about and between people and events also can be clarified by using introductory phrases.

Examples	
Description	Being 6 feet 6 inches tall and weighing 260 pounds, the freshman football player was selected by the coaching staff to be one of the starting defensive ends.
	By expanding and fluttering beautifully colored tail feathers, the male peacock hopes to attract a mate.
Cause and effect	Because of the low voter turnout, the party in power retained its majority.
	Caused by too many people using major appliances, the brownouts continued throughout the night and into the next day.
Definition	Having four sides of the same length, the square is one of the basic geometric designs used in architecture.

(continued)

Copyright © 2004 by Pearson Education, Inc.

	By crying and throwing toys, the child hoped his tantrum would force his parents to let him watch more cartoons.
Comparison	By acting rather than complaining, the newest employee was promoted before those with more seniority.
	After the conservatives won and the liberals lost, the school board voted to accept the new budget for the upcoming fiscal year.
Process	By calculating the jet stream position and isobar readings, the meteorologist put together her forecast.
	By counting deposits against expenditures, the bank teller balanced the cash drawer.
Persuasion	With skyrocketing tuition and cost of living increases, parents should start college funds for their children before they're born!
	As the IRS is increasing its tax rate on earnings, donating to charity is becoming a more attractive method of reducing taxable income.

▼ **PRACTICE 4**   **Identifying the Purpose of Introductory Phrases**

In the parentheses provided after each sentence, indicate how the introductory phrase helps to explain or clarify the independent clause by writing in the appropriate label: **description, cause and effect, definition, comparison, process,** or **persuasion.** Do not write in the same label twice.

1. As interest rates on loans and credit cards climb, it would be wise to

consolidate all bills into one payment to a single lending company.

(**persuasion**)

2. With snowcapped peaks and thick cloud cover, the Himalayas offer some

of the world's most spectacular scenery. (**description**)

3. By using sonar and dazzling speed, dolphins hunt successfully in groups

and as individuals. (**process**)

4. In foggy conditions or bright sunlight, driving lights have reduced the

number of automobile collisions. (**comparison**)

5. Because of not recruiting younger members, the gang eventually became

too old and too small to scare anyone. (**cause and effect**)

6. Consisting of a compartment for air and a breathing tube, the aqua lung has revolutionized undersea exploration. (**definition**)

▼ **PRACTICE 5** **Writing Sentences with Introductory Phrases**

Answers will vary.

Write five of your own sentences using an introductory phrase in front of the independent clause. Punctuate correctly. In the parentheses provided following each sentence, write in the label that best describes how the introductory phrase is helping to explain or clarify the independent clause. Use any of the labels you have studied, but don't use the same label twice.

1. _____

_____

_____

( )

2. _____

_____

_____

( )

3. _____

_____

_____

( )

4. _____

_____

_____

( )

5. _____

_____

_____

( )

Copyright © 2004 by Pearson Education, Inc.

▼ PRACTICE 6   Editing to Punctuate Introductory Phrases

In the following paragraph, add appropriate punctuation to the introductory phrases.

In the movie *Schindler's List*, the harshness of racism in World War II Nazi Germany was realistically brought to the screen. Throughout the movie, the idea that "the only good Jew is a dead Jew" was dramatized. During the war, Nazi Germany believed that all Jews were inferior, not only to Germans, but also to most of humanity. Because of this superior attitude, the only way to truly depict the violence of Nazi racism was to show the indiscriminate murder of the Jews in as realistic detail as possible. For example, in one scene, the Jews are herded like cattle into train cars and taken to a concentration camp where they are killed by poisonous gas before being incinerated in giant ovens. Because of the realistic interpretation, many moviegoers found the movie both moving and disturbing.

▼ PRACTICE 7   Editing to Punctuate Introductory Phrases

In the following paragraph, add appropriate punctuation to the introductory phrases.

After graduation from high school, prospective college students are faced with the dilemma of which university to attend. All things being equal, should a local or out of state school be considered? Of course, financial concerns are always a factor in the decision. Most importantly, should the money come from parents, loans, scholarships, grants, or some combination of all four sources? After all, accumulating debt prior to graduating just adds to the pressure of finding a job afterward.

CHAPTER REVIEW

▼ Use an introductory phrase, or phrases, to add information or to clarify or explain the basic idea in an independent clause.

▼ Introductory phrases can explain or clarify properties about or special relationships between persons and events, such as who, what, where, when, why, and how.

▼ Introductory phrases also can help explain or clarify properties about or special relationships between persons and events, such as description, definition, cause and effect, comparison, process, and persuasion.

▼ The introductory phrase, or phrases, should be separated from the independent clause with a comma.

Visit *The Write Start* Online!

For additional practice with the materials found in this chapter, visit our Website at:

http://www.ablongman.com/checkett

The Website also features additional readings, quizzes, writing activities, and Internet links, as well as a bulletin board and interactive chat.

For More Practice with Your Grammar and Writing Skills
Visit The Longman Writer's Warehouse

For further multimedia exercises and activities designed to improve your reading, thinking, writing, and grammar skills, visit The Longman Writer's Warehouse on the Web. The Writer's Warehouse offers an interactive handbook, an online journal, a bulletin board, and extensive coverage of the writing process. To take a tour, go to

http://longmanwriterswarehouse.com

Copyright © 2004 by Pearson Education, Inc.

11 Starting a Sentence with an Introductory Word

Another way to add variety and rhythm to your writing is by beginning a sentence with an **introductory word,** also called a **sentence modifier.** Although this technique is not used to combine sentences, it is important, nonetheless.

> **Examples**
>
> <u>Yes</u>, I will be going to the show.
>
> <u>Well</u>, I might buy a motorcycle instead of a car.
>
> <u>Obviously</u>, Einstein was an intelligent person by any standard.

Punctuating the Introductory Word

Notice that the introductory words in these examples are followed by a comma just as we saw in Chapter 9 when using the introductory dependent clause before the main clause and in Chapter 10 when using the introductory phrase.

When to Use Introductory Words

Introductory words are most often used to create sentence variety and rhythm, but they also can add useful information to a sentence.

Commonly Used Introductory Words	
Ah	Oh
Certainly	Sure, surely
Hmmm	Typically
However	Well
Nevertheless	Yes
Nonetheless	[Names of people and pets being addressed]
No	

Use the introductory word for the following five reasons:

1. To introduce an affirmative or negative reply

> <u>Yes</u>, the team has won three games in a row.
>
> <u>No</u>, I don't think I will be majoring in Refuse Disposal Management.

2. To address someone by name

> <u>Lennox</u>, bring the newspaper into the dining room.
>
> <u>Henrietta</u>, please come to the dinner table.

3. To express surprise or wonderment

> <u>Oh</u>, what a gigantic cake!
>
> <u>Ah</u>, I never suspected that the butler did it!

4. To express a contrast

> <u>However</u>, the business picked up during the next quarter.
>
> <u>Nevertheless</u>, I will continue to support the school board's decision.

5. To express a contemplative pause

> <u>Well</u>, I was actually thinking about buying a different model of car.
>
> <u>Hmmm</u>, that doesn't sound like something that would interest me.

▼
PRACTICE 1   Identifying and Punctuating Introductory Words

Underline the introductory word in each of the following sentences. Punctuate correctly.

1. <u>No</u>,taking the driver's exam is not possible until Monday morning.

2. <u>Ah</u>,that picture of the Orion Nebula is amazing.

3. <u>Nevertheless</u>,we are spending a full week in Toronto.

4. <u>Eugenia</u>,don't drive over the speed limit tonight.

5. <u>Yes</u>,the mechanic says he can fix the radiator.

6. <u>However</u>,the other team has a better pitching staff.

Copyright © 2004 by Pearson Education, Inc.

7. <u>Hmmm</u>,I can't decide on sausage or pepperoni on my pizza.

8. <u>Oh</u>,I think that news is fantastic.

9. <u>Well</u>,I might go hang gliding if the weather conditions are good.

10. <u>Mischa</u>,don't leave your dirty clothes on the floor.

▼ **PRACTICE 2**　　**Identifying the Purpose of Introductory Words**

Underline the introductory word in each of the following sentences. Punctuate correctly. In the parentheses following each sentence, identify one of the five reasons for using the introductory word you have learned: **affirmative or negative reply, address by name, surprise or wonderment, contrast, or contemplative pause.**

Example:　<u>Ah,</u> that's the biggest hamburger I've ever seen! (surprise or wonderment)

1. <u>Germaine</u>,please turn the air conditioning down.
   (**address by name**)

2. <u>Nevertheless</u>,the new supermarket will be built where the current children's amusement park is located. (**express a contrast**)

3. <u>No</u>,qualifying for the Olympic track team is based on how you do during the tryout meet next month. (**introduce a negative reply**)

4. <u>Ah</u>,this apple strudel is the best I've ever eaten.
   (**surprise or wonderment**)

5. <u>Hmmm</u>,I'm not sure I want to be away from my pets that long.
   (**contemplative pause**)

6. <u>However</u>,the rain washed away the topsoil as well as the grass seed.
   (**express a contrast**)

7. <u>Yes</u>,the German shepherd is a great guard dog.
   (**affirmative reply**)

8. <u>Well</u>,I might take History if it satisfies a graduation requirement.
   (**contemplative pause**)

9. <u>Oh</u>,the budget is already 20 percent over projected costs.
   (**surprise or wonderment**)

10. <u>Leonardo</u>,don't play with your food.
    (**address by name**)

Not all single words can be used as introductory words. For example, subordinating conjunctions (see Chapter 9) cannot be used as introductory words. These words must be part of a dependent clause and cannot be separated from the clause by a comma.

Examples

(Independent clause) The coroner examined the body thoroughly. He released the findings to the press.

(Made into a dependent clause) After the coroner examined the body thoroughly, he released the findings to the press.

(Incorrect use of the subordinating conjunction) After, the coroner examined the body thoroughly, he released the findings to the press.

(Correct use of an introductory word) Typically, the coroner examined the body before releasing the findings to the press.

▼ PRACTICE 3   Using Introductory Words

Answers will vary.

Choose appropriate introductory words from the examples given in this chapter and place them in front of the sentences below. Do not use the same one more than once. Punctuate correctly.

_____ the law will be carried out under the watchful eye of the police.

_____ that is something I will have to think about long and hard.

_____ Derek Jeter will hit at least one home run tonight.

_____ the nuclear reactor is functioning at 100 percent capacity.

_____ the committee will make a decision in lieu of the president's vote.

_____ go to the store and buy bread and milk.

_____ that behavior is not acceptable at any time.

_____ now that's what I call a gourmet meal.

▼ PRACTICE 4   Writing Sentences with Introductory Words

Answers will vary.

Create sentences using the introductory words from the examples given in this chapter. Do not use the same one more than once. Punctuate correctly.

1. _____

2. _____

Copyright © 2004 by Pearson Education, Inc.

3. _____

4. _____

5. _____

6. _____

7. _____

8. _____

▼ **PRACTICE 5**   **Editing to Add Introductory Words**

Answers will vary; sample answer given.

In the following paragraph, add introductory words to appropriate sentences. Remember, only add an introductory word to introduce an affirmative or negative reply, to address someone by name, to express surprise or wonderment, to express a contrast, or to express a contemplative pause. Be sure to punctuate correctly.

Taking on a car restoration project is a big responsibility at any age. **Well,** The

pressure is on not to spend money foolishly, especially when it is hard to come

by. **However,** Proper time management is important to ensure that the project is com-

pleted. Dealing with these constraints and knowing that in your hands is a

piece of history can lead to stress. Most kids, at fifteen, have not acquired

enough money to fund a restoration project, nor do they have an opportu-

nity to borrow the money. **Nevertheless,** By putting in long hours of strenuous work (mow-

ing lawns or cleaning gutters) you can earn enough money to get started.

Ah, The fact that your parents allow you to own an old car is an achievement in

itself! Just learning the basic skills is quite an accomplishment.

▼ **PRACTICE 6**   **Editing to Add Introductory Words**

Answers will vary; sample answer given.

In the following paragraph, add introductory words to appropriate sentences. Remember, only add an introductory word to introduce an affirmative or negative reply, to address someone by name, to express surprise or wonderment, to express a contrast, or to express a contemplative pause. Be sure to punctuate correctly.

Certainly, Country music is more popular than ever. The music of country artists

like Faith Hill, Mary Chapin Carpenter, and Garth Brooks has crossed over to

Surely,
the pop and soft rock audience. ⌃The steady, slow beat of traditional country

ballads has given way to a more upbeat and rhythmical style that has

Nonetheless,
attracted a much wider audience than ever before. ⌃As popular as country

music has become, it is becoming more widely accepted. Country artists are

beginning to make guest appearances with symphony orchestras.

CHAPTER REVIEW

Use an introductory word at the beginning of a sentence for the following
reasons:

▼ To introduce an affirmative or negative reply
▼ To address someone by name
▼ To express surprise or wonderment
▼ To express a contrast
▼ To express a contemplative pause

Do not confuse subordinating conjunctions, or dependent words, with
introductory words. Subordinating conjunctions are placed at the beginning
of an independent clause to change it to a dependent clause, and no punctuation is used. (Refer to Chapter 9 for a list of subordinating conjunctions.)

Visit *The Write Start* Online!

For additional practice with the materials found in this chapter, visit
our Website at:

http://www.ablongman.com/checkett

The Website also features additional readings, quizzes, writing activities,
and Internet links, as well as a bulletin board and interactive chat.

**For More Practice with Your Grammar and Writing Skills
Visit The Longman Writer's Warehouse**

For further multimedia exercises and activities designed to improve
your reading, thinking, writing, and grammar skills, visit The Longman
Writer's Warehouse on the Web. The Writer's Warehouse offers an
interactive handbook, an online journal, a bulletin board, and extensive
coverage of the writing process. To take a tour, go to

http://longmanwriterswarehouse.com

Copyright © 2004 by Pearson Education, Inc.

12 Adding Interrupters to the Sentence

Simple sentences are very good for conveying simple, straightforward ideas. Sometimes, though, reading several simple sentences in a row can be dull. Variety always makes writing more interesting, and a different method of adding variety is using interrupters. Some books also call this extra information "transitional expressions," or "parenthetical expressions," or "parenthetical information" because it can be placed in parentheses ( ). Most often, however, interrupters are preceded and followed by commas.

Interrupters are single words, phrases, or clauses often interrupting the flow of the basic clause.

Examples of Single-Word Interrupters

The exam, however, came to an end.

The opera diva, undoubtedly, could hold a single note for a long time.

The scientists, therefore, had a different reaction to the new discovery.

Examples of Phrase Interrupters

The coach, on the other hand, was not pleased with the team's performance.

The entire town, for instance, stopped watching television for a week.

The Southern writer William Faulkner, from Mississippi, wrote "The Bear."

Notice that interrupters most often are placed in between the subject and verb of the main clause. For further discussion of clause interrupters, see The Writer's Resources, Additional Punctuation Rules, Restrictive and Nonrestrictive Clauses (page 384).

Commonly Used Interrupters

Single Words	Phrases
also	as a matter of fact
besides	as a result
certainly	at last
consequently	believe me
eventually	by the way
finally	for example
furthermore	for instance
however	in fact
incidentally	on the other hand
likewise	to tell the truth
meanwhile	
naturally	
nevertheless	
subsequently	
therefore	
undoubtedly	
unfortunately	

Interrupters can be necessary or not necessary to the basic understanding of the main clause. If the interrupter is not necessary to understand the main clause, place commas around it. If the interrupter is necessary to understand the main clause, do not place commas around it.

Examples

The student, with a shocked expression, read the favorable comments on his paper. (unnecessary prepositional phrase—commas needed)

The boy with the red hair was the one riding the bike. (necessary phrase—commas not needed)

The surgeon, consequently, ordered more blood for the operation. (unnecessary single word—commas needed)

The student with the highest grades won the scholarship. (necessary prepositional phrase—commas not needed)

The boss, satisfied with employee morale, cancelled the company picnic. (unnecessary phrase—commas needed)

Copyright © 2004 by Pearson Education, Inc.

▼ **PRACTICE 1** Punctuating Interrupters

In the following sentences, use commas to set off the single-word interrupters from the basic idea of the sentence. Identifying the subject and the verb may help you select the interrupter.

1. World War II, naturally, is an event discussed to this day.

2. The United States and Japan, unfortunately, both were after dominance in the Far East.

3. Poor relations, meanwhile, developed between the two powers.

4. The two nations, subsequently, could not come to common agreement.

5. The Empire of Japan, therefore, attacked Pearl Harbor.

6. Although isolationist, the Congress, nevertheless, voted for a Declaration of War.

7. The United States, consequently, entered World War II on December 8, 1941.

8. The war, however, had begun in Europe in September of 1939.

9. The United States, eventually, would fight a war on two fronts: Asia and Europe.

10. After six years, the Allies, finally, defeated the Axis powers.

11. Today, the United States and Japan, however, are considered allies.

▼ **PRACTICE 2**   **Punctuating Interrupters**

In the following sentences, use commas to set off the phrase interrupters from the basic idea of the sentence. Identifying the subject and the verb may help you select the interrupter.

1. Robert Frost,for instance,is one of America's most beloved poets.

2. Frost,in fact,was from New England.

3. The poet,by the way,was funny, witty, and enjoyed poking fun at himself and others.

4. His poetry,on the other hand,often dealt with death and alienation.

5. "Desert Places," for example,is concerned with loneliness.

6. Frost,as a matter of fact,achieved his first success while living in England.

7. The poet,as a result,returned to America where his success continued.

8. Robert Frost,at last,had attained the status of a major poet worldwide.

▼ **PRACTICE 3**   **Punctuating Interrupters**

After reading each of the following sentences, decide if the interrupters are unnecessary or necessary. Punctuate correctly.

1. Our solar system,the only planetary system in this part of the galaxy,consists of nine major planets.

2. The nine planets,commonly grouped into the inner and outer planets, vary significantly in composition.

3. The inner planets,Mercury, Venus, Earth, and Mars,are composed primarily of rock and iron.

4. The outer planets,Jupiter, Saturn, Uranus, Neptune, and Pluto,are much larger and consist mainly of gas and ice.

5. Mercury not only is nearest the sun but also orbits the sun most quickly.

6. The morning star,Venus,is next closest to the medium-sized star.

7. The earth,with a myriad of life forms,is the only planet known to have abundant liquid water and oxygen.

8. Mars,by the way,once had water on its surface.

9. Jupiter's mass of 317 times that of earth makes it the largest of the planets.

10. Pluto,incidentally,is so distant from the sun and so cold that methane freezes on its surface.

Copyright © 2004 by Pearson Education, Inc.

| PRACTICE 4 | Writing Sentences with Interrupters |

Answers will vary.

Write a sentence for each of the following topics. From the list of Commonly Used Interrupters, provide an appropriate interrupter in each sentence. Do not use the same word or phrase twice. Punctuate correctly.

1. School _____

_____

2. Speeding _____

_____

3. Voting _____

_____

4. War _____

_____

5. Flowers _____

_____

6. Breakfast _____

_____

7. Math _____

_____

8. Cooking _____

_____

9. Pets _____

_____

10. Money _____

_____

| PRACTICE 5 | Writing Sentences with Interrupters |

Answers will vary.

Write a sentence for each of the following topics. From the list of Commonly Used Interrupters, provide an appropriate interrupter in each sentence. Do not use the same word or phrase twice. Punctuate correctly.

1. Automobiles _____

_____

2. Dating _____

_____

3. Vitamins _____

_____

4. Hobbies _____

_____

5. Sports _____

_____

6. Friends _____

_____

7. Art _____

_____

8. Computers _____

_____

9. Humor _____

_____

10. Clothes _____

_____

Copyright © 2004 by Pearson Education, Inc.

▼ **PRACTICE 6**   **Editing to Punctuate Interrupters**

Answers will vary; sample answer given.

In the following paragraph, place commas around any interrupter if it is unnecessary to the meaning of the main clause. If the interrupter is necessary to the meaning of the main clause, do not place commas around it.

Weight training is an excellent way to get in shape and stay in shape. However, you first need to check with your doctor and fitness expert to plan a routine that will work well for you. Proper stretching to increase flexibility should be the first activity when starting your routine. Stretching also will promote muscular development. Improved workout performance, a goal you should have, can be achieved with stretching, also. The best stretching, according to most fitness experts, starts with the muscles in the neck and works down to the ankles. After proper stretching, a ten-to-fifteen minute set of warmup exercises should be done. Only then should you begin weight training.

PRACTICE 7   Editing to Punctuate Interrupters

Answers will vary; sample answer given.

In the following paragraph, place commas around any interrupter if it is unnecessary to the meaning of the main clause. If the interrupter is necessary to the meaning of the main clause, do not place commas around it.

With every step as I walked down the road, breaking the crust on the top of the snow, my body became somewhat immune to the freezing cold. My boots, caked with snow, became heavier with every step, and my slacks, stiffened by a shellac-like frost, cracked at the slightest movement. My muffler, wrapped about my neck and face, grew more solid as the moisture of my breath froze within its warm and insulating softness. Leaning into the wind, forcing one step after another, I felt the sand-like snow piercing my face with needle-sharp harshness, making my cheeks red. My eyes were forced downward since there was no way of protecting them, and I grew dependent upon the tracks of others to find my way through the blinding wall of snow ahead of me.

CHAPTER REVIEW

▼ Interrupters are single words, phrases, or clauses often interrupting the flow of the sentence.
▼ Interrupters most often are placed between the subject and the verb.
▼ Interrupters can be necessary or unnecessary to the basic understanding of the sentence.
▼ If the interrupter is unnecessary to the basic understanding of the sentence, place commas on either side of it.
▼ If the interrupter is necessary to the basic understanding of the sentence, do not place commas around it.

Putting It All Together: Sentence Combining to Improve Paragraph Style

Combine the following groups of simple sentences using a combination of sentence combining strategies (coordination, subordination, and insertion of words and phrases). Omit repeated words, phrases, and unnecessary pronouns.

These exercises are taken from paragraphs from the professional essays in the "Additional Readings" section at the back of this book. When you have finished combining each group of sentences, you may compare your answer to the paragraph as it was written by the original author. A sample exercise has been done for you.

Sample Exercise

1. This happened several summers ago.
2. It was on one of those August evenings.
3. The evenings are endless.
4. The sun is hanging suspended.
5. The sun is above the horizon.
6. I made up my mind.
7. I decided to become beautiful.

Student Paragraph

On an August evening several summers ago, I decided to become beautiful. It was one of those endless evenings when the sun was hanging suspended above the horizon.

Original Paragraph as Written by Author

Several summers ago, on one of those endless August evenings when the sun hangs suspended just above the horizon, I made up my mind to become beautiful. (Grace Suh, "The Eye of the Beholder," paragraph 1)

Notice that both paragraphs are better written than if the original sentences had been organized into a paragraph.

The professional paragraph is somewhat better organized than the student example because the most important information (the decision to become beautiful) is contained in the independent clause while the less important information is subordinated in a series of introductory phrases and a dependent clause (Several summers ago) and (on one of those endless August evenings) and (when the sun hangs suspended just above the horizon).

In other words, it is more important to leave the readers with the idea of "becoming beautiful" than it is to let them know what type of evening it was.

▼ **PRACTICE 8**

Answers will vary.

1. The following sentences come from the essay "The Mute Sense" by Diana Ackerman, paragraph 8. Combine each group of sentences into one sentence. Then, combine these sentences into one paragraph.

Copyright © 2004 by Pearson Education, Inc.

1.1 I leaned against the flank of a boulder.
1.2 The flank was cool.
1.3 I fanned myself with my hat.

2.1 I could hear the drill of a woodpecker.
2.2 The sound was far away.
2.3 The drill was staccato.
2.4 The woodpecker was a Nutall's woodpecker.

_____

_____

_____

_____

_____

2. The following sentences are taken from "The Roommate's Death" by Jan Harold Brunvald, paragraph 5. Combine each group of sentences into one sentence. Then, combine these sentences into one paragraph.

1.1 The night was windy.
1.2 The night was especially dark.
1.3 Rain was threatening.

2.1 All went well for the girls.
2.2 The girls read stories aloud.
2.3 The girls read stories to the three little boys.
2.4 The girls were sitting for the three little boys.
2.5 The girls had no problem putting the boys to bed.
2.6 The boys were put to bed in the upstairs bedroom.

3.1 The boys were put to bed.
3.2 The girls settled down to watch television.

_____

_____

_____

_____

_____

3. The following sentences are taken from "The Eye of the Beholder" by Grace Suh, paragraph 26. Combine each group of sentences into one sentence. Then, combine these sentences into one paragraph.

1.1 I bought the skincare system.
1.2 I bought the foundation.
1.3 I bought the blush.
1.4 I bought the lipliner.
1.5 I bought the lipstick.

1.6 I bought the primer.
1.7 I bought the eyeliner.
1.8 I bought the eyeshadows.
1.9 The eyeshadows came in four colors.

2.1 The stuff filled a bag.
2.2 The bag was the size of a shoe box.

3.1 There was a cost.
3.2 The cost was a lot.

4.1 Estee handed me my receipt.
4.2 She handed it to me with a flourish.

5.1 I told her, "Thank you."

_____

_____

_____

_____

_____

4. The following sentences are taken from "The Culture of Violence" by Myriam Miedzian, paragraph 17. Combine each group of sentences into one sentence. Then, combine these sentences into one paragraph.

1.1 Our young boys watch TV.
1.2 They spend about twenty-eight hours a week watching TV.

2.1 They have seen an average of twenty-six thousand TV murders.
2.2 This is by the time they are eighteen.
2.3 These figures are an average.
2.4 The majority of murders are committed by men.
2.5 The majority is vast.

_____

_____

_____

_____

_____

5. The following sentences are taken from "Cyberspace: If You Don't Love It, Leave It" by Esther Dyson, paragraph 7. Combine each group of sentences into one sentence. Then, combine these sentences into one paragraph.

1.1 We should put this plainly.
1.2 Cyberspace is a destination.

Copyright © 2004 by Pearson Education, Inc.

1.3 The destination is voluntary.
1.4 This is reality.
1.5 This is many destinations.

2.1 You don't just get "onto the Net."
2.2 You have to go someplace.
2.3 The place is particular.

3.1 This has a meaning.
3.2 This meaning is that people can choose where to go.
3.3 This means that people can choose what to see.

4.1 Yes, the community has standards.
4.2 The standards must be enforced.
4.3 The standards should by set by cyberspace communities themselves.
4.4 The standards should not be set by courts.
4.5 The standards should not be set by politicians in Washington.

5.1 What we need is not Government control.
5.2 The control is over all these electronic communites.
5.3 We need self rule.

_____

_____

_____

_____

_____

Visit *The Write Start* Online!

For additional practice with the materials found in this chapter, visit our Website at:

http://www.ablongman.com/checkett

The Website also features additional readings, quizzes, writing activities, and Internet links, as well as a bulletin board and interactive chat.

For More Practice with Your Grammar and Writing Skills
Visit The Longman Writer's Warehouse

For further multimedia exercises and activities designed to improve your reading, thinking, writing, and grammar skills, visit The Longman Writer's Warehouse on the Web. The Writer's Warehouse offers an interactive handbook, an online journal, a bulletin board, and extensive coverage of the writing process. To take a tour, go to

http://longmanwriterswarehouse.com

PART 2

Writing Effective Paragraphs

In the preceding chapters, you have been practicing writing the basic sentence types that allow for communicating information with focus, clarity, variety, and rhythm. Sentences are good for conveying short pieces of information, but for longer, more developed ideas, a longer format such as the paragraph is necessary.

The next nine chapters in Part 2 will help you discover, understand, and write the basic paragraph. A paragraph can be a complete piece of writing by itself. However, paragraphs are usually grouped together in longer pieces of writing, for example, essays, letters, reports, research papers, and chapters in a novel or nonfiction work.

In Part 2, you will be introduced to the major elements and processes necessary to write effective paragraphs: prewriting; understanding the structure of a paragraph; creating an outline; writing first drafts; proofreading; and correcting sentence fragments, run-ons, and comma splices. You also will be introduced to the various modes (methods) of development writers use to examine topics:

▼ description
▼ narration
▼ examples
▼ classification
▼ process
▼ comparison and contrast
▼ definition
▼ persuasion (including cause and effect)

Each mode of development is discussed in its own chapter, and you often will be assigned to write a paragraph or essay in a particular mode. However, you should keep in mind that mode techniques are usually blended in most pieces of writing. For example, the following paragraph is predominantly descriptive, but it also exhibits a blend of other modes.

Copyright © 2004 by Pearson Education, Inc.

> The sprawling, white and brown Tudor mansion sat like a king atop the throne-like hilltop looking down upon its subjects. Unlike the mix of plain, wooden colonials and brick ranch houses surrounding it, the Tudor mansion was much more elegant and imposing. Its high arches, lead-traced windows, and fan vaults spoke to roots tracing back to Henry VIII.

The modes appear in the paragraph as follows:

Description: The phrases "sprawling, white and brown," "sat like a king atop the throne-like hilltop looking down upon its subjects," "plain, wooden," "brick ranch," "elegant and imposing," and "high arches, lead-traced windows, and fan vaults" describe the three styles of houses.

Classification and *Example:* The phrases "Tudor mansion," and "colonials and brick ranch houses" categorize the houses in the area by style.

Comparison and Contrast and *Persuasion:* The paragraph compares the elegant and stately style of the Tudor mansion to the relatively plain styles of the colonial and ranch houses. The reference to King Henry VIII also supports the contrasting styles. The writer makes the case that because of its style and historical roots, the Tudor mansion is "much more elegant and imposing" than the other two styles of house.

Definition: A topic can be defined by using one or more of the modes of development. Therefore, the Tudor mansion is defined through description, classification, example, comparison and contrast, and persuasion.

Before you begin to learn about writing paragraphs, let's examine ways to develop ideas and details that form the basis for a paragraph or other piece of writing.

Prewriting Activities

There are a variety of techniques that you can use to develop specific details for writing assignments. The development of a topic is influenced by the **purpose** of the assignment, as well as the **audience.** Often, more than one method of expanding a topic or developing details is necessary for writers. The techniques of **listing, clustering, cubing,** and **cross-examining** are summarized here. You should experiment with many of these techniques (and any others suggested by your writing teachers) in order to overcome writer's block. Later, in Chapter 13, the technique of *questioning* (asking the questions *who, what, when, where, why,* or *how* of the topic) is introduced.

Listing

For this strategy, write the topic at the top of a blank sheet of paper (or at the top of your computer screen). Then quickly list any idea that pops into your head. This is a form of free association; do not edit, correct, or revise. A list on the topic of musicianship may look like this

Musicianship			
performance	attention	strings	practice
anxiety	phrasing	cello	technique
concerts	dynamics	violin	emotion
conductors	interpretation	flutes	control
rehearsal	crescendo	brass	tension
orchestra	audience	oboes	tone
solo	musicians	percussion	intonation

Keep writing for ten minutes to inspire more thoughts. The act of writing actually helps thinking processes for many people. Next, look at your list and see which topics are related (such as technique, control, practice, interpretation, and dynamics). After you have chosen several ideas on your list that would best develop your topic, group them in the correct order (time/space, most to least important, and so on). This last step also helps you formally outline your topic.

Clustering (Mind Mapping)

This technique is similar to listing but is less structured. Write your topic in the center of a piece of paper. Place related ideas in nearby circles, then keep connecting the circles with lines, grouping those ideas that seem to be related. Note the following diagram on the topic of violence.

After studying the diagram or map, select the cluster of ideas that best develops the topic or thesis statement you have chosen. Further clustering on these selected terms may help expand your options. Additionally, you may wish to try another method of prewriting at this point.

Copyright © 2004 by Pearson Education, Inc.

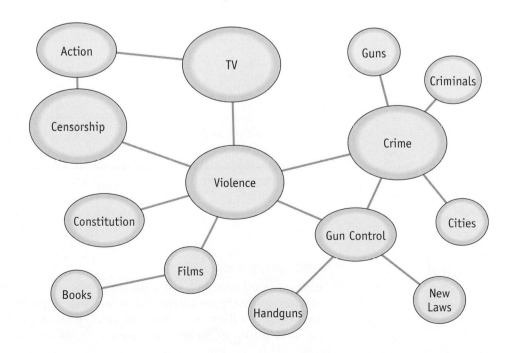

Choose one of the following topics, and write it in the center of a piece of paper. Then, cluster your ideas around it.

> A favorite holiday
> The color red
> The future
> A dream
> A best/worst boss
> A hero

Cubing

Another type of brainstorming uses a cube to generate new approaches to a topic. Imagine a six-sided cube with the following questions on each side:

Describe the topic: What does the subject look like? What is the size, color, shape, texture, smell, sound, and so forth? Which details are unique?

Compare or contrast it: What is your subject like? How does it differ from similar subjects? Give details.

Free-associate it: What does your subject remind you of? What further ideas do you think of?

Analyze it: What are the parts of the subject? How does each part function? How are the parts connected? What is the significance of this subject?

Argue for or against it: What are the arguments for or against your topic? What are the advantages and disadvantages?

Apply it: How can the subject be used?

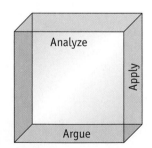

Approach your topic from each of the above six perspectives, freewriting your answers as you did with the techniques of listing or clustering and giving yourself 10 to 15 minutes to explore each idea. Do not worry about correctness at this point. Review your responses and see if any are suited to your assignment or inspire new ideas for the writing assignment.

Cross-Examining

This approach can be used with a partner or individually. It is a variation of the questioning form that is introduced in Chapter 13. The questions can be grouped depending on either the type of essay assigned or the type of essay you would like to write. Interview yourself or your partner regarding your topic.

Definition

1. How is the topic/subject defined or explained by the dictionary or encyclopedia?
2. How do most people define the topic informally?
3. How do I define the subject?
4. What is the history, origin, or background of the topic?
5. What are some examples of the topic?

Relationship

1. What is the cause of the topic/subject?
2. To what larger group or category does the subject belong?
3. What are the values or goals of the subject?
4. What are the effects of the subject?

Comparison and Contrast

1. What is the topic/subject similar to?
2. What is the topic different from?
3. What is the subject better than?
4. What is the subject worse than?
5. What is the subject opposite to?

Testimony

1. What do people say about the topic/subject?
2. What authorities exist on this topic?
3. Has anything been written on this subject?
4. What are the important statistics?
5. Is there any further research on the topic?
6. Have I had any personal experience on this topic?

Circumstance

1. Is this subject/topic possible?
2. Is the subject impossible?
3. When has this subject happened before?
4. What might prevent it from happening?
5. Why might it happen again?
6. Who or what is associated with the topic?

Not all of these questions will apply to every topic. Choose the questions that help develop your topic most thoroughly.

Brainstorming

Brainstorming is a process by which people develop ideas, supporting examples, or new topics by tossing out ideas for general discussion. It can be done individually or as a group. However, brainstorming is most useful when a group is working on a project and the group members need to combine their ideas and experiences.

▼ **PRACTICE**   **Brainstorming**

Break into groups of three or four. Choose a topic from one of the previous lists, or use a topic assigned by your instructor. The purpose of the exercise should be to find related subtopics and examples to develop the topic into a

Copyright © 2004 by Pearson Education, Inc.

paragraph or essay.* The members of the group should discuss the topic, taking turns mentioning related topics for five minutes. One member of the group should record the group's ideas.

Next, for each idea listed, each member of the group should try for five to ten minutes to think of an effective or creative example or supporting detail. The student who recorded the topics and examples can report the results to the rest of the class for comparison or general discussion.

---

*This activity can be modified to plan a debate strategy, propose ideas for a project, or as a part of peer editing.

Copyright © 2004 by Pearson Education, Inc.

The Paragraph

Many of the elements in longer pieces of writing such as essays are found in the paragraph. Thus the paragraph is a good model to use before learning to write longer pieces.

A **paragraph** is a group of sentences concerned with developing or expressing a single **topic** (one main idea). In fact, what you are reading right now is a paragraph. It is developing the concept of the paragraph! Generally, paragraphs can be as long as you want them to be, although most are usually 4 to 15 sentences in length. The key to writing a good paragraph is to make it long enough to develop the topic and no longer. This paragraph is between 4 and 15 sentences in length, and it is describing the elements that make up the paragraph.

There are two basic types of sentences in a paragraph: the **topic sentence** and **support sentences.** The topic sentence tells the reader what the main idea, or topic, of the paragraph is. Although there is no set place in the

133

paragraph for the topic sentence, making the topic sentence the first sentence in the paragraph will make organizing and developing the topic easier. The topic sentence is followed by support sentences that explain, clarify, and define the topic by using specific detail. Support sentences should demonstrate a variety of styles to show the relationship between the various pieces of information and to create rhythm (see Chapters 3 through 12). Exhibit 13–1 summarizes the elements and characteristics of a paragraph.

Exhibit 13–1

> **1.** A topic sentence announces one main idea (the topic).
> **2.** Support sentences use specific detail to develop the main idea.
> **3.** Sentence variety connects related ideas and adds rhythm.

Let's look at the characteristics of a basic paragraph. Specific points are illustrated in the bulleted comments following the paragraph.

> **Example Paragraph**
>
> Sophocles, the Greek dramatist, was greatly admired for his tragedies. *Oedipus* was his most famous tragedy, and Aristotle praised it as the finest example of dramatic irony. Sophocles wrote over 130 plays. Even though he was so prolific, his plays won over 20 first prizes at drama festivals.

▼ The first sentence is the topic sentence, and it announces the topic (Sophocles) and the **controlling idea** (which also contains the writer's attitude toward the topic: that Sophocles *was greatly admired* for his tragedies).

▼ The following three support sentences develop the controlling idea by (1) naming his most famous tragedy and explaining why it was praised by a famous critic; (2) giving the vast number of plays he wrote; and (3) giving the number of times his plays were rewarded.

▼ The sentences also exhibit variety. The first sentence contains extra information, between the commas. The second sentence is coordinated with the coordinating conjunction *and*. The third sentence is a simple sentence. The fourth sentence is subordinated by using an introductory dependent clause preceding the independent clause.

The Topic Sentence

The topic sentence has two parts: the **topic/subject** and the **controlling idea.** The topic is the subject of the paragraph. The controlling idea states what the writer will be developing about the subject of the paragraph, and it contains the writer's attitude toward the subject. The controlling idea limits what you can say about the topic subject so that you don't stray to other subjects or ideas.

> **Example**
>
> In a movie, music often enhances a romantic atmosphere.

The subject is "music." The controlling idea is "often enhances a romantic atmosphere." The attitude is "often enhances."

In a paragraph with this topic sentence, the controlling idea about the music is that it is romantic. The writer cannot talk about other aspects of the movie, such as violence, comedy, production costs, advertising, or attendance figures. The controlling idea forces the writer to talk only about those features of the music that developed the romantic aspects of the movie.

Let's look at another topic sentence.

Example

The Marshall Plan brought economic relief to Europe.

The subject is "the Marshall Plan." The controlling idea is that it "brought economic relief to Europe." In a paragraph with this topic sentence, the writer cannot write about European art, pollution, hunting, or vegetation. The writer must focus on economic factors that became successful because of the Marshall Plan.

Topic sentences missing a controlling idea lack focus and specific direction. Without a controlling idea, the writer's attitude about the subject can be unclear.

Examples

Soccer is a popular high school sport. (incomplete controlling idea—*popular* is an attitude only)

Michael Jordan is a basketball player. (no controlling idea—this is simply a statement of fact)

Soccer is a popular high school sport because it is relatively inexpensive to fund. (controlling idea: *cheap funding* makes soccer popular—the attitude)

Michael Jordan's diverse skills make him an exciting basketball player. (controlling idea: Jordan is exciting because of *diverse skills*—"exciting" is the attitude)

▼ **PRACTICE 1**   **Identifying Topics and Controlling Ideas**

In the following sentences, circle the topic/subject, and underline the controlling idea.

Example: (Swiss watches) are popular because of the fine craftmanship with which they are made.

  1. (Mud-slinging and personal attacks) turn off some people when it comes to politics.

  2. Many (students dislike high school) because of social cliques and favoritism for some students.

  3. (Families can help children) by being a support system for all their activities.

  4. (A hobby can assist people) in easing the stresses of everyday life.

Copyright © 2004 by Pearson Education, Inc.

5. (The movie was a success) because of the script, the acting, and the special effects.

6. (Vacation expenses can be reduced) by purchasing a good travel book.

7. (The depletion of the ozone layer) might cause global warming and an increase in skin cancers.

8. (Many current fads are driven) by how the rich and famous are portrayed in the media.

9. (Helping others) can make almost any profession a rewarding experience.

10. (Laws are effective) only if they are enforced fairly and equitably.

▼ **PRACTICE 2**   **Identifying Topics and Controlling Ideas**

In the following sentences, circle the topic/subject, and underline the controlling idea.

1. (Exercising) can be more enjoyable if done in a group.

2. The (fence) was built to keep the coyotes away from the livestock.

3. The (band) played an extra hour because their fans wouldn't let them off the stage.

4. Great teamwork has made the (United States' women's soccer team) an international success.

5. (Pizza) is a best selling fast food because of the variety of toppings available.

6. Versatility and size make the (laptop computer) a good business tool for travelers.

7. (Learning about long-term investing) can help people have a happier retirement experience.

8. (The Spanish Inquisition) impaired scientific thought for decades.

9. (Technology) has as many drawbacks as it does advantages.

10. (A quiet place) with good lighting can help students study more effectively.

▼ **PRACTICE 3**   **Rewriting Poor Topic Sentences**

Answers will vary.   The following sentences are inadequate as topic sentences because they lack a complete controlling idea. Turn them into topic sentences by adding a controlling idea to each.

1. The Final Four basketball tournament is exciting.

_____

_____

2. Dining out is enjoyable.

_____

_____

3. I attend college.

_____

_____

4. Live theater is dramatic.

_____

_____

5. My clothes are stylish.

_____

_____

6. I drive a Volvo.

_____

_____

7. Dr. Jonas Salk created a vaccine to combat polio.

_____

_____

8. Many new stadiums are being built with old stadium features.

_____

_____

9. Museums house many beautiful sculptures.

_____

_____

Copyright © 2004 by Pearson Education, Inc.

10. The final days of the Vietnam War were hectic.

_____

_____

▼ PRACTICE 4	Writing Topic Sentences

Answers will vary.

Write topic sentences for the following subjects. Don't forget to add the controlling idea.

1. Nuclear energy _____

_____

2. Presidential elections _____

_____

3. Rock music _____

_____

4. Jogging _____

_____

5. Farming _____

_____

6. Science fiction _____

_____

7. Fight against terrorism _____

_____

8. Tornadoes _____

_____

9. Vacationing _____

_____

10. Clothes _____

_____

Support Sentences

Support sentences follow the topic sentence and develop the subject using specific examples, details, and facts. These support ideas must be consistent with the controlling idea. In other words, the controlling idea unifies the paragraph by determining the kind of support ideas you can use in the support sentences.

Example

Police officers are most effective when helping citizens in their communities.

topic   controlling idea

Support sentences for this topic sentence would focus on *what* police officers do to help citizens and might include such activities as

a. finding lost/stolen property
b. solving crimes
c. preventing crimes

Six Important Support Questions

When writing a story, reporters ask six questions. The answers provide the focus that allows them to select the details, facts, and examples to develop the story with specific information. The six questions are **who, what, where, when, why,** and **how.**

After you have selected, or have been given, the topic you are to write about, decide on the controlling idea. To do this, choose which of the following reporter's questions allows you to write about the topic with the desired focus.

For instance, suppose your topic is an *important event*. In the support sentences, you could focus on

Who?

Who started the event?

Who attended/witnessed/participated in the event?

Who was affected by the event?

What?

What was the event?

What happened before/during/after the event?

What was special about the event?

Where?

Where did the event occur?

Did the location affect the event in any way?

Did the location have historical significance?

(continued)

Copyright © 2004 by Pearson Education, Inc.

When?

When did the event occur (A.M./P.M., day, month, year)?

Did the time frame add any special significance to the event?

Did the event coincide with a historically significant time?

Why?

Why did the event occur?

Why was the event important?

How?

How did the event happen?

How was the event funded?

How was the event advertised?

You can add your own focus to these questions if other ideas come to you. There is no need to limit yourself to the questions presented in the list.

Examples

1. Reading can help people become better educated.
2. Reading is best done in a quiet, secluded place.
3. Anyone interested in becoming a better writer should read as much as possible.

Although the topic/subject of each sentence, *reading*, is the same, the focus of the controlling idea is different. In sentence 1, the focus is on *what* reading can do for people (educate them); in sentence 2, the focus is on *where* reading is best accomplished (in a quiet, secluded place); and in sentence 3, the focus is on *who* (anyone interested in becoming a writer).

Creating the Working Outline of a Paragraph

Before you begin writing, you may want to sketch out the major ideas that will appear in your paragraph. This can help you discover whether you have a topic, controlling idea, and support ideas that work together for proper development. To create a **working outline,** list your topic, controlling idea, and support ideas in a ladderlike list.

Example

Topic: Dieting

Controlling idea: Can cause harmful effects

Support ideas: bulimia

              malnutrition

              psychological problems

In this paragraph, the harmful effects of dieting are discussed. This topic is developed and supported by using bulimia, malnutrition, and psychological problems as the negative outcomes that dieting can produce. The finished paragraph might look like this:

Dieting can cause many harmful effects. It can lead to a potentially deadly eating disorder called bulimia. This disorder is characterized by eating binges followed by self-induced vomiting or laxative abuse. Because the body is not ingesting the proper amounts of nutrients, malnutrition often occurs. Of course, physical problems are not the only negative effects caused by dieting. Stress and a poor self-image can lead to self-destructive psychological states requiring long-term medical help. The safest and most effective method to lose weight is eating balanced meals combined with a consistent exercise program.

▼ PRACTICE 5	Creating Working Outlines

Answers will vary.

To practice creating *working outlines*, add a controlling idea for each of the subjects listed below. Then, using the six reporter's questions, list three specific details that develop the controlling idea. Try to use all six of the reporter's questions. After you are finished, you will have a list of all the basic ideas that will go into the paragraph. This is called a *working outline* because the paragraph is still unfinished.

1. The *Star Wars* movies

Controlling idea: _____

a. _____

b. _____

c. _____

2. The United Nations

Controlling idea: _____

a. _____

b. _____

c. _____

3. Computers

Controlling idea: _____

a. _____

b. _____

c. _____

Copyright © 2004 by Pearson Education, Inc.

4. Abraham Lincoln

Controlling idea: _____

a. _____

b. _____

c. _____

5. Exercising

Controlling idea: _____

a. _____

b. _____

c. _____

6. Student loans

Controlling idea: _____

a. _____

b. _____

c. _____

7. Violence

Controlling idea: _____

a. _____

b. _____

c. _____

8. Course scheduling

Controlling idea: _____

a. _____

b. _____

c. _____

9. Recycling

Controlling idea: _____

a. _____

b. _____

c. _____

10. Vacations

Controlling idea: _____

a. _____

b. _____

c. _____

Writing the First Draft

To write your first draft of any one paragraph, combine the topic and the controlling idea listed in your working outline to create the topic sentence. Then, write a sentence for each of the specific detail ideas. These will be your support sentences used to develop the topic sentence. When you match your topic sentence with your support sentences, you'll have a **first draft,** or **rough draft,** paragraph.

> **Example**
>
> Topic: Civil War
>
> Controlling idea (Reporter's question—Who?): Leaders having an impact on war.
>
> A. Lincoln   B. Grant   C. Lee
>
> **Rough Draft Paragraph**
>
> The Civil War had three great leaders. President Lincoln believed that all men should be free. General Grant enjoyed drinking whiskey and smoking cigars. General Lee symbolized the belief that an aristocratic class should govern men of unequal status.

▼ **PRACTICE 6**   **Writing First Drafts**

Answers will vary.   On separate sheets of paper, using the ten examples you have created in Practice 5, turn each example into a short paragraph of four sentences.

Revising the First Draft

No one—not even professional writers—creates a perfect paragraph in the first draft. There are always some rough spots to smooth out—why else do

Copyright © 2004 by Pearson Education, Inc.

you think the first draft is called the rough draft? To improve what you wrote in your rough draft, you must revise.

As you revise, answer these four questions:

▼ Is the topic/subject clear?
▼ Will the controlling idea develop the subject adequately?
▼ Do my support sentences consist of specific facts, details, and examples?
▼ Is there sentence variety?

Let's look at our rough draft from the previous example and ask our four revision questions.

> **Example**
>
> (A) The Civil War had three great leaders. (B) President Lincoln believed that all men should be free. (C) General Grant enjoyed drinking whiskey and smoking cigars. (D) General Lee symbolized the belief that an aristocratic class should govern men of unequal status.

1. **Is the topic/subject clear?** The topic/subject is clear: Civil War leaders.
2. **Will the controlling idea develop the subject adequately?** There is no controlling idea that clarifies how the subject will be developed. The topic sentence is simply a statement of fact.
   Revised topic sentence with controlling idea: Three great leaders embodied the ideals of the North and South during the Civil War. (Now, the controlling idea clarifies that it is the beliefs of the three leaders that will be discussed.)
3. **Do my support sentences consist of specific facts, details, and examples?** Support sentences (B) and (D) consist of details that support the controlling idea. However, sentence (C) does not. General Grant's enjoying whiskey and cigars does not explain how his beliefs symbolized the North's beliefs.
   Revised support sentence: General Grant believed that all men should determine their own destiny. (This rewrite clarifies Grant's belief and mirrors Lincoln's belief as stated in sentence (B)).
4. **Is there sentence variety?** All the sentences in the paragraph are simple sentences. Although these sentences are grammatically correct, they don't add rhythm or help to link the ideas they express.
   Revised sentences demonstrating variety: (A) Three great leaders embodied the ideals of the North and South during the Civil War. (B) While President Lincoln detested the thought of war, he believed that all men should be free. (C) General Grant shared Lincoln's belief, for he believed that all men should determine their own destiny. (D) General Lee symbolized the belief that an aristocratic class should govern men of unequal status.

> **The Final Draft**
>
> Three great leaders embodied the ideals of the North and South during the Civil War. While President Lincoln detested the thought of war, he believed that all men should be free. General Grant shared Lincoln's belief, for he believed that all men should determine their own destiny. General Lee symbolized the belief that an aristocratic class should govern men of unequal status.

In this revision the information is presented more clearly, and the rhythm moves the reading along smoothly and quickly. This is a sign of mature, controlled writing.

▼ PRACTICE 7 — Revising First Drafts

Answers will vary.

On separate sheets of paper, revise the rough draft paragraphs you wrote in Practice 6.

Proofreading: The Final Step

After revising your rough draft into a final draft, there is still one last step you should accomplish before submitting your work.

You should always take time to make sure that your work does not have errors that will detract from its presentation. A great idea, one that professional writers use, is to have someone else read your finished writing. Sometimes, it is easier for someone else to see errors and inconsistencies than it is for the writer. Ultimately, the errors in your writing are your responsibility to find and correct. Typically, you should look for the following types of errors:

a. Sentence fragments; see Chapter 3 for a review of correcting sentence fragments.
b. Run-on sentences and comma splice sentences; see Chapter 4 for a review of correcting run-on and comma splice sentences. Use your computer's *grammarcheck* function to help you correct errors as you find them but don't rely on it entirely.
c. Spelling; use both your computer's *spellcheck* function and a dictionary to help you correct errors as you find them. Remember, *spellcheck* does not correct for meaning. If you use *lien* instead of *lean*, *spellcheck* will not correct the error because *lien* is spelled correctly even though it is not the word you meant to use.

▼ PRACTICE 8 — Correcting Sentence Fragments

Answers will vary.

Find and correct sentence fragments in the following paragraph. Neatly write your corrections in the text.

Facing the Night

I was eight years old the first time I had the biggest scare of my life. The thought of sleeping in the basement all by myself. I'll never forget that night. My brother was at the house of his best friend, and that left me in the "dungeon" all by myself. At first, I didn't think it would be that bad. Then, night came. There I was, lying in my bed in darkness. Where I could not see

Copyright © 2004 by Pearson Education, Inc.

my hand in front of my face. Soon, could hear every sound a dark, large, haunted and gloomy house makes. As my eyes adjusted to the darkness, enough light shining through the basement window let me see all the scary monsters on the wall. Quickly, I pulled the covers over my head and started to pray for sunlight. After a few minutes I heard a noise. The covers from my head only to see my brother standing in the doorway. His best friend was sick, so he had to come home. What a relief!

▼ **PRACTICE 9**   **Correcting Sentence Fragments**

Answers will vary.   Find and correct sentence fragments in the following paragraph. Neatly write your corrections in the text.

My Baby Brother

Nothing changed my life like the birth of my second brother. In July of 1999, my 32-year-old mother; announced she was pregnant. My brother Ryan and I thrilled by the thought of a baby; however, at the time we didn't realize what actually having a new member of the family involved. Didn't know about all the crying sessions or diaper changes. Soon afterwards, the newness of the baby and things started to get back to a routine. Went back to work. Ryan began staying after school for basketball practice. As for me, my life drastically. I became my mother's full-time baby-sitter.

▼ **PRACTICE 10**   **Correcting Run-On Sentences**

Answers will vary.   Find and correct the run-on sentence errors in the following paragraph. Neatly write your corrections in the text.

My Happiest Moment

The happiest moment of my life was the day I was married. The day started out a blustery 32 degrees. The sun was shining it looked to be a great day. First, we began decorating the hall, blowing up balloons and arranging tables my fiancé took his buddies to play a chilly round of golf. Next, the bridesmaids headed off to the beauty salon to get their hair and nails done to perfection. Time was moving very quickly there were still many projects that needed to be attended to before the wedding could begin. Finally, people began to arrive at the church they were wearing their finest dresses and suits. The ceremony was beautiful everything had fallen into place. The hardest part was over we would be heading for the reception to party away the tensions of all the hard work and worry that had gone into the planning. Before the night ended, my new husband and I made a toast we thanked each and every person for helping to make this a beautiful day that we would never forget.

▼ **PRACTICE 11**   **Correcting Run-On Sentences**

Answers will vary.   Find and correct the run-on sentences in the following paragraph. Neatly write your corrections in the text.

Mr. Unusual

Dennis Rodman, looming over the world at 6′8″, may be the most unusual looking person in America. As a star player in the NBA, he stands out like a garish, neon sign Rodman is widely acknowledged for his outlandish behavior as well as his looks. He has been suspended many times for abusing officials with offensive language and starting fights has been almost a monthly occurrence during games. Rodman is very outgoing the rumors about his nightlife are legend Madonna was even seen with him on several occasions. On the street, you might see him dressed in anything from a full-length mink coat or a wedding dress! Rodman loves the attention and he loves making millions of dollars each year as an NBA player and celebrity.

Copyright © 2004 by Pearson Education, Inc.

▼ PRACTICE 12	Correcting Comma Splice Errors

Answers will vary.

Find and correct the comma splice errors in the following paragraph. Neatly write your corrections in the text.

The Journey's End

It was early June, the sun was bright but not blistering on my face. The silent motion of the pedals of my bike moved me closer to my destination. It had been two months since my last visit with Bev, her usual shining face grew grim as she saw me approach. Her tone was one of concern, "Have you spoken to your mother today?" I was startled. She continued, "Your grandmother is in the hospital." I rushed home and called mother, she told me that grandmother was very ill, and I couldn't visit her without being accompanied by her. I refused to wait, I couldn't let my grandmother lay in a cold, indifferent room without being by her side, we were as close as mother and daughter.

▼ PRACTICE 13	Correcting Comma Splice Errors

Answers will vary.

Find and correct the comma splice errors in the following paragraph. Neatly write your corrections in the text.

The Dilemma of Modern Progress

Despite senseless tragedies and horrors, well-documented in history books, the twentieth century has been a time of continuing progression for humanity. Many wonderful advances, commonplace today, would have been beyond even the most imaginative of nineteenth century dreamers, there appears to be no slow down to this trend, moreover, new ideas are now being developed at an ever-increasing pace. Although most would agree these accomplishments are desirable, many so-called "time savers" can have us chasing our own tails, modern technology often produces more inconvenience than convenience because of our lack of understanding of the full scope of the impact that our inventions have on us.

▼ **PRACTICE 14** Correcting Spelling Errors

Find and correct the spelling errors in the following paragraph. Neatly write your corrections in the text.

Deserted Waters

    soothing   **deserted**
A place I find ~~sothing~~ is a ~~desserted~~ picnic area next to the river near

Old Town. Standing under the roof of a small pavilion, I can look out over

    rushing   **crash**
the dirty ~~ruhsing~~ water of the Mississippi River. I can hear the water ~~craxsh~~

as it hits the rocks with every wave. Surrounding me on the cracked concrete

    warped   **tables**
are half a dozen old, ~~warpped~~ picnic ~~talbles.~~ I can hear birds singing above

as they guard their nests hiding in the beams. On my left stand shabby

    leading
homes that once were vibrant mansions. The stairs ~~ledding~~ up to the front

    replaced
doors are missing, and the glass in the windows has been ~~rplaced~~ with

boards
~~boreds.~~ There is a lifeless playground, grass growing over the rusting equip-

    scene   **beautiful**
ment, behind me. The ~~seen~~ may look depressing, but it is a ~~beautifull~~ place

where I can relax.

▼ **PRACTICE 15** Correcting Spelling Errors

Find and correct the spelling errors in the following paragraph. Neatly write your corrections in the text.

The Sound of Music

                 to broaden   **can**
How does the music we listen ~~too broden~~ our minds? Music ~~an~~ make

    mellow
people happy, sad, ~~mello,~~ or even overjoyed. The words to a song tell a

    story
story; therefore, the outcome of a great ~~storey~~ means a great song to the

artist and listener. Music fills our lives; we hear it in doctors' offices,

elevators
~~elevaters,~~ and every time we turn the ignition key in our car. The music can

    classical   **or**   **western**
be rock, soul, ~~classicall,~~ bluegrass, ~~our~~ country and ~~wesstern.~~ Whatever your

                          your
taste, there is a style of music that will touch your heart and ~~you~~ soul.

Copyright © 2004 by Pearson Education, Inc.

▼ **PRACTICE 16**   **Correcting Errors**

Answers will vary.

The following paragraphs contain sentence fragment, run-on, comma splice, and spelling errors. Correct the errors you find. Neatly write your corrections in the text.

The Staff of Life

Bread is called "the Staff of Life" and the foodstuff is the most universal food known to man. Primiative man took centuries to discover how to identify seeds and how to grow them and adapt them to local enviroments.

Oats, barley, rye, and wheat breads are made threw the process of applying heat to a mixture of flower, grain, yeast, and water three kinds of bread were the first foods made by baking, flat bread, yeast bread, and quick bread are the three kinds, consequently, causing a surplus of food in homes. Bread sonn became a favorite food item to eat with all meals and they were a tasty and newtrisious treat.

Soon, bread production mover from the home to commercial bussiness, therefore, the amount of bread produced rose dramatically the numbers of loafs produced was staggering, it was an enormous boom. In the 1940s, newtrients and vitamens were added into commercial baking; reducing various deseases around the wrld. When bread is served in restarants, most loaves are not baked on the premises the bread is baked at a commercial bakary. With the amount of bread being eaten, is justified in beign called "the Staff of Life."

▼ **PRACTICE 17**   **Correcting Errors**

Answers will vary.

The following paragraphs contain sentence fragment, run-on, comma splice, and spelling errors. Correct the errors you find. Neatly write your corrections in the text.

Viva Las Vegas!

The trip my family tood to Las Vegas was one of the best times of my life, the plain landed, and my family and I stepped off into the cool night air of Las Vegas the gambling capitol of the world. Our baggage was picked up first, it seemed to take forever. Then, we took a cab to the most exotic hotel casino we had ever seen. The hotel casino; a giant castle, was called the Excalibur. In the front of the hotel, was a fire-breathing dragon during the evening, its mouth blew a flame that must have been 20 feet long.

The next day, we awoke to the beautiful dessert sun. After eating a huge breakfast. My sister and I went for a swim, and took in some of the attractions like the Treasure Island Casino Ship show. Which was a virtual reality ride. We also went to Circus-Circus and watched the acrobates high above the casino floor they did have a net but it was still exciting. After a delicious dinner, we saw a show starring Bette Midler it was so funny and entertaning. It was the perfect end to a perfect day. Which I will be looking forward to taking agan some day, I just hope it is with my family again.

CHAPTER REVIEW

▼ Write a topic sentence with a clear topic/subject and a controlling idea by which the subject can be developed.
▼ Choose the focus for the support details by using the six reporter's questions: who, what, where, when, why, and how.
▼ Write as many support sentences as are required to develop the topic. Be certain they contain specific facts, details, and examples.
▼ Check for sentence variety that clarifies relationships and adds rhythm.
▼ Revise when necessary, looking for paragraph unity.
▼ Proofread for grammar and spelling errors.
▼ Check for paper presentation: tears, creases, and smudges.

Topic Bank

The following paragraph writing assignments will suggest topics and help you practice the techniques you have learned in this chapter. Use the seven steps in the chapter review as you do your work.

As you write each paragraph, use the reporter's question in the parentheses as your focus. Remember to revise and proofread each paragraph.

1. (*Who?*) Describe a person. This can be a person you know, such as a parent, sibling, relative, friend, teacher, co-worker, or a historical person with whom you are familiar. In your topic sentence, name the person,

Copyright © 2004 by Pearson Education, Inc.

and write a controlling idea you wish to develop in the support sentences.

2. (*What?*) Describe an event. This can be an event from your own life, such as a religious ceremony, a graduation (see the photo on page 133), an operation, or a historical event with which you are familiar. In the topic sentence, name the event, and write a controlling idea you wish to develop in the support sentence.

3. (*Where?*) Describe a location. This can be a place that you know, such as your room, house, school, workplace, or a historical location with which you are familiar. In your topic sentence, name the location, and write a controlling idea you wish to develop in the support sentences.

4. (*When?*) Describe an important time. This can be a time in your life, such as your childhood, or teenage years, or a well-known time in history with which you are familiar. In your topic sentence, name the time frame, and write a controlling idea you wish to develop in the support sentences.

5. (*Why?*) Describe why something happened. This can be something that happened to you, someone you know, or the reason something happened in history. In your topic sentence, name the reason, and write a controlling idea you wish to develop in the support sentences.

6. (*How?*) Describe how something occurs or is done. This can be something you have accomplished or were witness to or how something happened historically. In your topic sentence, name the process, and write a controlling idea you wish to develop in the support sentences.

Writing Opportunities

Home

You want your sister, who lives across town, to accompany you on a shopping trip to a mall. Your sister doesn't like malls. She thinks they are too boring because all they have are women's clothing shops. In one of your e-mails, you include a paragraph convincing her of why she should meet you at the brand new mall that has just opened near your neighborhood.

School

Your Intro to Sociology professor wants you to visit a shopping mall and write one paragraph about the type of people who might be attracted by the different types of shops and services the mall offers.

Work

The owners of a shopping mall have hired the advertising agency you work for to attract customers to its newest mall. Write one paragraph of text to accompany the photograph above that will appear in a brochure advertising the grand opening of the mall.

Visit *The Write Start* Online!

For additional practice with the materials found in this chapter, visit our Website at:

http://www.ablongman.com/checkett

The Website also features additional readings, quizzes, writing activities, and Internet links, as well as a bulletin board and interactive chat.

For More Practice with Your Grammar and Writing Skills
Visit The Longman Writer's Warehouse

For further multimedia exercises and activities designed to improve your reading, thinking, writing, and grammar skills, visit The Longman Writer's Warehouse on the Web. The Writer's Warehouse offers an interactive handbook, an online journal, a bulletin board, and extensive coverage of the writing process. To take a tour, go to

http://longmanwriterswarehouse.com

Copyright © 2004 by Pearson Education, Inc.

14 Description

All paragraphs build on a topic. One way to build on a topic is by describing it in detail. Effective **description** creates images in the reader's mind by using specific details. Like a painter using color on a canvas, the writer uses words (the color) to create pictures in the reader's mind (the canvas).

Instead of merely writing

> The clouds flew by overhead.

A writer using good description might write

> The billowing clouds, like delicious mounds of white mashed potatoes, floated lazily by overhead as if they hadn't a care in the world.

The specific details help develop the word-painting that describes persons, places, things, and emotions. At times, writers want their meaning to convey a feeling of sadness. At other times, they might want to evoke a feeling of happiness, or frustration, or hope, or sarcasm. Effective description adds clarity, depth, and feeling to your writing.

Types of Description

There are two types of description: **objective** and **subjective.**

Objective description relies on factual detail without much embellishment.

Example

The snowman consisted of three round balls stacked one on top of the other. It stood 5 feet high. Its eyes were round stones, with a carrot serving as a nose. A baseball cap sat atop its head.

From this objective description, you can picture the snowman. However, it is difficult to recognize what emotion or impression the writer wants us to feel.

In contrast, subjective description creates an easily identifiable emotion or impression.

Example

The snowman's body consisted of three plump balls of fluffy, white snow stacked like an ice-cream cone. Its eyes were made from brightly colored stones, with a squiggly, pigtail, orange carrot serving as a nose. A fuzzy, red baseball cap with a crooked bill sat cockeyed on his head.

From this subjective description, it is clear that the writer wants the snowman to evoke a funny or happy emotion. Objective description tells what the writer actually sees. Subjective description shows how the writer feels.

Dominant Impressions

The content of your descriptive writing will be clearer and more enjoyable if you focus on just one **dominant impression.** In a descriptive paragraph, each support sentence should build on the dominant, or main, impression you created in the topic sentence. Adding descriptive detail helps writers achieve these dominant impressions. Writers convey the dominant impression to the reader by a word or phrase in the topic sentence of a paragraph and then support this word or phrase throughout the paragraph by using specific detail.

(No dominant impression) The sky was filled with dark, brooding clouds, and slivers of bright sunlight glistened toward the ground.

In this paragraph, the reader will not know the writer's intention. Is the writer trying to convey a negative or a positive mood?

Copyright © 2004 by Pearson Education, Inc.

> (Dominant impression) The sky was filled with dark, brooding clouds, and horrible flashes of lightning sent ugly scars across the horizon.

In this paragraph, the negative dominant impression is clear. Remember, the dominant impression is the overall feeling or emotional response that you want your reader to take away from your description. The words you choose to make your dominant impression should be specific enough to be easily understood; they should not be vague.

For example, the word "nice" has no specific meaning because it can mean almost anything. Nice can mean friendly, or pretty, or neat, or clean.

Examples

Topic sentences without dominant impressions:

Melody was a model.

It was evening in St. Louis.

The ball game was played.

The diamond necklace lay on the dresser.

Topic sentences with a dominant impression:

Melody was a glamorous model.

The evening in St. Louis was dreary.

The ball game was exciting.

The dazzling diamond necklace lay on the dresser.

Tip: A useful book to help you select better dominant impression words is a *thesaurus*. This is a reference book that contains lists of synonyms, homonyms, and antonyms for almost any word you can think of. You can find an inexpensive paperback thesaurus at any bookstore, or you can use an online thesaurus.

▼ **PRACTICE 1** **Using Specific Words to Create Dominant Impressions**

Answers will vary.

In the space to the right, replace the underlined, vague dominant impression word in the sentence with a more specific and descriptive word or phrase.

Example: **Vague:** The wedding dress was beautiful.

Specific: The wedding dress was dazzling.

1. The haunted house was scary.   Specific: _____

2. The thick, woolen blanket felt nice.   Specific: _____

3. My Uncle Jacob is fun.   Specific: _____

4. The bowl of chili tasted hot.   Specific: _____

5. Fiona's ballet practice was good.   Specific: _____

6. The actor's performance was bad.   Specific: _____

7. The band's music was <u>loud</u>.   Specific: _____

8. The dorm room was <u>messy</u>.   Specific: _____

9. The aquarium decorations were <u>pretty</u>.   Specific: _____

10. The chocolate mousse was <u>rich</u>.   Specific: _____

Sensory Images

Description creates images. It can tell the reader what a person, a place, or a thing

▼ Looks like
▼ Feels like
▼ Smells like
▼ Sounds like
▼ Tastes like

These **sensory images** are based on the five senses we are all familiar with: sight, touch, smell, sound, and taste. By using sensory images, writers can draw a more fully developed picture of what they are describing. Good description actually causes readers to remember similar persons, places, or things from their own experience. This personal interaction between the reader and the writing is a wonderful and powerful process.

Examples

Sight

    a. Nondescriptive: The model walked down the runway wearing a dress.

    b. Descriptive: The spaghetti-thin fashion model slinked down the long runway wearing a shining, cherry-red dress.

Touch

    a. Nondescriptive: The new bedsheets were uncomfortable.

    b. Descriptive: The new, stiff bedsheets felt like sandpaper scraping against my skin.

Smell

    a. Nondescriptive: Fred's car trunk smelled awful.

    b. Descriptive: Fred's car trunk smelled like a gym locker stuffed with rotten eggs.

Sound

    a. Nondescriptive: The band was loud.

    b. Descriptive: The band's ear-splitting punk music was loud enough to make your teeth vibrate.

Taste

    a. Nondescriptive: The bread tasted old.

    b. Descriptive: The bread tasted musty, like some moldy cheese I ate at my grandmother's house last year.

Copyright © 2004 by Pearson Education, Inc.

Answers will vary.

In the blank spaces below, rewrite the nondescriptive sentences by using various sensory images.

1. Nondescriptive: The boy's clothes didn't fit properly.

    Sight: _____

    _____

2. Nondescriptive: The car was not in good shape.

    Sight: _____

    _____

3. Nondescriptive: The tree bark felt rough.

    Touch: _____

    _____

4. Nondescriptive: The baby's skin was soft.

    Touch: _____

    _____

5. Nondescriptive: The odor of Fred's gym shoes was awful.

    Smell: _____

    _____

6. Nondescriptive: The perfume smelled good.

    Smell: _____

    _____

7. Nondescriptive: My younger brother was loud.

    Sound: _____

    _____

8. Nondescriptive: The storm made a lot of noise.

    Sound: _____

    _____

9. Nondescriptive: The breakfast pastries tasted good.

Taste: _____

_____

10. Nondescriptive: The fancy dinner was delicious.

Taste: _____

_____

Comparisons

Another device that writers use to describe something is **comparison,** also known as **figurative language.** Comparisons to well-known or everyday objects or images provide descriptions that readers can immediately recognize. Many writers find comparison the easiest descriptive tool because comparisons allow writers to provide clear ideas to the reader by tapping into images and emotions that the reader has already experienced. The three most effective figurative language devices are

▼ Simile
▼ Metaphor
▼ Personification

Simile

A **simile** is a comparison using either *like* or *as* to show a similarity between two different things. Notice how alike the words "simile" and "similarity" are.

> **Examples**
>
> My boss roars <u>like</u> a lion at his employees.
>
> The fog was <u>like</u> a blanket covering the city, so you couldn't see a thing.
>
> The runner was fast <u>as</u> a cheetah, and he won the race.
>
> The searchlight shined brightly <u>as</u> the sun, blocking our vision.

Metaphor

A **metaphor** is a stronger comparison between two things without using *like* or *as*. The implication is that one thing "is" the same as the other.

> **Examples**
>
> My boss <u>is</u> a lion, roaring at all his employees.
>
> The fog <u>was</u> a blanket covering the city, so you couldn't see a thing.

Personification

In **personification,** the writer gives human emotions or characteristics to animals, objects, or even ideas.

Copyright © 2004 by Pearson Education, Inc.

Examples

The tree <u>howled</u> in the wind.

Love <u>danced</u> in their eyes.

The bear <u>cheated</u> his rivals out of their food.

The house's windows <u>winked</u> at the passersby.

The car <u>rested</u> in the driveway after the long drive home.

▼ PRACTICE 3   **Using Figurative Language to Make Comparisons**

Answers will vary.

In the spaces below, create comparisons between the two objects in the parentheses using the figurative language device marked in boldface.

Example: (**simile**—raindrops/ball-bearings) <u>The raindrops sounded **like** steel ball-bearings smashing into the roof with a metallic bang!</u>

1. (**simile**—lake/glass) _____

_____

2. (**simile**—mansion/monster) _____

_____

3. (**metaphor**—airplane/bird) _____

_____

4. (**metaphor**—car/tiger) _____

_____

5. (**personification**—wind/caring person) _____

_____

6. (**personification**—stuffed animal/jolly person) _____

_____

▼ PRACTICE 4   **Analyzing Descriptive Writing**

The following paragraph is taken from a descriptive essay, "Halloween Havoc," by student writer Erin Nelson. The paragraph is jam-packed with expressive description that brings the special evening to life!

The spooky old houses come to life at night with gruesome decorations.

With grotesque carved faces, the jack-o'-lanterns give off an eerie glow.

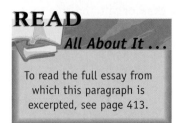

READ

All About It . . .

To read the full essay from which this paragraph is excerpted, see page 413.

Tombstones line the sidewalk, like a long narrow graveyard; beware of the bloody hand reaching out to grab intruders. Bats as black as the night sky fly in quick circles, darting in the air, and a black cat with razor sharp fangs crosses the path of unseen, terrified prey. The ghosts and the goblins sneak around monster-like trees, ready to snatch their next victim.

Descriptive Technique Questions

1. What is the topic?

Halloween—stated in the title, not in the paragraph.

2. What do you think is the dominant impression Nelson is attempting to describe?

Scary

3. Underline any figurative language techniques you find. How do they enhance the dominant impression?

Similes add descriptive images that support the "scary" dominant impression. The trees are also personified as they can "snatch their next victim."

▼ **PRACTICE 5**   **Analyzing Descriptive Writing**

In this paragraph from a descriptive essay, "New York—The Big Apple," by student writer Amber Barton, the cosmopolitan environs of New York City are compared to the rural area of Missouri in which she grew up.

The sights of New York City stimulate the senses; rural Missouri soothes them. From the Empire State Building to the subway system, the sights and sounds of New York City invigorate the spirit. The vision of Lady Liberty standing proudly in the East River with Ellis Island, its now silent companion, evokes pride in its visitors. The rich hills and valleys of rural Missouri are lovely, yet they pale in comparison to the stark beauty of New

Copyright © 2004 by Pearson Education, Inc.

York skyscrapers. A traveler would have to visit more than once to be able to take in all the diverse sights New York City has to offer.

Descriptive Technique Questions

1. What is the topic?

New York City

2. What do you think is the dominant impression Barton is trying to describe?

Excitement

3. Underline any figurative language techniques you find. How do they enhance the dominant impression?

Personification is used to give the reader a sense that New York City is actually "alive."

▼
PRACTICE 6   Analyzing Descriptive Writing

The following paragraph uses sensory images and figurative language to clarify and support the topic sentences. In this paragraph from the essay "The Mute Sense" from Diane Ackerman's 1990 book *The Natural History of the Senses,* the writer piles one descriptive device upon another until a full picture emerges. The first sentence in the paragraph is the topic sentence.

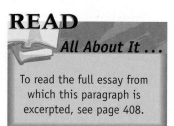

READ
All About It . . .

To read the full essay from which this paragraph is excerpted, see page 408.

Nothing is more memorable than a smell. One scent can be unexpected, momentary, and fleeting, <u>yet</u> conjure up a childhood summer beside a lake in the Poconos, <u>when</u> wild blueberry bushes teemed with succulent fruit, <u>and</u> the opposite sex was as mysterious as space travel; <u>another</u>, hours of passion on a moonlit beach in Florida, <u>while</u> the night-blooming cereus drenched the air with thick curds of perfume and high sphinx moths visited the cereus in a loud purr of wings; a third, a family dinner of pot roast, noodle pudding, and sweet potatoes, during a myrtle-mad August in a midwestern town, <u>when</u> both of one's parents were alive. Smells detonate softly in our memory like poignant land mines, hidden under the weedy mass of many years and experiences. Hit a tripwire of smell, and memories explode all at once. A complex vision leaps out of the undergrowth.

Descriptive Technique Questions

1. What is the topic?

Smells

2. What do you think is the dominant impression Ackerman is attempting to describe?

Memorable

3. Ackerman uses two similes. Can you identify them?

"The opposite sex was as mysterious as space travel," and "smells

detonate softly in our memory like poignant land mines."

4. Is the tone of the paragraph more objective or subjective? Cite examples of both.

More subjective than objective. Objective: "wild blueberry bushes

teemed with succulent fruit," "moonlit beach," "dinner of pot roast,

noodle pudding, and sweet potatoes." Subjective: "One scent can . . .

conjure up a childhood summer beside a lake," "night-blooming cereus

drenched the air with thick curds of perfume," "high sphinx moths

visited the cereus in a loud purr of wings," and "our memory . . . hidden

under the weedy mass of many years of experiences."

5. Ackerman uses very active verbs, such as "teemed," "drenched," "detonate," "explode," and "leap." How are these action words effective in supporting and clarifying the dominant impression Ackerman wants to give the reader?

These verbs are very dramatic, and they combine to stimulate visual

memory because of their ability to elicit memories from sensory

stimulation.

6. Identify the transitional words and phrases that help connect information and add rhythm to the sentences.

The writer primarily uses conjunctions to connect information and to

create rhythm. See underlining for examples.

Copyright © 2004 by Pearson Education, Inc.

PRACTICE 7 — Analyzing Descriptive Writing

The following paragraphs from Luis Rodriguez's essay, "The Ice Cream Truck," use many sensory images and figurative language devices to create a word-picture that is every bit as detailed as a fine painting. Although short, the paragraphs are packed with expressive sounds and sights. Explanations of terms in brackets are ours, not Rodriguez's.

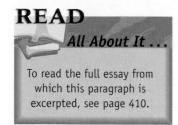

READ *All About It . . .*

To read the full essay from which this paragraph is excerpted, see page 410.

The Hills blistered below a haze of sun and smog. Mothers with wet strands of hair across their foreheads flung wash up to dry on weathered lines. Sweat-drenched men lay on their backs in the gravel of alleys, beneath broken-down cars propped up on cinder blocks. *Charrangas* [a Cuban style of music with violins] and *corridos* [a Mexican style of music] splashed out of open windows.

Suddenly from over a hill, an ice cream truck raced by with packs of children running beside it. A hurried version of "Old McDonald Had a Farm" chimed through a speaker bolted on the truck's roof. The truck stopped long enough for somebody to toss out dozens of sidewalk sundaes, tootie-fruities and half-and-half bars to the children who gathered around, thrusting up small, dirt-caked hands that blossomed open as their shrieks blended with laughter.

Then the truck's transmission gears growled as it continued up the slope, whipped around a corner and passed a few of us *vatos* [similar to "homeboys"] assembled on a field off Toll Drive. We looked over toward the echoes of the burdensome chimes, the slip and boom of the clutch and rasp of gears as the ice cream truck entered the dead-end streets and curves of Las Lomas.

Descriptive Technique Questions

1. What is the topic?

The ice cream truck

2. What do you think is the dominant impression Rodriguez is attempting to describe? Give some examples to support your answer.

   A hot, summer day in a poor, Mexican neighborhood. Words and images, such as "blistered," "haze," "sun," "wet strands of hair across their foreheads," "Sweat-drenched," in ¶ 1; and the image of the ice cream truck providing cold ice cream treats for the children in ¶ 2.

3. Identify the two personifications Rodriguez uses.

   In ¶ 3, "Then the truck's transmission gears growled," and "the echoes of the burdensome chimes."

4. Is the tone of the paragraphs more objective or subjective? Cite examples of both.

   More objective than subjective description. Objective: "a haze of sun and smog," "wet strands of hair across their foreheads," "flung wash up to dry on weathered lines," "sweat-drenched men lay on their backs in the gravel of alleys," "broken-down cars propped up on cinder blocks," "*Charrangas* and *corridos* splashed out of open windows," "children running beside it," "a speaker bolted on the truck's roof," and "the slip and boom of the clutch and rasp of gears." Subjective: "The Hills blistered," "thrusting up small, dirt-caked hands that blossomed open," "the truck's transmission gears growled," and "the echoes of the burdensome chimes."

A Ten-Step Process for Writing the Descriptive Paragraph

Experienced writers often follow a step-by-step process that helps them write effectively. As you develop as a writer, you will undoubtedly create your own process. In the meantime, this set of easy-to-follow guidelines will help you write an effective descriptive paragraph.

Writing the Descriptive Paragraph

1. Choose a topic. The topic should be a person, place, or thing (an idea, event, or situation).
2. Think about the topic, and choose the dominant impression (the overall feeling) you want your reader to experience.
3. Write a topic sentence with the dominant impression word included.
4. Make a list of the details you want to include in the paragraph that will support and clarify the dominant impression.

Copyright © 2004 by Pearson Education, Inc.

5. Put each of the details into a separate sentence.
6. Rewrite the sentences. Use sensory details and figurative language to create descriptive images.
7. Be certain that the sensory images and figurative devices support the dominant impression.
8. Proofread for punctuation errors, sentence fragments, and run-on sentences.
9. If possible, have another person read the paragraph. Ask him or her to point out any errors or unclear ideas. Rewrite, if necessary.
10. Prepare your finished paragraph for presentation to your instructor.

Example of the Ten-Step Process at Work

1. Topic: A person you have observed.
2. Dominant impression: joy
3. The man was **joyful** when he learned he had the winning lotto number.
4. Details: *facial expressions* (eyes and mouth); *mannerisms* (hand gestures and body language); *clothing* (style, color, accessories); *speech* (expressions and loudness).
5. a. The man smiled and his eyes lit up.
   b. He held his arms over his head and danced all around the store.
   c. He was wearing a yellow shirt, white pants, and a gold necklace matching the three gold diamond rings on each hand.
   d. He yelled and screamed about how happy he was to be a millionaire.

> **First Draft of Paragraph**
>
> The man was joyful when he learned he had the winning lotto number. He smiled, and his eyes lit up. He held his arms over his head and danced around the store. He was wearing a yellow shirt, white pants, and a gold necklace matching three gold diamond rings on each hand. He yelled and screamed about how happy he was to be a millionaire.

6. Support sentence rewrites:
   a. His smile <u>flashed like a beam of light</u>, and his eyes <u>twinkled</u>.
      ↑   ↑
      (simile)   (sight)

   b. He <u>waved</u> his <u>shaking</u> arms over his head as he danced around the store
      ↑   ↑
      (sight)   (sight)

   <u>like a statue made from Jell-O</u> that had suddenly come to life.
      ↑
      (simile)

   c. He wore a <u>bright-yellow</u>, <u>satin</u> shirt and <u>gleaming white</u> slacks
                    ↑   ↑   ↑
                 (sight)   (touch)   (sight)

   accented by a <u>shining</u> gold necklace matching three <u>sparkling</u>
                    ↑   ↑
                 (sight)   (sight)

   diamond rings on each hand.

   d. The <u>jewelry seemed to cry out</u>, "I'm rich! I'm a millionaire!"
                 ↑
          (personification)

7. Does the following list support the dominant impression of **joy?** Yes!!

flashed like a beam of light	satin
twinkled	gleaming white
waved	shining
shaking	sparkling
like a statue made from Jell-O	jewelry seemed to cry out "I'm rich . . ."
bright-yellow	

8. Proofread the paragraph.
9. Have someone else read the paragraph and make comments.
10. Rewrite the paragraph.

> **Final Draft of the Paragraph**
>
> The man was joyful when he learned he had the winning lotto number. His smile flashed like a beam of light, and his eyes twinkled. He waved his shaking arms over his head as he danced around the store like a statue made from Jell-O that had suddenly come to life. He wore a bright-yellow, satin shirt and gleaming white slacks accented by a shining gold necklace matching three sparkling diamond rings on each hand. The jewelry seemed to cry out, "I'm rich! I'm a millionaire!"

Now, compare this final paragraph to the original, and you can see how much more effective the final paragraph is. The dominant impression is clear, and the support sentences clearly describe the dominant impression.

▼ **PRACTICE 8**   **Writing a Descriptive Paragraph**

Answers will vary.

In this exercise you will use the step-by-step process described above. Following the ten steps, write one descriptive paragraph each for a person, place, and thing that you know very well. If you want to be adventurous, you can create a person from your own imagination. In other words, have some fun with it!

Person

Possible persons:

    a. An actor/actress
    b. An athlete
    c. An entertainer
    d. A relative
    e. A historical figure
    f. A circus performer
    g. A science fiction character
    h. A bodybuilder
    i. A movie monster
    j. A politician

  1. Choose a topic: _____

  2. Dominant impression: _____

Copyright © 2004 by Pearson Education, Inc.

3. Write a topic sentence with the dominant impression word included:

_____

_____

4. Choose three or four details that support the dominant impression:

a. _____

b. _____

c. _____

d. _____

5. Put each detail into a separate sentence:

a. _____

_____

b. _____

_____

c. _____

_____

d. _____

_____

6. Rewrite the sentences creating descriptive images by using sensory details and by using figurative language techniques you have practiced.

a. _____

_____

b. _____

_____

c. _____

_____

d. _____

_____

Put these sentences into paragraph form with the topic sentence first.

_____

_____

_____

_____

_____

_____

_____

7. Check to make sure the descriptive images support the dominant impression by making a list of the sensory details and figurative devices. Then evaluate the effectiveness of your images.

Dominant impression: _____

List of descriptive images: _____

_____

_____

_____

_____

_____

8. Now, proofread your paragraph, looking for punctuation errors, sentence fragments, run-on sentences, and spelling errors.

9. If possible, have another person read the paragraph. Ask them to point out any errors or unclear ideas. Rewrite, if necessary.

10. Write your final paragraph version:

_____

_____

_____

_____

_____

_____

Copyright © 2004 by Pearson Education, Inc.

![decorative bar] **CHAPTER REVIEW** ![decorative bar]

▼ Effective description creates images by using specific details.
▼ There are two types of description: objective and subjective.
▼ In descriptive writing, the topic is most clearly defined by creating one dominant impression.
▼ Effective description can be achieved through sensory images, based on the five senses: sight, touch, smell, sound, and taste.
▼ Figurative language also can help create effective description through the use of simile, metaphor, and personification.

Topic Bank

Place

Using the ten steps you have practiced, write a paragraph describing one of the following places or a place you choose.

1. An amusement park
2. A restaurant
3. A doctor's office
4. A rural setting
5. The zoo
6. The circus
7. A nightclub
8. A library
9. A grocery store
10. A business office

Thing

Using the ten steps you have practiced, write a descriptive paragraph for a thing. (Remember, a thing can be an idea, event, or situation.)

Possible things:

11. The atmosphere at a concert (see the photo on page 154)
12. A job interview
13. A romantic date
14. Oppression
15. A time of day
16. Christmas morning
17. A graduation ceremony
18. A wedding
19. A car wreck
20. Freedom

Writing Opportunities

Home

You are traveling through the West on summer vacation with your family. You are using a video camera to record the memorable sites you see, and you've also decided to keep a journal of the sites you experience to supplement the visual images. You spot an old barn set against the backdrop of the Rockies. Write a paragraph in your journal to describe the scene you have captured with your video camera.

School

Your geography instructor has given each member of the class a picture of an old barn set against the Rocky Mountains. Your assignment is to write a paragraph describing one prominent feature of the picture explaining how it reflects the spirit of the people who might live in the area.

Work

A mineral mining company wants to strip-mine the area in the photograph above. A government committee is considering whether to comply with their request. As an employee with the Department of the Interior, you have been given the task of writing a descriptive paragraph to help your agency's director convince the committee not to vote in favor of the project.

Copyright © 2004 by Pearson Education, Inc.

Visit *The Write Start* Online!

For additional practice with the materials found in this chapter, visit our Website at:

http://www.ablongman.com/checkett

The Website also features additional readings, quizzes, writing activities, and Internet links, as well as a bulletin board and interactive chat.

**For More Practice with Your Grammar and Writing Skills
Visit The Longman Writer's Warehouse**

For further multimedia exercises and activities designed to improve your reading, thinking, writing, and grammar skills, visit The Longman Writer's Warehouse on the Web. The Writer's Warehouse offers an interactive handbook, an online journal, a bulletin board, and extensive coverage of the writing process. To take a tour, go to

http://longmanwriterswarehouse.com

Copyright © 2004 by Pearson Education, Inc.

Narration

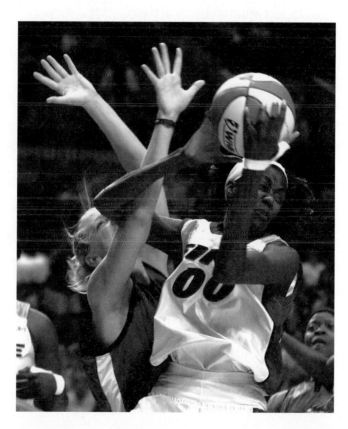

Writers use paragraphs to develop or express a main idea or topic. One way of doing so is through **narration.** Narration is simply the telling of a story, either to entertain or inform a reader. The stories in narrative paragraphs can be fiction (made up) or nonfiction (the retelling of an incident that actually happened). What's important, though, is that the story develops the topic of the paragraph.

The elements of a narrative paragraph are the same as those in any other type of paragraph:

▼ A topic sentence announcing the subject and controlling idea
▼ Support sentences using specific detail to develop the subject
▼ Sentence variety connecting related ideas and adding rhythm

The Point of the Story

There must be a point to every story; otherwise, no one will be interested in reading it. Therefore, every narrative paragraph you write must have a clear point or purpose. That purpose should always be to develop the topic and controlling idea of the paragraph. This might seem like an obvious and easy point to follow in a paragraph, but too many writers lose sight of it. The best way to get to the point of the story is to examine the topic sentence and see what makes it interesting to the reader. That will be the point of the story.

Exhibit 15–1 provides an example of a topic sentence for a narrative paragraph. The subject, controlling idea, and the point of the story are listed.

Exhibit 15–1

> **Example**
>
> When my mother had hip surgery, I assumed responsibility for running the household.
>
> > *Subject*: Running the household
> >
> > *Controlling idea*: Assuming responsibility for running the household
> >
> > *Point of the story*: Acting responsibly in a time of need

---

▼ **PRACTICE 1**   **Identifying the Point of a Story**

Answers will vary.

In the following topic sentences, underline the subject once, the controlling idea twice, and, in your own words, summarize what you think the point of the story is in the space provided.

1. I studied day and night for two weeks and passed all my exams with A grades.

Point of the story: _____

_____

2. I voted for the challenger even though he was behind in all the polls.

Point of the story: _____

_____

3. Although my first camping trip was not at all what I expected, I eventually had a good time.

Point of the story: _____

_____

4. I relied on my parents' advice when I bought my first car.

Point of the story: _____

_____

5. I read three fashion magazines before I went shopping for winter clothing.

Point of the story: _____

_____

▼ **PRACTICE 2**   **Writing Narrative Topic Sentences**

Answers will vary.   Write your own narrative topic sentences for the topics listed below. After you have finished, underline the topic once, the controlling idea twice, and, in your own words, summarize the point of your story in the space provided.

1. Topic: Driving _____

_____

Point of the story: _____

2. Topic: Working at a job _____

_____

Point of the story: _____

3. Topic: A hospital experience _____

_____

Point of the story: _____

4. Topic: Television _____

_____

Point of the story: _____

5. Topic: Video games _____

_____

Point of the story: _____

Developing the Narrative Paragraph

Once you've chosen the subject, controlling idea, and the point of the story, you must decide how to develop the subject. What details, facts, and examples will you choose to develop the story and get the point of the story across? The easiest way to develop a subject and maintain focus is to use the six reporter's questions: who, what, where, when, why, and how. (See Chapter 13, The Paragraph, for a broader discussion of the six reporter's questions.)

For the topic sentence example in Exhibit 15–1 presented earlier, the developing focus could be any of the following.

Copyright © 2004 by Pearson Education, Inc.

Examples

Who? Who assumed responsibility for running the household? (As the topic sentence states, the writer did.)

What? What household activities had to be done? (This might be a list of activities, such as paying bills, food shopping, cooking, cleaning, and babysitting.)

Where? Where were the activities finished? (The household has been identified.)

When? When were the activities completed? (The period encompassing the hospital stay and the convalescence time.)

Why? Why did the household activities have to be assumed? (Because the mother was in the hospital.)

How? How were the activities completed? (Did the writer use any special appliances to help out with the chores, or to do the chores in a particular order each day?)

From the list above, *who, where,* and *why* are obvious and probably do not need to be developed. The important features to develop would be *what* (what activities had to be done), *when* (how long did it take), or *how* (how were the activities taken care of). (For additional discussion of the importance of detail, see Chapter 14, Description.)

Model Narrative Paragraphs

The following are examples of paragraphs developed for the topic sentence in Exhibit 15–1 using different focus questions.

1. *Focus:* **What**—all the household chores and activities that needed to be done.

> When my mother had hip surgery, I assumed responsibility for running the household. First, I had to take care of a stack of bills for the month. After that, I planned a menu for the week, and I went to the supermarket to buy food. In addition to cooking daily meals, I prepared some meals in advance; afterward, I placed them in the freezer. I tried to clean part of the house each day, so I wouldn't have an overwhelming job on the weekend. Besides all of these chores, I had to take care of my younger sister and brother. Although I was very nervous at the thought of shouldering all these responsibilities, I was up to the challenge.

In this paragraph, the topic is developed using those activities that support the *what* focus question: paying bills, food shopping, cooking, cleaning, and babysitting. The list of chores is linked by the use of words and phrases that order the events: "first," "after that," and "in addition." Instead of a choppy list, the paragraph reads smoothly and rhythmically.

2. *Focus:* **When**—The period when the writer's mother was in the hospital, and the period when the mother was home recuperating but unable to help.

> When my mother had hip surgery, I assumed responsibility for running the household. The total time period for my running the house was four weeks. First, my mother had to stay in the hospital for an entire week; afterward, she came home, but she had to stay in bed for another week. Finally, when she could get out of bed, I had to be at her side to help her on short exercise walks. This lasted for two more weeks. All the while, I still had to do all the household chores by myself. After the four weeks had passed, my mother made me a special dinner, and she thanked me for being so mature in running the house. It was a proud day for both of us.

Notice that this paragraph uses "time" words and phrases to facilitate the development supporting the *when* focus question: "when," "time period," "four weeks," "entire week," "afterward," "another week," "two more weeks," "all the while," and "four weeks had passed." Also, notice the order of events is chronologically sound: the mother is in the hospital, then comes home, convalesces at home in bed, and, finally, gets out of bed to exercise.

3. *Focus*: **How**—How the chores were taken care of.

> When my mother had hip surgery, I assumed responsibility for running the household. I knew that I could not take care of everything, so I enlisted some help. My brother and sister were very young, so my Aunt Jessie came every other evening to help babysit; consequently, I could do laundry and prepare some meals for the following week. My neighbor and best friend, Celeste, also helped with food shopping and yard work. After my mother came home from the hospital, there was even more to do. So, every Saturday, I paid a maid service to come in and clean the house. When my mother finally was able to get up and around, we went for a walk, and she had tears in her eyes when she told me how proud she was of how I had handled all the responsibilities.

This paragraph develops the focus question *how* by describing how the chores were completed (the writer enlisted friends and relatives to help out): Aunt Jessie (babysitting), friend and neighbor Celeste (food shopping and yard work), and a maid service (housecleaning). Notice that this focus also could satisfy the *who* question. Often, one focus helps in developing ideas that are relevant to another focus.

The important aspect to remember is that each paragraph develops the same topic, yet uses information that places emphasis on a different aspect of the situation.

Transitional Expressions: Showing Time Sequence

Because narrative paragraphs relate a story, you usually present events in the proper order. That way, the reader can stay focused on the events without being confused about when things happened. To keep track of time and show readers the correct sequence of events, you need to use **transitional expressions.**

Copyright © 2004 by Pearson Education, Inc.

Commonly Used Transitional Expressions in Narration

after	first	soon
afterward	last(ly)	then
as	later	third
as soon as	meanwhile	upon
before	next	when
during	now	while
finally	second	

Exhibit 15–2

Transitional expressions are simply words and phrases that indicate when one event happened in relation to another.

PRACTICE 3   Identifying Transitional Expressions

Answers will vary.

The following paragraph is taken from a narrative essay, "Shattered Sanctuary," by student writer Stephanie Higgs. Underline the transitional expressions. Discuss how they help add rhythm and move the story from idea to idea smoothly.

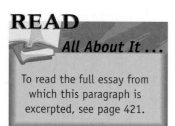

READ
All About It . . .

To read the full essay from which this paragraph is excerpted, see page 421.

Thunderstorms the previous night had settled into a steady, rhythmic rain shower by daylight. After finally getting the last child out the door and onto the school bus around 7:00 A.M., I was alone in the house following my predictable routine. First, I had put the dogs in the garage by 7:45 A.M. because I was leaving the house for a college art history class. Then, I heard the scraping of the vinyl floor trim on the French door against the ceramic floor tiles. Now, much like the sound of nails on a chalkboard, it is forever recorded in my memory coming back during waking and sleeping hours alike, to torture me. It makes no difference whether the door is actually opening or not because my mind will always believe that it is. Next, I remember calling out down the hallway to the kitchen, "What did you forget?" I guessed my husband had forgotten some important papers he needed for a meeting he had scheduled in Hazelwood that morning. As I rounded the corner, what I saw made fear rise in my throat like green bile forced up from the pit of my stomach. As soon as I saw them, panic increased my heart rate, bringing it

to ear-shattering crescendos until I thought I would go deaf or explode.
Incapacitating shock and disbelief bordering on denial paralyzed my entire
body as I stared at two masked black men wielding knives standing in my
kitchen breakfast room and heading straight toward me.

▼
| PRACTICE 4 | Identifying Transitional Expressions |

Answers will vary.

The following paragraph is taken from a narrative essay, "Small Town Views,"
by student writer Matt Grant. Underline the transitional expressions. Discuss
how they help add rhythm and move the story from idea to idea smoothly.

At first, the town of Sault Ste. Marie appeared large. A drive down the
main four-lane road through town revealed several restaurants, stores, and
businesses. Even though only a few streets intersected the main road, the
town seemed to sprawl before me. During my drive down Main Street, a fairly
new Wal-Mart stood out as one of the larger buildings. As soon as I passed
through town, on top of a large, grassy hill, Lake Superior State College
stood facing the divided highway that passed by town. Sitting on the hill,
the college seemed to appear larger and more majestic to cars passing by on
the highway. Finally, the Soo Locks controlled the north end of town, polic-
ing Lake Freighter traffic on the Saint Marys River. Yet, something was missing; the town was as quiet as night.

▼
| PRACTICE 5 | Editing for Time Sequence |

Answers will vary.

The following paragraph's topic is *how* the Spanish-American War began. The
sentences are out of chronological sequence. In their current order, the ideas
are not developed coherently, and the information is difficult to understand.
On a separate sheet of paper, rewrite the paragraph by reordering the sentences in proper time sequence, using transitional expressions from Exhibit
15–2 to help establish the proper order, link the ideas, and add rhythm.

This savage warfare frightened Americans, but the United States did not
intervene. The Cubans reverted to destroying their land to cause the Spanish
to leave. In the year 1898, America declared war on Spain. The Spanish

Copyright © 2004 by Pearson Education, Inc.

Army, which was commanded by General Valeriano Wyler, began capturing Cuban citizens and placing them in concentration camps. The war was an overwhelming victory for America and also for Cuba. The rebellion that arose in 1895 was the most devastating. Cubans had, for many years, attempted to overthrow Spanish rule. But, how the war actually began was the most interesting part of history. Thousands of Cubans died of disease and malnutrition.

▼ PRACTICE 6	Planning and Writing Narrative Paragraphs

Answers will vary.

Following are six writing exercises for narrative paragraphs. Each exercise will give you the development focus (who, what, where, when, why, and how) and a topic idea on which to write. Supply a topic for each of the focus questions. Next, complete a controlling idea for the topic you have selected. Then summarize, in your own words, what the point of the story will be. Afterward, write a topic sentence using the elements you have created. Finally, create support sentences that develop, explain, support, and clarify the point of the story.

1. (*Who?*) Personal heroes: either people you know or persons from history

   a. Topic: _____

   b. Controlling idea: _____

   c. Point of the story: _____

   d. Topic sentence: _____

   _____

   e. Development sentences: _____

   _____

   _____

   _____

   _____

   _____

2. (*What?*) An important decision you made that affected your life

   a. Topic: _____

b. Controlling idea: _____

c. Point of the story: _____

d. Topic sentence: _____

_____

e. Development sentences: _____

_____

_____

_____

_____

3. (*Where?*) A place that is meaningful in your life

a. Topic: _____

b. Controlling idea: _____

c. Point of the story: _____

d. Topic sentence: _____

_____

e. Development sentences: _____

_____

_____

_____

_____

4. (*When?*) An important time in your life

a. Topic: _____

b. Controlling idea: _____

c. Point of the story: _____

d. Topic sentence: _____

_____

Copyright © 2004 by Pearson Education, Inc.

e. Development sentences: _____

_____

_____

_____

_____

_____

5. (*Why?*) Why you are looking forward to the future

a. Topic: _____

b. Controlling idea: _____

c. Point of the story: _____

d. Topic sentence: _____

_____

e. Development sentences: _____

_____

_____

_____

_____

_____

6. (*How?*) How a task was completed

a. Topic: _____

b. Controlling idea: _____

c. Point of the story: _____

d. Topic sentence: _____

_____

e. Development sentences: _____

_____

_____

_____

_____

_____

▼ **PRACTICE 7**   **Analyzing Narrative Writing**

The following is a narrative paragraph taken from a chapter in a book titled *The Vanishing Hitchhiker: American Urban Legends and Their Meaning* (1981) by Jan Harold Brunvand, a folklorist and professor of English at the University of Utah. Brunvand has gathered examples of contemporary storytelling—strange, scary, funny, macabre, and embarrassing tales storytellers relate as true accounts of real-life experience. This excerpt is from an urban legend called "The Roommate's Death."

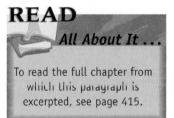

READ
All About It . . .

To read the full chapter from which this paragraph is excerpted, see page 415.

It was not long before the telephone rang. Linda answered the telephone, only to hear the heavy breathing of the caller on the other end. She attempted to elicit a response from the caller but he merely hung up. Thinking little of it and not wanting to panic Sharon, Linda went back to watching her television program, remarking that the caller had dialed a wrong number. Upon receiving the second call at which time the caller first engaged in a bit of heavy breathing and then instructed them to check on the children, the two girls became frightened and decided to call the operator for assistance. The operator instructed the girls to keep the caller on the line as long as possible should he call again so that she might be able to trace the call. The operator would check back with them.

Copyright © 2004 by Pearson Education, Inc.

Questions for Discussion

1. How does Brunvald order the events? Point out words and phrases that help the reader recognize the order of events as they occur.

The writer uses telephone calls to order the events. There are two

phone calls and a third is inferred. The first call is introduced in the first

sentence: "It was not long before the telephone rang." The second call

is introduced in sentence five: "Upon receiving the second call . . ." And

the third call is inferred by the operator in the last sentence: "The

operator would check back with them."

2. What is the primary focus of the paragraph: who, what, where, when, why, or how?

Answers will vary.

Suggestions for Writing

1. Rewrite the paragraph using appropriate transitional expressions from Exhibit 15–2. Reread both versions. Which reads more smoothly and rhythmically?

2. Rewrite the paragraph using a different focus than the one you selected for the answer to Question 2 in Questions for Discussion above.

▼ **PRACTICE 8**   **Analyzing Narrative Writing**

The following paragraph is taken from a narrative essay by Grace Suh. Suh works in academic publishing and as a poetry editor of the *Asian Pacific American Journal*. In this piece, Suh writes about her visit to a makeup counter in search of the transformation promised by the "priestesses of beauty."

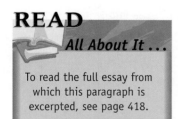

READ
All About It . . .

To read the full essay from which this paragraph is excerpted, see page 418.

And so, in an unusual exertion of will, I resolved to fight back against

the forces of entropy. I envisioned it as reclamation work, like scything

down a lawn that has grown into meadow, or restoring a damaged fresco.

For the first time in ages, I felt elated and hopeful. I nearly sprinted into

the nearby Nieman Marcus. As I entered the cool, hushed, dimly lit first floor

and saw the gleaming counters lined with vials of magical balm, the priest-

esses of beauty in their sacred smocks, and the glossy photographic icons

of the goddesses themselves—Paulina, Linda, Cindy, Vendella—in a wild, reckless burst of inspiration <u>I thought to myself</u>, Heck, why just okay? Why

not BEAUTIFUL?

Questions for Discussion

1. How does Suh order the events? Point out words and phrases that help the reader recognize the order of events as they occur?

The writer orders the events chronologically as they occur: first, the

writer resolves to do something about her looks; second, how she

feels about the project; third, she sprints to the department store;

fourth, she goes to the cosmetics counter; and lastly, her decision to

broaden her original desire to go for BEAUTIFUL, rather than just

attractive. See underlining for phrases.

2. What is the primary focus of the paragraph: who, what, where, when, why, or how?

Answers will vary.

Suggestions for Writing

1. Visit a cosmetics counter at a large department store. Take notes about the products and displays that you see there. How did the advertisements and the arrangements of the products induce you to "become beautiful" by using them? Did the salespeople themselves seem to conform to a particular ideal of beauty? Write a paragraph about your findings and read it to your class. Afterward, discuss the similarities and differences between the various reports made by members of your class.

2. Write a paragraph describing a time in which you made yourself look different than you normally do (this could be for a prom, wedding, or other special occasion). Did you act differently than you normally act? Did other people treat you differently? Was the experience enjoyable or not?

CHAPTER REVIEW

▼ Narration is the telling of a story, either to entertain or inform a reader.
▼ Narrative stories can be fiction (made up) or nonfiction (the retelling of an incident that actually happened).
▼ There must be a point to every story; otherwise, no one will be interested in reading it.
▼ Use the six reporter's questions (who, what, where, when, why, and how) to develop your story.
▼ Transitional expressions help develop the order of events that unfold in your story.

Copyright © 2004 by Pearson Education, Inc.

Topic Bank

Write a narrative paragraph about one or more of the following topics, or about a topic of your own choice.

1. A funny incident
2. A first date
3. An employment interview
4. An embarrassing moment
5. A tense athletic event (see the photo on page 173)
6. Your first day on a new job
7. Watching a scary movie
8. A family argument
9. Preparing for an important exam
10. Taking on a huge responsibility
11. The September 11, 2001, terrorist attacks
12. Taking a road test

Writing Opportunities

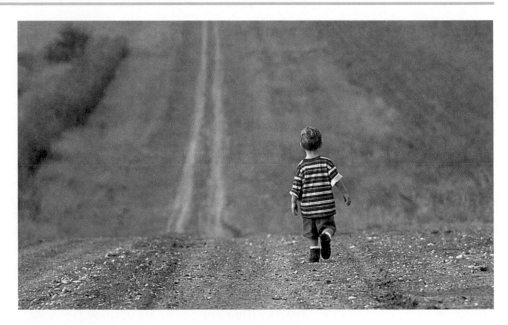

Home

You are looking through a family photo album when you come upon a picture of your son when he was little. The picture brings back a flood of memories. You pick up a pen and write a paragraph beneath the photograph that tells a brief story about why he was walking down the road alone.

School

The photographs taken by you and your fellow art students are going on display in the Fine Arts Building. You have been asked to choose someone else's picture and write a one-paragraph story about its subject matter. Your story will be typed on a card and affixed to the wall beneath the photo.

Work

You work for a movie studio that is going to release a new movie. The picture of the little boy on the road is going to be the advertising poster that will appear in movie theaters throughout the country. Write a one-paragraph "press release" detailing what the movie is about.

Visit *The Write Start* Online!

For additional practice with the materials found in this chapter, visit our Website at:

http://www.ablongman.com/checkett

The Website also features additional readings, quizzes, writing activities, and Internet links, as well as a bulletin board and interactive chat.

For More Practice with Your Grammar and Writing Skills
Visit The Longman Writer's Warehouse

For further multimedia exercises and activities designed to improve your reading, thinking, writing, and grammar skills, visit The Longman Writer's Warehouse on the Web. The Writer's Warehouse offers an interactive handbook, an online journal, a bulletin board, and extensive coverage of the writing process. To take a tour, go to

http://longmanwriterswarehouse.com

Copyright © 2004 by Pearson Education, Inc.

16 Using Examples

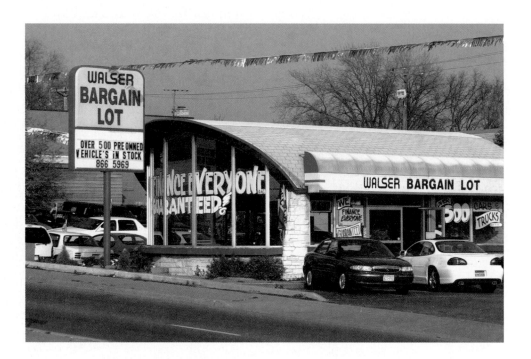

One of the most popular and effective methods for developing a topic is through the use of examples. The **example paragraph** can develop a topic quickly and clearly and help hold the reader's attention. Maybe you've heard a friend say, "My job is terrible." Your thought might be to question why your friend feels this way: "What makes the job so terrible? What does your friend have to do that makes her feel this way?" Your friend might respond with specific examples: the boss is a tyrant, working several hours after closing is a frequent demand, and the pay is low without any benefits. By recounting several examples, your friend supports and clarifies the general critical view of the job experience.

Detailed examples are used to convince, clarify, illustrate, or make concrete a general idea about the subject. For instance, the following subjects are accompanied by a list of examples that might be used to develop the subject in the paragraph.

Topic	Examples
Cars	Honda, Chrysler, VW
Wines	Bordeaux, Riesling, Merlot
Presidents	Washington, Lincoln, Truman
Houses	ranch, split-level, Tudor
Cheeses	gouda, mozzarella, cheddar

The Topic Sentence

The following is a topic sentence for an example paragraph. The subject, controlling idea, developing focus, and developing examples are given. (See Chapter 13 for clarification of the developing ideas of *who, what, where, when, why,* and *how.*)

Example

Topic sentence: President Roosevelt was a successful leader during World War II, overcoming many obstacles.

Subject: Franklin D. Roosevelt

Controlling idea: Overcoming problems

Developing focus: What

Developing examples: isolationists

Congress

illness

Finished Paragraph

President Roosevelt was a successful leader during World War II, overcoming many obstacles. For example, the American people were overwhelmingly isolationist, not wanting to go through the horrors that they remembered from World War I. Another hurdle was Congress's passing of a number of neutrality laws intended to prevent America from entering the war in Europe. Personal problems also had to be overcome. For instance, Roosevelt had to deal with poliomyelitis, a disease he had contracted in 1921. Eventually, Roosevelt's ideas won out when Congress passed his lend-lease legislation after Germany's defeat of France in 1940.

Each example helps to clarify, explain, and develop the controlling idea that President Roosevelt overcame adversity to be successful.

Transitional Expressions: Introducing Examples

Transitional expressions help to connect related ideas and add rhythm to a piece of writing. In the example paragraph above, transitional expressions, such as "for example," "another example," "for instance," and "eventually," are also used to announce to the reader that an example is forthcoming. Use

Copyright © 2004 by Pearson Education, Inc.

transitional expressions in your example paragraph so that the examples don't appear merely as a list. Examples should act in unison to develop the subject in the topic sentence.

Exhibit 16–1

Transitional Expressions for Example Paragraphs	
a case in point is _____	for example
another example of _____	for instance
another instance of _____	to illustrate
another illustration of _____	specifically

▼ **PRACTICE 1**	**Analyzing an Example Paragraph**

Answers will vary.

The following is an example paragraph written by a student. Read the paragraph, and check to see if it has all the elements for an example paragraph:

1. Topic sentence with controlling idea

2. A development focus

3. Three or four development examples

4. Transitional expressions

In the spaces provided after the paragraph, write in the elements that you have found.

In this paragraph from an example essay, "A Stroke of Bad Luck," Margaret Ewart relates how taking care of her father after his having a stroke affected her life.

> Shortly after I started taking care of my father, I came to realize that there was never any time for myself, much less my family. I rarely ever have the time to play with my children, help my daughter with her schoolwork, or spend time with my husband. My father requires a tremendous amount of my time, which prevents me from being a mother as well as being a wife. Most of the time I feel as if I am missing out on a great deal of my children's lives due to the fact that I have become a primary care giver. I have felt like a prisoner in my own home since the stroke. I have a great fear of leaving my home in the event that he may need me. My husband tries to take me out for dinner and a movie to give me some sense of relief from all of the stress, but I always decline. I would never be able to live with myself if something were

to happen to my father and I weren't at home to receive his call for help. Because I have become a recluse, our vacations are spent at home sitting by the phone. With the fear of leaving the house because of my new responsibilities, family members are reluctant to make plans with me due to the fact that I always have to decline. They began to treat me differently as well as see me as a different person.

Topic: _____

Controlling idea: _____

Development focus: _____

Development examples: _____

_____

_____

_____

Transitional expressions: _____

_____

_____

_____

Copyright © 2004 by Pearson Education, Inc.

PRACTICE 2   Analyzing an Example Paragraph

Answers will vary.

The following is an example paragraph written by a student. Read the paragraph, and check to see if it has all the elements for an example paragraph.

1. Topic sentence with controlling idea

2. A development focus

3. Three or four development examples

4. Transitional expressions

In the spaces provided after the paragraph, write in the elements that you have found.

In this paragraph from an example essay, "Seaside Sensation," Lora Smith recounts how the atmosphere in a seafood restaurant captures the "seaman's life."

The atmosphere in Crabby's Crab Shack, in Cherry Grove, North Carolina, exudes the seaman's life from top to bottom and everywhere in between. For example, walking on the crunchy peanut shells strewn all over the floor simulates the creaking deck of a ship. Another example of the "sea" décor can be found on the walls, for they are lined with hunks of driftwood, fishing poles, mounted sailfish and marlin, and paintings of seascapes and sailing vessels from around the world. To see the completeness of the setting, the patrons only have to look up! Specifically, the ceiling has been hung with fishing nets interlaced with twinkling Christmas lights. When the restaurant is darkened, it's as if you are gazing up into the vast, star-filled sky as seen from the deck of a ship. At Crabby's Crab Shack, the only thing missing is the gentle rocking of the sea.

Topic: _____

Controlling idea: _____

Development focus: _____

Development examples: _____

_____

_____

_____

Transitional expressions: _____

_____

_____

_____

▼ **PRACTICE 3**　　**Planning Example Paragraphs**

Answers will vary.　　For each of the following topics, choose a controlling idea and write a topic sentence. Afterward, choose a development focus (*who, what, where, when, why,* or *how*) and list three development examples. Do not use the same development focus idea more than once.

Example
Subject: Bad eating habits
Controlling idea: Cause illnesses
Topic sentence: Poor eating habits can cause many serious illnesses.
Development focus: What
Development examples: anorexia/bulimia
         diabetes
         osteoporosis

1. Topic: Favorite Rock Groups

Controlling idea: _____

Topic sentence: _____

_____

Development focus: _____

Development examples: _____

_____

_____

2. Topic: Vacation Locales

Controlling idea: _____

Topic sentence: _____

_____

Development focus: _____

Development examples: _____

_____

_____

3. Topic: Video Games

Controlling idea: _____

Topic sentence: _____

_____

Development focus: _____

Copyright © 2004 by Pearson Education, Inc.

Development examples: _____

_____

_____

4. Topic: <u>College Courses</u>

Controlling idea: _____

Topic sentence: _____

_____

Development focus: _____

Development examples: _____

_____

_____

5. Topic: <u>Job Hunting</u>

Controlling idea: _____

Topic sentence: _____

_____

Development focus: _____

Development examples: _____

_____

_____

6. Topic: <u>Studying</u>

Controlling idea: _____

Topic sentence: _____

_____

Development focus: _____

Development examples: _____

_____

_____

PRACTICE 4 | **Writing Example Paragraphs**

Answers will vary.

Complete this exercise on separate sheets of paper. Using the topic sentences, controlling ideas, development focuses, and development examples from Practice 3, write paragraphs for each subject. Use transitional expressions from Exhibit 16–1 to announce examples and create rhythm.

Example

Subject: <u>Bad eating habits</u>

Controlling idea: <u>Cause illnesses</u>

Topic sentence: <u>Poor eating habits can cause many serious illnesses.</u>

Development focus: <u>What</u>

Development examples: <u>anorexia/bulimia</u>

                                          <u>diabetes</u>

                                          <u>osteoporosis</u>

Finished Paragraph

Poor eating habits can cause many serious illnesses. For example, because many young girls are pressured to try to emulate fashion models, their lives are threatened by becoming anorexic and bulimic. It is not only young people who are threatened by eating-related diseases; in fact, both young adults and older adults can develop diabetes. Senior citizens are not exempt from problems, either. Specifically, osteoporosis often afflicts the elderly after many years of poor eating. In order to combat these diseases, eat a well-balanced diet, and don't snack on unhealthy foods between meals.

Using One Extended Example

Sometimes, you might want to use only one very detailed example to develop the topic rather than many shorter examples. This type of longer, more detailed example is called an **extended example.**

For instance, you might want to discuss how children's television programming can help educate preschool children. Instead of discussing many different programs, you could decide to focus on one program that is particularly effective. The most successful and popular program would be a good choice because your readers have most likely heard of it and would be more willing to accept what you have to say.

Example

Sesame Street continues to help preschool children learn to enjoy learning as well as to get a head start on their education. For instance, basic math processes, such as adding and subtracting, usually are illustrated with everyday objects, such as pieces of pie and fruit, for these are objects with which the toddlers are familiar. Another instance of blending instruction into the entertainment occurs at the beginning of each broadcast. Instead

(continued)

Copyright © 2004 by Pearson Education, Inc.

of advertisers sponsoring the show, the shows are "sponsored" by a different number and letter of the alphabet each day. The letter and number are integrated into the many sketches that pop up throughout the program. For example, Count Count, the vampire, will count bats, spiders, and lightning bolts, always emphasizing the "sponsoring" number. Another example occurs when a spelling game emphasizes words that contain the "sponsoring" letter. By mixing educational information with entertaining characters and skits, *Sesame Street* has helped millions of young boys and girls see learning as both fun and useful.

Notice, however, that whether many examples or one example is used, the same elements are used in the paragraph:

Subject: Children's educational television
Controlling idea: Helps children enjoy learning and learn some basics
Topic sentence: *Sesame Street* continues to help preschool children learn to enjoy learning as well as to get a head start on their education.
Development focus: What
Development example: *Sesame Street*

Also notice that transitional expressions are used to announce examples and keep the number of examples from appearing merely as a list.

PRACTICE 5   Writing Extended Example Paragraphs

Answers will vary.

On separate sheets of paper, write an **extended example** paragraph for each of the following topic sentences. The controlling idea has been included. Choose a developing focus (who, what, where, when, why, or how) and a development example that will develop the subject. Do not choose the same development focus question more than once. Don't forget to use transitional expressions.

1. Fear of flying has prevented me from visiting foreign countries.

2. Success means making many sacrifices.

3. Advertisements are often very misleading.

4. Today's athletes are better than those of the past.

5. College is much more difficult than high school.

6. Being a good son/daughter requires assuming responsibilities.

PRACTICE 6   Analyzing an Example Paragraph

In this paragraph from an essay, "The Culture of Violence," professional writer Myriam Miedzian relates how cultures influence the behavior of children. Answer the questions following the paragraph.

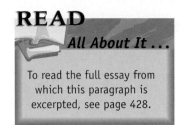

To read the full essay from which this paragraph is excerpted, see page 428.

Every child in the world is born into a particular culture and "from the moment of his birth the customs into which he is born shape his experience and behaviour," we are told by anthropologist Ruth Benedict. Throughout history people have known this intuitively, and so they have been careful to acculturate their children from the youngest age into a pattern of behavior that is acceptable to the group. We have in our own society some very clear and simple examples: Christian groups like the Hutterites and the Amish, or Jewish groups like the Hasidim want their children to grow up to be devoted primarily to religious rather than material values, to be sexually modest and completely chaste before marriage. They share a strong sense of community and commitment to taking responsibility for the well-being of all their members. Among the Hutterites and Amish there is a strong emphasis on non-violence. None of these groups allows their children to participate in the mainstream culture.

Questions for Discussion

1. What specific examples does Miedzian use to help support her idea that culture influences children's behavior?

   The writer lists a number of ethnic groups: "Christian groups like the

   Hutterites and Amish, or Jewish groups like the Hasidim."

2. Why don't the specific groups Miedzian mentions allow their children to mix with the mainstream culture?

   The desire is to acculturate children with the values of their own

   group.

3. Does the author use many transitional expressions? If so, point them out, and explain why they help connect ideas and add rhythm. Could the author have used more? Point out where in the paragraph she could have used additional ones and how they would have helped the paragraph.

   A few. "Throughout history," and "And so." They introduce new

   examples both historically and additionally. The transitional

   expressions add rhythm by creating compound and complex sentence

   structures. Probably. Answers will vary.

Copyright © 2004 by Pearson Education, Inc.

| PRACTICE 7 | Analyzing an Example Paragraph |

The following paragraph is from an essay, "Heroine Worship: The Age of the Female Icon," by professional writer Holly Brubach. In the essay, Brubach examines the rise of women as icons and role models in our starstruck culture. Answer the questions following the paragraph.

READ
All About It . . .

To read the full essay from which this paragraph is excerpted, see page 424.

An icon is a human sound bite, an individual reduced to a name, a face and an idea: Dale Evans, the compassionate cowgirl. In some cases, just the name and an idea suffice. Few people would recognize Helen Keller in a photograph, but her name has become synonymous with being blind and deaf to such an extent that she has inspired an entire category of jokes. Greta Garbo has gone down in collective memory as an exalted enigma with a slogan about being alone. Asking a man if that's a gun in his pocket is all it takes to invoke Mae West. Catherine Deneuve's face, pictured on a stamp, is the emblem of France. Virginia Woolf has her own T-shirt. Naomi Campbell has her own doll. Celebrity being the engine that drives our culture, these women have been taken up by the media and made famous, packaged as commodities and marketed to a public eager for novelty and easily bored. . . .

Questions for Discussion

1. What specific examples does Brubach use to help support her ideas about role models?

   See underlining.

2. How have these various female icons become famous in our culture?

   By being known, fairly or unfairly, by a single characteristic: a lunch-box portrait (Dale Evans), a saying (Greta Garbo), or a doll (Naomi Campbell).

3. Does the author use transitional expressions? If so, point them out, and explain why they help connect ideas and add rhythm. Could the author have used more? Point out where in the paragraph she could have used additional ones and how they would have helped the paragraph.

Only a few: "In some cases," in the second sentence, is used to

introduce the listing of famous female examples; and, in the third

sentence, the coordinating conjunction "but" to combine ideas. The

writer probably could have used more. Other answers will vary.

CHAPTER REVIEW

▼ Examples can develop a topic quickly and clearly and help hold the reader's attention.

▼ Transitional expressions can help connect examples, so that they do not appear as a list.

▼ Sometimes, it is better to use one detailed, extended example rather than many shorter ones.

Topic Bank

Write an example paragraph about one or more of the following topics, or about a topic of your own choice.

1. Buildings (function or architectural style)
2. Study habits
3. Phobias
4. Musical styles
5. Art (period, school, or medium)
6. Restaurants
7. Heroes (real or fictional)
8. Ecosystems
9. Celestial bodies
10. Signs (see the photo on page 188)

Copyright © 2004 by Pearson Education, Inc.

Writing Opportunities

Home

You have recently remarried, and the number of children in the family has doubled. Now there are four sons to add to your four daughters. To give this large and hungry new brood some breakfast variety, you travel to the nearest supermarket and make a one-paragraph inventory of the cereal possibilities, remembering that your children range in ages from five to sixteen years old, and their preferences are based on a number of different criteria: cartoon figures on the box, sugar content, numbers of colors, calories, or vitamin content.

School

Your Advertising & Marketing 205 professor wants you to go to the supermarket and write one paragraph detailing the various types of breakfast cereals and for what age group you think each is targeted based on the information on the box.

Work

Your boss at the consumer health agency is going to appear on a television show to talk about nutrition and breakfast cereals. So that she'll have some facts to use, she wants you to write one paragraph giving examples of a variety of breakfast cereals, and pointing out their good and bad nutritional qualities.

Visit *The Write Start* Online!

For additional practice with the materials found in this chapter, visit our Website at:

http://www.ablongman.com/checkett

The Website also features additional readings, quizzes, writing activities, and Internet links, as well as a bulletin board and interactive chat.

For More Practice with Your Grammar and Writing Skills
Visit The Longman Writer's Warehouse

For further multimedia exercises and activities designed to improve your reading, thinking, writing, and grammar skills, visit The Longman Writer's Warehouse on the Web. The Writer's Warehouse offers an interactive handbook, an online journal, a bulletin board, and extensive coverage of the writing process. To take a tour, go to

http://longmanwriterswarehouse.com

Copyright © 2004 by Pearson Education, Inc.

17

Classification

Some subjects are very complicated or contain many parts. A simple explanation or description of these subjects often is not enough for your readers to understand them fully. How, then, do you get your point across? Sometimes, you need to break a larger point into smaller points so you can explain it in your writing. **Classification** is the process of separating out smaller points from a larger concept and organizing these smaller points into easily recognized groups. These groups can be based on color, shape, kind, or any other type of category that readers will understand easily.

For instance, if you were asked to write a paragraph about the work of William Shakespeare, you could classify it into sonnets, histories, comedies, tragedies, dark comedies, and romances. Classifying his writing into smaller categories makes it easier to make a point about some aspect of his writing. Classifying can focus your writing into a specific area. For example, you could discuss his use of iambic pentameter in the sonnets as opposed to some of the plays.

Breaking Down a Topic

The same subject can be classified in a variety of ways. Whales can be classified as humpback, right, sperm, blue, sei, and pilot, among others. Food can be separated into meat, dairy, vegetables, fruits, and grains; trees into deciduous and coniferous; and music into soul, rock, alternative, jazz, classical, swing, and so on. It is important, however, to keep the units of classification of the same type.

> **Example**
> Dress slacks might be classified according to fabric: cotton, twill, wool.
>   Adding a category of *price range* would be inappropriate. Price does not belong with fabric.

PRACTICE 1   Identifying the Item That Does Not Belong

Look at each of the following groups of items. Circle the letter of the item that does not belong with the other members of the group.

Example

Shoes

a. wingtip

b. athletic

(c.) blue

d. high heel

The *color* blue does not belong with the *types of shoes*.

1. Highways

   a. one-lane

   b. two-line

   (c.) tollway

   d. four-lane

2. Fruit

   a. apples

   (b.) yellow

   c. pears

   d. grapes

3. Houses

   a. split-level

   b. ranch

   c. colonial

   (d.) brick

4. Money

   a. lira

   (b.) coins

   c. rupee

   d. yen

Copyright © 2004 by Pearson Education, Inc.

5. Politicians

  a. mayors

  b. senators

  (c.) lobbyists

  d. representatives

6. Boats

  a. yachts

  (b.) motorized

  c. schooners

  d. sloops

PRACTICE 2   Identifying the Item That Does Not Belong

Look at each of the following groups of items. Circle the letter of the item that does not belong with the other members of the group.

1. Musicals

  a. *Phantom of the Opera*

  b. *Evita*

  c. *Cabaret*

  (d.) *To Kill a Mockingbird*

2. Sports

  a. tennis

  (b.) workout

  c. football

  d. racquetball

3. Trees

  a. elm

  (b.) leaves

  c. oak

  d. Douglas fir

4. Nations

  a. Russia

  b. Australia

  c. Canada

  (d.) California

5. Oceans

  a. Atlantic

  (b.) Michigan

  c. Indian

  d. Pacific

6. Medical personnel

  a. nurse

  b. surgeon

  c. anesthetist

  (d.) accountant

The Topic Sentence

The classification paragraph begins with a topic sentence that clearly states the subject, how the subject will be divided, and why classifying the subject is important.

> **Example**
>
> To study the geologic evolution of the Earth more easily, we can classify rocks as igneous, sedimentary, and metamorphic.
>
> *Subject:* Rocks
>
> *Categories:* Igneous, sedimentary, metamorphic
>
> *Controlling idea:* To learn about the formation of the Earth

The entire paragraph might look like this:

> To study the geologic evolution of the Earth more easily, we can classify rocks as igneous, sedimentary, and metamorphic. The first type, igneous rock, is formed when a molten mass of rock (magma) from deep within the earth rises and fills in cracks close to the surface of the earth through a volcano. Magma cools rapidly and usually forms into a fine-grained, glasslike rock. Sedimentary rocks, the second category, are formed when other rocks disintegrate, and the particles from these rocks usually are carried by water into larger bodies of water where they settle on the bottom and form layers of rocks. Shale and sandstone are common sedimentary rocks. The last type, metamorphic rock, can be traced to a parent igneous or sedimentary rock and is formed through heat and pressure. For instance, the metamorphic rock slate is formed when shale is pressurized, over time, in a low-temperature environment.

▼ Into what categories does the writer classify the subject?
Igneous, sedimentary, and metamorphic rocks
▼ What does the writer say about the first category?
Igneous rock is formed by volcanic magma cooling near the earth's surface.
▼ What is said about the second category?
Sedimentary rock is formed from the particles of other rocks.
▼ When classifying, using examples is an excellent method of achieving clarity. What example of a sedimentary rock does the writer use?
Shale
▼ What information does the writer state about the third category?
Metamorphic rock is formed from other rocks by heat and pressure.
▼ What example is given to clarify the information?
Slate is formed from shale.

Note that the only categories of rocks discussed in the paragraph are those mentioned in the topic sentence. No new topics or subtopics were added.

Transitional Expressions: Linking Your Classifications

In classification paragraphs, transitional expressions help link your categories together so that they don't simply appear as a list. Transitional expressions also help focus the reader's attention on the variety of categories, types, kinds, and divisions.

Transitional Expressions for Classification			
The first type	can be categorized	the first kind	the first division
The second type	can be classified	the second kind	the second division
The last type	can be divided	the next kind	the final division

Copyright © 2004 by Pearson Education, Inc.

▼ PRACTICE 3   Identifying Transitional Expressions

List the transitional expressions you find in the example paragraph regarding types of rocks.

"The first type" (sentence 2) _____

"The second category" (sentence 4) _____

"The last type" (sentence 6) _____

▼ PRACTICE 4   Classifying

Answers will vary.

Groups can be classified in more than one way. Buildings, for example, can be classified by the activity that goes on in them (medical, office, school), or by the material out of which they are constructed (brick, stucco, wood). Think of three ways to classify each of the following groups:

Example

Friends
a. to whom you can tell any secret
b. who are "fair weather"
c. who are only "social"

1. Animals

    a. _____

    b. _____

    c. _____

2. Military personnel

    a. _____

    b. _____

    c. _____

3. Water

    a. _____

    b. _____

    c. _____

4. Clothing

a. _____

b. _____

c. _____

5. Fans

a. _____

b. _____

c. _____

Copyright © 2004 by Pearson Education, Inc.

▼ PRACTICE 5	Writing Topic Sentences

Answers will vary.

For the following groups, separate each into similar units of classification. Afterward, write a topic sentence for each one.

Example

Group: Oil paints

Unit of classification: <u>Color</u>

Categories: <u>Sunset red, forest green, sky blue</u>

Topic Sentence: <u>Because landscape painters want to capture nature realistically, oil paints come in a variety of colors, including sunset red, forest green, and sky blue.</u>

1. Group: Relatives

Unit of Classification: _____

Categories: _____

Topic Sentence: _____

_____

2. Group: Birds

Unit of Classification: _____

Categories: _____

Topic Sentence: _____

_____

3. Group: Restaurants

Unit of Classification: _____

Categories: _____

Topic Sentence: _____

_____

▼ **PRACTICE 6**   **Writing Classification Paragraphs**

Answers will vary.

On a separate sheet of paper, write a paragraph for each of the topic sentences you have written for Practice 5. Use examples to help in classifying the groups you chose. Don't forget to use transitional phrases to connect ideas and to add rhythm.

▼ **PRACTICE 7**   **Analyzing a Classification Paragraph**

In the following paragraph from a classification essay, "Michelangelo Madness," student writer Martin Brink takes a humorous look at tools used by homeowners. The tools are not classified by how helpful they are in making tasks easier but how they promote Murphy's Law by making any project frustrating and even dangerous.

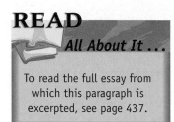

READ
All About It . . .

To read the full essay from which this paragraph is excerpted, see page 437.

A good rule of thumb (red and swollen by now) to follow is that any tools powered by fossil fuels—weed whackers, lawn mowers, edgers, and snow blowers—are temperamental by design. These helpful devices (a.k.a. "accidents waiting to happen") have starter cords to assist in starting the engine. According to the manual, the happy homeowner should pull the starter cord three or four times to prime the engine with gas. The manufacturer calls this activity "pre-ignition" because on the fifth pull, the engine is supposed to hum into full force. This activity should really be called "aerobic exercise" because the only thing demonstrating full force is the red-faced homeowner who is approaching unconsciousness after pulling on the starter cord fifty-seven times without so much as a puff of exhaust.

Classification Technique Questions

1. How does the writer classify power tools that use fossil fuels?

They all have "starter cords."

2. What do you think is the reaction the writer wants to get from his audience?

The humor in each situation. The writer probably assumes most people

have had similar experiences and can draw on their own predicaments

to find a common ground with those experiences the writer is

demonstrating.

3. What examples does the writer give for the tools that use fossil fuels? Does this make the essay more effective? Why or why not?

Weed whackers, lawn mowers, edgers, and snow blowers. Yes, because

many people probably own at least one of these machines, so they have

personal knowledge of and experience with them.

4. What other examples can you think of that might fit into the category?

Answers will vary.

5. Does the writer use any transitional devices to connect ideas and to add rhythm? If not, would the paragraph have been more effective if the writer had done so? Where in the paragraph would you suggest using a few?

No, the writer does not use transitional expressions.

Other answers will vary.

Copyright © 2004 by Pearson Education, Inc.

▼ **PRACTICE 8**   Analyzing a Classification Paragraph

In the following paragraph from a classification essay, "Who Else Is Going to Do It?" student writer Nicholas Wade extols the virtues of blue-collar workers. According to Wade, these talented construction workers provide places to work and live while experiencing many dangers on the job.

Pile drivers, carpenters, and millwrights are the <u>dedicated</u> blue-collar workers in the honorable field of construction. The first type of worker, the pile driver, lays the foundation for <u>massive</u> buildings. Unfortunately, working with <u>heavy</u> concrete pilings is a <u>risky</u> job, and many pile drivers have lost their lives performing this task. The second kind of blue-collar worker is the carpenter. They stand the walls, supply the roof, and prepare the interior. Carpenters often <u>suffer</u> <u>aching</u> joints and other early signs of aging. The last category of worker is the millwright. Millwrights install the machinery in office buildings and factories. Working with such heavy equipment is <u>dangerous</u> and often leads to <u>serious</u> injury.

Classification Technique Questions

1. What do you think is the writer's purpose in writing this paragraph?

To convince the reader that blue-collar construction workers are

important and have dangerous jobs.

2. How does the writer categorize blue-collar workers? What do the categories have in common?

Pile drivers, carpenters, and millwrights. All their jobs are dangerous.

3. Can you think of other categories of blue-collar workers? Is there a dangerous aspect to their jobs?

Answers will vary.

4. Identify any transitional devices the writer has used. How do they add to the effectiveness of the paragraph?

"The first type" (sentence 2); "The second kind" (sentence 4); "The last

category" (sentence 7). They organize the three types of workers

chronologically. This organization helps the reader remain focused on

the categories.

5. Does the writer's word choice support the serious tone? Point out some examples.

Yes, see underlining.

Copyright © 2004 by Pearson Education, Inc.

▼ **PRACTICE 9**   **Analyzing a Classification Paragraph**

In the following paragraph from a classification essay, "The Plot Against People," by professional writer Russell Baker, inanimate objects are classified as things that break, get lost, and malfunction—on purpose! Although short, the paragraph has many examples to support Baker's contention that inanimate objects can confound unsuspecting humans at any moment.

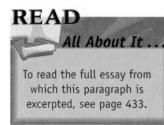

READ

All About It . . .

To read the full essay from which this paragraph is excerpted, see page 433.

> It is not uncommon for a pair of <u>pliers to climb</u> all the way from the cellar to the attic in its single-minded determination to raise its owner's blood pressure. <u>Keys have been known to burrow</u> three feet under mattresses. Women's purses, despite their great weight, <u>frequently travel through six or seven rooms to find hiding space under a couch.</u>

Classification Technique Questions

1. Personification (giving human qualities to nonhuman things) is a technique that writers use to enhance their writing. Point out some examples of personification in the paragraph. How do they enhance the tone (serious, humorous, sarcastic, ironic) of the paragraph?

See underlining. The tone is humorous. It's as if the objects are

planning these things to annoy us.

2. How does word choice support the tone of the paragraph? Give examples.

"Single-minded determination," "burrow . . . under mattresses," and

"great weight" are all exaggerations that enhance the humorous tone.

3. What other inanimate objects can you think of, and how do they confound you?

Answers will vary.

4. The paragraph is short. Would the paragraph have been more effective if Baker had developed each item more fully? Explain.

Answers will vary.

5. What do you think was Baker's purpose in writing this essay?

To entertain by giving us humorous situations that we can identify with

because we have all most likely experienced such exasperating

activities.

Suggestions for Writing

1. Using one of your answers from Question 3 in the classification technique questions above, write a paragraph about some inanimate object that confounds or frustrates you.
2. With some of your classmates, write a paragraph about an inanimate object that confounds or frustrates a group of people.

PRACTICE 10   Analyzing a Classification Paragraph

In the following paragraph from a classification essay, "Relatively Speaking," by sociology teacher Jan Borst, the definition of family is explored. In an age of so many divorces and remarriages, the traditional family is undergoing fundamental changes. Borst raises some serious issues that such families confront including what to call people and what their responsibilities are in the new "unconventional" families. The paragraph attempts to define Borst's daughter's new marriage consisting of her new husband's daughter and her two daughters.

Questions arise as to who is family. Will our daughter's new family be a family of four, made up of those who live in the house? Or a family of five— the four plus the child who visits on weekends? In their home, who is the real parent? Who sets the rules? When does the mother relinquish some of her parenting role to her husband? When does the stepparent step in; when does he or she back off? How much time should the visiting child spend alone with her father and how much time with her new family?

Classification Technique Questions

1. How does Borst classify her daughter's new family?

Borst uses a number of possibilities: the number of people in the family

(It varies from four to five depending on the time of the week), and by

who is the "real" parent (there are four of them—parents and step-

parents—at any given time).

2. What problems are suggested by the categories?

Disciplining, rulesetting, and visitation.

3. What problems will they have in deciding how to name or identify their relationships?

Answers will vary.

4. Borst poses questions about her daughter's situation. Why is this more effective than supplying her own answers?

Many readers will come from split families, and they will have their own

experiences in similar situations.

5. Do you know of people who have faced this same dilemma? What were some of their problems and solutions?

Answers will vary.

Suggestions for Writing

1. In her paragraph, Borst mentions that her daughter's family will have three children, including one who stays only on the weekends. Write a paragraph classifying some of the problems other family members will have in trying to include this girl as a full-fledged member of the family.

2. Multiracial families are becoming more common. What kinds of issues similar to Borst's daughter's do they have to face? Write a paragraph classifying these issues. If you can suggest some solutions, do so.

Copyright © 2004 by Pearson Education, Inc.

░░░░░░░░░░░░ **CHAPTER REVIEW** ░░░░░░░░░░░░

▼ Large or complicated subjects can be made more manageable and easier to understand by classifying them into smaller units: types, kinds, categories, or divisions.

▼ It is important to classify a group into smaller units of the same type.

▼ Classification paragraphs begin with a topic sentence that clearly states the subject, how the subject will be divided, and why classifying the subject is important.

▼ In classification paragraphs, transitional expressions focus on categories, types, kinds, and divisions. Transitional expressions connect ideas and add rhythm to the writing.

Topic Bank

Write a classification paragraph about one or more of the following topics, or about a topic of your own choice.

1. Fans at a sporting event
2. Bosses
3. Athletic shoes
   (see the photo on page 202)
4. Successes or failures
5. Sit-coms

6. Clothes
7. Dates you've had
8. Co-workers
9. Movies
10. Problems of a new student or employee

Writing Opportunities

Home

For your visit to your child's "Parent's Day" at school, you've been asked by the teacher to talk about the various types of jobs at the company where you are employed. You decide to bring the two photographs on page 215 accompanied by a written paragraph classifying the various categories that the workers in the photographs represent.

School

Your Business 333 professor has given you an assignment to create your own manufacturing company. Your first task is to write a paragraph that identifies both the product you will be making and the types of workers necessary to make and bring your product to market.

Work

As the personnel director of your company, the president has instructed you, because of declining profits, to downsize the number of employees by ten percent in each job classification. You decide that your first step should be to write a paragraph classifying the job categories in each of the three divisions of the company.

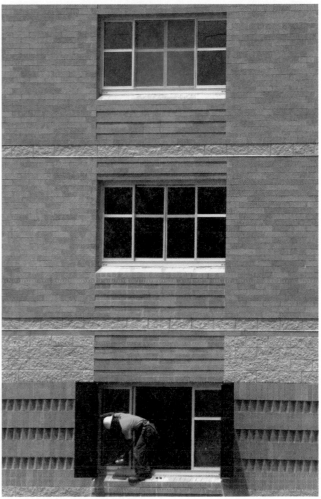

Copyright © 2004 by Pearson Education, Inc.

Visit *The Write Start* Online!

For additional practice with the materials found in this chapter, visit our Website at:

http://www.ablongman.com/checkett

The Website also features additional readings, quizzes, writing activities, and Internet links, as well as a bulletin board and interactive chat.

For More Practice with Your Grammar and Writing Skills
Visit The Longman Writer's Warehouse

For further multimedia exercises and activities designed to improve your reading, thinking, writing, and grammar skills, visit The Longman Writer's Warehouse on the Web. The Writer's Warehouse offers an interactive handbook, an online journal, a bulletin board, and extensive coverage of the writing process. To take a tour, go to

http://longmanwriterswarehouse.com

18 Process

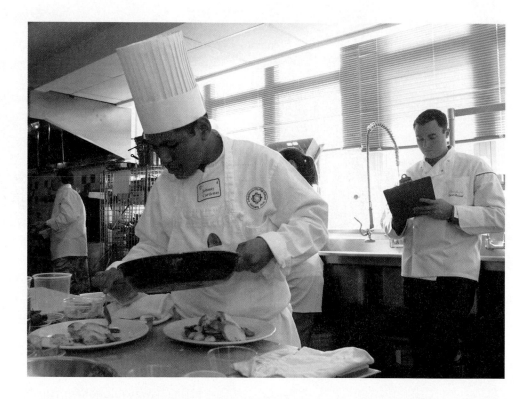

Have you ever had to explain to a friend how to perform a specific task? Perhaps you had to explain how to play a video game or how to use a certain type of equipment. Think about how you would give that explanation in writing. You would have to provide a step-by-step account. Now, consider how such an account might apply to your writing for school or work. Sometimes, you might be called on to explain how you performed a certain science experiment, how a car should be maintained, or how a meeting with a client was conducted. All of these writing situations involve a process.

Process explains the steps necessary to complete a procedure, an operation, or an event. Process is an important method when you are asked to develop ideas in areas such as science, technology, sports, medicine, and business. For example, you may be asked to explain how stars are born and how they eventually die; or, you may be asked to write about the bus boycott during the Civil Rights movement; or, you may have to give a report illustrating how to assemble a piece of machinery.

Types of Process

There are two kinds of process descriptions: **directional** and **informational.** *Directional* process explains to the reader how to do something: how to bake a cake, how to tune a car engine, or how to write a process essay. The goal of directional process is to enable readers to do something or to duplicate some process after they have followed the directions.

Informational process explains to the reader how something was made or how an event occurred, or how something works: how a treaty between two countries was finalized, how the Panama Canal was built, or how a laser is used in medical procedures. Readers are not expected to be able to actually repeat or duplicate the process explained, but they should be able to understand the process.

▼ **PRACTICE 1** Identifying Directional and Informational Process

In the space provided to the left, identify each topic as directional **(D)** or informational **(I).**

1. __D__ How to install gas logs in a fireplace

2. __I__ How Dr. Jonas Salk developed the polio vaccine

3. __D__ How to balance a checkbook

4. __I__ How the automobile was developed by Henry Ford

5. __I__ How lightning forms

6. __D__ How to sew a dress from a pattern

7. __D__ How to build a brick barbecue

8. __D__ How to read the stock market page

9. __I__ How to begin a hobby

10. __I__ How prisoners were tried during the Spanish Inquisition

---

▼ **PRACTICE 2** Identifying Directional and Informational Process

In the space provided to the left, identify each topic as directional **(D)** or informational **(I).**

1. __I__ How to study for an exam

2. __I__ How to be a friend

Copyright © 2004 by Pearson Education, Inc.

3. ___D___ How to send e-mail using a computer

4. ___D___ How to repair a clock

5. ___I___ How the War of the Roses occurred

6. ___D___ How to fill out a job application

7. ___D___ How to register to vote

8. ___I___ How to plan for a vacation

9. ___D___ How to make candied apples

10. ___I___ How photosynthesis works

Organizing the Process Paragraph

Both directional and informational process paragraphs are developed according to the order in which the steps of the process occurred. Adhering to chronological order avoids confusion. For example, in describing how to change a tire, the instructions would not occur as suggested by the list on the left; rather, they would follow the chronological steps as listed on the right:

Poor Sequence	Chronological Sequence
1. Replace the hubcap	1. Remove the hubcap
2. Replace lug nuts and tighten	2. Unscrew and remove lug nuts
3. Replace with spare tire	3. Remove flat tire
4. Unscrew and remove lug nuts	4. Replace with spare tire
5. Remove flat tire	5. Replace lug nuts and tighten
6. Remove the hubcap	6. Replace the hubcap

▼ **PRACTICE 3**   **Using Chronological Order**

Here are two lists of steps for process paragraphs. They are not in chronological order. Number the steps in the proper order in the spaces provided to the left. If you find any steps that should not be included, write an "X" in that space.

1. Sending an e-mail using a computer is an easy method of communication.

___4___ Move the cursor to the text box and begin composing your message.

___5___ Finally, click on the "send" icon.

___3___ Move your cursor to the "subject" box, and type in a subject word or phrase.

_2_ Move your cursor to the "to" box, and type the addressee's e-mail address.

_1_ First, click on the "Compose Message" icon.

2. Alice became a good student through hard work and sticking to a schedule.

_4_ Each evening, she studied between 7 and 10 o'clock.

_2_ During class, she always took notes.

_X_ She spent many hours drinking coffee in the Student Center.

_1_ In the morning before class, she looked over her notes from the day before.

_3_ After class each day, she did research in the library for one hour.

PRACTICE 4   Using Chronological Order

Here are two lists of steps for process paragraphs. They are not in chronological order. Number the steps in the proper order in the spaces provided to the left. If you find any steps that should not be included, write an "X" in that space.

1. How pearls are created is both a fascinating and unusual process.

_3_ The particle acts as an irritant.

_1_ Pearls are produced inside certain bivalve mollusks, such as an oyster.

_2_ A small particle, like a grain of sand, lodges in the mollusk's soft tissue.

_5_ Either spherical or irregular pearls are formed depending on the shape of the particle.

_X_ Pearl coloration varies widely, the most prized shades being white, black, rose, and cream.

_4_ The irritant becomes coated with layer upon layer of lustrous nacre.

2. While stopping smoking is difficult, it can be achieved by breaking some old habits and by establishing some new ones.

_X_ Treat yourself to a thick, rich, strawberry milkshake.

_5_ Instead of smoking while talking on the telephone, twirl a pencil with your fingers. Pretend it's the cigarette you normally hold when on the phone.

Copyright © 2004 by Pearson Education, Inc.

_____2_____ Instead of having a cigarette the first thing in the morning, go for a brisk walk around the neighborhood.

_____4_____ After lunch, suck on a piece of hard candy instead of having a smoke.

_____1_____ Begin by making a list of when and where it is that you normally smoke.

_____7_____ If all else fails, see your doctor about wearing a nicotine patch.

_____6_____ Finally, before you go to bed, do 50 pushups and eat a piece of fruit.

_____3_____ On the way to work, keep your mind off having a cigarette and use the tape deck or CD to learn a new language.

Transitional Expressions: Connecting the Steps

Now that you have the steps of your process in the correct order, you need to connect them in your paragraph so that they follow each other chronologically. Transitional expressions are extremely helpful in connecting these steps.

Commonly Used Transitional Expressions for Process			
afterward	before	initially	to begin
as	begin by	later	until
as soon as	during	meanwhile	upon
at first	finally	next	when
at last	first, second, third, etc.	now	while
at this point	following	then	

The Topic Sentence

Now that you know how to make smooth transitions between the steps of the process, you are ready to put the paragraph together. Both directional and informational paragraphs begin with a topic sentence that clearly states what the reader should be able to do or understand after reading the steps of the process and why the process is important.

Example

Great dough, a delectable sauce, and a variety of delicious toppings are the three things you need to make a gourmet pizza.

The entire paragraph might read like this:

Great dough, a delectable sauce, and a variety of delicious toppings are the three things you need to make a gourmet pizza. First, in a large bowl, pour $^1/_2$ cup of warm water, 1 package yeast, and 1 teaspoon of sugar. Mix well, and wait about 5 to 7 minutes to allow the yeast and sugar to activate. Next, add 2 cups flour, $^1/_2$ teaspoon salt, 2 tablespoons olive oil, and another $^1/_2$ cup of warm water to the yeast mixture. With a fork, stir the mixture until all the water is absorbed. Now, spread flour on a pastry board or table. Dust your hands with flour, and empty the dough onto the floured mixing surface. Knead the dough for about 10 minutes. Put the dough back into the bowl, drizzle some olive oil over the surface, cover with a towel, and place the bowl in a draft-free area. The dough will be ready in 45 minutes. Second, prepare the sauce. Over medium heat in a saucepan, sauté a minced clove of garlic in 2 tablespoons olive oil. Then, add one 14-ounce can of crushed tomatoes, one 3-ounce can of tomato paste, and basil, parsley, oregano, salt, and pepper to taste. After this, reduce heat to low, cover, and simmer for 1 hour, stirring occasionally until sauce thickens. Third, assemble the pizza and toppings. Remove the dough from the bowl, punch it down, and spread it in a 12- to 14-inch diameter circle on a floured surface. With a spoon, spread the sauce liberally over the dough's surface. Then, add some tasty toppings such as cooked bacon, Italian sausage, ground beef, pepperoni, shrimp, pineapple, peppers, onions, mushrooms, broccoli, cauliflower, and olives. Finally, top with shredded cheese, such as mozzarella or provolone, and bake at 475° for 15 minutes, until the cheese melts. Mangia!

▼
PRACTICE 5   Analyzing a Process Paragraph

Answer the following questions about the preceding paragraph.

1. What process does the paragraph explain?

How to make a pizza

2. Is this process paragraph intended to be directional or informational?

Directional

3. How many steps are there in the process? Name them.

Three steps: making the dough, making the sauce, assembling the

pizza and toppings.

4. Identify the transitional expressions in the paragraph.

"First" (sentence 2); "Next" (sentence 4); "Now" (sentence 6);

"Second" (sentence 10); "Then" (sentence 12); "After this" (sentence 13);

"Third" (sentence 14); "Then" (sentence 17); "Finally" (sentence 18)

Copyright © 2004 by Pearson Education, Inc.

In the following paragraph from a process essay, "How to be Successful at Kicking the Smoking Habit," student writer Stephanie Higgs outlines the reasons people begin smoking before tackling the daunting procedure to end the habit.

People smoke for many reasons; therefore, it is important for smokers to identify the reasons why they smoke. Analyzing the origin of the habit is the first positive step toward kicking the habit. For most people, smoking is a learned behavior; consequently, smokers tend to come from families where one or more of their parents were smokers. The majority of them are anxious people who started smoking because it seemed to provide a temporary release from current or future distress and uncertainties. Some tobacco users started smoking to be cool and to fit in with the crowd; likewise, others started smoking because they enjoyed the taste of tobacco after trying it. While others did not necessarily enjoy the act of smoking, they felt addicted to the nicotine and needed to continue to satisfy their cravings. Now, with the origin of the habit exposed, the smoker is empowered with the knowledge of why he or she smokes and each can seek out healthier alternatives to satisfying needs.

Process Technique Questions

1. What is the process that is being explained?

   Identifying why people smoke.

2. Is the paragraph directional or informational?

   Informational

3. How many steps or reasons are discussed? What are they?

   Six: learned behavior, families wherein smoking occurs, anxious

   people, to be cool (to fit in), enjoy the taste, and addiction to nicotine.

4. Identify any transitional expressions that are used. Do they help organize the information chronologically?

   "first . . . step" (sentence 2); "while" (sentence 6); "now" (sentence 7)

5. What transitional expressions would be more effective, and where would you place them in the paragraph?

Answers will vary.

Copyright © 2004 by Pearson Education, Inc.

▼ PRACTICE 7   Writing an Informational Process Paragraph

Answers will vary.

On a separate sheet of paper, write an informational process paragraph for one of the informational process topics you identified in either Practice 1 or Practice 2. Remember, use transitional expressions to order your steps and to connect related ideas.

▼ PRACTICE 8   Analyzing a Process Paragraph

In the following paragraph from a process essay, "A Step-by-Step Guide to Photography," student writer Stephanie Weidemann clarifies the steps necessary to produce visually effective prints.

A photographer must set the scene, correctly develop the negative, and creatively enlarge the print to achieve a worthwhile photograph. First, using a grey card, measure the light that the camera is reading from the scene. Adjust the aperture so that the light meter is floating in the center of its scale; this insures the picture will not be under or over exposed. Next, great care must be given when developing the negative. No light must ever reach the negative during the developing process. In complete darkness, the film is loaded onto a developing reel and placed into a series of chemical liquids that develop and fix the negative. After this, the negative is enlarged. The process is achieved by first placing the negative into an enlarger, followed by shining a light through the negative onto resin coated paper. By manipulating the amount of light and time, the photographer can create a variety of special effects. The paper is then run through another series of chemical liquid baths and allowed to dry.

Process Technique Questions

1. What process is being explained in the paragraph?

   Producing a photograph from a negative.

2. Is the paragraph intending the process to be directional or informational?

   Directional

3. How many steps are explained?

   Three: setting the scene, developing the negative, and enlarging the

   print.

4. Identify any transitional expressions that are used. Do they help organize the information chronologically?

   "First" (sentence 2); "Next" (sentence 4); "After this" (sentence 7);

   "by first" (sentence 8); "is then" (sentence 10); "and then" (sentence 10)

5. Would other transitional expressions be more effective? Which ones would you add, and where would you place them?

   Answers will vary.

▼
PRACTICE 9   **Writing a Directional Process Paragraph**

Answers will vary.

On a separate sheet of paper, write a directional process paragraph for one of the directional process topics you identified in either Practice 1 or Practice 2. Remember, use transitional expressions to order your steps and to connect related ideas.

▼
PRACTICE 10   **Analyzing Process Writing**

In the following paragraphs from an essay, "How to Cram," Jill Young Miller gives advice about a "cherished" college pastime . . . cramming for an exam. Although not a good idea, last minute cramming seems to be an irresistible activity for most harried college students. This being the case, Miller suggests that there are a few steps that make the otherwise dubious process bear more fruit.

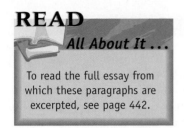

READ
All About It . . .

To read the full essay from which these paragraphs are excerpted, see page 442.

Experiment with memory techniques. They impose structure on new information, making it easier to remember at test time. The "house" method is one of the oldest. Let's say you want to remember a list of sequential events for a history exam. Try to imagine the events taking place in separate but connected rooms of your house. When the test asks you to recall the events, take a mental amble through the rooms.

Another simple technique involves acronyms. You may have learned the names of the Great Lakes (Huron, Ontario, Michigan, Erie, and Superior) with this one: HOMES.

Try some proven learning strategies. Richard Yates, a counselor and time management expert at Cleveland State University, recommends the SQ3R method: survey, question, read, recite, review. Survey the material to formulate a general impression; rephrase titles and headings into questions; read through the material quickly to find the main points and the answers to your questions; recite those main ideas, taking brief notes; and review. Even when you're pressed for time, the strategy can help. "It may take a little longer," says Yates, "but it's worth the effort."

Process Technique Questions

1. Is the information in the three paragraphs intended to be directional or informational?

   Directional

2. How many steps are in the process described in the third paragraph?

   Five

3. In paragraph two, the acronym method is explained. But there also is an acronym in paragraph three. What is it, and what does it represent?

   SQ3R: survey, question, read through the material, recite the main

   ideas, and review.

4. The author does not use transitional devices to connect the steps in the processes she describes. Which transitional devices would you choose to help organize the steps in the process?

   Answers will vary.

Copyright © 2004 by Pearson Education, Inc.

▼ **PRACTICE 11** **Analyzing Process Writing**

In the following paragraphs from an essay, "Conversational Ballgames," author Nancy Masterson Sakamoto discusses cultural differences between conversations in Japan and in the United States. Pay attention to how Sakamoto explains the subtle differences between the two processes that on the surface may seem similar, but in actuality, are completely different.

READ *All About It ...*

To read the full essay from which these paragraphs are excerpted, see page 439.

A western-style conversation between two people is like a game of tennis. If I introduce a topic, a conversational ball, I expect you to hit it back. If you agree with me, I don't expect you simply to agree and do nothing more. I expect you to add something—a reason for agreeing, another example, or an elaboration to carry the idea further. But I don't expect you always to agree. I am just as happy if you question me, or challenge me, or completely disagree with me. Whether you agree or disagree, your response will return the ball to me.

And then it is my turn again. I don't serve a new ball from my original starting line. I hit your ball back again from where it has bounced. I carry your idea further, or answer your questions or objections, or challenge or question you. And so the ball goes back and forth, with each of us doing our best to give it a new twist, an original spin, or a powerful smash.

A Japanese-style conversation, however, is not at all like tennis or volleyball. It's like bowling. You wait for your turn. And you always know your place in line. It depends on such things as whether you are older or younger, a close friend or a relative stranger to the previous speaker, in a senior or junior position, and so on.

When your turn comes, you step up to the starting line with your bowling ball, and carefully bowl it. Everyone else stands back and watches politely, murmuring encouragement. Everyone waits until the ball has reached the end of the alley, and watches to see if it knocks down all the pins, or only some them, or none of them. There is a pause, while everyone registers your score.

Process Technique Questions

1. What is the specific process the paragraphs explain?

Conversation

2. Is the explanation of the two different conversational processes intended to be directional or informational?

Informational

3. What are the sports processes that Sakamoto uses to clarify her points about both American and Japanese conversational styles?

Tennis and bowling

4. Identify any transitional expressions that Sakamoto uses to help connect and organize her ideas.

"But" and "as" in the first paragraph; "And then" and "And so" in the

second paragraph; "however" and "and so on" in the third paragraph;

"When," "until," and "while" in the fourth paragraph.

CHAPTER REVIEW

▼ A process explains the steps necessary to complete a procedure, an operation, or an event.

▼ There are two kinds of process descriptions: directional and informational.

▼ Directional process explains how to do something. The goal of directional process is to enable readers to do something or to duplicate some process after they have followed the directions.

▼ Informational process explains how something was made, how an event occurred, or how something works. Readers are not expected to be able to repeat or duplicate the process, but they should be able to understand it.

▼ Because process paragraphs are organized chronologically, transitional expressions help connect ideas in proper order and add rhythm to the writing.

▼ Both directional and informational process paragraphs begin with a topic sentence that clearly states what the reader should be able to do or understand after reading the steps of the process and why the process is important.

Topic Bank

Write a process paragraph about one or more of the following topics, or about a topic of your own choice.

Copyright © 2004 by Pearson Education, Inc.

1. How to wash a car
2. How to plan a budget
3. How to cook a specific meal (see the photo on page 216)
4. How to repair an appliance
5. How to cut someone's hair
6. How a camera works
7. How to meet new people
8. How a bill becomes a law
9. How a bird builds a nest
10. How the war in Afghanistan was conducted

Writing Opportunities

Home

You and your spouse want to film your daughter's college graduation ceremony and the party at your home afterward. Additionally, your two youngest children want to be a part of the "crew." Write a paragraph describing the process that the four of you will follow to do a good job of filming the events.

School

The student senate at your school wants to make a short video to be shown at freshman orientation in hopes of inducing more students to become active in campus organizations. You have been chosen to direct the shoot. Write a paragraph explaining to the student senate the process that you want to follow to make the video.

Work

The chief operating officer (CEO) of a new computer software company has hired your public relations company to make a video to introduce their new product line. The CEO wants to be filmed sitting at her desk as she introduces the company and its products to the consumer. Before you and your crew arrive at the company offices, you will need her to make certain arrangements to make the shoot successful and less time-consuming. Write a paragraph to the CEO explaining the process she will need to accomplish prior to your arriving for the shoot.

Visit *The Write Start* Online!

For additional practice with the materials found in this chapter, visit our Website at:

http://www.ablongman.com/checkett

The Website also features additional readings, quizzes, writing activities, and Internet links, as well as a bulletin board and interactive chat.

For More Practice with Your Grammar and Writing Skills
Visit The Longman Writer's Warehouse

For further multimedia exercises and activities designed to improve your reading, thinking, writing, and grammar skills, visit The Longman Writer's Warehouse on the Web. The Writer's Warehouse offers an interactive handbook, an online journal, a bulletin board, and extensive coverage of the writing process. To take a tour, go to

http://longmanwriterswarehouse.com

Copyright © 2004 by Pearson Education, Inc.

19

Comparison and Contrast

Often in your writing you will need to discuss an object, idea, or item not in terms of its own features, but in terms of how it relates to another object, idea, or item. This type of writing can be a challenge because it forces you to think about each item on its own, as well as about the ways in which the items relate to one another. Are they alike? Are they different? How? Although you will often need to compare and contrast several items at one time in your writing, this chapter focuses on comparing and contrasting just two items, for the sake of simplicity.

Deciding to Compare or to Contrast

The two main tools you use in this type of writing are **comparison and contrast.** When you compare things, you are looking for similarities. When you contrast things, you are looking for differences. For example, consider two shirts. In comparing them, you might notice that they are both white, have collars, and have buttons. When contrasting them, you might notice that they are made of different materials, that only one has buttons on the collar, and that one is a dress shirt and the other is a casual shirt. Comparison and contrast, therefore, assists the reader in understanding one person, place, feeling, idea, or object in relation to another.

▼ **PRACTICE 1**   **Comparing or Contrasting**

Answers may vary, but the following are the most popular approaches.

Look at the following pairs of topics. Decide whether it would be better to compare or contrast each pair.

	Compare	*Contrast*
1. My friends Bob and Carl	X	
2. Antarctica and the Sahara Desert		X
3. Concrete and rubber		X
4. Beef and fish		X
5. Internet search engines Yahoo! and Google	X	
6. Idaho and Yukon Gold potatoes	X	
7. French and California wines	X	
8. Nurses and doctors		X
9. Jogging and walking		X
10. Apples and oranges		X

▼ **PRACTICE 2**   **Comparing or Contrasting**

Look at the following pairs of topics. Decide whether it would be better to compare or contrast each pair.

	Compare	*Contrast*
1. Board games Monopoly and Careers	X	
2. Attorney and judge		X
3. Movie star and rock star	X	
4. Swimming in a pool or a lake		X
5. Oral exam and essay exam		X

Copyright © 2004 by Pearson Education, Inc.

6. Coin collecting and stamp collecting	X	
7. Canada and the United States		X
8. Soccer and rugby	X	
9. Running shoes and walking shoes	X	
10. Chicago and New York style pizza		X

The Topic Sentence

The comparison/contrast paragraph begins with a topic sentence that clearly states the two items being compared or contrasted and explains why comparing or contrasting them is important. Here is an example of a topic sentence for a comparison/contrast paragraph.

> When parents choose between a two-year college and a four-year college for their child, cost is often a deciding factor.

This topic sentence clearly states the two items for comparison: two-year and four-year colleges. "Cost" is the factor mentioned that indicates how the writer is going to compare the two types of colleges.

The entire paragraph might look like this:

> When parents choose between a two-year college and a four-year college for their child, cost is often a deciding factor. Tuition is a major cost when deciding on which college to attend. At a four-year college, tuition is a flat fee that can run anywhere from $8,000 to $24,000 depending on the size and selectivity of the school. The student can take from 24 to 36 credit hours per year and the tuition charge will not vary. In addition to tuition costs, room and board adds to the expenses at the four-year college. Room and board can run from $4,000 to $10,000 per year depending on the school's dormitory and apartment facilities. Consequently, the cost for tuition and room and board at a four-year college can run between $12,000 and $34,000. Unlike four-year colleges, two-year colleges charge by the credit hour, usually ranging from $37 to $48 per credit hour; therefore, a student taking between 24 and 36 credit hours per year will pay between $900 and $1,800 per year in tuition. Another major difference between four-year and two-year colleges is that most two-year colleges do not have dormitories. They are known more as "commuter schools" because students live at home and drive to school each day. Because most families do not have to adjust their budgets for children who are going to college but still living at home as they did during high school, there is no "additional" cost for room and board. Even if parents charge room and board to their college student living at home, the charge is usually somewhat reduced, say $200 per month. This would add an additional $2,000 to the cost. Thus the expense for a two-year college, including room and board and tuition, would be between $900 and $3,800 per year.

▼ **PRACTICE 3**   **Writing Compare and Contrast Topic Sentences**

Answers will vary.

Compose both comparison and contrasting topic sentences for the pairs of items listed below.

Example

Topic: Two Friends

a. Julio and Angelina have very different study habits. (Contrast)

b. Aretha and Maurice have similar exercise routines. (Comparison)

1. Two Musical Groups

a. _____

b. _____

2. Two Restaurants

a. _____

b. _____

3. Two School Courses

a. _____

b. _____

▼ **PRACTICE 4**   **Writing Compare and Contrast Topic Sentences**

Answers will vary.

Compose both comparison and contrasting topic sentences for the pairs of items listed below.

1. Two Vacation Spots/Resorts

a. _____

b. _____

2. Two Bosses

a. _____

b. _____

3. Two Types/Styles of Clothes

a. _____

b. _____

Copyright © 2004 by Pearson Education, Inc.

Organizing Comparisons and Contrasts

Once you know what comparisons and contrasts you are going to use, you need to organize your thoughts and decide how to present them. There are two commonly used organizational plans for comparison and contrast paragraphs: **block** and **point-by-point.** The block method presents information about one item first, then uses this information for comparison or contrast when presenting information about the second item in the second half of the paragraph. The point-by-point method presents the information about both items together, creating an ongoing series of comparisons and contrasts.

Block Method

In the preceding paragraph about two-year and four-year colleges, the block method is used. Notice that the cost elements of the four-year college are discussed in the first half of the paragraph (without mention of the two-year college). Afterward, the same cost elements concerning the two-year college are discussed in the second half of the paragraph.

The block method is illustrated in this manner:

Topic Sentence: When parents choose between a two-year college and a four-year college for their child, cost is often a deciding factor.

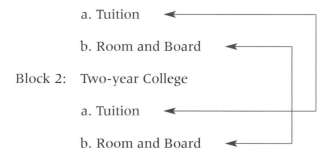

Block 1: Four-year College

    a. Tuition

    b. Room and Board

Block 2: Two-year College

    a. Tuition

    b. Room and Board

Remember, when using the block method, you discuss all the factors in the first item of comparison in the first part of the paragraph without mentioning the second item in the comparison. Then, in the second half of the paragraph, discuss each point regarding the second item in the comparison, remembering to make reference to each item that was mentioned in the first half of the paragraph. This will connect the two items of the comparison so that the paragraph will not seem to be about two items that have nothing to do with one another.

Point-by-Point Method

In the point-by-point method, each point concerning each item being compared is followed by the similar point concerning the second item in the comparison. For example, in a paragraph comparing four-year and two-year colleges, as each cost element of the four-year college is mentioned, it is compared to the same cost element at the two-year college. In this way, the comparison between the elements is continually made.

The point-by-point method is illustrated in this manner:

Topic Sentence: When parents choose between a two-year college and a four-year college for their child, cost is often a deciding factor.

Point 1: Tuition

    a. Four-year College Tuition

    b. Two-year College Tuition

Point 2: Room and Board

    a. Four-year College Room and Board

    b. Two-year College Room and Board

Using the point-by-point method, the paragraph might be written like this:

> When parents choose between a two-year college and a four-year college for their child, cost is often a deciding factor. Tuition is a major cost when deciding on which college to attend. At a four-year college, tuition is a flat fee that can run anywhere from $8,000 to $24,000 per year depending on the size and selectivity of the school. The student can take from 24 to 36 credit hours per year, and the tuition charge will not vary. However, two-year colleges charge by the credit hour, usually ranging from $37 to $48 per credit; therefore, a student taking between 24 and 36 credit hours per year will pay between $900 and $1,800 per year in tuition. In addition to tuition costs, room and board adds to the expenses at the four year college. Room and board can run from $4,000 to $10,000 per year depending on the school's dormitory and apartment facilities. In contrast, most two-year colleges do not have dormitories. They are known more as "commuter schools" because students live at home and drive to school each day. Because most families do not have to adjust their budgets for children who are going to college but still living at home as they did during high school, there is no "additional" cost for room and board. Even if parents charge room and board to their college student living at home, the charge is usually somewhat reduced, say $200 per month. This would add an additional $2,000 to the cost. Thus the expense for a two-year college, including room and board and tuition, would be between $900 and $3,800 per year.

Notice that in the point-by-point method, each item in the elements to be compared is developed in the same order. It is important to keep the order consistent to avoid confusion.

Transitional Expressions: Connecting Your Comparisons and Contrasts

Transitional expressions are important because they stress either comparison or contrast, depending on the type of paragraph you are writing.

Copyright © 2004 by Pearson Education, Inc.

Transitional Expressions Showing Comparison

again	in addition
and	in the same way
also	like
as well as	likewise
both	neither
each	similar to
equally	similarly
furthermore	so
just as	the same
just like	too

Transitional Expressions Showing Contrast

although	nevertheless
but	on the contrary
despite	on the other hand
different from	otherwise
even though	still
except for	though
however	whereas
in contrast	while
instead	yet

▼

PRACTICE 5	Using Transitional Expressions Showing Contrast

Answers will vary.

The following paragraph is difficult to understand because of a lack of transitional expressions that stress *contrast*. On separate paper, add proper transitional expressions that show contrast. To achieve variety, do not use the same transitional expression more than once.

The United States has many historical places of interest. They are more modern than those in Mexico. The Statue of Liberty is barely a century old. The pyramids found in Tenochtitlán are at least a millennium old. Another historic place to visit in the United States is Philadelphia where many of the events of the American Revolution occurred. It is over two hundred years old. Guanajuato, in Mexico, is historic because many events of the Mexican

Revolution happened there. Walking down Guanajuato's streets is just like going back in time. The houses and roads are four and five hundred years old. Many of the houses have been ravaged by time, and the ancient roads polished shiny by the winds of time.

| PRACTICE 6 | Using Transitional Expressions Showing Comparison |

Answers will vary.

The following paragraph is difficult to understand because of a lack of transitional expressions that stress *comparison*. On separate paper, add proper transitional expressions that show comparison. To achieve variety, do not use the same transitional expression more than once.

The occupations of cosmetologist and nurse may seem very different, but they share many common attributes. The cosmetologist makes the client's appearance better by using the proper grooming techniques. The nurse uses the latest medical procedures when treating a patient. A cosmetologist's client often feels depressed or anxious about his or her appearance. By using the coloring products appropriate to the client's complexion and age, the cosmetologist can change a person's appearance dramatically, making people feel good about themselves once again. The nurse makes the patient feel better by administering the proper medications or exercise appropriate for the patient's problem and age group. Both the cosmetologist and the nurse make the people in their care feel better about themselves.

| PRACTICE 7 | Analyzing a Contrast Paragraph |

In the following paragraph from an essay, "'The Jury' Is In!" student writer Carol Hoxworth contrasts two novels by popular writer John Grisham. Hoxworth focuses on character development as a crucial difference between the two stories.

In *The Runaway Jury,* the character development is superb because Grisham alludes to certain aspects of the characters' personalities throughout the development of the plot. One of the strong points of this novel is being fed only enough information about them at the crucial time; therefore, a desire is created within the reader to know each character more

Copyright © 2004 by Pearson Education, Inc.

intimately and how they will relate to the rest of the story. In contrast, *The Testament* has a glaring lack of character development from the very beginning of the novel. There is some confusion in the first few chapters as to who the main characters are. Instead of revealing the nature of each personality throughout the book, Grisham gives bland, generic, and brief descriptions of each. There also seems to be an overabundance of characters who truly are not necessary to the development and enrichment of the plot, so the desire to know the characters better and to see how the plot relates to them is not achieved.

Contrast Technique Questions

1. What is the writer contrasting in the paragraph? Is there a topic sentence that clearly states the items for contrast? If not, write one for the paragraph.

   Two novels by John Grisham. No. Answers will vary.

2. What organizational pattern does the writer use, point-by-point or block?

   point-by-point

3. How does the writer make a smooth transition to the second part of the paragraph?

   By using the contrast traditional expression "In contrast" (sentence 3).

4. Does the writer use enough specific examples to develop and clarify the contrast?

   While the author talks about "character," in general terms, no specific characters are offered as examples.

▼
PRACTICE 8   Analyzing a Comparison Paragraph

In the following paragraph from an essay, "Commercial vs. Residential Real Estate," student writer Nancy Smith compares two aspects of her job that on the surface might seem quite different but, in reality, are very similar.

Marketing costs for commercial real estate are paid for by the company; similarly, in residential real estate, costs are usually picked up by the company, as well. Like residential real estate, commercial real estate sends out thousands of flyers advertising property for lease or sale. For example, both commercial and residential agents mail advertising brochures to area residents and other agents announcing available properties. Both commercial and residential agents can work alone or share commissions with other agents when a property is sold, rented, or leased.

Comparison Technique Questions

1. What is the writer comparing in the paragraph? Is there a topic sentence that clearly states the items for comparison? If not, write one for the paragraph.

Who pays for the commercial and residential real estate marketing

costs—the company or the agent. Yes, the first sentence.

2. What organizational pattern does the writer use, point-by-point or block?

Point-by-point

3. How does the writer transition smoothly so that the points do not seem like merely a list of items strung together?

By using transitional expressions: "similarly" (sentence 1); "like"

(sentence 2).

4. Does the writer use enough specific examples to develop and clarify the comparison?

Yes, the author mentions "flyers" and "brochures."

▼ **PRACTICE 9**   *Analyzing a Contrast Paragraph*

In the following paragraph from an essay, "Throughout the Years," student writer Meghan Burrows contrasts the changing aspects of her relationship with her father as she grew from a young girl into an adolescent.

Copyright © 2004 by Pearson Education, Inc.

When I was little, Dad often was my coach for soccer, softball, volleyball, and basketball. If not the designated coach, he would be on the sidelines helping out. We used to play catch every evening before and after dinner. Going for a ride to Wal-Mart or to the car wash was always a treat. But as I grew older, being "Daddy's Little Girl" wasn't so easy; in fact, it became a source of distance between us. Going through adolescence isn't easy for anyone, and I was no exception. The first time I remember feeling less close to my father was the day my body decided to take the plunge into womanhood. Because I felt scared and embarrassed, the last person whom I wanted to find out was my father. Needless to say, he found out. I think that was the day it came home to him that I was no longer going to be his little girl. As the next few years went by, I realized that I could make my own decisions. I could decide when to go to bed, when and what to eat, what clothes to wear, and what sports to play.

Contrast Technique Questions

1. What is the writer contrasting in the paragraph? Is there a topic sentence that clearly states the items for contrast? If not, write one for the paragraph.

   Activities that she did with her Dad when she was young as contrasted

   with those things she did on her own when she reached adolescence.

   There is no topic sentence defining the specific contrast points.

   Student topic sentences will vary.

2. What organizational pattern does the writer use, point-by-point or block?

   Block

3. How does the writer transition smoothly from the first part of the paragraph to the second half of the paragraph so that the contrasting points are connected?

   By using transitional expressions: "But as I grew older" (sentence 5)

   and "The first time" (sentence 7)

4. Does the writer use enough specific examples to develop and clarify the contrasts?

Yes, the author mentions activities when she was a girl, such as sports

and driving with her father to Wal-Mart, and she mentions the things she

did on her own as an adolescent, such as deciding when to go to bed,

what to wear, and what to eat.

▼ **PRACTICE 10**   **Analyzing and Writing Comparison Paragraphs**

In the following paragraph from an essay, "Grant and Lee: A Study in Contrasts," professional historian Bruce Catton focuses on the differences between the two great Civil War generals. However, Catton does, on occasion, comment on the similarities between the two leaders.

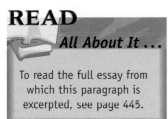

READ
All About It . . .

To read the full essay from which this paragraph is excerpted, see page 445.

> Lastly, and perhaps greatest of all, there was the ability, at the end, to turn quickly from war to peace once the fighting was over. Out of the way these two men behaved at Appomattox came the possibility of a peace of reconciliation. It was a possibility not wholly realized, in the years to come, but which did, in the end, help the two sections to become one nation again . . . after a war whose bitterness might have seemed to make such a reunion wholly impossible. No part of either man's life became him more than the part he played in their brief meeting in the McLean house at Appomattox. Their behavior there put all succeeding generations of Americans in their debt. Two great Americans, Grant and Lee—very different, yet under everything very much alike. Their encounter at Appomattox was one of the great moments of American history.

Comparison Technique Questions

1. What is the writer comparing in the paragraph? Is there a topic sentence that clearly states the items for comparison? If not, write one for the paragraph.

Ulysses S. Grant and Robert E. Lee, the two military commanders for

the North and South during the Civil War. Yes, although Grant and Lee

are not specifically mentioned. It might have been a more effective

topic sentence had the author done so.

Copyright © 2004 by Pearson Education, Inc.

2. What organizational pattern does the writer use, point-by-point or block?

Point-by-point

3. Point out transitional expressions the writer uses to connect ideas and to add rhythm. Are there any that the writer could have used to achieve smooth transitions? If so, which ones and where would they be placed for greatest effectiveness?

"again" (sentence 3); "very different" (sentence 6); "very much alike"

(sentence 6). Yes. Answers will vary.

4. Does the writer use enough specific examples to develop the comparison?

Only in general terms—that both men put peace utmost on the agenda.

The writer does not give any specifics.

Suggestions for Writing

1. Write a paragraph comparing two moral, social, economic, or political disagreements that have been or might become conflicts.
2. Write a paragraph on why the two items you chose in Question 1 are so difficult to resolve. Concentrate on explaining, not taking either side or trying to persuade the reader to adopt a particular solution.

▼ PRACTICE 11   Analyzing and Writing Contrast Paragraphs

In the following paragraph from an essay, "Hasta la Vista, Arnold," professional writer Margaret Talbot suggests that recent movies have signaled a shift toward female action heroes. This trend might reveal changing cultural attitudes; however, she worries that this trend might also reinforce stereotypes.

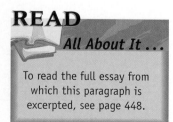

READ
All About It . . .

To read the full essay from which this paragraph is excerpted, see page 448.

For actresses, the new availability of action roles is a boon, but not an unmitigated one. Action movies propel a few of them into the salary stratosphere as nothing else can. They still don't occupy the same gilded bracket as, say, Schwarzenegger, Stallone, or—God help us—Jim Carrey, all of whom make $20 million a film. But Sandra Bullock did take home $12.5 million for *Speed 2: Cruise Control,* and Sigourney Weaver got $11 million for *Alien Resurrection.* On the other hand, the roles can be, well, a bit robotic. Elizabeth Hurley had fun playing a jokey action heroine in silver lamé boots but says

Copyright © 2004 by Pearson Education, Inc.

she's not especially eager to sign up for a lot of rock-'em-sock-'em block-busters. "I really prefer to do a scene that you can get your teeth into, rather than just waiting around for things to blow up. Action films can be a little tedious." Minnie Driver agrees. In *The Flood,* she plays, of all things, a church restorer who manages to save her work and her town from rising waters and marauding robbers. She says she liked playing a character who was "definitely not a damsel in distress," and she's encouraged by the prospect of more parts for "women who can be strong across the board without being bitches." Still, Driver says she "wouldn't necessarily do another action thriller," because she's "interested in movies that are more about character. Though I have to say that if it involved somebody more like Sigourney Weaver's character in the *Alien* movies, I'd make an exception. That role, and Sigourney in it, has such grace and passion. It's never cheesy." Weaver herself worries that action movies may not embrace women who, like Ripley, project a sinewy tenacity rather than something more traditionally feminine. "The important thing in introducing new female action heroes," Weaver says, "is that they don't try to make us too glamorous, put us all in see-through uniforms or something."

Contrast Technique Questions

1. Is there a topic sentence that clearly states the items being contrasted? If not, write a topic sentence for the paragraph.

   Yes, new (stated) versus traditional (inferred) action roles for women.

   _____

   _____

2. What organizational pattern does the writer use, point-by-point or block?

   Point-by-point

3. Does the writer use a transitional expression to smoothly move from point to point? If not, which ones would you choose, and where would you place them?

   Yes. "On the other hand" (sentence 5); "like" (sentence 15).

   _____

4. In the paragraph, the writer notes Sigourney Weaver's worry that Holly-wood will not "embrace women who . . . project a sinewy tenacity rather than something more traditionally feminine." What is Weaver worried about? What exactly is being contrasted here?

Answers will vary.

Suggestions for Writing

1. Write a paragraph contrasting some recent action movies starring women with those mentioned in the paragraph you have just read. Do they support or differ from what the writer suggests about female heroes?
2. Write a paragraph focusing on this question: How do action movies define the difference between masculinity and femininity? What, then, do action movies say about the traditional characteristics of gender division?

CHAPTER REVIEW

▼ Comparison and contrast assists the reader in understanding one person, place, feeling, idea, or object in relation to another.
▼ When comparing, you are looking for similarities.
▼ When contrasting, you are looking for differences.
▼ There are two commonly used organizational patterns for comparison and contrast paragraphs: point-by-point and block.
▼ In comparison and contrast paragraphs, transitional expressions are important because they stress either comparison or contrast, depending on the type of paragraph you are writing.
▼ Comparison and contrast paragraphs begin with a topic sentence that clearly states the two items being compared or contrasted and why comparing or contrasting them is important.

Topic Bank

Write a comparison or contrast paragraph about one or more of the following topics, or about a topic of your own choice.

1. Two pieces of art
2. Two members of your family
3. Two magazines (see the photo on page 230)
4. Your past and present position on a social or political issue
5. Two schools you have attended
6. Two bosses or two co-workers
7. A widely held belief and its real meaning
8. Two places you have lived (cities, houses, countries)
9. Two forms of government (local, state, or national)
10. Two novels

Writing Opportunities

Copyright © 2004 by Pearson Education, Inc.

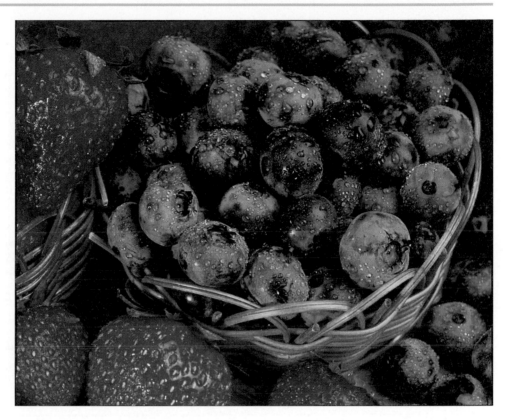

Home

The community council in your town has decided to raise funds by publishing and selling a book of recipes from local townspeople. As you are known as the best dessert maker in the community, the committee has asked you to write a paragraph comparing the variety of uses of the blueberry versus the strawberry.

School

For your final exam in Home Economics 314, you had to make one dessert using blueberries and one dessert using strawberries. Additionally, you were instructed to write a paragraph comparing the two efforts.

Work

As communications director for the National Association of Fruit Growers, your current challenge is to put together a brochure extolling the virtues of people including a variety of fruits in their daily diet. Research indicates that most people only think of blueberries and strawberries as dessert fruits. Write a paragraph that makes a case for the blueberry and the strawberry as an "anytime food," compared to apples, bananas, and oranges.

Visit *The Write Start* Online!

For additional practice with the materials found in this chapter, visit our Website at:

http://www.ablongman.com/checkett

The Website also features additional readings, quizzes, writing activities, and Internet links, as well as a bulletin board and interactive chat.

For More Practice with Your Grammar and Writing Skills
Visit The Longman Writer's Warehouse

For further multimedia exercises and activities designed to improve your reading, thinking, writing, and grammar skills, visit The Longman Writer's Warehouse on the Web. The Writer's Warehouse offers an interactive handbook, an online journal, a bulletin board, and extensive coverage of the writing process. To take a tour, go to

http://longmanwriterswarehouse.com

20 Definition

Copyright © 2004 by Pearson Education, Inc.

Often, the writer uses words, terms, or concepts that his or her audience may not fully understand. To explain clearly what these words and terms mean is to **define** them.

For example, you might use the term *quasar*, a star-like object that emits powerful blue light and often radio waves; or, you might use *griffin*, a fabulous, mythological beast with the head and wings of an eagle and the body of a lion.

Simple Definitions

Simple definitions are basic one- or two-sentence definitions, such as those you might find in a dictionary. There are three types of simple definitions:

1. **Synonym definition** supplies another simpler word that means the same thing. For example, *ubiquitous* means *everywhere*; *cacophony* means *noise*.
2. **Class definition** places a word or term in a broad group or class that readers will readily understand, and then provides a specific detail that differentiates the original word or term from other members of that class. For example, a *convertible* is a *car* with a *top that goes up and down*. In this definition, *convertible* is the term being defined. It is put into a class of similar things (cars), and then it is distinguished from other cars, such as sedans, because it has a top that goes up and down.
3. **Definition by negation** begins by saying what a given word or term is *not* before saying what the word or term actually is. For example: A bagel isn't just a doughnut-shaped piece of bread. It's actually a unique type of bread that's boiled before it's baked.

Definition is important because clear communication depends on clear understanding. Precise language is essential if you are to understand what someone else means. The same word can have multiple meanings, so it is essential that you define those kinds of terms for your reader.

▼
PRACTICE 1   **Using Synonym Definitions**

Use a synonym definition to define each of the following terms.

Example: Chagrined: <u>To be chagrined is to be embarrassed.</u>

1. Dichotomy: <u>**To be divided into two contradictory parts or opinions.**</u>

2. Blunder: <u>**To make a mistake.**</u>

3. Literal: <u>**The most obvious meaning of a word.**</u>

4. Rustic: <u>**Relating to the rural or country life or people.**</u>

5. Malevolent: <u>**To act maliciously.**</u>

▼
PRACTICE 2   **Using Class Definitions**

Using a class definition, define the following terms.

Example: Martini: <u>A martini is a cocktail made with gin and vermouth.</u>

1. Robin: <u>**A robin is a bird having a red breast and gray and black upper plumage.**</u>

2. Banana: <u>**A banana is an elongated, edible fruit having a thick yellow-to-red skin and white pulp.**</u>

3. Shark: <u>**A shark is a marine carnivorous fish having a cartilage skeleton and scratchy skin.**</u>

4. Dictionary: <u>**A dictionary is a reference book containing an alphabetized list of words and their definitions.**</u>

5. Prude: <u>**A prude is a person who is excessively concerned with appearing proper, modest, or righteous.**</u>

▼ PRACTICE 3	Using Definitions by Negation

Answers will vary.

For each of the following terms, write a definition by negation.

Example: Hero: A hero is not just someone performing an act of bravery; it is also someone taking care of his or her daily responsibilities.

1. Moral (to be): _____

_____

2. Freedom: _____

_____

3. Knowledgeable (to be): _____

_____

4. Grades: _____

_____

5. A job: _____

_____

Copyright © 2004 by Pearson Education, Inc.

Extended Definition

Sometimes, terms such as *self-esteem, love, free speech,* and *macroeconomics* can require much more developed definitions if they are to be fully understood. A simple, one-sentence dictionary definition may not suffice. Instead, you may need to use an entire paragraph to define such terms adequately. This longer type of definition is called an **extended definition.** Extended definition can be accomplished by means of any of the **modes of development:** description, example, comparison and contrast, process, and so forth.

To help define your term, you might

a. describe some of its parts or elements
b. explain its process

c. compare and/or contrast it to other like terms

d. give some examples

e. explain what it is not

You may use one of these modes to develop your definition, or you may use as many modes in the paragraph as you find necessary. For example, if you were writing an extended definition paragraph for the term *soul music,* you might choose one or several of the following strategies:

▼ Compare or contrast soul music to other kinds of music, such as blues, alternative rock, and jazz.

▼ State some examples of well-known soul hits.

▼ Describe its parts: lyrics, themes, musical motifs.

A simple definition for *soul music* might be "music relating to or characteristic of African American culture." This definition does not give the reader the full flavor of just how soul music represents a part of the American culture. An extended definition might expand on this idea:

> Soul music is a combination and merging of gospel and blues, two African American musical styles. While blues praised the worldly desires of the flesh, gospel extolled the virtues of spiritualism. This opposition of themes was melded into wide ranging and extremely diverse style, full of passion, pride, and optimism mixed with the historical emotion of pain and discrimination.

Whatever concept you are defining, use only those modes and strategies that are necessary to define the concept fully. Do not use techniques solely for the sake of variety.

The Topic Sentence of an Extended Definition

The definition paragraph begins with a topic sentence that clearly states the term(s) being defined, the mode of development that will be used to define the term(s), and why defining the term is important. Because there are many different reasons for supplying a reader with a definition, and because there are many different types of terms you might want or need to define in your writing, your topic sentence must clarify why you're defining a given term. For example, are you defining:

▼ A specialized term that is unfamiliar to most people, such as *lasik eye surgery* or *superstring theory*

▼ An abstract term that can have a variety of meanings, such as *freedom* or *indifference*

▼ A concept that is often misunderstood, such as *liberalism* or *Generation X*

▼ A new slang or cultural term, such as *extreme sport* or *anime*

Here is an example of a topic sentence for a definition paragraph about being a high school freshman:

> Entering new surroundings, being harassed by upper classmen, and having four long years of school ahead of you make being a high school freshman a dreadful experience.

The entire paragraph might look like this:

> Entering new surroundings, being harassed by upperclassmen, and having four long years of school ahead of you make being a freshman a dreadful experience. Freshmen become very confused when rushed to find classes in a labyrinth of unfamiliar hallways. They act like mice attempting to find their way through a complicated maze. Additionally, harassment by upperclassmen makes running the maze even more of a challenge. Veteran students play pranks on the unsuspecting newcomers, such as asking them for elevator and hall passes. Finally, being a freshman means having four more years of headaches. Just because you are new, teachers will have little leniency in regard to the quantity of homework given and the quality of the homework returned. All three factors contribute to the realization that being a high school freshman is a dreadful existence.

In this paragraph, the term being defined is "high school freshman," and the mode of development is by example and description, using typical events that happen to freshmen.

▼ PRACTICE 4   Writing Definition Topic Sentences

Answers will vary.

Write a topic sentence for each of the definitions you wrote for Practice 3.

1. Moral (to be):

_____

_____

2. Freedom:

_____

_____

3. Knowledgeable (to be):

_____

_____

4. Grades:

_____

_____

5. A job:

_____

_____

Copyright © 2004 by Pearson Education, Inc.

In the following paragraph from an essay, "My Hot Flathead," student writer Trevor Campbell defines a specific type of automobile engine not only by its design and horsepower output but through its cultural importance.

After World War II, countless GI's returned home with extra money to spend. Almost overnight, custom shops sprang up in southern California catering to the Flathead owner. The Flathead-powered Ford was cheap and plentiful, making this motor a prime candidate to customize. Within a few years, the Ford Flathead V-8 became the popular choice among custom builders; this power plant combined with a light-bodied chassis was considered a winning combination at the dragstrip. Success is often copied, a circumstance which, in turn, further established the Flathead presence.

Definition Technique Questions

1. Does this paragraph have a topic sentence that states the term to be defined? If not, how does the writer introduce the term?

   The third sentence would be a good topic sentence. The first two sentences give information about the historical times that existed when the engine became popular.

2. What is the mode of development for the paragraph?

   Informational process: World War II soldiers returning home. Description: the engine was cheap, plentiful, a popular choice, easy to customize, and a winning combination when coupled to a light-bodied chassis.

3. In what larger class of items would you put the Flathead powered Ford?

   Automobile engines.

4. What made the Flathead engine so popular?

   It was cheap, plentiful, easy to customize, and powerful.

Copyright © 2004 by Pearson Education, Inc.

▼ **PRACTICE 6**   Analyzing a Definition Paragraph

In the following paragraph from an essay, "The Perfect Store," student writer Jeanette Weiland defines the perfect store in terms of pricing. According to Weiland, low price is important, but there are also other aspects of pricing that put the customer in a buying mood.

While shopping at a perfect store, customers are generally sold products at an inexpensive price. Shoppers are typically offered items that are clearly marked with price tags on each separate package. This allows customers to rapidly and easily choose the product that gives them the best buy. There aren't any reasons to look for the price on the store shelf and then have to worry about whether or not the item matches the price tag. A perfect store does not only honor its own sales coupons, but it also accepts other department store advertised prices and coupons. This gives the customers the convenience of shopping at one store instead of having to go to two or three. No matter what store they are shopping at, these pricing policies offer shoppers an opportunity to receive the best possible price.

Definition Technique Questions

1. Does this paragraph have a topic sentence stating the term to be defined? What is the mode of development?

   Yes, the perfect store. Process—how the customer is sold merchandise

   and how the customer can evaluate by price.

2. How many different pricing policies does the writer mention?

   Two: clearly marked prices on the items, and the store honors

   competitors' coupons and advertised prices.

3. In which sentence does the writer define by negation? Point out what it is that the perfect store not only does not do, but also what it does do for its customers.

   Sentence 5. It not only honors its own coupons and advertised prices,

   but it does so for its competitors' coupons and advertised prices as

   well.

Answers will vary.

In the following paragraph from an essay, "Discrimination Is a Virtue," professional writer Robert Keith Miller takes a deep and thoughtful look at the meaning of the often-misused word *discrimination*. Miller points out that the overuse, misuse, and misunderstanding of this word is so widespread that most people have probably never thought about its true meaning. This improper use of the term carries with it negative social consequences.

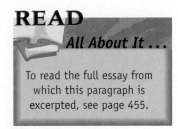

READ *All About It . . .*

To read the full essay from which this paragraph is excerpted, see page 455.

We have a word in English which means "the ability to tell differences." That word is *discrimination*. But within the last 30 years, this word has been so frequently misused that an entire generation has grown up believing that "discrimination" means "racism." People are always proclaiming that "discrimination" is something that should be done away with. Should that ever happen, it would prove to be our undoing.

Definition Technique Questions

1. A term's *denotation* is its direct, definite, and easily understood meaning, while its *connotation* is those ideas that are suggested by the word in addition to its essential meaning. In the paragraph, what is *discrimination*'s denotation and what is its connotation?

   Denotation: "discrimination" is the ability to tell differences.

   Connotation: "discrimination" means racism.

2. Miller suggests that doing away with "discrimination" would have awful consequences for all of us. What are some of the consequences you can think of?

   Answers will vary.

3. Miller suggests, then, that discrimination, when properly defined, is beneficial for society. How can discrimination be a positive force?

   Answers will vary.

Suggestions for Writing

1. Think of two words that you are apt to confuse, such as *lay/lie; there/their; leave/let; bring/take;* and *scratch/itch.* Check out the correct use of the words

and then write a paragraph defining them. Your topic sentence is ready-made: The two words are commonly confused.

2. Slang has become more and more a part of everyday speech, and much of it is specialized, used by a particular group. Select a slang word that you or your friends use and define it, explaining how it is both used and mis-used or misunderstood by those outside of your group.

<table>
<tr><td>▼ **PRACTICE 8**</td><td>**Analyzing Definition Paragraphs**</td></tr>
</table>

Answers will vary.

In these paragraphs from a 1982 essay, "The Handicap of Definition," syndicated columnist William Raspberry defines the main reason many black children do not have good self-images and explains the impact this has on their feelings about future success. While the famous people Raspberry mentions may no longer be in the public eye as much as they used to be, the idea he suggests is still relevant to today's athletes and entertainers.

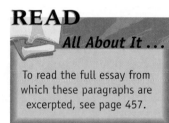

READ
All About It . . .

To read the full essay from which these paragraphs are excerpted, see page 457.

Let me explain quickly what I mean. If a basketball fan says that the Boston Celtics' Larry Bird plays "black," the fan intends it—and Bird probably accepts it—as a compliment. Tell pop singer Tom Jones he moves "black" and he might grin in appreciation. Say to Teena Marie or The Average White Band that they sound "black" and they'll thank you.

But name one pursuit, aside from athletics, entertainment or sexual performance in which a white practitioner will feel complimented to be told he does it "black." Tell a white reporter he writes "black" and he'll take a writing course. Tell a white lawyer he reasons "black" and he might sue you for slander.

What we have here is a tragically limited definition of blackness, and it isn't only white people who buy it.

Definition Technique Questions

1. The author, William Raspberry, is black. Does knowing this make a difference in how you interpret these paragraphs? What if the author were white?

Answers will vary.

2. In the paragraph in Practice 7, Miller suggests that discrimination, when properly defined, is beneficial for society. Do you think this idea applies equally to the term "black"?

Answers will vary.

Copyright © 2004 by Pearson Education, Inc.

3. How does Raspberry build his definition of the word "black"?

He uses examples from music, sports, and entertainment of what

"black" means.

4. If you're a black student, do you and your friends use the term "black" in the way that Raspberry suggests? If you're a non-black student, do you feel blacks use the term "black" in the way Raspberry suggests?

Answers will vary.

CHAPTER REVIEW

▼ Clearly explaining a word, term, or concept that a reader might not fully understand in your writing is known as defining.

▼ There are many types of definitions. Some short, dictionary-type definitions are synonym definitions, class definitions, and definition by negation.

▼ Some terms and concepts require more than a short, one-sentence definition. You may need to use an entire paragraph to define them adequately. This is called an extended definition.

▼ Extended definition can be accomplished by means of any of the modes of development: description, example, comparison and contrast, process, and so forth.

▼ Definition paragraphs begin with a topic sentence that clearly states the term being defined, the mode of development, and why defining the term is important.

Topic Bank

Write a definition paragraph about one or more of the following topics, or about a topic of your own choice.

1. Success or failure
2. A political or social issue, like animal rights or the environment (see the photo on page 247)
3. A good or bad roommate
4. A technical or medical term
5. A terrorist
6. A new form of art or music
7. A good or bad teacher, parent, friend
8. A good or bad movie, concert, party
9. Heroism or cowardice
10. A sports term

Writing Opportunities

Home

You want to hang a print of Magritte's painting in your family room. You are talking about the painting's content by e-mail with your spouse who is away on a long business trip. Your spouse is unsure about hanging the painting because the content sounds so unusual. So, you send him a scanned copy of the painting with an accompanying paragraph defining what you think the content means.

School

Your Psych 205 professor comes into class one day and displays a slide of Magritte's painting on the overhead. He directs you to write a paragraph defining what you think the artist is like by the contents of the painting. He also instructs that you can, if you like, define by negation—pointing out what you think the artist would not be like based on the painting's contents.

Work

As a new, summer tour guide at the art museum, you find out that your job will include giving brief talks about a variety of paintings. Your schedule indicates that your first stop will be Magritte's surreal painting. Write a paragraph that you will memorize to help you define surrealism for your tour group.

Copyright © 2004 by Pearson Education, Inc.

Visit *The Write Start* Online!

For additional practice with the materials found in this chapter, visit our Website at:

http://www.ablongman.com/checkett

The Website also features additional readings, quizzes, writing activities, and Internet links, as well as a bulletin board and interactive chat.

For More Practice with Your Grammar and Writing Skills Visit The Longman Writer's Warehouse

For further multimedia exercises and activities designed to improve your reading, thinking, writing, and grammar skills, visit The Longman Writer's Warehouse on the Web. The Writer's Warehouse offers an interactive handbook, an online journal, a bulletin board, and extensive coverage of the writing process. To take a tour, go to

http://longmanwriterswarehouse.com

Copyright © 2004 by Pearson Education, Inc.

21 | Persuasion (Including Cause and Effect)

When writers use **persuasion,** they are trying to convince someone else that their point of view or belief is correct. Persuasion can be *informal, semiformal,* or *formal.* Think of informal persuasion as verbally convincing someone else of your point of view. For example, you and your friends or members of your family may try to convince each other about which college basketball team should be number one or which restaurant has the best pizza. Commercials on radio and television also are types of informal persuasion. So are public service advertisements for nonprofit organizations and most political advertisements.

Formal persuasion is usually called **argumentation.** This type of persuasion requires not only arguing for your own beliefs but also arguing directly against someone else's beliefs. Argumentation uses evidence from secondary sources (information often found in the library) that are cited by using a formal documentation process (MLA or APA, for example). Research papers, analytical essays, and certain business reports fall into this category.

However, in this chapter, we are interested in a semiformal type of persuasion that falls somewhere in between the two mentioned above. Persuasion requires a bit more logical thought and organization than that expressed around the kitchen table in informal arguing. However, it does not have the rigid requirements that occur with the use of quotations and the accompanying documentation needed in formal argumentation.

Persuasion is one of the most common types of writing in school. Students are required to argue for and against ideas in quizzes, papers, and examinations. Therefore, learning the fundamentals of the persuasive paragraph is one of the most important skills you can learn.

Building the Persuasive Paragraph

The **topic sentence** states the writer's conclusion or point of view about a particular topic. The writer's conclusion can be for or against (pro or con) the idea concerning the topic. Therefore, the topic sentence is the key to a successful persuasive paragraph. The verbs used in a persuasive topic sentence are most often *should/should not* or *must/must not.*

Examples

The pending legislation on the right of citizens to carry concealed handguns should be defeated.

This paragraph will argue against (con) citizens having the right to carry concealed handguns.

Employers should provide day care for their employees.

This paragraph will argue for (pro) companies providing day care for the children of their employees.

Euthanasia should be legalized because of our constitutional rights of personal freedom.

This paragraph will argue for (pro) physician assisted suicide.

Athletics should not receive more funding than academics.

This paragraph will argue against (con) sports receiving more money than academics.

▼ **PRACTICE 1**   **Writing Persuasive Topic Sentences**

Answers will vary.   For the ten topics listed below, write either a pro (for) topic sentence or a con (against) topic sentence. Try to write five sentences pro and five con.

1. Topic: Instant replay in sports

_____

_____

2. Topic: Mandatory drug testing in schools/workplace

_____

_____

3. Topic: A federally regulated Internet

_____

_____

4. Topic: National ban on smoking

_____

_____

5. Topic: Reinstitution of the military draft

_____

_____

6. Topic: Elderly drivers

_____

_____

7. Topic: Interstate highway speed limits

_____

_____

8. Topic: Paying college athletes

_____

_____

9. Topic: National identification cards

_____

_____

10. Topic: Clubs/organizations excluding certain groups for membership on the basis of race, religion, or ethnic origin

_____

_____

Copyright © 2004 by Pearson Education, Inc.

In the following paragraph from a persuasive essay, "Nuke Nuclear Energy," student writer Danny Butler's argument is concerned with the nuclear fuel industry.

> Because of waste management problems, the nuclear fuel industry must not be revived. Many researchers see nuclear energy as the source of power for the future because it can greatly lessen the consumption of other fuels. A typical nuclear reactor can produce many times more energy than plants using other materials such as fossil fuels. Although this new form of energy can help to preserve diminishing resources, it leads to a new problem of waste management. The fission of radioactive materials causes leftover wastes that can remain radioactive for many years. Waste management has already become a problem that will have to be faced by generations to come; we must decide which is more important, a new energy source, or the survival of life on Earth.

Persuasion Technique Questions

1. Identify the topic sentence. Does it clearly state whether the author is for or against the topic?

Sentence one. Yes, the author states that the nuclear fuel industry must not be revived.

2. Do the support sentences support the writer's position?

The writer uses the first sentence to state the opposition's point of view. Then, he uses the next two sentences to refute the opposition's position by introducing the negative aspects of nuclear waste material.

3. Point out any sentences that are simply informational and that do not support the author's position.

Sentences two and three give information about the opposition's point of view that the writer will refute later.

Copyright © 2004 by Pearson Education, Inc.

▼ **PRACTICE 3**   **Analyzing a Persuasive Paragraph**

In the following paragraph from a persuasive essay, "The Revolt of the Black Bourgeoisie," professional writer Leonce Gaiter confronts stereotypical thinking.

READ
All About It . . .

To read the full essay from which this paragraph is excerpted, see page 459.

Yes, there are the beginnings of a new candor about our culture, but the question remains, How did one segment of the African-American community come to represent the whole? First, black society itself placed emphasis on that lower caste. This made sense because historically that's where the vast majority of us were placed; it's where American society and its laws were designed to keep us. Yet although doors have opened to us over the past 20 years, it is still commonplace for black leaders to insist on our community's uniform need for social welfare programs, inner-city services, job skills training, etc. Through such calls, what has passed for a black political agenda has been furthered only superficially; while affirmative action measures have forced an otherwise unwilling majority to open some doors for the black middle class, social welfare and Great Society-style programs aimed at the black lower class have shown few positive results.

Persuasion Technique Questions

1. What is a "stereotype"?

   An idea many have about a thing, another person, or a group that is

   often untrue or partially untrue.

2. How does the use of stereotypes hurt successful African-Americans?

   The "lower caste" of African-American society has come to represent

   all of the African-American society, even the middle and upper class.

3. Whom does Gaiter blame for this stereotypical thinking?

   Black political leaders, whose agenda seems to be limited to Great

   Society-style programs aimed at the lower class.

The Pro/Con List

Once you have decided on the topic, it is vital that you know the major argument points on either side of the issue regardless of whether you know which side you are going to take. For example, if the topic is nuclear energy, list as many points for either side that you can think of.

Topic: Nuclear Energy

Pro (For) List	Con (Against) List
Cheaper fuel costs	Radioactive waste
Less dependence on foreign oil	Causes unemployment in traditional fossil fuels industry
Creates high-tech jobs	Nuclear accidents
Saves natural resources	Nuclear weapons proliferation
Ensures strong nuclear arsenal	Theft of nuclear materials by terrorists
	Environmental pollution

Once you have listed as many points as you can think of, consider the points on both sides of the argument, and choose the side you wish to argue for. Decide which points you will use in your paragraph to support your topic.

PRACTICE 4   Making Pro/Con Lists

Answers will vary.

Create a pro/con list for each of the following topics. Think of as many items for each list as you can.

1. Topic: Sex education should be taught in elementary school.

Pro	Con
_____	_____
_____	_____
_____	_____
_____	_____
_____	_____
_____	_____

2. Topic: Women should be allowed to fight as infantry soldiers.

Pro	Con
_____	_____
_____	_____
_____	_____

_____   _____

_____   _____

_____   _____

3. Topic: The drinking age should be reduced to 18 years of age.

Pro   **Con**

_____   _____

_____   _____

_____   _____

_____   _____

_____   _____

_____   _____

4. Topic: English should be America's official language.

Pro   **Con**

_____   _____

_____   _____

_____   _____

_____   _____

_____   _____

5. Topic: The government should provide health insurance for all citizens.

Pro   **Con**

_____   _____

_____   _____

_____   _____

_____   _____

_____   _____

Copyright © 2004 by Pearson Education, Inc.

Support in Persuasion Paragraphs

Persuasion paragraphs need to demonstrate the different types of support used to convince readers. These include *answering the opposition, referring to an authority, predicting consequences, presenting facts,* and *giving examples.* Although you probably will never use all of them in one paragraph, you will use them when you write persuasively.

1. **Answering the opposition:** At times, the best way to persuade your reader is to respond to an opponent's point. This also shows your reader that you are aware of your opponent's side of the issue, not just your own.
2. **Referring to an authority:** An authority is a person or a group that is considered an expert on the subject and will give an unbiased opinion.
3. **Predicting consequences:** Predicting consequences can help your reader agree with your point of view and disagree with your opponent's.
4. **Presenting facts:** Facts are those things that actually exist or have existed, such as people, places, things, and events. A *fact* differs from an *opinion* in a quite significant way. An opinion is the way we think about, or interpret, facts. For instance, it is a fact that the United States Congress removed our currency from the gold standard in 1978. That fact cannot be argued. However, whether you think it was a good idea to remove the gold standard is your opinion, and that can be argued. Whether your *opinion,* or your opponent's *opinion,* is the more persuasive, the *fact* remains that the gold standard was removed in 1978.
5. **Giving examples:** Good examples can develop an idea quickly and clearly and help convince your reader of your point of view. Examples also are used to clarify, illustrate, or make concrete a general idea about the subject. Therefore, be certain that your examples support your position or convincingly argue against your opponent's position.

PRACTICE 5   **Distinguishing Fact from Opinion**

Write an **F** for *fact* or an **O** for *opinion* in the space to the left of each item in the following list.

1. __F__ There are nine known planets in our solar system.

2. __F__ The Congress of the United States consists of the Senate and the House of Representatives.

3. __F__ I am 6 feet tall.

4. __O__ Wolves make great pets.

5. __F__ Water freezes at 32 degrees Fahrenheit and 0 degrees Celsius.

6. __O__ I am the greatest basketball player in my state.

7. __O__ Hurricanes are more frightening than tornadoes.

8. __O__ Laughter is the best medicine.

9. ___O___ Pastrami is better sandwich meat than ham.

10. ___F___ Neil Armstrong was the first man on the moon.

▼ **PRACTICE 6**   **Analyzing a Persuasive Paragraph**

Answers will vary.

In the following paragraph from a persuasive essay, "Cyberspace: If You Don't Love It, Leave It," Esther Dyson attempts to persuade the reader that cyberspace communities evolve and take on the characteristics of earthly communities.

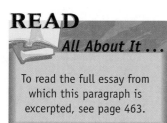

READ *All About It . . .*

To read the full essay from which this paragraph is excerpted, see page 463.

Cyberspace communities evolve just the way terrestrial communities do: People with like-minded interests band together. Every cyberspace community has its own character. Overall, the communities on Compuserve tend to be more techy or professional; those on America Online, affluent young singles; Prodigy, family oriented. Then there are independents like Echo, a hip, downtown New York service, or Women's Wire, targeted to women who want to avoid the male culture prevalent elsewhere on the Net. There's SurfWatch, a new program allowing access only to locations deemed suitable for children. On the Internet itself, there are lots of passionate noncommercial discussion groups on topics ranging from Hungarian politics (Hungary-Online) to copyright law.

Persuasion Technique Questions

1. Dyson compares the cyberspace community to a real earthly community. List the issues a real community faces. Are these the same issues that exist in a cybercommunity? Discuss their similarities and differences. What issues are unique to each?

Answers will vary.

_____

_____

2. Point out sentences in which Dyson uses opinion and those in which she uses facts to support her topic. Which does she use more frequently, fact or opinion? How convincing is her support evidence?

Three sentences use opinion (sentences 1, 2, and 3), two use fact

(sentences 5 and 6), and one uses both (sentence 4). Answers will

vary.

Copyright © 2004 by Pearson Education, Inc.

▼ PRACTICE 7	Analyzing a Persuasive Paragraph

Answers will vary.

In the following paragraph from a persuasive essay, "Don't Give Up the Right to Carry," student writer Tim Schuette tries to persuade his audience that giving citizens the right to carry concealed guns will reduce the crime rate.

The opposition is worried that the crime rate will increase overall with a concealed weapon law. However, after passing concealed weapon laws, states have seen a decrease in crime. John Lott, who has never been a member of the National Rifle Association (N.R.A.), is an economist at the University of Chicago. Lott examined gun laws and crime in 3,054 U.S. counties. He found that "not only did violent crime drop after states relaxed concealed weapon laws, but . . . after five years murder was down 15%, rape 9%." If Missouri residents could carry a concealed weapon, crime would likely decrease.

Persuasion Technique Questions

1. The writer does not state his attitude (pro or con) about the topic directly in a topic sentence. State in your own words what you think the author's attitude is about the topic.

   Answers will vary.

   _____

   _____

2. How convincing are the support points that the writer makes? How many of the types of support does the writer use? How convincing are the support points that the writer makes? Do quotes and statistics seem more convincing than opinion?

   Answers will vary depending on the student's answer to #1.

   _____

   _____

Organization Patterns

Once you have made your pro/con list and have chosen the type of evidence you want to use to support your topic, you will need to organize your paragraph for an effective presentation. There is no defined pattern that a writer has to use when writing persuasively. However, several patterns logically come to mind that will organize your points into a convincing persuasive paragraph.

Pattern 1: Using only support points that argue for your point of view (only pro-list items if you are arguing for a point of view, or using only con-list items if you are arguing against a point of view).

Pattern 2: Stating only your opposition's support points (either pro or con) and arguing against them.

Pattern 3: Alternating use of support points for your side of the argument and listing your opponent's points and arguing against them. This is a hybrid of patterns 1 and 2.

Once you have chosen your organization pattern, select several points from the appropriate list or lists and write sentences for each. Arrange the sentences according to the organization pattern you have selected.

The following are three persuasive paragraph examples using the pro/con list on page 264. Each paragraph is organized according to one of the three patterns you have studied.

Pattern 1 Persuasive Paragraph: Against Nuclear Energy (Con-List Items)

Topic Sentence
Con Item

Con Item
Conclusion
Con Item

Con Item

Example

Fact
Consequence
Conclusion

Conclusion

Nuclear energy should not be restored because of radioactive waste disposal problems and the possibility of a nuclear reactor accident. One of the problems with nuclear energy is waste management. Radioactive waste can remain dangerous for thousands of years; therefore, safe disposal sites must meet rigid safety standards to keep the public safe. Sites must be deep in the ground to shield the public from possible radiation exposure, and the sites must be immune to earthquake damage. Such sites are hard to find and expensive to maintain. In addition to the waste disposal problem, nuclear accidents pose a real danger to people living near nuclear reactors. In 1986, in the Ukrainian town of Chernobyl, a nuclear reactor accident put thousands at risk of radioactive poisoning. A radiation cloud spread over northern Europe and Great Britain. Thirty-one Soviet citizens died, and over 100,000 had to be evacuated from surrounding areas. The dangers involved in the long term control and management of such a volatile substance as radioactive materials make it a very risky proposition. Until more trustworthy safeguards can be developed in both the operation and waste disposal of radioactive substances, nuclear energy should remain a thing of the past.

Pattern 2 Persuasive Paragraph: Arguing Against the Opposition (Pro-List Items)

Topic Sentence
Opposition/Argument

Answering Opposition
Using a Fact
Consequence
Opposition/Argument

Answering Opposition (Fact)

Despite the possible benefits to society, nuclear energy should not be restored as a fuel source. Many scientists and researchers claim nuclear energy is desirable as an energy source because it creates enormous amounts of power from small resources. While this may be true, there are other costs that outweigh the purely monetary. In 1986, in the Ukrainian town of Chernobyl, a nuclear reactor accident killed 31 Soviet citizens and caused 100,000 people to be evacuated. A radioactive cloud covered much of northern Europe and Great Britain. Military leaders in Washington, D.C. state that a nuclear energy industry will also ensure a continuous source of radioactive material necessary to maintain our nuclear weapons arsenal for the defense of the nation. However, every year there are reports of nuclear byproducts missing from

Copyright © 2004 by Pearson Education, Inc.

<table>
<tr><td>Possible Consequence</td><td></td></tr>
<tr><td>Possible Consequence</td><td></td></tr>
<tr><td>Conclusion</td><td></td></tr>
</table>

government inventories. Terrorist enemies of the United States could use this material to build nuclear weapons with which to threaten us. Also, the plans for building, running, and producing nuclear reactors for energy could be used to produce materials for making nuclear weapons and might be stolen and used by unfriendly nations. The potential for disaster far outweighs the potential benefits coming from a nuclear energy industry. Nuclear energy is not a safe or practical energy source.

Pattern 3 Persuasive Paragraph: Alternating Your Points with Arguing Against the Opposition's Points (Pro- and Con-List Items)

Topic Sentence
Con Item
Con Item
Conclusion

Opposition/Argument

Answering Opposition Using a Fact

Consequences

Opinion
Answering Opposition (Fact)

Possible Consequence
Opposition/Argument

Answering Opposition (Opinion)

Conclusion

Despite the possible benefits to society, nuclear energy should not be restored as a fuel source. One of the problems with nuclear energy is waste management. Radioactive waste can remain dangerous for thousands of years; therefore, safe deposit sites must meet rigid safety standards to keep the public safe. Sites must be deep in the ground to shield the public from possible radiation exposure, and the sites must be immune to earthquake damage. Many scientists and researchers claim nuclear energy is desirable as an energy source because it creates enormous amounts of power from small resources. While this may be true, there are other costs that outweigh the purely monetary. In 1986, in the Ukrainian town of Chernobyl, a nuclear reactor accident killed 31 Soviet citizens and caused 100,000 people to be evacuated. A radioactive cloud covered much of northern Europe and Great Britain. Nuclear weapons proliferation is another problem if nuclear energy production is increased. Every year there are reports of nuclear byproducts missing from government inventories. Terrorist enemies of the United States could use this material to build nuclear weapons with which to threaten our security. Economists like to say that increasing the nuclear energy industry will create more high tech jobs, but the same industry will cause widespread unemployment in traditional fossil fuel industries like coal, oil, and gas. The potential for both disaster and a negative impact on the economy should convince lawmakers to prohibit the return of nuclear energy as a fuel source.

PRACTICE 8 Writing Persuasive Paragraphs

Answers will vary.

On separate sheets of paper, write a persuasive paragraph for three of the topics below using a separate organization pattern for each. Write your completed draft on the lines provided.

Topics

The academic year should/should not be extended to 12 months with 2 weeks vacation every 3 months.

Tobacco and alcohol advertising should/should not be regulated.

Young people should/should not be given college tuition money for public service just because soldiers are given tuition money for military service.

All guns should/should not be licensed and registered with the authorities.

Prayer should/should not be allowed in public schools.

Welfare recipients should/should not have to have a job to receive benefits.

Grades should/should not be abolished as the method for judging student performance.

Marijuana should/should not be legalized for medical use.

All coursework should/should not transfer to any other college in the country.

Same-sex couples should/should not be allowed to legally marry.

Persuasive Paragraph—Pattern 1

_____

_____

_____

_____

_____

_____

_____

_____

_____

Persuasive Paragraph—Pattern 2

_____

_____

_____

_____

_____

_____

_____

_____

_____

Copyright © 2004 by Pearson Education, Inc.

Persuasive Paragraph—Pattern 3

_____

_____

_____

_____

_____

_____

_____

_____

_____

_____

Transitional Expressions for Persuasion

Transitional expressions are useful in connecting related ideas and for adding rhythm to the paragraph so that it reads more smoothly.

Transitional Expressions for Persuasive Writing		
Answering the Opposition and Referring to Authority	**Predicting Consequences and Stating Conclusions**	**Facts and Examples**
according to. . .	consequently	another. . .
although	in conclusion	because
nevertheless	therefore	finally
of course	thus	first
on the other hand		for
others may say. . .		last
		next
		second
		since
		third

PRACTICE 9   Using Transitional Expressions

Answers will vary.

Rewrite the three persuasive paragraphs from Practice 8 using transitional expressions as appropriate.

Pattern 1 Rewrite

_____

_____

_____

_____

_____

_____

_____

_____

_____

Pattern 2 Rewrite

_____

_____

_____

_____

_____

_____

_____

_____

Copyright © 2004 by Pearson Education, Inc.

Pattern 3 Rewrite

_____

_____

_____

_____

_____

_____

_____

_____

Persuasive Logic: Cause and Effect Reasoning

Often, when attempting to persuade someone about a belief or point of view you hold, you are also trying to convince them by pointing out special relationships that different things or events share. In persuasion, **cause** and **effect** reasoning can be a powerful tool in convincing your reader that your point of view is both logical and reasonable.

Cause and effect development explains the reasons behind *why* something occurs: **cause** analysis develops *why* something happens, and **effect** analysis explains *the results and consequences* stemming from the causes. These are called **causal relationships,** and they help us understand why things happen in the world around us and the possible consequences that may occur in the future.

For example, a writer might ask the question, "Why did President Clinton lie to the American public?" as a way of finding out the possible causes of this problem. (*Possible causes:* he didn't define his actions with Monica Lewinsky as "having sex"; he didn't want the First Lady, Hillary Rodham Clinton, to find out about his relationship with Ms. Lewinsky; he did not want to be embarrassed publicly in the press; he didn't want history to focus on this aspect of his presidency.) The writer also might ask, "What will happen because President Clinton lied to the American public?" as a way of figuring out the possible events that might occur in the future stemming from the lying. (*Possible effects:* he might have been impeached for "high crimes and misdemeanors"; history books might focus on this aspect of his presidency rather than his successes with domestic and foreign affairs; the Democratic Party might find it harder to get legislation passed through Congress; Democratic candidates might find it difficult to get elected or re-elected to office.)

Obviously, the search for cause and effect answers can be a complex undertaking. More than one explanation can be found and, often, all the answers fit. This can be helpful in achieving thorough development of the issue. In persuasion, thoroughly developing your point of view can help you persuade your reader that your side of the issue has been both logically and reasonably stated.

Causal Chains

Whether you are focusing on cause or effect, it is helpful, before you begin writing, to develop a **causal chain.** A causal chain demonstrates the series of events that can develop between things and can help clarify the relationships that exist between them, as well.

Example		
Causes		**Effects**
Too many unpaid bills	can lead to	increased physical tension.
Increased physical tension	can lead to	severe headaches.
Severe headaches	can lead to	nausea and loss of appetite.
Nausea and loss of appetite	can lead to	physical and mental fatigue.
Physical and mental fatigue	can lead to	health problems.

In the example above, notice how an effect can become a cause for the next effect, and so on. Things and events do not exist in a vacuum isolated from the other things and events around them. Yes, we can focus on cause, and we can focus on effect, but for your insights to be most persuasive, it will be helpful during your argument to share with the reader the knowledge you have learned from the causal chain.

Once readers know *why* something has happened and the consequences that might occur, they are much more likely to accept your persuasive conclusions about the topic. In other words, they are clear as to why you think the way you do, and "understanding" an issue is often half the battle to "accepting" the arguer's ideas concerning the issue.

Problems to Avoid

When using cause and effect reasoning, do not confuse **chronological sequence** and **coincidence** with true cause and effect relationships.

In chronological sequence, do not assume that because one event follows another in time that the first event causes the second to occur.

> **Example**
>
> After I attend a movie, I read in the paper several days later that another movie star has died. Therefore, my going to the movies causes actors to die. (There are literally thousands of movie stars spanning decades of time. One movie star is likely to die on almost any day of the week and, because they are famous, their passing also is likely to be reported in newspapers. So the chances of a movie star's death being reported at about the same time as you do anything, not just attending a movie, is a likely occurrence.)

With coincidence, do not assume that because one thing occurs that it is the cause for another thing that occurs, that a cause and effect relationship exists between them.

Copyright © 2004 by Pearson Education, Inc.

> **Example**
> Every time a black cat crosses my path, something bad happens to me. (Bad things indeed may happen to you, but the proverbial "black cat," as a cause of bad luck, is a superstition that has no basis in reality. Your "bad luck" is probably due to your not being properly prepared for the events in your life or possibly just being at the wrong place at the wrong time—chance occurrence.)

Transitional Expressions for Cause/Effect Writing

There are several transitional expressions you will find useful when writing about causes or effects.

Cause	Effect
because	as a consequence of
causes, caused by	as a result (of)
the reason . . .	consequently
since	then
	therefore

The Topic Sentence in a Cause/Effect Paragraph

After choosing your subject and figuring out some ideas using one or more of the prewriting techniques you have learned, you will need to decide whether you are going to focus on causes or effects. The topic sentence will announce your purpose to the reader, and it will clarify the paragraph's development.

> **Examples**
> *Focus on Causes:*
> Proper nutrition, regular exercise, and a positive attitude can lead to a long, healthful life. (This paragraph will develop *proper nutrition, regular exercise, and a positive attitude* to show how each "causes" a *long, healthful life*.)
>
> *Focus on Effects:*
> A long, healthful life can increase earnings potential, intelligence levels, and an active retirement period. (This paragraph will develop *earnings potential, intelligence levels, and an active retirement period* as "effects" or "results" of a *long, healthful life*.)

▼ **PRACTICE 10**   **Writing a Paragraph Focusing on Causes**

Answers will vary.   This practice will help you develop a paragraph that focuses on causes.

> **1.** Pick one of the following topics: divorce; poor job performance; disinterest in politics.

2. List as many causes of your topic choice as you can think of.

a. _____

b. _____

c. _____

d. _____

e. _____

3. If any of the causes in your list are merely chronological or coincidental, draw a line through them.

4. Write a topic sentence that focuses on causes.

_____

_____

5. Write a sentence for each of the remaining causes in your list.

_____

_____

_____

_____

_____

_____

6. On a separate sheet of paper, rewrite your sentences into paragraph form.

Copyright © 2004 by Pearson Education, Inc.

| PRACTICE 11 | Writing a Paragraph Focusing on Effects |

This practice will help you develop a paragraph that focuses on effects.

Answers will vary.

1. Pick one of the following topics: drug abuse; dieting; organizational skills.

2. List as many effects of your topic choice as you can think of.

a. _____

b. _____

c. _____

d. _____

e. _____

3. If any of the effects in your list are merely chronological or coincidental, draw a line through them.

4. Write a topic sentence that focuses on effects.

_____

_____

5. Write a sentence for each of the remaining effects in your list.

_____

_____

_____

_____

_____

6. On a separate sheet of paper, rewrite your sentences into paragraph form.

CHAPTER REVIEW

▼ Writers use persuasion to try to convince others that their point of view is correct.
▼ Persuasion can be informal, semiformal, or very formal.
▼ The topic sentence in a persuasive paragraph states the writer's conclusion or point of view about a particular topic.
▼ Answering the opposition, referring to an authority, predicting consequences, facts, and examples are types of evidence.
▼ A fact differs from an opinion. An opinion is the way we think about, or interpret, facts.
▼ To present a persuasive paragraph convincingly, the ideas must be organized into a pattern that offers the evidence and ideas in an effective manner.
▼ Cause and effect reasoning can be a powerful tool in convincing your reader that your point of view is both logical and reasonable.
▼ Cause analysis explains the reasons _why_ something occurs.
▼ Effect analysis explains _the results and consequences_ stemming from causes.
▼ Transitional expressions help organize and connect ideas. They also add rhythm to writing so it reads more smoothly.

Topic Bank

Write a paragraph about one or more of the following topics, or about a topic of your own choice.

Persuasion

1. Mandatory drug testing should/should not be allowed at schools.
2. Instant replay should/should not be used in all professional sports.
3. Controversial organizations (Communist Party, Ku Klux Klan) should/should not be allowed to advertise in campus publications.
4. National identification cards will/will not help prevent terrorism.
5. Women should/should not be allowed to be combat soldiers in the military services.
6. Affirmative action should/should not be implemented for college enrollment.
7. The legal drinking age should/should not be eighteen years of age.
8. Marijuana should/should not be legalized for medical purposes.
9. English should/should not be legally designated as the official language of the United States.
10. Health insurance should/should not be made available for all citizens of the United States.

Causes of . . .

1. drug abuse
2. the increasing high school dropout rate
3. test anxiety
4. high taxation
5. road rage
6. divorce
7. spousal abuse
8. a high teen pregnancy rate
9. low unemployment
10. high prison populations

Effects of . . .

1. prejudice
2. pollution (see the photo on page 280)
3. a school grading system
4. over-prescribing antibiotics
5. high speed limits
6. high interest rates
7. international trade agreements
8. alcohol abuse
9. a tornado
10. a large corporation leaving a small town

Copyright © 2004 by Pearson Education, Inc.

Writing Opportunities

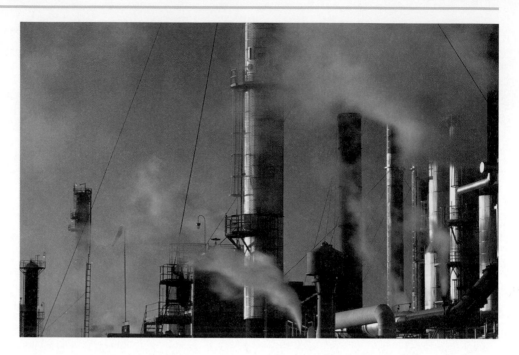

Home

The factory near your home has been releasing foul-smelling clouds of smoke for nearly three months. You have phoned City Hall on several occasions to complain, but nothing has been done. In an attempt to persuade the mayor of your city to look into the air pollution caused by the factory, write one paragraph detailing the problems associated with the factory's smokestacks.

School

Your Biology 101 professor's assignment sheet states that each student must find a potential source of pollution (air, water, or land) in the local community, and write a one-paragraph report detailing the potential hazardous conditions. The report should try to persuade people in the community that action needs to take place to correct the problem. You decide to write about the fumes coming from the smokestacks at the local chemical factory just outside of town.

Work

You work for the Environmental Protection Agency (EPA). Write a one-paragraph report convincing your boss to bring action against the factory in the photograph for violation of air pollution standards.

Visit *The Write Start* Online!

For additional practice with the materials found in this chapter, visit our Website at:

http://www.ablongman.com/checkett

The Website also features additional readings, quizzes, writing activities, and Internet links, as well as a bulletin board and interactive chat.

**For More Practice with Your Grammar and Writing Skills
Visit The Longman Writer's Warehouse**

For further multimedia exercises and activities designed to improve your reading, thinking, writing, and grammar skills, visit The Longman Writer's Warehouse on the Web. The Writer's Warehouse offers an interactive handbook, an online journal, a bulletin board, and extensive coverage of the writing process. To take a tour, go to

http://longmanwriterswarehouse.com

Copyright © 2004 by Pearson Education, Inc.

PART 3

Writing Effective Essays

Writing effective paragraphs is very useful when it comes to memos, short-answer exams, and brief writing assignments, but many business reports and longer college writing assignments require multiple paragraphs to explain many ideas.

Just as we joined together sentences to form a paragraph, we can join together paragraphs into a longer piece of writing called an *essay*.

Copyright © 2004 by Pearson Education, Inc.

Copyright © 2004 by Pearson Education, Inc.

22

The Essay

Business and academic writing often requires considerable length to fully express a variety of complex ideas. Length in academic writing, in particular, often demands two to three pages in the form of an essay.

An **essay** is a written composition made up of a number of paragraphs that develop a particular subject. Therefore, an essay can be developed using the same methods demonstrated in the preceding chapters dealing with writing single paragraphs.

Although an essay can have any number of paragraphs, we will use a five-paragraph model to introduce the basic elements of the essay.

The Five-Paragraph Essay

Almost all essays should have a **title.** The title should pique the reader's interest. It should be a catchy or dramatic phrase, usually two to six words;

longer titles can become wordy and cumbersome to read. If you can't come up with something clever or dramatic, pick several of the key words from your thesis sentence and use them. It's a good idea to wait until your essay is finished before you create the title. That way you give yourself enough time to fully understand the point of your essay and come up with the most appropriate title.

When writing your title, do the following:

1. Capitalize the first word and all other words except articles (a, an, the) and prepositions (of, on, to, in).
2. Center the title on the page and leave two spaces between it and the introductory paragraph.

Do not put quotation marks on either side of the title, and do not underline it.

Most essays begin with an **introductory paragraph.** Its purpose is to introduce the reader to the topic of the essay. The paragraph consists of *introductory sentences* and the *thesis sentence.*

After the introductory paragraph comes the **body paragraphs.** Their purpose is to develop, support, and explain the topic idea stated in the thesis sentence. Body paragraphs consist of a *topic sentence* followed by *support sentences.*

The essay ends with a **concluding paragraph.** Its purpose is to bring the essay to a conclusion that gives the reader a sense of completeness. The most common methods for concluding an essay are emphasizing one of the following: *a call to action, a warning, a prediction,* or an *evaluation* of the important points.

The Introductory Paragraph

The purpose of the **introductory paragraph** is to introduce the reader to the topic of the essay. This can be accomplished through a series of introductory sentences followed by the thesis sentence.

The Thesis Sentence

The most important element in an essay is the **thesis sentence** because it sets the tone for the entire essay. It states what the writer is going to explain, clarify, or argue for or against about the essay's topic. While there is no rule about which paragraph to place the thesis sentence in, it is usually placed near the end of the first paragraph. This placement makes your thesis the last element of your essay's introduction. This is important. After all, the thesis sentence is a roadmap for the entire essay, and you should want the reader to understand what your essay is about. A good thesis sentence:

▼ announces the overall topic/subject.
▼ states the importance of the topic/subject (the writer's attitude toward the subject).
▼ can outline the organizational structure of the entire essay.
▼ asserts only one main idea.
▼ expresses the topic as an opinion that can be discussed.
▼ is *not* expressed as a fact.
▼ is *never* expressed as a question.

> **Examples**
>
> Preventive maintenance will help increase the resale value of your car.
>
> Knowing you have inherited a genetic disease can help you plan for the future.
>
> Computers have effectively reduced the cost of communications for most businesses.

PRACTICE 1   Analyzing Thesis Sentences

In the space provided after each example, explain why each thesis sentence is constructed improperly. Write "Correct" in the space if you think the example is a good thesis.

1. Is St. Louis an exciting city in which to live?

Not a good thesis because it is in the form of a question.

2. The St. Louis Cardinals are a professional baseball team.

Not a good thesis because it is a statement of fact.

3. Many people have different opinions on whether St. Louis is a good place to raise a family.

Not a good thesis because the writer's position is not clear.

4. St. Louis is a popular tourist city because of the nightlife and the historical sites.

Correct.

5. St. Louis has not fully utilized its riverfront for barge traffic; the civic leadership has not dealt effectively in revitalizing the north side of the city.

Not a good thesis because it asserts two main ideas.

6. St. Louis has a rich social, political, and cultural history.

Not a good thesis because its subject matter is too broad.

7. St. Louis is known as the "Gateway to the West."

Not a good thesis because it is a statement of fact.

8. The Gateway Arch was a sound financial investment.

Correct.

9. St. Louis is strategically located in the middle of the country.

Not a good thesis because it does not clearly define the topic.

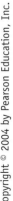
Copyright © 2004 by Pearson Education, Inc.

10. Visitors enjoy St. Louis because of the international flavor of its restaurants.

Correct.

Expressing an Attitude in the Thesis Sentence

The writer's **attitude** is simply how the writer feels about the topic at hand. The verb in the thesis sentence usually starts to express the writer's attitude about the subject. For example, the verbs *are/are not, is/is not, should/should not,* and *can/cannot,* begin to tell you how the writer feels about the subject. Perhaps the topic is good citizenship, and the writer thinks that reading a newspaper each day will make people better informed about community affairs, thus making them good citizens. The verb and the words after the verb finish expressing the writer's attitude. So, the verb "will make," when tied to the idea of "good citizen," expresses the writer's attitude that "reading a newspaper" will make people good citizens. As a writer, your attitude expresses both why the subject is important to you and also why you think the subject should be important to the reader.

> **Examples**
>
> In the following thesis sentences, the words that express attitude are italicized.
>
> 1. Breakfast *is the most important* meal of the day.
> 2. <u>Psycho</u> *is a scary* movie because of the shower scene.
> 3. Vitamin supplements *can help* you feel more energized.
> 4. Vitamins *have no* role in whether or not you feel more energized.
> 5. Ford *makes better* trucks than Chevrolet.

▼ **PRACTICE 2**   **Identifying the Writer's Attitude**

Underline the words that express attitude in each of the following thesis sentences.

1. Organically grown fruits and vegetables <u>are healthier</u> than those chemically treated.

2. Students who study on a daily basis <u>are more successful</u> on exams than students who cram.

3. Hybrid fuel automobiles <u>will help reduce</u> America's dependence on foreign oil.

4. Metal detectors <u>should not be installed</u> in schools throughout the nation.

5. Warning labels on CD and DVD packaging <u>are a violation</u> of free speech.

6. Society during the "good old days" <u>was not any better</u> than today.

7. Playing violent video games <u>can be harmful</u> to young people's perception of reality.

8. Working at a part-time job while going to school <u>promotes</u> a sense of responsibility.

9. Global warming <u>could have a negative effect</u> on the earth's ecosystems.

10. Learning a different language <u>helps</u> students learn about other cultures.

The Essay Map in the Thesis Sentence

Because you are learning to write a five-paragraph essay with three body paragraphs, the three-item essay map in the thesis sentence will both organize and limit your essay's discussion of the topic. Each of the three essay map items becomes the subject of each of the three body paragraphs. The essay map automatically organizes the essay for you and limits its scope.

Examples

In the following sentences, the essay map is italicized.

1. To be safe during a tornado alert, people should *go to the basement, hide inside an interior room closet,* or *get underneath a heavy piece of furniture.*
2. *Intelligence, dedication,* and *hard work* are necessary ingredients for a successful career.
3. Because of an *excessive military budget, poor farming methods,* and *inadequate international trade strategies,* Communism was a failure in Russia.

▼ PRACTICE 3   Analyzing the Essay Map

Read the following thesis sentences to see if the essay map items explain, clarify, or support the writer's attitude about the topic. If the essay map does explain, clarify, or support the writer's attitude about the topic, write **correct** in the space provided. If not, indicate what is wrong.

Example: Thesis Sentence: *St. Louis is an exciting city to visit because of clouds, elm trees, and cats.*

Topic: St. Louis

Attitude: An **exciting** city to visit

Why: Clouds, elm trees, cats (the three-item essay map)

Problem: The three essay map items are not exciting reasons to visit the city.

Copyright © 2004 by Pearson Education, Inc.

1. A vegetarian diet is healthier than one with meat because of temperature, salt, and water retention.

   Salt and water retention may be related as unhealthy aspects of eating

   meat versus vegetables, but temperature is not a viable reason

   supporting a vegetarian diet.

2. Expanding your vocabulary, learning about new places, and developing a better writing style makes reading a valuable activity.

   Correct

3. Weekly household chores help children learn math, tuna salad, and opera houses.

   These three essay map items do not support why household chores

   help children in any way.

4. Cultural awareness, civic responsibility, and volunteerism make coin collecting an interesting hobby.

   Obviously, the three essay map items are not related to coin collecting.

5. Maintaining a successful professional sports career is difficult because of talented newcomers, the constant travel, and the aging process.

   Correct

Putting It All Together

It is vital that your thesis sentence be constructed properly. Without a good thesis sentence, the essay cannot succeed. To check your thesis sentence, ask this question:

Do the **essay map items** explain or support why the writer has chosen his **attitude** about the **topic**?

Examples

Poor	Voting and military service are important activities for all citizens. (two topics, no essay map)
Better	Voting is an important responsibility for all citizens. (one topic and clear attitude, no essay map)
Best	Voting is an important responsibility for all citizens because it gives people a voice in how the government is run, removes ineffective politicians from office, and influences political decision making. (one topic, clear attitude, three-item essay map)
Poor	Many students work while going to school. (statement of fact, no attitude, no essay map)
Better	Working, while going to school, can teach students valuable lessons. (one topic, clear attitude, no essay map)
Best	Working, while going to school, can teach students responsibility, organizational skills, and teamwork. (one topic, clear attitude, three-item essay map)
Poor	Are regular automobile oil changes really necessary? (question—not a clear opinion, no essay map)
Better	Regular oil changes can keep a car running better. (one topic, a clearly stated opinion, no essay map)
Best	Regular oil changes can keep a car running more efficiently, improve gas mileage, and reduce long-term maintenance costs. (one topic, clear attitude, three-item essay map)

PRACTICE 4   Analyzing Thesis Sentences

In each of the following thesis sentences, underline the topic once, circle the attitude, and underline the essay map twice. On the line provided, indicate if any element is missing.

1. Broccoli and oranges are (good) sources for vitamins.

   No essay map.

2. Playmaking, speed, and bench-clearing brawls make ice hockey an (exciting) sport.

3. The Rolex is considered by many as a (better) wristwatch than the Breitling.

   No essay map.

4. College students go to class, study, and write papers.

   No attitude.

5. Laptop computers (are good buys because of portability.)

   No essay map.

Copyright © 2004 by Pearson Education, Inc.

6. Solar power (should be a governmental priority) because of diminishing fossil fuels, environmental pollution, and skyrocketing costs.

_____

7. Bungee jumping (is a dangerous activity.)

No essay map.
_____

8. The St. Louis Rams, Green Bay Packers, and Pittsburgh Steelers are football teams.

No attitude.
_____

9. Are savings bonds (better) investment instruments than annuities because of interest, safety, and liquidity?

A thesis sentence cannot be a question.
_____

10. Humor, social satire, and musicality made the Beatles (popular long) (after their breakup as a rock group.)

_____

▼ **PRACTICE 5**   **Rewriting Thesis Sentences**

Answers will vary.

From Practice 4, rewrite those sentences that do not meet the necessary criteria for an effective thesis sentence. Number your finished sentences.

_____

_____

_____

_____

_____

_____

_____

_____

_____

_____

_____

_____

PRACTICE 6   **Writing Thesis Sentences**

Answers will vary.

Write thesis sentences for the following topics. Use the criteria for writing an effective thesis sentence that you have studied.

1. A movie you have seen

_____

_____

2. A social issue you are interested in

_____

_____

3. A job you have or would like to have

_____

_____

4. A famous person you admire

_____

_____

5. A piece of artwork you like

_____

_____

Introductory Sentences

In the introductory paragraph, the thesis sentence is introduced by **introductory sentences.** The introductory sentences should catch the reader's attention and clarify your tone (humorous, serious, or satiric). Some effective techniques for introducing the thesis sentence are as follows:

▼ *Shocking statistics or statements*

> One of every four babies in America is born out of wedlock. Fifty percent of teenage deaths involve alcohol. More Americans die and are injured in automobile accidents than from all diseases combined. It's time something is done about these national tragedies. (*Place thesis sentence here*)

Copyright © 2004 by Pearson Education, Inc.

▼ *A series of questions*

> Tired of the same old political promises? Are the current politicians in Washington, D.C. not representing your concerns? Are you thinking about not voting in the upcoming elections? Maybe you simply need to find a new direction. *(Place thesis sentence here)*

▼ *A common problem or misconception*

> Most people think welfare only goes to poor people living in the inner city. They believe that welfare recipients have no job and are hopelessly lazy, and that welfare recipients are poorly educated and lack skills necessary to hold a job. What you don't realize about welfare and who gets it may shock you. *(Place thesis sentence here)*

PRACTICE 7   **Writing Introductory Sentences**

Answers will vary.   Write introductory sentences for each of the following thesis sentences. Try to create at least three sentences that lead logically to the thesis sentence.

1. Expanding your vocabulary, learning about new places, and developing a better writing style make reading a valuable activity.

   _____

   _____

   _____

   _____

   _____

   _____

2. Solar power should be a governmental priority because of diminishing fossil fuels, environmental pollution, and skyrocketing costs.

   _____

   _____

   _____

   _____

   _____

   _____

3. Maintaining a successful professional sports career is difficult because of talented newcomers, the constant travel, and the aging process.

_____

_____

_____

_____

_____

_____

The Body Paragraphs

The **body paragraphs** get their organization from the three-item essay map located in the thesis sentence. Each topic for each body paragraph is taken from the essay map in the thesis sentence. There are two types of sentences in the body paragraph: the _topic sentence_ and _support sentences._

The Topic Sentence

The **topic sentence** tells the reader what the main idea, or topic, of the paragraph is. Although there is no set place in the paragraph for the topic sentence, making the topic sentence the first sentence in the paragraph will make organizing and developing the topic easier.

The topic sentence has two parts: the _topic/subject_ and the _controlling idea._ The **topic** is the subject of the paragraph taken from the essay map in the thesis sentence. The **controlling idea** states what the writer will be developing about the subject of the paragraph. The controlling idea limits what you can say about the subject so that you don't stray to other subject areas.

Topic sentences missing a controlling idea lack focus and specific direction. Without a controlling idea, the writer's attitude about the subject can be unclear.

> **Examples**
>
> Soccer is a popular high school sport. (no controlling idea— <u>popular</u> is too ambiguous)
>
> Michael Jordan was a popular basketball player. (no controlling idea—simply a statement of fact)
>
> Soccer is a popular high school sport because it is relatively inexpensive to fund. (controlling idea: <u>cheap funding</u> makes soccer popular)
>
> Michael Jordan's diverse skills made him an exciting basketball player. (controlling idea: Jordan is exciting because of <u>diverse skills</u>).

Support Sentences

Support sentences follow the topic sentence and develop the subject using specific examples, details, and facts. These support ideas must be consistent with the controlling idea. In other words, the controlling idea unifies the

Copyright © 2004 by Pearson Education, Inc.

paragraph by determining the kind of support ideas you can use in the support sentences.

Example

Police officers <u>are most effective when helping citizens in their</u> <u>communities.</u>

topic   controlling idea

Support sentences for this topic sentence would focus on *what* police officers do to help citizens and might include such activities as

    a. finding lost/stolen property
    b. solving crimes
    c. preventing crimes

Six Important Support Questions

When writing a story, reporters ask six questions. The answers provide the focus that allows them to select the details, facts, and examples to develop the story with specific information. The six questions are *who, what, where, when, why,* and *how.*

After you have selected, or have been given, the topic you are to write about, decide on the controlling idea. To do this, choose which of the following reporter's questions allows you to write about the topic with the desired focus.

For instance, suppose your topic is An Important Event. In the support sentences, you could focus on

Who?   Who started the event?

Who attended/witnessed/participated in the event?

Who was affected by the event?

What?   What was the event?

What happened before/during/after the event?

What was special about the event?

Where?   Where did the event occur?

Did the location affect the event in any way?

Did the location have historical significance?

When?   When did the event occur (A.M./P.M., day, month, year)?

Did the time frame add any special significance to the event?

Did the event coincide with a historically significant time?

Why?   Why did the event occur?

Why was the event important?

How?   How did the event happen?

How was the event funded?

How was the event advertised?

You can add your own focus to these questions if other ideas come to you. There is no need to limit yourself to the preceding list.

Copyright © 2004 by Pearson Education, Inc.

Examples

1. Reading can help people become better educated.
2. Reading is best done in a quiet, secluded place.
3. Anyone interested in becoming a better writer should read as much as possible.

Although the topic subject of each sentence, Reading, is the same, the focus of the controlling idea is different. In sentence 1, the focus is on *what* reading can do for people (educate them); in sentence 2, the focus is on *where* reading is best accomplished (in a quiet, secluded place); and, in sentence 3, the focus is on *who* (anyone interested in becoming a writer).

For a more developed discussion of body paragraphs and outlining, see Chapter 13.

The Concluding Paragraph

An essay should not suddenly stop after you have finished discussing the last body paragraph topic. You should leave your reader with a feeling of completion. Use the concluding paragraph to emphasize why your essay is important. The **concluding paragraph** can help convince your reader that your ideas are valid. The concluding paragraph should not introduce new points; developing new points is the function of the body paragraphs. However, the concluding paragraph should give the points you have made a dramatic purpose. Also, it is not necessary to restate the thesis sentence and essay map items at the end of your essay unless you are doing a longer paper. In a short, five-paragraph essay, the reader is not likely to forget three points.

Just as there were several introductory techniques you could use in the introductory paragraph, there also are several concluding techniques that you can use in the concluding paragraph. These include:

▼ Call to action
▼ Warning
▼ Prediction
▼ Evaluation

Call to Action

You are actually asking the reader to take action, to do something.

Example

New subdivisions are necessary to house the burgeoning population in our suburbs, but the wholesale destruction of mature trees simply to make building easier is not an acceptable construction practice. <u>Call your local alderperson, and complain about this anti-environmental practice.</u> It takes 20 to 30 years for a sapling to mature into a fully foliaged shade tree.

Warning

You are warning the reader that there is the possibility of something adverse happening.

> **Example**
>
> Buying products and services on the Internet is becoming commonplace. The amount of money being spent online is doubling every year. The main reason for the Internet's popularity for consumers is convenience. However, be careful when giving out credit card numbers on the Internet. <u>Unauthorized use of credit cards is a growing problem for Internet shoppers.</u> Make sure that the online business you are dealing with has a secure server for credit information. Your economic security is at stake.

Prediction

You "look into the future," so to speak, and predict outcomes stemming from the topic.

> **Example**
>
> The new suburban vans are becoming bigger every year. They look like off-road vehicles with glandular problems. The extra roominess inside the vans is great for large families, hauling Little League teams, and traveling with lots of luggage. But the larger vehicles are hard to handle, and their greater bumper height and extra weight cause more damage to regular-sized cars when accidents occur. <u>Because of the proliferation of these monster-vans, insurance rates will surely rise in the near future.</u> Suburban van manufacturers should begin to study ways to counter this potential negative impact on all drivers.

Evaluation

You summarize the importance of the overall topic.

> **Example**
>
> Studying plants in the Amazon rainforest has had and will continue to have many benefits for society. <u>New drugs to combat disease are an important result of these studies. Additionally, new antibiotics are needed to replace those that bacteria have become resistant to because of overuse.</u> Synthetic derivatives also can be developed from studying the new drugs. The Amazon rainforest is a valuable resource for all the world.

Sample Student Essay

The following is a student essay demonstrating all the elements of an effectively written essay that you have learned in this chapter. The key elements and concepts are noted in the margin and underlined in the text of the essay.

In this essay, student writer Nancy Smith relates the emotionally devastating effects of finding out that her 3-year-old son has cancer, followed by the equally disturbing period of surgery and treatment.

The Ravages of Childhood Cancer

Shocking Statistic	<u>Nearly one-third of all children diagnosed as having a childhood malignancy die.</u> This number strikes fear into the heart of any parent unfortunate enough to have to face such awful news about their child. <u>Most everyone has been a patient in a hospital, but a grave uncertainty about leaving alive is not a common experience.</u> Being told, "If there is a type of cancer to have, this is the kind," is of little comfort. The "C" word is frightening in any context. Diagnosis, surgery, and treatment are <u>terrifying</u> experiences for the family of a child having cancer.
Shocking Statement	
Introductory Paragraph Thesis Sentence with Three-Item Essay Map "Terrifying" Is the Attitude Controlling Idea: "What"	
Topic Sentence: "Diagnosis"	<u>We had taken him to Cardinal Glennon Children's Hospital for testing to find out a diagnosis.</u> When he had not felt good over the past month, cancer was not even a remote thought in any of our minds. Apparently, it was for the doctors. Nurses tried five times before successfully finding a vein that would hold the IV tube. Derek cried out of pain and fear. I could feel myself becoming nauseous as I tried to comfort him. Next, we moved to the ultrasound room where Derek, exhausted from the IV ordeal, slept soundly. The doctor inspected the screen. Yes! There it was. A tumor the size of a quarter. Wilms tumor, otherwise known as cancer of the kidney, was Derek's diagnosis.
Support Sentences: The Ordeal of the Diagnostic Procedure	
Topic Sentence: "Surgery"	<u>As the day of the surgery arrived, the family gathered at the hospital.</u> We were told the operation to remove the tumor and infected kidney would take two to three hours. Although sedated, Derek looked at me longingly through frightened eyes. I was surrounded by my entire family, but I never felt more vulnerable. Three hours passed, then four, with no word. My hand trembled uncontrollably as I tried to sip from my coffee cup; I could not stop the tears welling in my eyes. Finally, after five hours, the surgeon entered the waiting room and told us the results. He was fairly certain they had gotten all of the tumor. If all went well, Derek would start chemotherapy and be released from the hospital in two weeks.
Body Paragraphs #1, #2, #3	
Support Sentences: Emphasis on "Time"	
Topic Sentence: "Treatment"	<u>Derek's treatment consisted of six radiation therapy sessions and chemotherapy spread over a one and a half year period.</u> The radiation came first—once a day for six consecutive days. The procedure only lasted a few minutes; however, thirty minutes after the session Derek would vomit every fifteen minutes for hours. His little body would convulse like a dying snake's. His little voice split the air with terrifying screams. The chemotherapy started early and lasted all day. The medicine was administered through a port-catheter in his chest. After the chemo was injected, Derek would be sick for days.
Support Sentences: The Difficulty of Treatment	
Call to Action Concluding Paragraph	It's been five years since the operation, and there has been no sign of a tumor on his remaining kidney. The prognosis is good. Doctors and scientists still do not know all the causes of the various forms of cancer. Research is needed at all levels, so give generously to the Cancer Foundation. Someone once said that a statistic is a victim without the tears. Your continued support of cancer research will help eliminate future statistics.
Prediction	

Copyright © 2004 by Pearson Education, Inc.

Sample Student Essay

In the following essay, student writer Rebecca Eisenbath revisits a horrendous time in our history—the genocide of six million people based on their race, religion, or nationality at the hands of Adolf Hitler and the Nazis before and during World War II.

First, read the essay. Then, answer the questions following the essay.

The Holocaust: The Ashes Remain

Most people know that World War II began in September of 1939 when Germany invaded Poland. But the year 1933 may not ring any bells; however, the event that began that year surely would: the beginning of the Holocaust. Over the next decade, six million people would be exterminated in what became euphemistically known as "the Final Solution." The Holocaust remains one of the most devastating events in human history due to its horrendous policies, number of victims, and the terrible effect it continues to have on the survivors and the people around the world.

Germany's horrendous policies led to the decision to commit genocide. Hitler and his followers believed their Aryan race was the only one that deserved to rule other "inferior" races, and they made slave laborers of those different than themselves. They blamed the Jews for their economic problems, so Reinhard Heydrich, the Chief of Reich Security, thought up the idea of mass extermination in prisoner camps. This policy came to be known as the "Final Solution." All Jews had to wear an identification badge or armband emblazoned with a yellow Star of David. They either were herded into traincars and taken to the extermination camps, or they were imprisoned in ghettos and killed by bands of SS military units.

The Holocaust also was alarming because of the numbers and types of people it claimed. The total death toll was over six million. Although they are the most written about because of the sheer numbers that were killed, the "Final Solution" did not stop with the Jews. Catholics, Poles, Czechs,

Gypsies, homosexuals, and even the mentally ill were shot, gassed, poisoned, and tortured until merciful death came.

Near the end of the war, when the Allies overran German-held countries, they liberated the concentration camps. What they found inside, emaciated prisoners, huge ovens filled with human bones, and mass graves overflowing with bodies, devastated many of the liberators. Many of these men had to undergo years of psychological treatment to deal with the horrors of the camps. The Jewish survivors were sent to Palestine after the war to try and rebuild their lives. Three years later, the State of Israel was recognized by the United Nations. The survivors of the Holocaust, although never forgetting their pain (how could they with camp numbers tattooed on their forearms?), never lost hope.

Even today, the world cannot escape what happened so many decades ago. In 1993, two museums commemorating the Holocaust were dedicated in the United States. Yet, the practice of genocide still exists as wars rage in parts of Asia, Africa, and Europe. Nations must learn from the past or, as we are seeing today, we will be doomed to repeat it. Be an advocate for peace, and let your congresspersons know how you want them to act.

Questions

1. What type of introductory technique does the writer use?

A shocking statistic: over six million people were exterminated.

2. Write the thesis sentence on the line below.

The Holocaust remains one of the most devastating events in human history due to its horrendous policies, number of victims, and the terrible effect it continues to have on the survivors and people around the world.

3. Identify the topic in the thesis sentence.

The Holocaust.

Copyright © 2004 by Pearson Education, Inc.

4. Identify the attitude.

Most devastating events.

5. What are the three essay map items?

Horrendous policies, number of victims, and the terrible effect it

continues to have on the survivors.

6. Write the three topic sentences of the three body paragraphs on the lines below. Underline the topic in each sentence.

Germany's horrendous policies led to the decision to commit genocide.

The Holocaust also was alarming because of the numbers and types of

people it claimed. Near the end of the war, when Allies overran

German-held countries, they liberated the concentration camps.

7. Choose the method by which the writer develops the topic in each of the body paragraphs: who, what, where, when, why, or how?

Body paragraph 1 **What the horrendous policies led to**

Body paragraph 2 **Who was affected by the Holocaust**

Body paragraph 3 **How the liberators and survivors were affected**

8. What technique(s) does the writer use in the concluding paragraph?

The essay concludes with a warning: learn or be doomed to repeat

history, and a call to action: contact your congresspersons.

PRACTICE 9   Analyzing an Essay

Sample Student Essay

In the following essay, student writer Tim Schuette explores why exercising properly can benefit your health.

First, read the essay. Then, answer the questions following the essay.

Effective Exercising

Are you overweight? After cutting the grass, are you exhausted? Are you

unable to keep up with your friends or your children? Would you like to feel

younger? Exercising the upper body, abdominal, and leg muscles correctly is

important for proper functioning.

The most important muscles to exercise in the upper body are the triceps, biceps, and pectorals. The triceps and biceps, located in the upper arm, work as a team so that your arm can flex at the elbow. Exercising only one or the other of these muscles can reduce flexibility and can facilitate injuries like "tennis elbow." When you exercise the chest, you need to use an equal amount of weight in each hand and do the exact number of repetitions so that neither right nor left pectoral muscle will dominate the other. When this happens, "pulled" muscle injuries occur more often. The upper body muscles will work freely and efficiently when exercised proportionately.

The abdominal muscles are significant because they support the entire body. Therefore, you need them to simply sit upright in a chair. The abdominals consist of eight separate muscles that must be exercised for total effectiveness. The upper and lower muscles, known as the "six pack," are located from navel to chest, and they support your body front to back. The oblique muscles are located on either side of the "six pack" and assist in supporting the body when bending left or right. If your back is constantly hurting or you simply want to lose that "spare tire," then exercising the abdominals is essential.

The three major muscles in the legs give you the ability to stand, walk, run, and jump. The rectus femoris and the semitendinous are located in the upper leg. The gastrocnemius better known as the calf muscle, is located in the lower leg. The upper leg muscles make the leg bend at the knee, and the lower leg muscles make the foot moveable. If the muscles are worked unevenly, they can become damaged; additionally, injured or weakened leg muscles can cause shin splints and hip problems. Also, the leg muscles must be exercised properly when you are younger, so that more problems won't occur as you get older.

Copyright © 2004 by Pearson Education, Inc.

No single muscle works by itself; therefore, it is important to exercise all your muscles and their group partners evenly. If your muscles are worked correctly, you will lose weight, have more energy, and feel younger. A total workout only takes about thirty minutes, three times per week. Exercise regularly. Your body deserves it!

Questions

1. What type of introductory paragraph technique does the writer use?

series of questions

2. Write the thesis sentence on the line below.

Exercising the upper body, abdominal muscles, and leg muscles correctly is important for proper functioning.

3. Identify the topic in the thesis sentence.

Exercising

4. Identify the attitude.

Is important

5. What are the three essay map items?

Upper body

Abdominal

Leg Muscles

6. Write the three topic sentences of the three body paragraphs on the lines below. Underline the topic in each sentence.

The most important <u>muscles</u> to exercise in the upper body are the triceps, biceps, and pectorals. The <u>abdominal muscles</u> are significant because they support the entire body. The <u>three major muscles</u> in the legs give you the ability to stand, walk, run, and jump.

7. Choose the method by which the writer develops the topic in each of the body paragraphs: who, what, where, when, why, and how.

Body paragraph 1 **How to exercise the upper body muscles**

Body paragraph 2 **Where the abdominal muscles are located**

Body paragraph 3 **What the leg muscles do**

8. What technique(s) does the writer use in the concluding paragraph?

Call to action: it is important to exercise. Prediction: if you exercise

properly, you will lose weight, have more energy, and feel younger.

CHAPTER REVIEW

▼ An essay consists of a number of paragraphs that develop a particular topic.

▼ Almost all essays should have a title.

▼ Most essays begin with an introductory paragraph. Its purpose is to introduce the reader to the topic of the essay.

▼ The introductory paragraph consists of introductory sentences and the thesis sentence.

▼ The thesis sentence names the topic of the essay, gives the writer's attitude toward the topic, and organizes the body paragraphs through the use of an essay map.

▼ The essay map items become the topics for the body paragraphs.

▼ Introductory sentences introduce the thesis by piquing the reader's interest through using a shocking statistic or statement, a series of questions, or by stating a common problem or misconception.

▼ Body paragraphs develop, support, and explain the topic idea stated in the thesis.

▼ Body paragraphs consist of topic sentences and support sentences.

▼ Topic sentences have two parts: the topic/subject and the controlling idea.

▼ The controlling idea unifies the paragraph by determining the kind of support ideas the writer can use in the support sentences.

▼ To support and develop the body paragraphs, the six reporter's questions can be used: who, what, where, when, why, and how.

▼ The essay ends with a concluding paragraph. Its purpose is to bring the essay to a conclusion that gives the reader a sense of completeness.

▼ The most common methods for concluding the essay are to emphasize one of the following: a call to action, a warning, a prediction, or an evaluation of the important points.

Topic Bank

Write a five-paragraph essay using one of the following thesis sentences, or a thesis sentence of your own.

1. Political negotiation should help solve the Israel-Palestine issue.

2. Skateboarding can be very dangerous without proper equipment (see the photo on page 285).

3. A positive attitude can help you achieve your goals.

4. Space exploration benefits mankind because of the inventions stemming from it.

5. Past performance is the best indicator of future behavior.

6. Listening to classical music can help you achieve better math scores.

7. Content warning labels on CDs are worthwhile.

Copyright © 2004 by Pearson Education, Inc.

8. Living in a dorm is a better way to learn good social skills than sharing an apartment.
9. Art is a waste of time unless it adds to your job skills.
10. A poor teacher is a good excuse for failing a class.

Writing Opportunities

Home

You convince your spouse to take you to your 25th high school reunion. It's a formal affair, strictly tuxedos and gowns. From 7 in the evening until 2 in the morning, you and your old classmates dance to the music popular the year you graduated and reminisce about the good old days at Smarmy High. When you return home, you are so excited about what you have witnessed that you decide to write about the experience and send copies to all your friends and relatives around the country. In hopes of organizing the vast amount of details in your mind, and remembering your writing class from college, you decide to write a five-paragraph essay using the thesis sentence with three-item essay map.

School

You are a reporter for your school newspaper. Your editor wants a five-paragraph column detailing the major events at the year's biggest campus social activity, the Homecoming Formal Dance. You decide to make the Homecoming Queen the focus of your story.

Work

As a freelance writer, you'll take any assignment as long as the money is right or the subject interests you. For the right price, the editor of a popular national magazine, concerned with "the rich and famous," has convinced you to write a five-paragraph article about the movie industry's Academy Awards Ceremony. You decide that the focus of your article will be the crowds, the parade of stars, and the unfolding pageantry.

Visit *The Write Start* Online!

For additional practice with the materials found in this chapter, visit our Website at:

http://www.ablongman.com/checkett

The Website also features additional readings, quizzes, writing activities, and Internet links, as well as a bulletin board and interactive chat.

For More Practice with Your Grammar and Writing Skills
Visit The Longman Writer's Warehouse

For further multimedia exercises and activities designed to improve your reading, thinking, writing, and grammar skills, visit The Longman Writer's Warehouse on the Web. The Writer's Warehouse offers an interactive handbook, an online journal, a bulletin board, and extensive coverage of the writing process. To take a tour, go to

http://longmanwriterswarehouse.com

Copyright © 2004 by Pearson Education, Inc.

The Writer's Resources

Copyright © 2004 by Pearson Education, Inc.

GRAMMAR

Nouns

Nouns are words that stand for people, places, or things. They can be singular or plural.

Nouns		
	Singular	**Plural**
Person	man	men
	cousin	cousins
	girl	girls
Place	cave	caves
	beach	beaches
	forest	forests
	yard	yards
	mountain	mountains
Thing	ring	rings
	computer	computers
	discussion	discussions
	truth	truths
	sport	sports
	idea	ideas
	vacation	vacations
	conversation	conversations

To **form the plural of most nouns,** you simply add an –*s* or –*es* to the end of the word. However, there are some exceptions:

1. Nouns ending in –*f* or –*fe* form the plural by adding –*ves*:

half	halves
knife	knives

2. Hyphenated nouns (names that are formed by joining several short words with hyphens "-") form plurals by adding –*s* or –*es* to the main word in the phrase:

mother-in-law	mothers-in-law
sergeant-at-arms	sergeants-at-arms

3. Some nouns form plurals in other ways, such as by changing the spelling of the plural form. These are sometimes called irregular forms of plural nouns:

foot	feet
child	children
criterion	criteria

| woman | women |
| man | men |

4. Other nouns do not change at all when forming the plural. These exceptions must simply be memorized:

fish	fish
deer	deer
shrimp	shrimp

Nouns can also be classified as *proper* and *common*. **Proper nouns** are the specific names or titles of people, places, or things, and they are capitalized. **Common nouns** are general terms for people, places, or things, and they are not capitalized.

Common Nouns	Proper Nouns
singer	Sheryl Crow
beach	Corona Del Mar
magazine	*Time*
student	Julianne

▼
PRACTICE 1   Identifying Nouns

Underline the nouns in the following sentences.

Example: The <u>family</u> travels to the <u>mountains</u> every <u>weekend</u>.

1. They pack up the family <u>van</u>, drive two <u>hours</u>, and arrive at the small <u>cabin</u> in <u>Big Bear Lake</u>.

2. The <u>weekend</u> is spent relaxing in the fresh <u>air</u>.

3. The four <u>children</u> spend their <u>time</u> hiking, skiing, swimming, or reading, depending on the <u>season</u>.

4. The <u>parents</u> try to relax as they do the <u>yardwork</u>, repair the <u>cabin</u>, and prepare <u>meals</u> for the <u>children</u>.

5. When they get <u>home</u>, the <u>kids</u> are relaxed but the <u>parents</u> are exhausted.

6. The next <u>weekend</u> the <u>family</u> plans a <u>trip</u> to the <u>beach</u>.

7. On <u>Saturday</u> <u>morning</u>, the <u>van</u> is filled with inner <u>tubes</u>, boogey <u>boards</u>, beach <u>towels</u>, beach <u>chairs</u>, and picnic <u>baskets</u>.

8. The <u>drive</u> to the <u>beach</u> is an hour <u>trip</u> through the <u>maze</u> of Southern California <u>freeways</u>.

Copyright © 2004 by Pearson Education, Inc.

9. Arriving at the sheltered <u>cove</u>, the <u>girls</u> throw their <u>towels</u> on the <u>sand</u> and dash down to the <u>shore</u>, shrieking as the cold <u>waves</u> splash around their <u>ankles</u>.

10. After spending the <u>day</u> swimming and resting on the <u>shore</u>, they gather around the <u>fire</u>, munching on <u>hot dogs</u> and <u>s'mores</u>.

11. As the <u>sun</u> sets into the firey <u>ocean</u>, the <u>group</u> gathers its sandy <u>belongings</u> and staggers to the <u>car</u> for the gritty <u>ride</u> home.

▼ **PRACTICE 2   Using Nouns**

Fill in the blanks with appropriate nouns. Compare your answers with those of a classmate to see how the results vary depending on the vocabulary chosen. **Answers will vary.**

The new _____ are becoming bigger every

_____. They look like _____ with

_____. The extra _____ inside the

_____ are great for _____, _____

and _____. But the larger _____ are hard to

handle, and their greater _____ and _____

make for more damage to _____ when _____

occur.

For the original paragraph, see p. 298.

Pronouns

A **pronoun** is a word that takes the place of, or refers to, a noun. The word or words that the pronoun refers to are known as the **antecedent(s)** of the pronoun.

> **Example**
>
> <u>Fariba</u> said that <u>she</u> did not understand the question. (<u>she</u> is the pronoun, and <u>Fariba</u> is its antecedent)

Pronouns can be divided into several categories. The most common categories are *personal pronouns, relative pronouns, demonstrative pronouns, indefinite pronouns,* and *reflexive pronouns.*

Personal Pronouns

Personal pronouns are those that refer to a person (*I/me, you, he/him, she/her, it, we/us,* and *they/them*). *Personal pronouns* are divided into three forms, depending on how they are used in a sentence. These forms are **subjective** (pronoun used as a subject), **objective** (pronoun used as an object), or **possessive** (the pronoun indicates possession/ownership).

Subjective Pronouns

	Singular	Plural
1st person	I	we
2nd person	you	you
3rd person	he, she, it	they

Objective Pronouns

	Singular	Plural
1st person	me	us
2nd person	you	you
3rd person	him, her, it	them

Possessive Pronouns

	Singular	Plural
1st person	my (mine)	our (ours)
2nd person	your (yours)	your (yours)
3rd person	his (his)	their (theirs)
	her (hers)	
	its (its)	

The following examples demonstrate the uses of these three types of personal pronouns:

I frequently listen to music when I drive. (subjective pronoun; the pronoun is used as a subject)

They enjoy decorating their home. (subjective pronoun)

Dave is starting to annoy you. (objective pronoun; the pronoun is the object of the sentence)

He gave the same gift to him. (objective pronoun)

That is my sweater. (possessive pronoun; the pronoun shows ownership or possession)

He borrowed her keys. (possessive pronoun)

The keys are hers. (possessive pronoun)

▼ **PRACTICE 1   Identifying Personal Pronouns**

In the following sentences, underline subjective pronouns once, objective pronouns twice, and possessive pronouns three times. Some sentences may contain more than one type.

Copyright © 2004 by Pearson Education, Inc.

1. He came home from work.

2. His new car was covered with oak leaves.

3. As she walked to the water cooler, her shoe came off and slid under a desk.

4. They decided that not participating in the parade was a better decision for them.

5. It will not be as surprising to you after they explain the rules.

6. Would you like to eat at your place or ours?

7. We sold their horses for them while they were in Europe.

8. It was never my intention to buy his car for you.

9. It's never a good idea to put all of your investments into one stock.

10. I thought the best plan for you would be to go with them to the game.

▼

| PRACTICE 2 | Using Personal Pronouns |

Circle the correct form of personal pronoun in the following sentences.

1. The Governor accepted an interview with Lisa and (he, him).

2. (She, Her) and Ellen want to be firefighters.

3. After the rehearsal, Luis and (he, him) went to the coffee shop.

4. The contractors left (their, his) tools on the desk.

5. These statistics helped (her, she) and (me, I) with our research paper.

6. That estimate seemed very expensive to my sister and (I, me).

7. Marc installed the CD and then returned it to (he, him).

8. His parent's questions caught Terrance and (we, us) by surprise.

9. It seemed as if an unresolved problem was causing difficulties between my father and (I, me).

10. The restored painting had regained (its, their) glorious colors.

Relative Pronouns
Relative pronouns are those pronouns used to introduce a qualifying or explanatory clause.

Relative Pronouns

who	Used as a subject in reference to people
whom	Used as an object in reference to people
which	Used as a subject in reference to things
that	Used as a subject in reference to people or things
whoever	Used as a subject in reference to an uncertain number of people
whichever	Used as a subject in reference to an uncertain number of things

The following examples illustrate the use of relative pronouns:

Who made the phone call? (*Who* is used as the subject)
The phone call was made by *whom*? (*Whom* is used as the object)
Which tastes better to you? (*Which* is used as a subject referring to things)
I don't like *that*! (*That* is used as the object referring to a thing)

PRACTICE 3   Using Relative Pronouns

Write the correct relative pronoun in the following sentences.

Example: The scientist <u>who</u> is studying AIDS received a grant.

1. **Which** field of study has he chosen as a major?

2. For **whom** did he buy this bicycle?

3. **Whoever** wants to go to the concert may go.

4. The biology lab **that/which** I attend is three hours long.

5. He did not know **that** the performance had been cancelled.

6. At **whom** did the clown throw the cream pie?

7. **Who** will take the originals to the copy room?

8. He will marry **whomever** his friends approve of.

9. Give the money to **whomever** you choose.

10. For **whom** are those gifts piled in the closet?

11. To **whom** was he singing?

12. **Who** would prefer skiing to snowboarding?

13. Fred chose the major **that** best suited his interests.

Copyright © 2004 by Pearson Education, Inc.

14. ___Whoever___ has been trained in computer support technology will get the job.

15. The committee will hire ___whomever___ best fits the job description.

16. ___Who___ is pounding on the door?

17. ___Which___ set of problems are the most difficult?

18. Lorraine did not know ___whom___ to ask to the backward dance.

19. The children could not decide ___which___ toys to take on their vacation.

20. ___Who___ will be going to Gulf Breeze for spring break?

Demonstrative Pronouns

Demonstrative pronouns are used to point out or specify certain people, places, or things.

Demonstrative Pronouns

Singular	Plural
this	these
that	those

▼ **PRACTICE 4**   **Using Demonstrative Pronouns**

Write the correct demonstrative pronoun in the following sentences.

1. ___This___ book (in my hand) gives the latest statistics on the dangers of second-hand smoke.

2. He spent the afternoon staring at ___that___ picture across the room.

3. ___Those___ flowers in the valley only bloom in the early fall.

4. The police found ___this___ puppy (in my car) on the side of the highway.

5. ___That___ was the most important discovery of the century.

6. ___Those___ apples in the truck are still green.

7. Why didn't you take ___these___ cookies to our new neighbor?

8. ___Those/these___ small tattoos are the least painful to apply.

9. His cockatiel will only eat ___these/those___ special seeds.

10. To whom do ___these___ keys belong?

Indefinite Pronouns

Indefinite pronouns do not refer to a specific person or thing; they refer to general or indeterminate people, places, or things.

Indefinite Pronouns

These pronouns do not refer to a specific person.

Singular

everyone	someone	anyone	no one
everybody	somebody	anybody	nobody
everything	something	anything	nothing
each	another	either	neither

Singular or Plural

all	more	none
any	most	some

Plural

both	few	many	several

▼ **PRACTICE 5   Using Indefinite Pronouns**

Write the correct indefinite pronoun in the following sentences.

1. _____**Everyone**_____ should do his or her best work for each class.

2. The rules do not apply equally to _____**everyone**_____ in this society.

3. _____**Anyone**_____ can learn to use a computer if he or she takes the appropriate classes.

4. _____**All**_____ of the new homes have a three-car garage.

5. He sold _____**all**_____ of the CDs in one hour.

6. Her two children came home from school hungry, so she fixed snacks for _____**both**_____ of them.

7. _____**No one**_____ could stop them from finishing the race!

8. Jon consulted several sources; _____**each**_____ of them consistently supported limitations on handgun ownership.

9. _____**Most**_____ arguments are flawed.

10. _____**All**_____ of the salesmen were very aggressive.

Copyright © 2004 by Pearson Education, Inc.

Reflexive Pronouns

The reflexive form adds –*self* or –*selves* to the pronoun and is used to indicate action performed to or on the antecedent.

Reflexive Pronouns		
	Singular	**Plural**
1st person	(I) myself	(we) ourselves
2nd person	(you) yourself	(you) yourselves
3rd person	(he) himself	(they) themselves
	(she) herself	
	(it) itself	

The following examples illustrate the use of the reflexive pronoun:

> We gave *ourselves* a party to celebrate the end of the school year.
> Vinh found *himself* in an impossible situation.

The reflexive pronoun form can also be used to intensify meaning. When a reflexive pronoun is used this way it is called an **intensifier.**

> The instructor *herself* found the concepts confusing.
> Raoul *himself* had made the engine.

▼ PRACTICE 6   Using Reflexive Pronouns

Write the correct reflexive pronoun in the following sentences.

1. Aliesha ____**herself**____ was astounded at how quickly she learned the concepts.

2. My children and I painted the room ____**ourselves**____.

3. Oksana found ____**herself**____ alone in a strange city.

4. The goal is for the students to edit the essay ____**themselves**____.

5. Although I enjoy cooking, I cannot cook all meals by ____**myself**____.

6. The computer turns ____**itself**____ off after one hour.

7. Do you consider ____**yourself**____ exempt from the laws that apply to everyone else?

8. The cat could open the door by ____**itself**____.

9. Though he hates to write in English, Kahn ____**himself**____ wrote the entire research paper.

10. The professor did not consider ____**himself/herself**____ an expert on all subjects.

Pronoun-Antecedent Agreement

It is important that pronouns agree with their antecedents. For example, the singular antecedent *everyone* must be used with the singular pronouns *he* or *she*.

The following examples illustrate sentences in which pronouns agree with the antecedent:

> If *someone* works late at night, *he* or *she* may not be able to concentrate in class the next morning.
>
> Or
>
> When Adam works late at night, *he* is not able to concentrate in class the next morning.
>
> *Each* ticket holder stood in line waiting for *his* or *her* refund.
>
> *Many* were angry that *their* efforts had not been rewarded.

▼ **PRACTICE 7   Pronoun-Antecedent Agreement**

Fill in the blanks with the correct pronouns. Underline the antecedent of each pronoun.

Example: All <u>students</u> must do _____**their**_____ assigned reading before class.

1. Each soccer <u>player</u> gave _____**his or her**_____ best effort in the world cup match.

2. <u>Jennifer</u> referred to recent local social conflict in _____**her**_____ history project.

3. <u>Anyone</u> can learn to dance if _____**he or she**_____ has a patient instructor.

4. <u>Someone</u> left _____**his/her**_____ clothes all over the locker room.

5. The <u>managers</u> want us to attend _____**their**_____ sales meeting next week.

6. Although the average <u>consumer</u> wants the best price, _____**he/she**_____ may not shop carefully enough to find one.

7. <u>Lana</u> and <u>Patricia</u> gave _____**their**_____ opinions to Alicia.

8. The creative writing <u>students</u> turned in _____**their**_____ portfolios.

9. She grows <u>tomatoes</u> and green <u>beans</u>; _____**they**_____ taste best fresh from the garden.

10. _____**She/He**_____ is going to the dance with _____**her/his**_____ date.

Copyright © 2004 by Pearson Education, Inc.

▼ **PRACTICE 8** **Pronoun-Antecedent Agreement**

Correct any errors in pronoun reference in the sentences below. Put a **C** in the blank if the sentence has no error in pronoun reference.

                                         its

Example: _____ The business has ~~their~~ problems.

             its

1. _____ The jury delayed ~~their~~ verdict.

                                   their

2. _____ Mr. Billings' students are planning for ~~its~~ field trip to the science center.

                   its

3. _____ The crowd roared ~~their~~ approval as the ball dropped in Times Square.

4. __**C**__ The group of friends has continued to share their lives over many years.

                     its

5. _____ The family did not take ~~their~~ annual vacation to the beach this year.

                     its

6. _____ The soccer team is at ~~their~~ best during challenging tournaments.

                             its

7. _____ The faculty of the college argued over ~~their~~ grading policies all semester.

8. __**C**__ The musicians performed the difficult symphony as well as they could.

                     its

9. _____ Our committee changes ~~their~~ decision every month.

10. __**C**__ The student council is working on an award banquet for its members.

▼ **PRACTICE 9** **Pronoun-Antecedent Agreement**

Write the correct pronoun in the blank, and write the antecedent of the pronoun in the column on the right.

1. The school is doing ____**its**____ best to improve   __**school**__ student retention.

2. Each political movement has ____**its**____   __**movement**__ supporters and detractors.

3. Anyone can conquer ____**his/her**____ fear of   __**Anyone**__ technology.

4. Many women are returning to school to achieve _____ women _____

_____ their _____ personal goals.

5. Each country has _____ its _____ own flag.   _____ country _____

6. The two teams recovered _____ their _____ equipment   _____ teams _____

after the game.

7. Someone left _____ his/her _____ keys in the empty   _____ Someone _____

classroom.

8. Soap operas manipulate _____ their _____ viewers'   _____ Soap operas _____

emotions.

9. Louisa plans to pick up _____ her _____ dry cleaning   _____ Louisa _____

next week.

10. When will we know the results of _____ our _____   _____ we _____

evaluations?

▼ **PRACTICE 10**   **Writing Sentences with Pronoun-Antecedent Agreement**

Referring to the previous practice patterns, write ten similar sentences, making sure to match each pronoun to the appropriate antecedent. Underline the pronoun and circle the antecedent.

1. **Answers will vary.** _____

_____

2. _____

_____

_____

3. _____

_____

4. _____

_____

5. _____

_____

6. _____

_____

Copyright © 2004 by Pearson Education, Inc.

7. _____

_____

8. _____

_____

9. _____

_____

10. _____

_____

▼
PRACTICE 11   Editing for Pronoun Use

Edit the following paragraph to correct pronoun use. The first sentence has been done for you. The correct answer is in parentheses. Some sentences are correct. (The following paragraphs are from a student essay, "A Stroke of Bad Luck" by Margaret Ewart.)

On August 25, 1997, I received a phone call that changed the lives of ~~anyone~~ (everyone) in my family. My father had a stroke while traveling from North Carolina to Mississippi. After the detailed phone conversation about my father's condition, I realized that as a supportive and caring daughter, I ~~one~~ needed to be at my father's side. Looking at my frail father, partially paralyzed and unable to take care of his own personal needs, I became aware that I ~~you~~ had to take care of him throughout the rest of his life. Making the decision to become a primary care giver affected my family by the changes in a father-daughter role, and the loss of family time, which resulted in new attitudes among all family members.

▼
PRACTICE 12   Editing for Pronoun Use

Edit the following paragraph to correct pronoun use. The first sentence has been done for you.

Shortly after I started taking care of my father, I came to realize that there was never any time for ~~me~~ (myself), much less my family. I rarely ever have the time to play with my children, help my daughter with her school work or spend time with my husband. My father requires a tremendous amount of my time, which prevents me from being a mother as well as being a wife. Most of the time I feel as if I am missing out on a great deal of ~~mine~~ **my** children's lives, due to the fact that I have become a primary care giver. I have felt like a prisoner in ~~our~~ **my** own home since the stroke. My husband and I have a great fear of leaving ~~my~~ **our** home in the event that he may need us. My husband tries to take me out for dinner and a movie to give me some sense of relief from all of the stress, but I always decline. Due to ~~her~~ **my** fear of leaving the house because of my new responsibilities, family members are reluctant to make plans with me. They have begun to treat me differently and to see me as a different person.

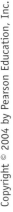

▼ **PRACTICE 13** **Editing for Pronoun Use**

Edit the following (concluding) paragraph for pronoun usage. The first sentence has been done for you.

As each day brings new obstacles and solutions, ~~you~~ (I) have overcome almost ~~anyone~~ (every one) of them. What was once a difficult situation has become part of everyday life for ~~them~~ **me**. In the midst of taking care of my father, I have realized that ~~you~~ **I** can't help him unless I can help ~~oneself~~ **myself**. I was becoming extremely exhausted trying to take care of ~~anything~~ **everything**, and I was losing myself. Finally, I realized that I didn't need to be around my father that much, and ~~you~~ **I** could do something to better ~~oneself~~ **myself**. Going back to school was the first thing that came into my mind, and I said, "Why not?" So I enrolled in school. I have made a special schedule for my family, my father, my school, and most importantly, myself. Emotionally, I am the happiest that I have ever been in my life, which reflects on ~~any~~ **each** member of ~~your~~ **my** family.

Copyright © 2004 by Pearson Education, Inc.

Verbs ESL

A **verb** is a word indicating action, feeling, or being. Verbs can be divided into three classes: action verbs, linking verbs, and helping verbs (see Chapter 3). Additionally the form of the verbs can indicate the time of the action: **present, past,** or **future** (also known as **tense**). Each of these tenses has many forms that we use every day.

The most commonly used tenses are **simple present** and **simple past:**

Present Tense

Verbs in the Simple Present Tense

Sample verb: to think

	Singular		**Plural**
1st person	I	think	we think
2nd person	you	think	you think
3rd person	he*		they think
	she	thinks	
	it		

*Use an -s or -es ending on the verb when the subject is *he, she,* or *it,* or the equivalent.

▼ **PRACTICE 1   Using the Present Tense**

Write the present tense of the verb in parentheses in the following sentences. (This exercise is taken from a paragraph by student Jeanette Weiland.)

1. While shopping at a perfect store, customers ___**are**___ (to be) generally sold products at an inexpensive price.

2. Shoppers ___**are**___ (to be) typically ___**offered**___ (to offer) items that are clearly marked with price tags on each separate package.

3. This ___**allows**___ (to allow) customers to rapidly and easily choose the product that ___**gives**___ (to give) them the best buy.

4. There ___**are not**___ (to be, not) any reasons to look for the price on the store shelf and then have to worry about whether or not the item ___**matches**___ (to match) the price tag.

5. A perfect store ___**does**___ (to do) not only honor its own sales coupons, but it also ___**accepts**___ (to accept) other department store advertised prices and coupons.

6. This _____**gives**_____ (to give) the customers the convenience of shopping at one store instead of having to go to two or three.

7. No matter what store they _____**shop**_____ (to shop) at, these pricing policies _____**offer**_____ (to offer) shoppers an opportunity to receive the best possible price.

▼ **PRACTICE 2**   **Using the Present Tense**

Write the present tense of the verb in parentheses in the following sentences. The following paragraph is by student Amber Barton. (In some cases, the present progressive form may be used.)

1. The sights of New York City _____**stimulate**_____ (to stimulate) the senses.

2. Rural Missouri _____**soothes**_____ (to soothe) them.

3. From the Empire State Building to the subway system, the sights and sounds of New York City _____**invigorate**_____ (to invigorate) the spirit.

4. Lady Liberty _____**stands**_____ (to stand) proudly in the East River with Ellis Island, its now silent companion, and _____**evokes**_____ (to evoke) pride in its visitors.

5. The rich hills and valleys of rural Missouri _____**are**_____ (to be) lovely.

6. They _____**pale**_____ (to pale) in comparison to the stark beauty of New York skyscrapers.

7. A traveler would _____**have**_____ (to have) to visit more than once to be able to take in all the diverse sights New York City has to offer.

Past Tense
Regular Verbs

Regular verbs are those verbs that form the past tense by adding –ed or –d. The **simple past tense** is used to refer to an action that began and ended at one time period in the past.

> **Past Tense of Regular Verbs**
> Sample verb: to dance
>
> | | **Singular** | **Plural** |
> | --- | --- | --- |
> | 1st person | (I) danced | (we) danced |
> | 2nd person | (you) danced | (you) danced |
> | 3rd person | (he, she, it) danced | (they) danced |

Copyright © 2004 by Pearson Education, Inc.

In addition to simple forms, there are other present and past verb forms. The following table illustrates the most commonly used verb tenses. Each tense expresses a specific time or duration. Students for whom English is a second language should practice the use of each tense in spoken and written English.

Common Verb Tenses
Sample verb: to talk

Tense	First Person Singular	Sample Sentence
present	I talk	I like to talk in a group.
present progressive	I am talking	I am talking on the phone now!
present perfect	I have talked	I have talked about this often.
present perfect progressive	I have been talking	I have been talking since dawn!
past	I talked	I talked to him last night.
past progressive	I was talking	I was talking about my car.
past perfect	I had talked	I had talked before I decided.
past perfect progressive	I had been talking	I had been talking before they sang.
future	I will talk	I will talk to you tomorrow.
future progressive	I will be talking	I will be talking all morning tomorrow.
future perfect	I will have talked	I will have talked enough by then.
future perfect progressive	I will have been talking	I will have been talking for three hours by the time the meeting is over.

Irregular Verbs

Many irregular verbs (more than 100 in English) do not form the past tense by adding –ed, or –d. Some verbs do not change form at all, or they form the past tense by changing the spelling of the entire word (*stem-changing verbs*). The following table lists the most commonly used irregular verbs.

An Alphabetical List of Irregular Verbs

Simple Form	Simple Past	Past Participle
arise	arose	arisen
be	was, were	been
bear	bore	borne/born
beat	beat	beaten/beat
become	became	become
begin	began	begun
bend	bent	bent
bet	bet	bet*
bid	bid	bid
bind	bound	bound
bite	bit	bitten
bleed	bled	bled
blow	blew	blown

*See page 330.

Simple Form	Simple Past	Past Participle
break	broke	broken
breed	bred	bred
bring	brought	brought
broadcast	broadcast	broadcast
build	built	built
burst	burst	burst
buy	bought	bought
cast	cast	cast
catch	caught	caught
choose	chose	chosen
cling	clung	clung
come	came	come
cost	cost	cost
creep	crept	crept
cut	cut	cut
deal	dealt	dealt
dig	dug	dug
do	did	done
draw	drew	drawn
eat	ate	eaten
fall	fell	fallen
feed	fed	fed
feel	felt	felt
fight	fought	fought
find	found	found
fit	fit	fit*
flee	fled	fled
fling	flung	flung
fly	flew	flown
forbid	forbade	forbidden
forecast	forecast	forecast
forget	forgot	forgotten
forgive	forgave	forgiven
forsake	forsook	forsaken
freeze	froze	frozen
get	got	gotten*
give	gave	given
go	went	gone
grind	ground	ground
grow	grew	grown

Copyright © 2004 by Pearson Education, Inc.

*See page 330.

Simple Form	Simple Past	Past Participle
hang	hung	hung
have	had	had
hear	heard	heard
hide	hid	hidden
hit	hit	hit
hold	held	held
hurt	hurt	hurt
keep	kept	kept
know	knew	known
lay	laid	laid
lead	led	led
leave	left	left
lend	lent	lent
let	let	let
lie	lay	lain
light	lit/lighted	lit/lighted
lose	lost	lost
make	made	made
mean	meant	meant
meet	met	met
mislay	mislaid	mislaid
mistake	mistook	mistaken
pay	paid	paid
put	put	put
quit	quit	quit*
read	read	read
rid	rid	rid
ride	rode	ridden
ring	rang	rung
rise	rose	risen
run	ran	run
say	said	said
see	saw	seen
seek	sought	sought
sell	sold	sold
send	sent	sent
set	set	set
shake	shook	shaken
shed	shed	shed
shine	shone/shined	shone/shined

*See page 330.

Simple Form	Simple Past	Past Participle
shoot	shot	shot
show	showed	shown/showed
shrink	shrank/shrunk	shrunk
shut	shut	shut
sing	sang	sung
sit	sat	sat
sleep	slept	slept
slide	slid	slid
slit	slit	slit
speak	spoke	spoken
speed	sped/speeded	sped/speeded
spend	spent	spent
spin	spun	spun
spit	spit/spat	spit/spat
split	split	split
spread	spread	spread
spring	sprang/sprung	sprung
stand	stood	stood
steal	stole	stolen
stick	stuck	stuck
sting	stung	stung
stink	stank/stunk	stunk
strike	strove	striven
string	struck	struck/stricken
strive	strung	strung
swear	swore	sworn
sweep	swept	swept
swim	swam	swum
swing	swung	swung
take	took	taken
teach	taught	taught
tear	tore	torn
tell	told	told
think	thought	thought
throw	threw	thrown
thrust	thrust	thrust
understand	understood	understood
undertake	undertook	undertaken
upset	upset	upset
wake	woke/waked	woke/waked

Copyright © 2004 by Pearson Education, Inc.

Simple Form	Simple Past	Past Participle
wear	wore	worn
weave	wove	woven
weep	wept	wept
win	won	won
wind	wound	wound
withdraw	withdrew	withdrawn
wring	wrung	wrung
write	wrote	written

*The following are some differences in verb forms between American English and British English.

American	British
bet-bet-bet	*bet-bet-bet* OR *bet-betted-betted*
fit-fit-fit	*fit-fitted-fitted*
get-got-gotten	*get-got-got*
quit-quit-quit	*quit-quitted-quitted*

American: *burn, dream, kneel, lean, leap, learn, smell, spell, spill, spoil are usually regular: burned, dreamed, kneeled, leaned, leaped, etc.*

British: simple past and past participle forms of these verbs can be regular but more commonly end with **-t:** *burnt, dreamt, knelt, leant, leapt, learnt, smelt, spelt, spilt, spoilt.*

Source: Azar, Betty S., *Understanding and Using English Grammar*, Volume A. Third edition. Englewood Cliffs, New Jersey: Prentice Hall Regents. 18–19.

Some irregular verbs do not follow the stem-changing pattern:

Irregular Verbs That Do Not Change Their Form
(All end in -*t* or -*d*)

Present Form	Past Form	Past Participle
bet	bet	bet
cost	cost	cost
cut	cut	cut
fit	fit	fit
hit	hit	hit
hurt	hurt	hurt
quit	quit	quit
spread	spread	spread

The Verb Be

Because the verb *be* is used so often, as a helping verb, linking verb, as well as to form verb tense, it is useful to see how irregular the form is.

To Be (Infinitive form)

	Present Tense		Past Tense	
	Singular	Plural	Singular	Plural
1st person	I **am**	We **are**	I **was**	We **were**
2nd person	You **are**	You **are**	You **were**	You **were**
3rd person	He, she, it, **is**	They **are**	He, she, it **was**	They **were**

▼ PRACTICE 3   Choosing the Correct Verb Form

Supply the past form of the past tense or the participle in the following sentences.

Example: (sing) For her recital, the soprano <u>sang</u> a variety of arias.

1. (go) Yesterday we _____**went**_____ to the beach.

2. (go) All summer we have _____**gone**_____ to beaches on the coast.

3. (ride) We _____**rode**_____ the waves with boogie boards for hours in the morning.

4. (blow) The wind _____**blew**_____ violently all afternoon.

5. (lose) We _____**lost**_____ our umbrella and all of our towels.

6. (leave) We _____**left**_____ the beach after searching up and down the shore for our belongings.

7. (swim) Normally, we have _____**swum**_____ all afternoon during a beach outing.

8. (drive) Yesterday, we _____**drove**_____ home, exhausted and windblown, but ready to return today.

9. (be) Why _____**were**_____ you absent for three weeks?

10. (lie) The book _____**lay**_____ on the desk yesterday.

▼ PRACTICE 4   Using the Past Tense of Regular and Irregular Verbs

Write the past tense of the verbs in parentheses in the following sentences, taken from a student paragraph.

1. When my mother _____**had**_____ (to have) hip surgery, I _____**assumed**_____ (to assume) responsibility for running the household.

Copyright © 2004 by Pearson Education, Inc.

2. I ___**knew**___ (to know) that I ___**could**___ (can) not take care of everything.

3. I ___**enlisted**___ (to enlist) some help.

4. My brother and sister ___**were**___ (to be) very young, so my Aunt Jessie ___**came**___ (to come) every other evening to help babysit.

5. Consequently, I ___**could**___ (can) do laundry and prepare some meals for the following week.

6. My neighbor and my best friend, Celeste, also ___**helped**___ (to help) with food shopping and yard work.

7. After my mother ___**came**___ (to come) home from the hospital, there ___**was**___ (to be) even more to do.

8. So, every Saturday, I ___**paid**___ (to pay) a maid service to come in and clean the house.

9. When my mother finally ___**was**___ (to be) able to get up and around, we ___**went**___ (to go) for a walk.

10. She ___**had**___ (to have) tears in her eyes when she ___**told**___ (to tell) me how proud she ___**was**___ (to be) of how I ___**had**___ ___**handled**___ (to have, to handle) all the responsibilities.

▼ **PRACTICE 5**   **Using the Past Tense of Regular and Irregular Verbs**

Convert the underlined present tense verbs to the past tense. The first sentence has been done for you. This student paragraph was from an essay written by Erin Nelson.

The spooky old houses <u>come</u> (came) to life at night with gruesome

                                                     gave

decorations. With grotesque carved faces, the jack-o'-lanterns <u>give</u> off an

                lined

eerie glow. Tombstones <u>line</u> the sidewalk, like a long narrow graveyard; a

            reached   **flew**

bloody hand <u>reaches</u> out to grab intruders. Bats as black as the night sky <u>fly</u>

in quick circles, darting in the air, and a black cat with razor-sharp fangs
crossed

<u>crosses</u> the path of the unseen, terrified prey. The ghosts and the goblins
sneaked, snuck

<u>sneak</u> around monster-like trees, ready to snatch their next victim.

In the following paragraphs from the same student essay, underline all of the present tense verbs, and convert them to the past tense. The first sentence has been done for you.

The wind begins (began) to whip, and the branches of the trees begin

(began) to sway like the bones of a forgotten skeleton. The fallen dead

whirled   **rolled**

leaves whirl around like a vicious tornado. When the fog rolls in, the eyes

began   **came**   **made**

begin to play tricks. A monster! With the fog comes the mist that makes you

chilled down to the bone.

                        echoed

        Screams echo from all directions. A witch, a vampire, and a ghost

flew   **disappeared**

fly by; consequently, they disappear down the dark damp street. The hairy

        howled   **moaned**   **came**

werewolf howls, and the musty old mummy moans. Next comes Freddy—with

blood dripping from his razorblade fingers.

                        was   **took**

        One night of the year is all it takes to get the heart pounding and the

                              was

blood flowing. To be out on this night is quite a fright.

Additional Practice for Complex Verb Forms
Present Perfect/Past Perfect

How to form the present/past perfect:

Present perfect tense:	*has* or *have* + past participle of the main verb
	Has talked (singular)
	Have talked (plural)
Past perfect tense:	*had* + past participle of the main verb
	Had talked (singular and plural)

When to Use the Present/Past Perfect Tenses

The **present perfect tense** is used to describe an action that started in the past and continues to the present time. It can also be used to describe an action that has recently taken place or an action in which the exact past time is indefinite.

Julia has played with the symphony for five years.

This sentence means that Julia began playing with the orchestra five years ago and is still playing with the symphony today.

Copyright © 2004 by Pearson Education, Inc.

> Asim <u>has traveled</u> to Pakistan several times recently.

This sentence indicates no specific time for the travel mentioned. If the specific time were to be emphasized, the simple past would have been used.

> Asim <u>traveled</u> to Pakistan last December.

The **past perfect tense** is used to describe an action that occurred in the past before another point in time in the past or before another past activity.

> Julia <u>had played</u> with the symphony for five years before she retired.

This sentence means that Julia played in the symphony for five years, and then she retired. All of this activity took place in the past.

▼

PRACTICE 7   Using the Present and Past Perfect Tenses

In the following sentences, circle the correct form of the verb tense: past perfect, present perfect, simple past, or simple present.

1. Elena prefers to wear contact lenses; she (wore, (has worn)) them for several years.

2. Dane (sang, (has sung)) in the chorus of the musical for two years.

3. Yesterday, George ((bought), has bought) a new computer.

4. Susan (was, (has been)) a teacher for 20 years this September.

5. The Governor flew to North Dakota and (has driven, (drove)) miles before he reached Grand Forks.

6. The news commentator announced that the dictator ((fled,) has fled) the country sometime in the last 24 hours.

7. The news commentator also reported that the dictator (fled, (had fled)) the country before the army arrived in the capital.

8. The year David graduated, he was given a new computer; he (planned, (had planned)) for this purchase for four years.

9. Insook says she (found, (has found)) the perfect house.

10. Insook said she (has found, (had found)) the perfect house before the winter weather arrived.

▼ **PRACTICE 8**   **Using the Correct Tense**

In the following paragraph fill in the blanks with the correct form of the present perfect, simple present, or simple past tense.

Since Beatrice arrived in the United States from Colombia, she __has studied__ (to study) at this college for two years. In that time, she __has taken__ (to take) many courses. First, she __studied__ (to study) English, primarily, taking a few mathematics courses to complete her requirements. After her English improved, she __studied__ (to study) many other subjects, such as sociology, computer technology, and education. For several months, she __has tutored__ (to tutor) many students who are new immigrants to this country. Additionally, she __has learned__ (to learn) that she enjoys working with small children. Even though she __studied__ (to study) to be a lawyer in Colombia, she now __plans__ (to plan) to become an elementary school teacher, so that she can continue her work with immigrant children.

Forming the Passive Voice

The **passive voice** is chosen when the actor of the sentence is not important or when the writer wishes to avoid naming the subject.

In the passive voice, the object of an active verb becomes the subject of the passive verb. The form of the verb becomes *be* + **past participle**.

		s	v	o
Active:		Carol tells the story.		

		s	v	o
Passive:		The story was told by Carol.		

Use of the Active Voice Compared with the Passive Voice

In the **active voice** the subject of the sentence does the acting (action verb/transitive verb).

In the **passive voice** the subject is acted upon.

The students finished the project. (subject is *students;* active verb is *finished*)

The project was finished by the students. (subject is *project* [acted upon by the students]; passive verb is *was finished*)

Most writing is done in the active voice for direct, concise expression.

Copyright © 2004 by Pearson Education, Inc.

The following list shows the conversion of the active to the passive for the important verb tenses:

	Active	**Passive**
Present	Carol tells the story.	The story is told by Carol.
Present progressive	Carol is telling the story.	The story is being told by Carol.
Present perfect	Carol has told the story.	The story has been told by Carol.
Simple past	Carol told the story.	The story was told by Carol.
Past progressive	Carol was telling the story.	The story was being told by Carol.
Past perfect	Carol had told the story.	The story had been told by Carol.
Future	Carol will tell the story.	The story will be told by Carol.
Future progressive	Carol will be telling the story.	The story is going to be told by Carol.
Future perfect	Carol will have told the story.	The story will have been told by Carol.

Going to is often used instead of *will*.

▼ **PRACTICE 9**   **Writing Sentences with Active Verbs (Voice)**

The following sentences are written in the passive voice. Rewrite each in the active voice.

1. The car was fixed by the mechanic.

 The mechanic fixed the car.

2. The wedding will be planned by his fiancée and her mother.

 His fiancée and her mother will plan the wedding.

3. The test is given by the instructor.

 The instructor gives the test.

4. The plans for the house had been created by the architect.

 The architect had created the plans for the house.

5. The sermon was delivered by the pastor.

 The pastor delivered the sermon.

6. His new car was polished every day, even when it rained.

He polished his new car every day, even when it rained.

7. Monique's records were misplaced by the Human Resource Department.

The Human Resource Department misplaced Monique's records.

8. The diamond ring was stolen by her envious friend.

Her envious friend stole the diamond ring.

9. The cello was tuned before the concert started.

She tuned the cello before the concert started.

10. The homes in the area were overpriced before the recession.

Before the recession, realtors overpriced the homes in the area.

11. The child's feelings were easily hurt.

Anyone could easily hurt the child's feelings.

▼ PRACTICE 10   Writing Sentences with Passive
                 Verbs (Voice)

The following sentences are written in the active voice. Rewrite each in the passive voice.

1. Josh ate the strawberry shortcake.

The strawberry shortcake was eaten by Josh.

2. Congress voted to increase Social Security payments.

The vote to increase Social Security payments was made by Congress.

3. The doctors isolated the virus causing the disease.

The virus causing the disease was isolated by the doctors.

4. The youngest player won the chess tournament.

The chess tournament was won by the youngest player.

5. The skiers chose the hardest, steepest run.

The hardest, steepest run was chosen by the skiers.

6. He revised the report several times before presenting it to the class.

The report was revised several times before being presented to the class.

Copyright © 2004 by Pearson Education, Inc.

7. Every night when he unloads the dishwasher, he breaks a bowl or a plate.

Every night when the dishwasher is unloaded, a bowl or a plate is broken.

8. The manager overpriced the new shipment of clothes.

The new shipment of clothes was overpriced (by the manager).

9. The new company collected the trash and recycling on Tuesday instead of Wednesday.

Trash and recycling is collected (by the new company) on Tuesday

instead of Wednesday.

10. The family locked the door every day after they had been robbed.

The door was locked every day after the family had been robbed.

▼ **PRACTICE 11   Using the Correct Verb Form and Tense**

Underline all the verbs in the following paragraph. Change the tense of the verb from past to present. Additional changes in the paragraph may be necessary as well.

stands   **try**   **is happening**
Time <u>stood</u> still as I <u>tried</u> <u>to reconcile</u> in my mind what <u>was happening</u>
                    this

in my cheery breakfast nook on that dreary Tuesday morning; a traumatic
              is happening here   **is being changed**
event <u>happened</u> there; consequently, my life <u>has been changed</u> forever.
              had felt
Before this event, I <u>felt</u> snug and secure in my roomy, comfortable two story

home, peacefully nestled on three gently rolling acres where my loyal and in-
                              are
timidating German shepherds <u>were</u> on patrol, in a private neighborhood near

suburban St. Louis. Two young men and their decision <u>to invade</u> my home
are taking
<u>took</u> all of that away from me.

▼ **PRACTICE 12   Using the Correct Verb Form and Tense**

Verb tenses may vary.

In the following paragraph, supply the correct form/tense of the verb in the spaces provided. The first sentence has been done for you. Be careful to use the perfect tenses when appropriate.

Perceptions of a small town all too often <u>are</u> (to be) the same.

Moviemakers __**create/have created**__ (to create) the ideal vision of what

a rural American town should _____**look like**_____ (to look like), and society _____**believes**_____ (to believe) what moviemakers create.

I _____**lived/have lived**_____ (to live) in a large town most of my life; my

experience with small towns only _____**involved**_____ (to involve) driving

through them on vacation. What I _____**saw/have seen**_____ (to see) during my

trips _____**gave/has given**_____ (to give) me the same perception as most of

society. My limited views would soon _____**be**_____ (to be) ex-

panded when my first experience away from home _____**landed**_____ (to

land) me in a small Michigan town, on the U.S.-Canadian border.

Subject-Verb Agreement

Subjects and verbs in the present tense (as well as in the past and future) should agree in number. Thus, singular subjects require verbs with singular endings, and plural subjects require verbs with plural endings. The following sentences illustrate correct subject-verb agreement:

> The *woman* (singular subject) *takes* (singular verb form) a cab.
> The *men* (plural subject) *take* (plural verb form) a cab.

▼ PRACTICE 13   Using Subject-Verb Agreement

In each of the following sentences, choose the correct form of the verb in the parenthesis. First, underline the subject and decide whether it is singular or plural. Next, underline the verb form that correctly agrees with the subject.

Example: He always (carry, carries) a credit card in his wallet.

1. They (work, works) at the factory on the north side of town.

2. The group (walk, walks) in the mall every morning.

3. The senate (vote, votes) on legislation.

4. He (eat, eats) at the diner every Thursday after work.

5. The boy (run, runs) to the schoolyard to play basketball.

6. She (look, looks) like a skilled basketball player.

7. The team (eat, eats) steak and potatoes prior to each game.

8. The band (play, plays) at a local club every Friday.

9. His class (meet, meets) three times per week.

10. People (vote, votes) every four years in the presidential election.

Copyright © 2004 by Pearson Education, Inc.

▼ **PRACTICE 14   Using Subject-Verb Agreement**

Find and correct the errors in subject-verb agreement in the following paragraph. First, underline the subject in each sentence. Next, find the verb and correct those verbs that do not agree with the subject. The first sentence has been done for you.

come
The spooky old <u>houses</u> ~~comes~~ to life at night with gruesome decora-

give
tions. With grotesque carved faces, the <u>jack-o'-lanterns</u> ~~gives~~ off an eerie

glow. Tombstones line the sidewalk; beware of the bloody hands, for they

fly
may grab intruders. <u>Bats</u> as black as the night sky ~~flies~~ around in the air, and

crosses
a black <u>cat</u> with razor-sharp fangs ~~cross~~ the path of terrified prey. The <u>ghosts</u>

sneak
and the <u>goblins</u> ~~sneaks~~ around monster-like trees, ready to grab their next

victim with ease.

Compound Subject-Verb Agreement

In a sentence there may be more than one subject **(compound subject),** and the verb form chosen must agree in tense and number with the subjects.

If the compound subjects are connected by *and,* the verb is usually plural.

> Fredric and Elise *are* working together on the project.

However, if the compound subjects are thought of as a unit, a singular verb is used.

> Macaroni and cheese *is* a favorite dish for children.

If the compound subject is connected with the *either/or, neither/nor, not only/but also,* correlative conjunctions, the verb must agree with the following rules:

If both subjects are singular, the verb is singular.

> Either Fredric or Elise *is* going to turn in the project to the boss.

If both subjects are plural, the verb is plural.

> The violins and cellos *need* to rehearse their parts with the conductor.

If one subject is singular and the other is plural, the verb agrees with the subject closest to the verb.

> My sisters or my friend *plans* all my formal gatherings.

▼ **PRACTICE 15**   **Using Subject-Verb Agreement with Compound Subject**

Circle the correct verb in each sentence.

Example: During the summer, parents and children (look, looks) forward to vacation.

1. At the high school, students and a teacher (work, works) on a project in archeology.

2. The committee and the administrators (plan, plans) the social activities for the year.

3. Both the lack of exercise and eating too much rich food (cause/causes) serious health problems.

4. Whining, begging, and nagging (indicate, indicates) a lack of problem-solving skills.

5. Television and junk food (is, are) a bad diet combination.

6. Peanut butter and jelly (is, are) his favorite sandwich.

7. His mother and father, on the other hand, often (enjoy, enjoys) going out to the show.

8. Not only children but also adults (need, needs) to be aware of the level of violence in the media.

9. My co-workers or my supervisor (are, is) going to advise me.

10. A banana or raisins (make, makes) a high-energy snack.

▼ **PRACTICE 16**   **Using Subject-Verb Agreement with Compound Subject**

In each sentence put two lines under the verb that agrees with the subject.

Example: The adults and children in the family often (selects, <u>select</u>) a Mexican restaurant for dinner.

1. Rice, refried beans, and corn cakes (<u>accompany</u>, accompanies) the serving of enchiladas.

2. Either flour tortillas or fried tortillas (<u>come</u>, comes) with dinner.

3. Flan, fried ice cream, or pastry (<u>is</u>, are) served as dessert.

4. In American restaurants, hot dogs or hamburgers (<u>seem</u>, seems) to be a favorite lunch.

Copyright © 2004 by Pearson Education, Inc.

5. French fries or, in some cases, hash browns (<u>complement</u>, complements) the burgers.

6. Either catsup, mustard, or both (<u>add</u>, adds) to the uniquely American flavor.

7. As a beverage, a soda or a shake (complete, <u>completes</u>) the order.

8. Neither Wendy's nor Burger King (deserve, <u>deserves</u>) the reputation of McDonald's.

9. Often, McDonald's, Wendy's, and Burger King (<u>compete</u>, competes) for business at the same intersection.

10. Enchiladas as well as burgers for dinner (<u>have</u>, has) been known to ruin many diets!

▼ PRACTICE 17   Editing for Subject-Verb Agreement

Edit the following paragraph for subject-verb agreement. (The first sentence has been done for you.) Some sentences may be correct. The following paragraphs are taken from a student essay, "Nuke Nuclear Energy" by Danny Butler.

The question of nuclear energy ~~are~~ (is) a debate that has caused protests and conflicts since its discovery. Nuclear energy ~~have~~ **has** the potential to be a remarkably effective energy source. Using the products of fission (the splitting of atoms to create energy) military experts ~~has~~ **have** used nuclear energy for the manufacturing of defense weapons. Resources such as wood, oil, coal, and other fossil fuels can be preserved with the use of nuclear energy to produce power. Despite the possible benefits to society, nuclear energy ~~are~~ **is** extremely dangerous due to the possibility of explosion causing mass pollution, creation of nuclear weapons, and production of radioactive waste.

▼ PRACTICE 18   Editing for Subject-Verb Agreement

Edit the following paragraph for subject-verb agreement. The first sentence has been done for you.

Several military and political leaders have suggested that nuclear energy can greatly ~~contributes~~ (contribute) to world peace by allowing for countries to have nuclear defense systems. According to this theory, when an aggressive

launches
nation ~~launch~~ a nuclear attack, the opposing nation will always have time to

counterattack, thus creating a stalemate. Weapons of mass destruction

have
created from nuclear energy ~~has~~ the potential to cause such severe damage

that the entire planet could be affected. Scientists estimate that the nuclear

explosions in a major nuclear war could kill 500 million people. But four

billion more people could starve to death in the next century because of

has
nuclear winter. Nuclear energy ~~have~~ the potential to cause irreversible

cause
damage to the Earth. Because this damage could possibly ~~causes~~ the extinc-

Is
tion of all life, nuclear energy ~~are~~ not a safe and practical energy source.

▼ **PRACTICE 19   Editing for Subject-Verb Agreement**

Edit the following (concluding) paragraph for subject-verb agreement. The first sentence has been done for you.

The debate over nuclear energy <u>are</u> (is) sure to be a very important

topic in years to come. Standing up against using nuclear energy can possi-

bly lead to the eventual abolishment of many nuclear weapons as well as the

learn
protection of the environment. Hopefully, we ~~learns~~ from our mistakes and

will not repeat the tragic catastrophes of such accidents as that in Chernobyl.

By finding alternate sources of energy, we can solve the nuclear energy

help
crisis and ~~helps~~ to save the resources for generations to come.

Adjectives   ESL

An **adjective** is a word that modifies (or describes) a noun or pronoun. Although adjectives usually come before the nouns they describe, they can also follow the noun (in the predicate of the sentence).

> The *glistening* ocean sparkled in the sunset.
> The coffee tasted *bitter*.

Adjectives can be **objective** (describing nouns with sensory details) or **subjective** (describing concepts, feelings, ideas in more general terms). Both are useful in good writing and enhance meaning, especially in combination.

Copyright © 2004 by Pearson Education, Inc.

Objective Adjectives	Subjective Adjectives
glowing	beautiful
crashing	harsh
stabbing	painful
twisted	ugly
strident	annoying
tender	loving

▼ **PRACTICE 1   Using Adjectives**

Complete each of the following sentences with an appropriate adjective from the list below. Use each adjective once.

beautiful	painful	young	red	large
brilliant	stuffy	rusted	broken	creative

1. The ____**brilliant**____ star shone in the cold, night sky.

2. The actress was ____**creative**____.

3. Hawks and eagles are ____**large**____ birds of prey.

4. The ____**rusted**____ metal on the rail of the shipwreck began to separate from the hull.

5. My dog had a ____**red**____ rash on his hind legs.

6. The loss of the championship game was very ____**painful**____ after the winning season.

7. The room became warm and ____**stuffy**____ after all the students arrived.

8. The ____**beautiful**____ glowing sunset over the ocean was her favorite view.

9. A ____**broken**____ window was the only clue to the robbery.

10. When the kitten was ____**young**____, he would bounce on the furniture.

▼ **PRACTICE 2   Identifying Adjectives**

Underline the adjectives in the following passage from the student essay by Stephanie Higgs.

1. Thunderstorms the previous night had settled into a steady, rhythmic shower by daylight.

2. I was alone in the house following my <u>predictable</u> routine.

3. Then, I heard the scraping of the <u>vinyl</u> floor trim on the <u>French</u> door against the <u>ceramic</u> tiles.

4. As I rounded the corner, what I saw made fear rise in my throat like <u>green</u> bile forced up from the pit of my stomach.

5. As soon as I saw them, panic increased my <u>heart</u> rate, bringing it to <u>ear-shattering</u> crescendos until I thought I would go deaf or explode.

6. <u>Incapacitating</u> shock and disbelief bordering on denial paralyzed my <u>entire</u> body.

7. I stared at two masked men wielding knives, standing in my <u>breakfast</u> room and heading straight toward me.

8. Walking past the <u>wall</u> phone, in one <u>deft</u> move, they dropped the receiver to the floor and were right in front of me with a <u>cold</u>, <u>steel</u> blade to my throat.

READ
All About It ...

To read the full essay from which these sentences are excerpted, see page 421.

9. While looking into the <u>cold</u>, <u>dark</u> eyes of the one who seemed to be in charge, I heard someone who strangely sounded like me, asking, "What are you here for?"

10. Gripped by the <u>icy</u> fingers of insanity, I heard myself laughing as I was pushed down onto my <u>bedroom</u> floor.

Adverbs ESL

An **adverb** is a word that modifies (describes) a verb or an adjective. Often adverbs end in *–ly*. Another test to identify adverbs is to ask if it answers one of the questions *where, how,* or *when*. Adverbs describe the action of a passage; in some cases they refer to other adverbs to intensify meaning. As with adjectives, the careful use of effective adverbs can improve the style.

Lisa stormed *angrily* up the stairs. (modifies the verb *stormed*)
He was *very* cold. (modifies the adjective *cold*)
The guests were *too* early to dinner. (modifies the adverb *early*)

Commonly Used Adverbs

happily	harshly	quietly	sadly	rudely
softly	perfectly	poorly	politely	slowly
sadly	loudly	quickly	carefully	very

Copyright © 2004 by Pearson Education, Inc.

▼
PRACTICE 1   Using Adverbs

Complete each of the following sentences with an appropriate adverb from the list below. Use each adverb once.

softly	loudly	menacingly	rudely	dangerously
honestly	perfectly	poorly	swiftly	carefully

1. The bird chirped _____**softly**_____.

2. The intruder glared ____**menacingly**____ at the inhabitants.

3. She sang _____**loudly**_____ during the concert.

4. The school bus full of children rocked __**dangerously**__ back and forth.

5. The figure in the drawing was shaped _____**carefully**_____.

6. _____**Honestly**_____, I did not know where I put my keys!

7. The _____**perfectly**_____ phrased melody drifted from the practice room.

8. The crowd jeered _____**rudely**_____ at the referee when he overlooked the foul.

9. _____**Poorly**_____ planned, the ceremony dragged on for hours.

10. The students left the classroom _____**swiftly**_____, before the teacher could assign more homework.

▼
PRACTICE 2   Using Adverbs in a Paragraph

Choose one sentence in the previous exercise as a topic sentence. Then write a ten-sentence descriptive/narrative paragraph using adverbs in each sentence to modify your verbs and adjectives. Do not forget that intensifiers, such as *very*, are also useful adverbs. Underline your adjectives and circle your adverbs. (See Chapters 14 and 15 for descriptive and narrative techniques.) Compare your answers with those of fellow students.

Answers will vary.

_____

_____

_____

_____

_____

_____

_____

_____

_____

Conjunctions

A conjunction is a connecting word. There are three categories of conjunctions discussed in this text: *coordinating conjunctions, subordinating conjunctions,* and *adverbial conjunctions* (also known as conjunctive adverbs).

Coordinating conjunctions (see list below) join two equal words or groups of words. See Chapters 4 and 7 for extensive instruction and practice with these conjunctions.

Coordinating Conjunctions

but	or	yet	for	and	nor	so

Examples

Gloria is sweet, *but* she becomes angry if she is deceived.

The students brought bread, cheese, fruit, *and* chocolate to the picnic.

Subordinating conjunctions connect a dependent clause/idea with an independent clause. See a list of the most commonly used subordinating conjunctions below. Refer to Chapter 9 for a thorough discussion of the use of these conjunctions.

Subordinating Conjunctions

after	if	when
although	since	whenever
as	though	wherever
because	unless	whether
before	until	while

Examples

Before the game was over, several members of the team were injured.

Her test scores improved *because she had begun to get more sleep.*

Adverbial conjunctions are connecting words that transition from one idea to the next, or from one independent clause to another, by adding emphasis or direction. See the following list for the most frequently used adverbial conjunctions. Refer to Chapters 6 and 11 for thorough discussion and practice with the use of these conjunctions.

Copyright © 2004 by Pearson Education, Inc.

Adverbial Conjunctions

accordingly	incidentally	similarly
additionally	indeed	still
also	likewise	then
anyway	meanwhile	thereafter
besides	moreover	thus
certainly	nevertheless	undoubtedly
finally	next	
furthermore	nonetheless	
hence	now	
however	otherwise	

Examples

The winter days dragged in February; *additionally*, blizzards left six feet of snow on the ground.

Nevertheless, the stores began to advertise sandals and summer dresses.

Interjections

Interjections are words that express intense or sudden feelings or reactions. These words are often expressed forcefully, as in *Help!* or *Watch out!* and are followed by exclamation points if they are the entire sentence. If the words are attached to a sentence, they are followed by a comma. (See Chapter 11 regarding introductory words.)

Interjections are rarely used in formal expository writing. They are most often used in narrative or creative writing in which there is realistic dialogue.

Examples

Wait! You forgot your receipt!

Well, now what should I do?

Clauses and Phrases

Independent and Dependent Clauses

A **clause** is a group of related words containing both a subject and a verb. There are two types of clauses: *independent clauses* and *dependent clauses*. **Independent clauses** can stand alone as a complete sentence. A **dependent clause** (or subordinate clause) begins with subordinating words/conjunctions and cannot stand alone as a sentence (see Chapter 9 for more information on dependent clauses).

Examples

We went shopping during the holidays. *Independent clause*
   (subject is *we;* verb is *went*).

although we went shopping during the holidays *Dependent clause*
   (subordinating conjunction is *although;* subject is *we;* verb is *went*)

Carl and Louisa were often late to class. *Independent clause*
   (subject is *Carl and Louisa*; verb is *were*)

because Carl and Louisa were often late to class *Dependent clause*
   subordinating conjunction is *because;* subject is *Carl and Louisa;*
   (verb is *were*)

Phrases

A **phrase** is a group of related words missing a subject, verb, or both subject and verb. Phrases are used in sentences to complete thoughts or add descriptive detail; they may be restrictive or nonrestrictive (See: Additional Punctuation Rules, Interrupters, on page 384.) To avoid problems with ambiguous meaning or errors in punctuation, phrases must be carefully placed next to the noun, verb, or other parts of speech to which the phrase refers.

There are several types of phrases used as modifiers in sentences: *prepositional phrases, participial phrases, gerund phrases, infinitive phrases*, and *absolute phrases*.

Commonly Used Phrases

Prepositional Phrase

Prepositions connect a noun or pronoun to the rest of the sentence, often showing location or time. A **prepositional phrase** contains the preposition (*in, on, over, before, after,* etc.) and its object. (See Additional Practice with Prepositions in the following section, and a list of prepositions on page 356.)

Examples

He waited *for the train.*

The cat prefers to stay *in the house.*

They enjoy going out *for pizza after the football games.*

Participial Phrase

A **participial phrase** is a group of words consisting of a participle and its completing words. All verbs have present participle and past participle forms.

Examples

Staring at the blank computer screen, Martin found himself unable to
   finish his essay. (present participle form)

Interrupted by the demands of her hungry two year old, she could not
   finish reading the paper. (past participle form)

Walking down the hall, he was hit by the door as it flew open at the
   end of class.

Bewildered by the question, the student could not finish the test.

Copyright © 2004 by Pearson Education, Inc.

Gerund Phrase

A **gerund** is the *–ing* form of a verb that functions as a noun in the sentence. A **gerund phrase** includes a gerund and its complete words.

> **Examples**
>
> *Dancing* is her favorite activity. (*Dancing* functions as the subject of the sentence)
>
> *Writing a collection of poems* remains Sophia's secret hobby. (The gerund phrase functions as the subject of the sentence)
>
> Employees will not be paid without *completing the weekly projects.* (The gerund phrase functions as the object of the preposition *without*)

In some cases, the possessive form of a noun or pronoun precedes a gerund:

> **Examples**
>
> The parents were thrilled with *their son's removal of all tattoos.*
>
> *Her dancing in the moonlight* amazed the children.

Infinitive Phrase

An **infinitive phrase** is a group of words consisting of *to* plus a verb and its completing words. An infinitive phrase can function as a noun, adjective, or adverb.

> **Examples**
>
> *To read* is the best way to study grammar. (The infinitive phrase functions as a noun, the subject of the sentence)
>
> Disneyland is one of the best places *to visit while on vacation.* (The infinitive phrase functions as an adjective and modifies the noun *places*)
>
> Her daughter was too nervous *to play the piano in front of an audience.* (The infinitive phrase functions as an adverb, modifying the adjective *nervous*)

Absolute Phrase

An **absolute phrase** is a group of words consisting of a noun or pronoun and a participle (not the regular verb form) plus any other completing words. Absolute phrases modify the entire sentence and cannot be punctuated as a complete sentence.

> **Examples**
>
> *Their project nearly completed,* the painters began to clean their equipment. (notice the past participle *completed* used in the phrase)
>
> The violinist, *her arms and shoulders aching with pain,* practiced long hours every night. (the present participle *aching* is used in this verb phrase)

▼ PRACTICE 1   Identifying Phrases and Clauses

In the blank to the side of each group of words, write **IC** if the group is an independent clause, **DC** if the group of words is a dependent clause, and **P** if the group of words is a phrase. If the group of words is a phrase, identify the type of phrase.

Examples P (prepositional) under the floor.

1. _____IC_____ he was born near Los Angeles, California

2. __P (infinitive)__ to purchase a new car

3. _P (prepositional)_ until the day he died

4. _____DC_____ even if she used the material provided

5. _P (participle)_ hidden in the loft

6. _P (gerund or participle)_ playing badminton

7. _____DC_____ when the long winter finally ends

8. _P (absolute)_ the weather being harsh and changeable

9. _____DC_____ while she sat by the ashes of the fire

10. _P (infinitive)_ to complete the assignment

▼ PRACTICE 2   Writing Sentences with Phrases and Clauses

Convert the dependent clauses and phrases from the previous practice into complete sentences, using correct punctuation. Underline the phrase or dependent clause in the finished sentence. Label the independent clauses as correct.

1. C _____

2. **Answers will vary.** _____

3. _____

4. _____

5. _____

6. _____

7. _____

8. _____

9. _____

10. _____

Copyright © 2004 by Pearson Education, Inc.

▼ PRACTICE 3   Identifying Phrases and Clauses

In the following paragraph from Chapter 20, "Definition," underline phrases once, identifying the type of phrase over the words, and underline the dependent clauses twice. The first sentence has been done for you.

Prep.
Soul music is a combination and merging <u>of gospel and blues</u>, two
Adj.
<u>African American musical styles.</u> <u>While blues praised the worldly desires</u>
Prep.   **Prep.**
<u>of the flesh</u>, gospel extolled the virtues <u>of spiritualism</u>. This opposition
Prep.   **Prep.**
<u>of themes</u> was melded <u>into wide ranging and extremely diverse style</u>,
Adj.   **Adj.**
<u>full of passion, pride, and optimism</u>, <u>mixed with the historical emotion</u>
Prep.
<u>of pain and discrimination</u>.

Misplaced and Dangling Modifiers

Misplaced modifying phrases modify the wrong word in a sentence or are placed so that it is not clear which word is being described.

Example	Incorrect:	The courier delivered the material to the vice president *in the red envelope.*
	Correct:	The courier delivered the material *in the red envelope* to the vice president.

Dangling modifying phrases do not seem to modify anything in the sentence, or they may appear to describe a word that makes no logical sense. Dangling modifiers usually occur at the beginning of the sentence. To correct the sentence, add the correct subject/verb to the phrase, **or** restructure the sentence for accurate meaning.

Example	Incorrect:	*After painting the house,* the furniture was rearranged.
	Correct:	*After painting the house,* we rearranged the furniture.

▼ PRACTICE 4   Correcting Misplaced and Dangling Modifiers

The sentences below have misplaced or dangling modifying phrases. Underline the misplaced/dangling phrases and rewrite the sentences so that the meaning is clear and accurate.

Example: David fed the birds <u>in his robe and slippers</u>.

<u>In his robe and slippers</u>, David fed the birds.

1. The waiter swept the crumbs away from the couple <u>on the tablecloth</u>.

The waiter swept away the crumbs <u>on the tablecloth</u> in front of the

couple.

2. <u>Walking down the hall</u>, the door hit her in the face.

As she <u>walked down the hall</u>, the door hit her in the face.

3. <u>Working on his homework</u>, the dog barked all evening.

<u>Working on his homework</u>, he heard the dog bark all evening.

4. The saleswoman sold the suit to the customer <u>that needed mending</u>.

The saleswoman sold the suit <u>that needed mending</u> to the customer.

5. We enjoyed the performance in the theater <u>which we had paid twenty dollars to see</u>.

In the theater, we enjoyed the <u>twenty dollar</u> performance.

6. <u>Singing in the shower</u>, the cat suddenly dashed across the room, and the dog began to howl.

When he began <u>singing in the shower</u>, the cat suddenly dashed across

the room, and the dog began to howl.

7. The car is in the garage with two cartons of ice cream <u>unlocked</u>.

The <u>unlocked</u> car is in the garage with two cartons of ice cream.

8. <u>Wrapped up in a mummy costume</u>, I enjoyed my son's preparations for Halloween.

I <u>wrapped my son in a mummy costume</u> and enjoyed his preparations

for Halloween.

9. <u>While enjoying the family picnic</u>, the table suddenly fell to the ground.

While we were <u>enjoying the family picnic</u>, the table suddenly fell to the

ground.

10. The teacher gave the students an essay exam <u>which was unprepared</u>.

The teacher gave the <u>unprepared</u> students an essay exam.

Copyright © 2004 by Pearson Education, Inc.

▼ **PRACTICE 5**   Avoiding Dangling and Misplaced Modifiers

In this paragraph by student writer Stephanie Weidermann, combine the following sentences by converting at least one of the sentences to a phrase or clause. Be careful to avoid misplaced or dangling modifiers. When sentence combining, first cross out all repeated words and phrases after they have been stated once and change verb forms if necessary.

> **Example**   A photographer achieves a worthwhile photograph.
> The photographer sets the scene.
> He correctly develops the negative.
> He creatively enlarges the print.

One correct option: (By setting the scene,) (correctly developing the negative,) and (creatively enlarging the print,) a photographer can achieve a worthwhile photograph.

1.1   First, the photographer measures the light that the camera is reading.

1.2   The light is from the scene.

1.3   The photographer uses a gray card.

(Using a gray card,) the photographer measures the light from the

scene that the camera is reading.

2.1   The aperture should be adjusted.

2.2   The meter should be floating in the center of its scale.

2.3   This ensures the picture will not be under or over exposed.

The aperture should be adjusted so that the meter is floating in the

center of its scale, (ensuring the picture will not be under or over exposed.)

3.1   The film is loaded onto a developing reel.

3.2   This is done in complete darkness.

3.3   The film is placed into a series of chemical liquids.

3.4   The liquids develop and fix the negative.

(In complete darkness,) the film is loaded onto a developing reel, then

placed into a series of chemical liquids (which develop and fix the negative).

4.1   Next, the negative is enlarged.

4.2   The enlarging process is achieved by placing the negative into an enlarger.

4.3   This is followed by shining a light through the negative onto paper.

4.4 The paper is resin coated.

> **Next, the negative is enlarged (by placing the negative into an enlarger,)**
>
> **(followed by shining a light through the negative onto paper.)**

5.1 The photographer can create a variety of special effects.

5.2 The photographer manipulates the amount of light.

5.3 The photographer manipulates the amount of time.

> **(By manipulating the amount of light and time,) the photographer**
>
> **can create a variety of special effects.**

6.1 The paper is run through another series of chemical liquid baths.

6.2 The paper is finally allowed to dry.

> **(After being run through another series of liquid baths,) the paper**
>
> **is finally allowed to dry.**

Types of Sentences

There are four basic types of sentences: simple, compound, complex, and compound-complex.

The Simple Sentence

A *simple sentence* contains one independent clause. An independent clause consists of a subject, a verb (or compound subjects or verbs), and sufficient meaning to stand on its own as a complete idea. (See Chapter 3 for a detailed discussion and exercises.)

> **Examples**
> The ship sailed into port.
> A tree fell during the storm.

The Compound Sentence

Compound sentences contain two independent clauses. These independent clauses can be combined using a process called **coordination.** There are three methods of coordination: combining two independent clauses with a comma and a coordinating conjunction, combining two independent clauses with a semicolon, and combining two independent clauses with a semicolon, followed by an adverbial conjunction and comma. (See Chapters 4, 5, and 6 for a detailed discussion and exercises.)

Copyright © 2004 by Pearson Education, Inc.

> ### Examples
>
> The bird landed on the branch, **and** it warbled a beautiful song.
>
> Satellites circle the earth; the Space Shuttle can be considered a satellite.
>
> She intended to turn in the paper on time; **however,** her car broke down on the way to school.

The Complex Sentence

Complex sentences combine an independent clause and a dependent clause using a process called **subordination.** There are two common methods of subordination: adding a dependent clause after an independent clause, and preceding the independent clause with a dependent clause and a comma. (See Chapter 9 for a detailed discussion and exercises.) The dependent clauses are *italicized* in the examples below.

> ### Examples
>
> The students could not enter the building *because the smokers had created a toxic cloud of tobacco smoke in front of the door*.
>
> *If the team wins the game*, the students will cheer the athletes.

The Compound-Complex Sentence

A *compound-complex* sentence combines a complete *compound sentence* with a dependent clause or a complete complex sentence.

> ### Examples
>
> The bird landed on the branch, and it warbled a beautiful song while the cat crouched on the ground below.
>
> If the team wins the game, the students will first cheer the athletes and then they will head into town for pizza and hamburgers.

Additional Practice with Prepositions ESL

Prepositions and Prepositional Phrases

Common Prepositions

about	before	despite	of	to
above	behind	down	off	toward(s)
across	below	during	on	under
after	beneath	for	out	until
against	beside	from	over	up
along	besides	in	since	upon
among	between	into	through	with
around	beyond	like	throughout	within
at	by	near	till	without

> ```
>                      S         V
> (a) The student studies *in the library.*
>                        PREP   O of PREP
>                               (NOUN)
>                   S      V
> (b) We enjoyed the party *at your house.*
>                          PREP    O of PREP
>                                  (NOUN)
>
> (c) We went **to the zoo in the afternoon.**
>                 (place)      (time)
>
> (d) **In the afternoon,** we went to the zoo.
> ```
>
> An important element of English sentences is the prepositional phrase. It consists of a preposition **(PREP)** and its object **(O).** The object of a preposition is a noun or pronoun.
>
> In (a): *in the library* is a prepositional phrase.
>
> In (c): In most English sentences "place" comes before "time."
>
> In (d): Sometimes a prepositional phrase comes at the beginning of a sentence.

▼ **PRACTICE 1**   **Identifying Prepositional Phrases**

Find the subjects (**S**), verbs (**V**), objects (**O**), and prepositional phrases (**PP**) in the following sentences. Underscore the prepositional phrases.

            S V   O   PP

Example: Jack put the letter in the mailbox.

        S   V   PP

1. The children walked to school.

        S   V   O

2. Beethoven wrote nine symphonies.

        S   V   O   PP

3. Mary did her homework at the library.

        S   V   PP

4. Bells originated in Asia.

          S   V   O   PP

5. Chinese printers created the first paper money in the world.

        S V   PP   PP   PP

6. The cat ran up the stairs, into the family room, and over the sofa.

                                         V   S

7. Before Spring arrives in the midwest, there can be many bitter snowstorms
    PP
in March.

      S   V   PP

8. (You) Do not come to class without your textbook, your notebook, your

pen, and your homework.

                  PP   V   S

9. Throughout the community, there are many individuals who would like

to explore new career options.

     S   V   O   PP

10. He found his glasses under the sofa cushions.

Copyright © 2004 by Pearson Education, Inc.

▼ **PRACTICE 2**   **Identifying Prepositional Phrases**

In the following student paragraph by Trevor Cambell, label the subjects (S) and verbs (V), and underline and label the prepositional phrases (PP). The first sentence has been done for you.

    PP   **S**   **V**   **PP**

After World War II, countless GI's returned home with extra money to

                S   **V**   **PP**

spend. Almost overnight, custom shops sprung up in southern California,

       PP   **S** **V**

catering to the Flathead owner. The Flathead-powered Ford was cheap and

                              PP

plentiful, making this motor a prime candidate to customize. Within a few

     S   **V**   **PP**

years, the Ford Flathead V-8 became the popular choice among custom

    S

builders; this power plant, combined with a light-bodied chassis, was

                         PP   **S** **V**

considered a winning combination at the dragstrip. Success is often copied,

               PP

a circumstance which, in turn, further established the Flathead presence.

▼ **PRACTICE 3**   **Writing a Paragraph and Identifying Prepositional Phrases**

Write a ten-sentence paragraph in the space provided. You may use a paragraph you have written for another assignment in this class. (See Chapters 13 through 21 for topics and techniques.) Analyze each sentence for subjects (S), verbs (V), and prepositional phrases (PP).

Answers will vary.

_____

_____

_____

_____

_____

_____

_____

_____

_____

Preposition Combinations   ESL

Here is a list of preposition combinations with adjectives and verbs.

Preposition Combinations with Adjectives and Verbs

A   *be* absent from
accuse of
be accustomed to
be acquainted with
be addicted to
be afraid of
agree with
be angry at, with
be annoyed with
apologize for
apply to, for
approve of
argue with, about
arrive in, at
be associated with
be aware of

B   believe in
blame for
be blessed with
be bored with

C   *be* capable of
care about, for
be cluttered with
be committed to
compare to, with
complain about
be composed of
be concerned about
be connected to
consist of
be content with
contribute to
be convinced of
be coordinated with
count (up)on
cover with
be crowded with

D   decide (up)on
be dedicated to
depend (up)on
be devoted to
be disappointed in, with
be discriminated against
distinguish from
be divorced from
be done with

dream of, about
be dressed in

E   *be* engaged to
be envious of
be equipped with
escape from
excel in
be excited about
excuse for
be exposed to

F   *be* faithful to
be familiar with
feel like
fight for
be filled with
be finished with
be fond of
forget about
forgive for
be friendly to, with
be furnished with

G   *be* grateful to, for
be guilty of

H   hide from
hope for

I   *be* innocent of
insist (up)on
be interested in
be involved in

J   *be* jealous of

K   *be* known for

L   *be* limited to
look forward to

M   *be* made of, from
be married to

O   object to
be opposed to

P   participate in
be patient with
be polite to
pray for

Copyright © 2004 by Pearson Education, Inc.

Preposition Combinations with Adjectives and Verbs *(continued)*

	be prepared for		*be* scared of
	prevent from		stare at
	prohibit from		stop from
	protect from		subscribe to
	be proud of		substitute for
	be provided with		succeed in
	provide with	**T**	take advantage of
R	recover from		take care of
	be related to		*be* terrified of
	be relevant to		thank for
	rely (up)on		*be* tired of, from
	be remembered for	**U**	*be* upset with
	rescue from		*be* used to
	respond to	**V**	vote for
	be responsible for		
S	*be* satisfied with	**W**	*be* worried about

▼ PRACTICE 1   Using Preposition Combinations

Fill in the blanks with the correct preposition combination. The verb has been indicated. Supply the correct form of the verb to *be* (if necessary) and the preposition. The first one has been done for you.

1. Shirley (be absent) <u>was absent from</u> class last week.

2. The students (be accustomed) <u>**were**</u> (not) <u>**accustomed to**</u> writing in a foreign language.

3. The exam (be composed) <u>**is composed of**</u> questions from the text as well as lecture material.

4. Deirdre could not (decide) <u>**decide upon**</u> which classes to take for next semester.

5. Paul and Stephanie (be devoted) <u>**are devoted to**</u> their daughter Lydia.

6. The family (be excited) <u>**is excited about**</u> the upcoming reunion.

7. Ramon could not (forgive) <u>**forgive**</u> Teresa <u>**for**</u> taking his money.

8. The president will (be remembered) <u>**be remembered for**</u> the scandal with the intern.

9. The instructor (be satisfied) **is satisfied with** the progress of her students.

10. Helen (be terrified) **is terrified of** the film *Psycho*.

▼ **PRACTICE 2   Using Preposition Combinations**

Use the given preposition combination correctly in a sentence. Be careful with subject-verb agreement and pronoun-antecedent agreement.

Example: (be relevant to) Your comments <u>are not relevant to</u> the discussion.

1. (be acquainted with) **Answers will vary.**

   _____

2. (be aware of) _____

   _____

3. (believe in) _____

   _____

4. (be concerned about) _____

   _____

5. (depend on) _____

   _____

6. (be disappointed in) _____

   _____

7. (excuse for) _____

   _____

8. (be finished with) _____

   _____

9. (be known for) _____

   _____

10. (respond to) _____

Copyright © 2004 by Pearson Education, Inc.

Articles ESL

Articles are a type of word that introduces a noun and indicates whether it is specific or countable. (Most frequently used articles are *a*, *an*, and *the*.)

Basic Article Usage

I. Using Articles: Generic Nouns

Ø means no article is used.

| **Singular Count Noun** | (a) *A banana* is yellow.* |

A speaker uses generic nouns to make generalizations. A generic noun represents a whole class of things; it is not a specific, real, concrete thing but rather a symbol of a whole group.

| **Plural Count Noun** | (b) Ø *Bananas* are yellow. |

In (a) and (b): The speaker is talking about any banana, all bananas, bananas in general. In (c), the speaker is talking about any and all fruit, fruit in general.

| **Noncount Noun** | (c) Ø *Fruit* is good for you. |

Notice that no article (Ø) is used to make generalizations with plural count nouns and noncount nouns, as in (b) and (c).

II. Using *A* or *Some:* Indefinite Nouns

| **Singular Count Noun** | (d) I ate *a banana*. |

Indefinite nouns are actual things (not symbols), but they are not specifically identified.

| **Plural Count Noun** | (e) I ate *some bananas*. |

In (d): The speaker is not referring to "this banana" or "that banana" or "the banana you gave me." The speaker is simply saying that s/he ate one banana. The listener does not know nor need to know which specific banana was eaten; it was simply one banana out of that whole group of things in this world called bananas.

| **Noncount Noun** | (f) I ate *some fruit*. |

In (e) and (f): *Some* is often used with indefinite plural count nouns and indefinite noncount nouns. In addition to *some*, a speaker might use **two, a few, several, a lot of,** *etc.,* with plural count nouns, or **a little, a lot of,** *etc.,* with noncount nouns.

*Usually ***a/an*** is used with a singular generic count noun:
Examples:
> **A window** *is made of glass.* **A doctor** *heals sick people. Parents must give* **a child** *love.* **A box** *has six sides.* **An apple** *can be red, green, or yellow.*

The is sometimes used with a singular generic count noun (not a plural generic count noun, not a generic noncount noun). Generic ***"the"*** is commonly used with, in particular:
(1) species of animals: ***The whale*** *is the largest mammal on earth.*
> ***The elephant*** *is the largest land mammal.*

(2) inventions: *Who invented* **the telephone? the wheel? the refrigerator? the airplane? The computer** *will play an increasingly large role in all our lives.*
(3) musical instruments: *I'd like to learn to play* **the piano.**
> *Do you play* **the guitar?**

III. Using *The:* Definite Nouns

Singular Count Noun   **(g)** Thank you for *the banana.*

A noun is definite when both the speaker and the listener are thinking about the same specific thing.

Plural Count Noun   **(h)** Thank you for *the bananas.*

In (g): The speaker uses *the* because the listener knows which specific banana the speaker is talking about, i.e., that particular banana which the listener gave to the speaker.

Noncount Noun   **(i)** Thank you for *the fruit.*

Notice that *the* is used with both singular and plural count nouns and with noncount nouns.

General Guidelines for Article Usage

(a) ***The sun*** is bright today. Please hand this book to *the teacher.* Please open *the door.* Jack is in *the kitchen.*	GUIDELINE: Use *the* when you know or assume that your listener is familiar with and thinking about the same specific thing or person you are talking about.
(b) Yesterday I saw *some dogs.* ***The dogs*** were chasing *a cat.* ***The cat*** was chasing *a mouse.* ***The mouse*** ran into *a hole.* ***The hole*** was very small.	GUIDELINE: Use *the* for the second mention of an indefinite noun*; in (b): first mention = *some dogs, a cat, a mouse, a hole* second mention = *the dogs, the cat, the mouse, the hole*
(c) INCORRECT: *The apples are my favorite fruit.* CORRECT: ***Apples*** are my *favorite fruit.*	GUIDELINE: Do not use *the* with a plural count noun (e.g., *apples*) or a noncount noun (e.g., *gold*) when you are making a generalization.
(d) INCORRECT: *The gold is a metal.* CORRECT: ***Gold*** is a metal.	
(e) INCORRECT: *I drove car.* CORRECT: I drove *a car.* I drove *the car.* I drove *that car.* I drove *his car.*	GUIDELINE: Do not use a singular count noun (e.g., *car*) without: (1) an article (*a/an* or *the*); OR (2) *this/that;* OR (3) a possessive pronoun.

*The is not used for the second mention of a generic noun. COMPARE:
  (1) What color is *a banana* (*generic noun*)? *A banana* (*generic noun*) is yellow.
  (2) Tom offered me *a banana* (*indefinite noun*) or an apple. I chose *the banana* (*definite noun*).

▼ **PRACTICE 1**   **Using Articles**

In the following dialogues, determine whether the speakers would use **a/an** or **the**.

1. A: I have ____an____ idea. Let's go on ____a____ picnic Saturday.

B: Okay.

Copyright © 2004 by Pearson Education, Inc.

2. A: Did you have fun at ___the___ picnic yesterday?

B: Sure did. And you?

3. A: You'd better have ___a___ good reason for being late!

B: I do.

4. A: Did you think ___the___ reason Jack gave for being late was believable?

B: Not really.

5. A: Where's my blue shirt?

B: It's in ___the___ washing machine. You'll have to wear ___a___ different

shirt.

6. A: I wish we had ___a___ washing machine.

B: So do I. It would make it a lot easier to do our laundry.

7. A: What happened to your bicycle? ___The___ front wheel is bent.

B: I ran into ___a___ parked car when I swerved to avoid ___the___ big

pothole in the street.

A: Did you damage ___the___ car?

B: A little.

A: What did you do?

B: I left ___a___ note for ___the___ owner of ___the___ car.

A: What did you write on ___the___ note?

B: My name and address. I also wrote ___an___ apology.

8. A: Can you repair my car for me?

B: What's wrong with it?

A: ___The___ radiator has ___a___ leak, and one of ___the___ windshield

wipers doesn't work.

B: Can you show me where ___the___ leak is?

9. A: Have you seen my boots?

B: They're in ___the___ closet in ___the___ front hallway.

▼ **PRACTICE 2** **Using Articles**

Complete the sentences with **a/an**, **the**, or **Ø**. (Ø means no article.)

1. __Ø__ beef is a kind of __Ø__ meat.

2. __The__ beef we had for dinner last night was excellent.

3. Jack is wearing __a__ straw hat today.

4. Jack likes to wear __Ø__ hats.

5. __A__ hat is __an__ article of clothing.

6. __Ø__ hats are __Ø__ articles of clothing.

7. __The__ brown hat on that hook over there belongs to Mark.

8. Everyone has __Ø__ problems in __Ø__ life.

9. My grandfather had __a__ long life.

10. That book is about __the__ life of Helen Keller.

11. Tommy wants to be __an__ engineer when he grows up.

12. The Brooklyn Bridge was designed by __an__ engineer.

13. John Roebling is __the__ name of __the__ engineer who designed the Brooklyn Bridge. He died in 1869 from __an__ infection. He died before __the__ bridge was completed.

14. __Ø__ people wear __Ø__ jewelry to make themselves more attractive.

15. __The__ jewelry Diana is wearing today is beautiful.

16. Mary is wearing __a__ beautiful ring today. It is made of __Ø__ gold and rubies. __The__ gold in her ring was mined in Canada. __The__ rubies came from Burma.

17. One of the first things you need to do when you move to __a__ new city is to find __a__ place to live. Most __Ø__ newspapers carry __Ø__ advertisements (called "want ads") for __the__ apartments that are for rent. If you find __an__ ad for __a__ furnished apartment, __the__ apartment will probably contain __a__ stove and __a__ refrigerator. It will also probably have __Ø__ furniture such as __Ø__ beds, __Ø__ tables, __Ø__ chairs, and maybe __a__ sofa.

Copyright © 2004 by Pearson Education, Inc.

18. My wife and I have recently moved to this city. Since we're going to be here for only __a__ short time, we're renting __a__ furnished apartment. We decided that we didn't want to bring our own furniture with us. __The__ apartment is in __a__ good location, but that's about the only good thing I can say about it. Only one burner on __the__ stove works. __The__ refrigerator is noisy, and __the__ refrigerator door won't stay closed unless we tape it shut. __The__ bed sags in the middle and creaks. All of the rest of __the__ furniture is old and decrepit too. Nevertheless, we're still enjoying living in this city. We may have to look for __Ø__ another apartment, however.

CAPITALIZATION AND NUMBERS

Capitalization

1. Capitalize proper nouns, the names of people, places, and specific products.

> Fredric Chopin
> Sacramento, California
> German class
> Fords

2. Capitalize the days of the week, names of months, and the titles of holidays.

> Saturday, August 28
> Friday the 13th
> Christmas holiday

3. Capitalize the first word of every sentence.

> The dog, cat, and birds all began to bark, growl, and chirp at once.

▼ PRACTICE 1   Correcting Capitalization

Correct the capitalization errors in the following sentences.

1. Every friday, the sociology class met in the eisenhower library.
       F   E   L
[corrections: F (friday), E (eisenhower), L (library)]

2. The rent-a-car company used fords, chevrolets, and buicks.
[corrections: F (fords), C (chevrolets), B (buicks)]

3. Julie's birthday fell on saturday, august 14.
[corrections: S (saturday), A (august)]

4. ludwig van beethoven wrote nine symphonies.
[corrections: L (ludwig), B (beethoven)]

5. In chicago, the sears tower is the tallest skyscraper.
[corrections: C (chicago), S (sears), T (tower)]

6. The vice president of international business incorporated slashed the budget.
[corrections: V (vice), P (president), I (international), B (business), I (incorporated)]

7. Next summer, we hope to camp at yellowstone national park.
[corrections: Y (yellowstone), N (national), P (park)]

8. The lincoln memorial and jefferson memorial are impressive historic sites in washington, d. c.
[corrections: L (lincoln), M (memorial), J (jefferson), M (memorial), W (washington), D C (d. c.)]

9. The categories for general education courses are communication, mathematics, social science, and humanities.

10. Angelina is from bulgaria, but she has lived in the united states for two years.
[corrections: B (bulgaria), U (united), S (states)]

Copyright © 2004 by Pearson Education, Inc.

▼ **PRACTICE 2**   **Correcting Capitalization**

Correct the errors in capitalization in the following paragraph.

        M
       many scientists and researchers claim nuclear energy is desirable as

an energy source because it creates enormous amounts of power from small

         W
resources. while this may be true, there are other costs that outweigh the

          I   **U**   **C**
purely monetary. in 1986, in the ukrainian town of chernobyl, a nuclear

         S
reactor accident killed 31 soviet citizens and caused 100,000 people to be

       A   **E**   **G**
evacuated. a radioactive cloud covered much of northern europe and great

B   **N**
britain. nuclear weapons proliferation is another problem if nuclear energy

        E
production is increased. every year there are reports of nuclear byproducts

        E   **U**   **S**
missing from government inventories. enemies of the united states could use

this material to build nuclear weapons with which to threaten our security.

Numbers

1. Numbers (instead of words) should be used for dates, street addresses, page numbers, telephone numbers, and time stated in terms of A.M. and P.M. (words are used with the phrase "o'clock").

> August 29, 2003
> 321 Walnut St.
> page 34
> 12:00 A.M.
> 922-8000

2. Use numbers for figures above 100 (although some authorities tell us to spell out numbers that can be expressed in one or two words).

> 1,000 pages to be completed
> Twenty-four hours
> $15.99 per ticket
> $20,000 or Twenty thousand dollars

3. Use numbers in a short passage in which several numbers are used.

> On the initial placement test, Julia scored 75, Celia scored 60, and Luis scored 85.

4. Never begin a sentence with a number.

> 25 students filled the course. (Incorrect)
> Twenty-five students filled the course. (Correct)

▼ **PRACTICE 1   Correcting Number Errors**

Correct the number errors in the following sentences.

Forty-five
1. ~~45~~ truck drivers participated in the salary dispute talks.

4272
2. Meldrick lives at ~~forty-two seventy-two~~ Main Street.

$37.00
3. The contestant won ~~thirty-seven dollars~~ playing the lottery.

$8.00
4. Tickets for the tour cost ~~eight dollars~~.

10:30
5. The program began at ~~ten-thirty~~, Eastern Standard Time.

one
6. We should meet for lunch at ~~1:00~~ o'clock; the restaurant will be too **twelve** crowded at ~~12:00~~ o'clock.

Seven hundred and fifty
7. ~~750~~ students dressed in caps and gowns stood nervously in line, waiting to enter the auditorium.

2:30
8. Lisa crept into the house, through the family room window, at ~~two-thirty~~ A.M.

1950's
9. Oil was discovered on his ranch in the ~~nineteen fifties~~.

Two hundred and sixty thousand
10. ~~260,000~~ ancient Chinese artifacts were packed into the crates.

▼ **PRACTICE 2   Correcting Number Errors**

Correct any errors with numbers in the following paragraph.

The Yukon Territory is located in northwestern Canada. The vast area **186,300** (~~one hundred and eighty six thousand, three hundred~~ square miles) is bordered by Alaska and British Columbia. Its mineral wealth and scenic **two** vistas are ~~2~~ of its main attractions. Forests cover about forty percent of the total land area. A subarctic climate prevails with severe winters and hot **9**   **13** summers, and the annual precipitation ranges from ~~nine~~ to ~~thirteen~~ inches.

Copyright © 2004 by Pearson Education, Inc.

ADDITIONAL PUNCTUATION RULES

Basic rules of punctuation and sentence structure are covered in Chapters 4–12, where periods, semicolons, commas, question marks, and exclamation points are discussed.

The Apostrophe

The **apostrophe** is used to indicate contractions or possession/ownership.

1. Some words can be combined, usually in informal writing, by using an apostrophe. This is a contraction.

   > *Isn't* this strange? (is + not)
   > We *couldn't* drive any farther. (could + not)

2. Add an apostrophe plus *s* to a noun to indicate possession.

   > *Anna's* papers were left in the office.

3. To a plural noun ending in *s*, add only an apostrophe to indicate possession.

   > *Parents'* advice often is ignored.

4. For some words, an apostrophe plus *s* should be added to a singular word ending in *s*. This is most often true for a proper name.

   > The *Billings's* recipe book

5. Apostrophe plus *s* can be used to form the plurals of figures, letters, and words being treated as words in isolation. (It is also acceptable to leave out this apostrophe.)

   > Many students are not satisfied with C's.
   > The 1970's were confusing years.
   > Don't use so many "okay's" when you speak.

▼ PRACTICE 1   Correcting Apostrophe Errors

Correct any apostrophe errors in the following sentences. (Some sentences may be correct.)

C   1. The Smiths in this society are very difficult to track down individually.

    2. December 31, 1999, was a very exciting New Year's Eve!

Who's
3. ~~Whose~~ your favorite football team?

You're
4. ~~Your~~ right!

5. If she wasn't on time, she should've been.

Correct the apostrophe errors in the following sentences.

1. What's his name?

2. The 1960's brought about changes in many institutions in our society.

3. In your essays, change the *a lot's* to words such as *many* or *several*.

4. When you change batteries, align the *+'s* and *−'s* correctly.

5. It's not correct to omit necessary apostrophes.

6. Students' questions are usually not frivolous.

7. The man's shoes were made of leather.

8. Mr. Lewis'**'s** donation to the walkathon was very generous.

9. The families' plans for a joint vacation were put on hold.

10. George and Shirley's relationship is very unpredictable.

Correct the apostrophe errors in the following sentences. (Some sentences may be correct.)

's
1. The boss plan was to intimidate his employees.

2. The months' work was destroyed by a computer virus.

3. Luis frequently asked his father-in-law's advice.

4. The ladies' raincoats dripped in the hall closet.

5. The sisters' reunion in San Antonio was a fantastic success.

C **6.** The minivan is theirs; the Porsche is yours.

7. The sun's rays began to filter through the clouds.

C **8.** The shirts for the boys were destroyed in the washing machine.

Copyright © 2004 by Pearson Education, Inc.

C **9.** Louisa is suffering from the terrible twos.

10. The class's spirit improved after their papers were returned.

Quotation Marks

1. Use **quotation marks** to set apart written words or the spoken words in dialogue.

> My mother wrote, "We will be traveling in our mobile home."
>
> Jung said, "I need to change my grammar text."

2. Periods and commas are placed inside the quotation marks, whereas semi-colons and colons are placed outside the quotation marks. If the quoted material is a question, place the question mark inside the quotation marks. However, if the quoted material is part of a longer sentence that asks a question, put the question mark outside the quotation marks.

> "Do the bats fly at night?" he asked.
>
> Did I hear you ask, "Do the bats fly at night?"
>
> He politely remarked, "I would like tea"; however, his wife asked for coffee.
>
> In his short story "Hills Like White Elephants," the male character makes several references to a "simple operation" as a solution to an inconvenient pregnancy, as a way to convince his girlfriend that the operation posed no risk, and as a way to keep his life uncomplicated.

3. Use quotation marks to set apart titles of essays (except for the title of your own essay), articles in magazines, short stories, short poems, songs, and chapter headings.

> The class discussed "My Life on the Streets" for two days.
>
> "Music of the Night" is her favorite song in *Phantom of the Opera*.
>
> The poem "Fire and Ice" by Frost illustrates two types of anger and destruction.
>
> "Letters From a Birmingham Jail" is an essay that effectively illustrates argumentation.

4. Quotation marks or italics can be used to set apart a word, phrase, or letter being discussed.

> Do not follow the conjunction "although" with a comma.
>
> Descriptive words such as "brilliant," "glowing," and "illuminating" support the dominant impression of "light."

5. Uncommon names/nicknames and words used in irony or sarcasm should be surrounded by quotation marks.

"Buzz" McCarthy prefers to shave his head.

His crime of adultery almost made him "public enemy number one."

6. Single quotation marks should be used to indicate a quotation within a quotation.

Tasha said, "My favorite song is 'Layla' performed by Eric Clapton."

▼ PRACTICE 1   Using Quotation Marks

Wherever necessary, add quotation marks to the following sentences. Put a C in front of any correct sentence.

_____ **1.** Two of the best short stories in our anthology are "Hills Like White Elephants" by Hemingway and "Chrysanthcmums" by Steinbeck.

_____ **2.** The new sign reads "Please Do NOT Park on the Driveway!"

_____ **3.** "Brillig" and "slithy toves" are "portmanteau" words created by Lewis Carroll.

_____ **4.** The superintendent reported, "Most students in the city have improved their test scores."

_____ **5.** The *St. Louis Post Dispatch* carries a hysterical column entitled "Your Serve" in the Food section.

_____ **6.** At the end of the visit, the doctor stated firmly, "Cut back on the caffeine and get more exercise!"

___C___ **7.** The Fox Theater is performing *Annie Get Your Gun* this fall.

_____ **8.** "Spring is the most beautiful time of the year in the Midwest!" she exclaimed.

_____ **9.** The songs on "The White Album" by the Beatles are still quite popular.

_____ **10.** Please compare the short stories "Yellow Wallpaper" by Gilman and "Story of an Hour" by Chopin for your final essay in the "Gender Communication" unit.

Copyright © 2004 by Pearson Education, Inc.

▼ **PRACTICE 2**   **Using Quotation Marks**

Add quotation marks as necessary in the following sentences, taken from a student essay on a poem by Robert Frost. Also correct the quotation marks and italics/underlining in the Works Cited material at the end of the exercise.

1. In Robert Frost's poem "After Apple-Picking," the analogy between a person's life and the seasons is well paralleled.

2. The problem is whether to attach to the "After" of the title a finality (death) or a shorter pause that has at its core a continuation.

3. According to Alvan Ryan, "Few of Frost's protagonists are passive victims, nor do they escape into a romantic dream world; we see them at a moment of crisis …" (136).

4. In the first two lines, "the two-pointed ladder's sticking through a tree/ Toward heaven still" (1-2) could be seen as an affirmation of something joyously attained after hard work is finished.

5. Additionally, note that the woodchuck in the poem is only hibernating; he will awaken from this form of "death" in the spring to resume life.

6. As Lawrance Thompson writes, "Most of the Puritans were more bold than talented in their attempts to prove that art is concerned with directing the individual to apprehension; that art is therefore a means to knowledge and truth…" (32).

7. The frustration and weariness sets in because of the emotional let-down occurring when the farmer realizes that the original goal of picking the "ten thousand fruit" (30) was not possible.

8. The lines, "No matter if not bruised or spiked with stubble,/ went surely to the cider-apple heap/ As of not worth" (34-36) indicate that the fruit of our life's work will often be discarded despite how good and noble our intentions may have been.

9. But the farmer says, "I am done with apple-picking now" (6).

10. It is important to note that the line ends with the word "now," not "forever."

Works Cited

Ryan, Alvan S. "Frost and Emerson: Voice and Vision." Critical Essays on Robert Frost. Ed. Phillip Gerber. Boston: G.K. Hall, 1982. 124–37.

Thompson, Lawrance. "Robert Frost's Theory of Poetry." Robert Frost: A Collection of Critical Essays. Ed. James Cox. Englewood Cliffs: Prentice-Hall, 1962. 16–35.

Copyright © 2004 by Pearson Education, Inc.

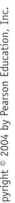

▼ PRACTICE 3　　Correcting Apostrophe and Quotation Mark Errors

Correct the apostrophe and quotation mark errors in the following sentences.

1. My Uncle Silas wrote, "I'll be in St. Louis on Wednesday evening."

2. Mark's car was left in the parking lot overnight.

3. The winning dragster was driven by Bud "The Snake" Collins.

4. The Jones's prize heifer won the Blue Ribbon at the county fair.

5. The short story "Mrs. Garland's Garden" appeared in *Horticulture* magazine.

6. Studying all night for the exam is not what I wanted to do.

7. Slang expressions, such as "dissed" and "way cool," should not be used in formal writing.

8. The 1960's saw the rise of hippies and the counterculture in American society.

9. Marva said, "My favorite saying is P. T. Barnum's 'Never Give a Sucker an Even Break.'"

10. Lawyers' legal advice is usually based on case law.

▼ PRACTICE 4　　Using Correct Punctuation

Add the correct punctuation to the following student paragraph (taken from a student essay "Don't Give Up the Right to Carry" by Tim Schuette).

  P   **B**

  proposition b will allow people twenty-one or older, who have never

been convicted of a felony, the ability to carry a concealed weapon if they

     twelve   **P**

pass a background check and 12 hour handgun safety course. people opposed

 P **B**   **T**

to proposition b believe criminals will have easier access to weapons. the

             P

danger for police officers will greatly increase. people will misuse the guns;

      V **P**   **B**

therefore, the crime rate will increase. vote yes for proposition b because crim-

inals already have guns, police support concealed weapons, and the crime rate

will decrease.

Parentheses

1. **Parentheses** are used to set off specific details giving additional information, explanations, or qualifications of the main idea in a sentence. This would include words, dates, or statements.

> Many students name famous athletes as heroes (Sammy Sosa, Mark McGwire, and Maurice Green, for example).
>
> *Tom Sawyer* (1876) is one of Mark Twain's most enduring works.

2. Notice that the period for the sentence is placed outside the closing parenthesis when the enclosed information occurs at the end of the sentence and is not a complete sentence itself. If the enclosed information is a complete sentence, the period is placed inside the closing parenthesis.

▼ **PRACTICE 1** **Using Parentheses**

Insert parentheses when necessary in the following sentences. The first item has been done for you.

1. Three new students (Marta, Eric, and Elena) were admitted to the class.

2. The rich desserts (Bavarian chocolate cake, chocolate cream pie, and peach melba) were added to the menu.

3. Johann Sebastian Bach (1685–1750) is the featured composer for tonight's concert.

4. The appendix (pp. 300–385) provides additional exercises for the text.

5. They thought she died from the "joy that kills" (Chopin 344).

6. Women were restricted by the social role required of wives in the Victorian period (1837–1901).

7. The media (television, magazines, newspapers, radio, and the Internet) play a crucial role in each election.

8. The four brothers (Thomas, Robert, Steven, and John Corey) have grown up with one sister (Amy).

9. His explanation of the "silent phase" (see page 646) in language learning is very helpful for new teachers.

10. Wolfgang Amadeus Mozart (1756–1791) composed his favorite piano concerto.

Copyright © 2004 by Pearson Education, Inc.

▼ **PRACTICE 2   Using Parentheses**

Insert parentheses when necessary in the following sentences.

1. In *definition*(the rhetorical mode which explains or clarifies meaning)the strategies of narration, description, and comparison/contrast can all be used.

2. So many cities in Europe(Rome, for example)are too rich in artifacts and history to be appreciated on a one-day tour.

3. Many students suffer from "test taking anxiety"(a condition which is much like "performance anxiety" for musicians).

4. Jane Austen's two most well-known novels(*Pride and Prejudice* and *Sense and Sensibility*)have both been made into successful films.

5. He plans to major in herpetology(the study of snakes).

6. The following is an analysis of the Robert Frost poem "After Apple-Picking," from his book of poems *North of Boston*(1914).

7. The paper also cites outside sources and uses MLA documentation format (see Chapter 16 in your text).

8. Denotative language (the use of words in their accepted, dictionary defined sense)is complemented by connotative language(the use of words which have or develop associations and implications apart from their explicit sense).

9. Thus, the heart represents love("She has given her heart to her partner"), empathy("he has a lot of heart"), or courage("She has the heart of a lion"—this is also a metaphor).

10. In this poem, are people or things(animals, etc.)portrayed as good or evil or indifferent?

Brackets

1. **Brackets** are used in quoted material to set apart editorial explanations.

   The tenor sang "Angel of Music" [original version sung by Michael Crawford] for his encore.

2. Brackets are also used to indicate editorial corrections to quoted material. The word "sic" (which means "thus") placed next to an error in quoted

material means that the mistake appeared in the original text and that it is not the writer's error.

> The dean wrote, "All faculty must teach sumer [sic] school."

▼ **PRACTICE 1   Using Brackets**

Insert brackets where necessary in the following sentences.

1. In his instructions, the professor made the following explanation: "Each answer will be wort[sic]25 points."

2. According to Davidson, "He [the Irish hero Cuchulain]became horrible, many shaped, strange, and unrecognizable" (84).

3. The Vice President for Instruction wrote the following memo: "All faculty must fellow[sic]the graduates into the stadium."

4. According to Public Citizen, a watchdog group that does not accept corporate or government support, "Using trade flow data to calculate job loss under NAFTA[The North American Free Trade Agreement]yields net job destruction numbers in the hundreds of thousands" ("Talking Points").

5. "The hypothesis of a killer instinct," according to a commentator summarizing a recent conference on the anthropology of war, is "not so much wrong as irrevelant[sic]"

6. Lori Wallach, director of Public Citizen's Global Trade Watch, stated in a Senate Commerce Committee meeting, "Thus, even if Congress opposes permanent normal trade relations with China, U.S. exporters would obtain the potential benefits China must provide other nations if it enters the WTO [World Trade Organization]while retaining the effective U.S. trade enforcement mechanisms forbidden under the WTO, such as Section 301" ("Testimony").

▼ **PRACTICE 2   Using Parentheses and Brackets**

Add parentheses and brackets where appropriate in the following sentences.

1. World War II(1939–1945)was divided into two main theaters of conflict.

2. The historian wrote, "Napoleon was exiled to the Island of Elbi[sic]"

3. Many famous presidents(Washington, Lincoln, and Roosevelt)are quoted in speeches by political candidates.

4. The coach said, "The Fighting Irish[Notre Dame]will be a tough opponent next week."

5. The student wrote "I threw the paper on the grownd[sic]yesterday."

6. Brian analyzed the performance of the concerto by Dvorak(as performed by Rostropovich).

7. The President stated, "She [the Vice-President] described the financial crisis."

8. The erratic weather(rain, wind, and sudden snow storms) in Missouri makes it difficult to plan outdoor activities.

9. The reporter wrote, "The sailors were innured[sic]in the explosion."

10. These popular shoes(Reebok, Adidas, and Naturalizer)were available in a variety of sizes.

The Dash

1. The dash is used to set apart parenthetical information that needs more emphasis than would be indicated by parentheses.

> Irina's new teacher—a dynamic sociology teacher—helped her to understand American society.

2. Use a dash before a statement that expands on or summarizes the preceding statement (this could also include ironic or humorous comments).

> He studied for the exam for two days—then fell asleep before he finished!

▼ **PRACTICE 1   Using the Dash**

Add dashes to the following sentences.

1. Alexis Jordan and I do not believe this is an exaggeration is a genius.

2. She is running I think in the 10K race.

3. Anna-Lee and Jake have traveled to every state I am not kidding!

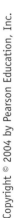Copyright © 2004 by Pearson Education, Inc.

4. Marjo and Marc met Gayle and Larry in Denver, Colorado, for vacation‸ luckily they all like mountains!

5. He turned in the financial report‸and I know this is true‸before the dead-line.

6. Brenda indicated‸in fact she insisted‸that the patient see a specialist.

7. Sergei arrived‸so we were told‸an hour ago.

8. Every morning‸so he says‸Andrew runs 3 miles.

9. Is dinner‸if you can call it that‸ready?

10. Never‸and I mean never‸open an attachment on e-mail!

▼ **PRACTICE 2** **Using the Dash**

Add dashes to the following sentences.

1. The caretakers of society‸mothers, teachers, nurses‸are devalued in modern society.

2. There is only one way to do this‸his way‸so we are forced to agree.

3. If you eat a heavy dinner‸as you usually do when we eat at a restaurant‸ you will be unable to sleep later!

4. Oksana‸the only Russian student in the class‸prefers to study poetry.

5. Please try to remember‸although you never do‸to take the phone with you when you take the car.

6. When Grandpa‸the best story-teller at the family gatherings‸begins to talk about life on the farm, even the grandchildren listen.

7. A first date‸as you well know‸can be a tense experience.

8. Television‸the bane of modern existence‸can hypnotize an entire family.

9. Although the emphasis of the class was composition skills‸prewriting, drafting, and revising‸the class took time every week to debate current events.

10. The elephant and the gorilla‸two of the most powerful animals in the jungle‸are also vegetarian!

The Hyphen

1. Hyphens are used to join descriptive adjectives before a noun.

> a well-written play
> a forty-year-old woman

2. Do not use a hyphen when the descriptive phrase includes an adverb that ends in *–ly*.

> a quickly changed opinion
> a beautifully designed home

3. Check the dictionary for compound words that always require a hyphen.

> compound numbers (twenty-five, fifty-six)
> good-for-nothing
> father-in-law (mother-in-law, and so on)
> President-elect

4. Some words with prefixes use a hyphen; check your dictionary if you are unsure.

> ex-husband
> non-English-speaking
> All-American

5. Use a hyphen to separate syllables at the end of a line. Do not divide a one-syllable word.

> Do not forget to review dependent clauses and subordinate con-junctions.

PRACTICE 1   Using Hyphens

Add hyphens where needed in the following sentences. The first sentence is done for you.

1. My brother-in-law will leave for Florida next week.

2. The seventeen-year-old driver was nervous on the highway.

3. The old violin was a very well-constructed instrument.

Copyright © 2004 by Pearson Education, Inc.

4. The scientist prefers up-to-date results.

5. She stared into the blue-green water.

6. When the cleaners arrived at the house, they did not know how to dis-arm the security system.

7. Every year his tax forms were rapidly completed; then, he waited to see if he would be audited.

8. Hal's ex-wife never saw him again.

9. At age forty-nine her mother discovered that she really wanted to be a gardener rather than a nurse.

10. Even though it was not a particularly well-written essay, the concepts were unusual.

▼ **PRACTICE 2**   **Identifying Hyphen Errors**

Indicate whether hyphens are used correctly in the words below. Write C for correct and I for incorrect.

1. all-inclusive   C

2. re-dress (dress again)   C

3. brilliantly-stated   I

4. pre-1950   C

5. re-dress (set right)   I

6. anti-gun control   C

7. night-shift   I

8. badly-shaken   I

9. cedar-shingles   I

10. kilowatt-hours   C

Underlining or Italics

1. The titles of books, magazines, journals, movies, works of art, television programs, CDs, plays, ships, airplanes, and trains should be underlined.

The Sun Also Rises
Good Housekeeping
The New York Times
The Last Supper
Tapestry
Buffy the Vampire Slayer
Queen Mary

2. There are some exceptions to this rule: the Bible, titles of legal documents (including the U.S. Constitution), and the title of your own essay on your title page.

3. Also, underlining is equivalent to or a symbol for *italics*, which may be used instead of underlining.

▼ **PRACTICE 1**   **Using Underlining and Italics**

In the following Works Cited entries, correct the underlining/italics when necessary and add quotation marks when appropriate. The first item has been done for you.

1. Davidson, Hilda Ellis. Myths and Symbols in Pagan Europe: Early Scandinavian and Celtic Religions. Syracuse, NY: Syracuse UP, 1988.

2. Fox, Robin. "Fatal Attraction: War and Human Nature." The National Interest Winter 1992/93: 11–20.

3. Grossman, Lt. Col. Dave. On Killing: The Psychological Cost of Learning to Kill in War and Society. Boston: Little, Brown, 1995.

4. McCauley, Clark. "Conference Overview." The Anthropology of War. Ed. Jonathan Haas. Cambridge: Cambridge UP, 1990. 1–25.

5. Metraux, Alfred. "Warfare, Cannibalism and Human Trophies." Handbook of South American Indians. Ed. Julian H. Steward. Vol. 5. New York: Cooper Square, 1963. 383–409.

6. Mitchell, Timothy. Colonizing Egypt. Berkeley: U of California P, 1991.

7. Sagan, Eli. Cannibalism: Human Aggression and Cultural Form. New York: Harper and Row, 1974.

8. Stoessinger, John G. Why Nations Go to War. New York: St. Martin's, 1993.

9. Sun Tzu. The Art of War. Trans. Samuel B. Griffith. London: Oxford UP, 1971.

Copyright © 2004 by Pearson Education, Inc.

10. Van Creveld, Martin. <u>The Transformation of War</u>. New York: Free Press, 1991.

▼ **PRACTICE 2**   **Using the Dash, Hyphen, and Underlining**

Add dashes, hyphens, and underlining where needed in the following sentences. Some sentences may be correct.

1. The fifteen-year-old cat sat on top of the television most of the day and night.

C 2. In the event of a nuclear accident, it is important to listen for broadcasts about emergency procedures.

3. Jack Nicklaus ‸ the greatest golfer of all times ‸ is also a successful golf course designer.

4. Singer Bob Dylan wrote a novel titled <u>Tarantula</u>.

5. Her son-in-law always dropped by on Saturday to mow the lawn.

6. Sela baked four dozen cookies for her younger sister's camping trip ‸ then it rained!

7. <u>Dawson's Creek</u> was a very popular television program for younger adults.

8. Jim Thorpe was the first All-American of Native American extraction.

9. The long jump winner at the Senior Olympics was seventy-two years old.

10. Jose's new wrestling coach ‸ a woman ‸ competed for four years at Dellwood College.

Interrupters: Restrictive and Nonrestrictive Clauses and Phrases (Modifiers)

1. Sentences may be interrupted by clauses or phrases that clarify or provide additional meaning. These clauses usually begin with the relative pronouns *who, whom, which,* or *that*. These are also known as **restrictive and nonrestrictive clauses/phrases**.

> They did not know the man *who was speaking.*
> Their dog, *which was barking all night,* annoyed the neighbors.

2. **Restrictive clauses** are essential to identify nouns or to complete the meaning of the sentence. These clauses simply follow the nouns or ideas they are modifying. No commas are used to set off restrictive clauses.

> **clause**
> In the line, the young woman *who was wearing a red bandana and hoop earrings* needed a ticket. (This relative clause is essential to identify which woman needed a ticket)
> **phrase**
> The film *showing at the Rialto* is very provocative. (This descriptive phrase is necessary to identify which film/theater is under discussion)

3. **Nonrestrictive clauses/phrases** are not essential to complete the meaning of the sentence. You can remove them from the sentence, and the basic meaning of the sentence will remain clear. Because they are nonessential, these phrases or clauses are always set off by commas.

> **clause**
> Linda and Burt, *who just returned from Alaska,* would go on another vacation tomorrow. (This relative clause is not essential because it just adds interesting details to the sentence; without it, the meaning of the sentence is still clear)
> **phrase**
> The cockatiels, *chirping loudly to the music of the nearby television,* should live for up to twenty years. (This verb phrase is nonessential, supplying interesting details but not essential information)

4. Most clauses beginning with *that* are not set off with commas.

> Where is the report *that he left on the the desk this morning*?

▼ **PRACTICE 1**   **Punctuate Restrictive and Nonrestrictive Clauses and Phrases**

Punctuate the phrases or clauses in the following sentences correctly, putting commas only around nonessential phrases and clauses. Some sentences may be correct.

C 1. A person who insists on piling papers on any available space can be difficult to live with.

2. Mrs. Collins,who once dreamed of being an anthropologist,now works at the local bookstore.

3. The Alamo,the site of the famous battle,is a popular tourist attraction in San Antonio.

4. Calculus 101,which is required for many majors,is a very demanding course for most college freshmen.

5. He reminds me of my son,who always enjoys a spirited discussion of film. (The answer differs, depending on the number of sons!)

Copyright © 2004 by Pearson Education, Inc.

6. Asim, who took Composition 102 last semester, passed the course easily even though English is not his first language.

C 7. The storm racing up the eastern seaboard threatened South Carolina with dangerous winds.

8. The class, nodding and yawning, woke up quickly when the teacher announced a pop-quiz.

9. Fariba, who is from Iran, enjoyed meeting Svetlana, who is from Bulgaria.

C 10. Pet dogs that run away at any opportunity should be fenced.

▼ **PRACTICE 2**   **Punctuating Restrictive and Nonrestrictive Clauses and Phrases**

Create a sentence including the phrase or clause given. Determine whether the phrase or clause is restrictive or nonrestrictive in your sentence; then, punctuate the sentence correctly. The first sentence has been done for you.

1. who ran up the stairs

    The young man who ran up the stairs had just finished his final exam.

2. crying in the corner

    Answers will vary. _____

3. which he had not known

    _____

4. that he detested

    _____

5. singing in the shower

    _____

6. wearing a purple coat

    _____

7. which creaked and moaned

    _____

8. who remained silent

    _____

9. howling in the dark

_____

10. a difficult problem

_____

▼ **PRACTICE 3** **Punctuating Restrictive and Nonrestrictive Clauses and Phrases**

Combine the following sentences, inserting phrases and clauses when necessary and punctuating correctly. Omit any repeated words or phrases. The first group of sentences has been done for you.

1.1 Being a freshman can be a dreadful experience.

1.2 Freshmen are entering new surroundings.

1.3 Freshmen are harassed by upperclassmen.

1.4 Freshmen have four long years ahead of them.

Freshmen, who enter new surroundings, can have a dreadful

experience, being harassed by upperclassmen, and facing four long

years ahead of them.

2.1 The new suburban vans are becoming bigger every year.

2.2 The vans look like off-road vehicles with glandular problems.

Answers will vary.

_____

_____

3.1 There is extra roominess inside the vans.

3.2 The roominess is great for large families.

3.3 The roominess is great for hauling Little League teams.

3.4 The roominess is great for traveling with lots of luggage.

Answers will vary.

_____

_____

4.1 However, the larger vehicles are hard to handle.

4.2 Their greater bumper height makes extra weight.

Copyright © 2004 by Pearson Education, Inc.

4.3 The extra weight makes for more damage to regular-sized cars.

4.4 The damage results when accidents occur.

Answers will vary.

_____

_____

_____

5.1 These monster-vans are proliferating.

5.2 This proliferation will surely cause insurance rates to rise.

5.3 The rates will rise in the near future.

Answers will vary.

_____

_____

_____

6.1 Higher insurance rates will affect all drivers.

6.2 The impact will be negative.

6.3 Suburban minivan manufacturers should begin to study ways to counteract this problem.

Answers will vary.

_____

_____

_____

WORDS AND MEANING — ESL

Commonly Misspelled Words

The following is a list of words that are difficult to spell:

across	grammar	possible
address	height	prefer
answer	illegal	prejudice
argument	immediately	privilege
athlete	important	probably
beginning	integration	psychology
behavior	intelligent	pursue
calendar	interest	reference
career	interfere	rhythm
conscience	jewelry	ridiculous
crowded	judgment	separate
definite	knowledge	similar
describe	maintain	since
desperate	mathematics	speech
different	meant	strength
disappoint	necessary	success
disapprove	nervous	surprise
doesn't	occasion	taught
eighth	opinion	temperature
environment	particular	thorough
embarrass	optimist	thought
exaggerate	perform	tired
familiar	perhaps	until
finally	personnel	weight
government	possess	written

▼ PRACTICE 1   Identifying Correctly Spelled Words

Circle the correctly spelled word in each of the following pairs.

1. arguement   (argument)

2. seperate   (separate)

3. (judgment)   judgement

4. privelege   (privilege)

5. writen   (written)

6. jewelery   (jewelry)

7. sucess   (success)

8. desparate   (desperate)

9. (occasion)   ocasion

10. embarass   (embarrass)

Copyright © 2004 by Pearson Education, Inc.

▼ **PRACTICE 2**   **Identifying Correctly Spelled Words**

Circle the correctly spelled word in each of the following pairs.

1. (weight) wieght

2. untill (until)

3. (thought) thot

4. (thorough) thorugh

5. rhithem (rhythm)

6. preform (perform)

7. mathmatics (mathematics)

8. grammer (grammar)

9. goverment (government)

10. (optimist) optomist

▼ **PRACTICE 3**   **Correcting Misspelled Words**

Cross out any misspelled words and rewrite them correctly.

answered   **behavior**
1. He ~~ansered~~ the questions about his odd ~~behaviour~~.

              pursue career
2. David wants to ~~pursu~~ a ~~carer~~ in computer science.

                                          conscience
3. The student struggled with a troubled ~~consience~~.

        exaggerate   height   **ridiculous**
4. Don't ~~exagerate~~ your ~~hieght~~ by wearing those ~~ridiculus~~ shoes!
    Grammar
5. ~~Grammer~~ and spelling problems make the writer look uneducated.

              disapproved
6. The children ~~disaproved~~ when their parents began to dance.

              surprising   **mathematics**
7. He had a ~~suprising~~ knowledge of ~~mathmatics~~.

                          opinion   particularly
8. On one occasion, Beth's ~~opinon~~ was ~~paticulary~~ essential.
          rhythm
9. The ~~rhithem~~ of Maya Angelou's speech enhances the beauty of her poetry.

              tired thought   **weight**
10. He was so ~~tird~~ he ~~thot~~ that the ~~weiht~~ of his eyelids was overwhelming.

Words That Sound Alike

Many words in English are pronounced alike but are spelled very differently. These words need special study or memorization. The following list includes word pairs that pose problems for all writers.

Words	Definition	Example
aural/oral		
aural	having to do with hearing	The doctor said that he needs testing for *aural* skills.
oral	having to do with speech/the mouth	He had to give an *oral* presentation.

buy/by

buy (verb)	to purchase	They *buy* shoes whenever there is a sale.
by (preposition)	past; near; not later than	The dog sits *by* the door.

capital/capitol

capital (adjective)	fatal; major	The class debated *capital* punishment. The college is making *capital* improvements.
capital (noun)	money; leading city	He invested his *capital* in the stock market. Sacramento is the *capital* of California.
capitol (noun)	a legislative building	The *capitol* building in Washington D.C. is often visited by tourists.

complement/compliment

complement (noun)	something that adds to or completes	The drapery *complements* the furniture.
compliment (verb)	to express praise or admiration	He rarely gives *compliments*.

passed/past

passed (verb)	to move ahead	The jeep *passed* the car on the highway.
past (noun)	time before present	The *past* haunted him.
past (preposition)	beyond	The boys ran *past* the graveyard.
past (adjective)	not current	The storms were dangerous this *past* year.

plain/plane

plain (adjective)	clear; ordinary	The letter lay on the table in *plain* sight.
plain (noun)	flat land with few trees	Early settlers lived in sod homes on the *plains*.
plane	flat/level surface; aircraft; degree of development	As part of her geometry assignment she was told to plot a line through a *plane*. He was afraid of *planes*. They talk on different *planes*.

presence/presents

presence	being present; a person's way of behavior	Her *presence* calmed the child. The president has a hypnotic *presence*.

Copyright © 2004 by Pearson Education, Inc.

Presents	gifts	Piles of *presents* were stacked under the Christmas tree.

principal/principle

principal (adjective)	main; most important	The *principal* idea is truth. The *principal* violinist led the orchestra.
principal (noun)	the head administrator of a public elementary or high school; amount of money	The *principal* is rarely popular. The *principal* earns interest in the account.
principle (noun)	a comprehensive and fundamental law, doctrine; a primary source; an ingredient that exhibits or imports a characteristic quality	Faith is a complex *principle*.

rain/reign/rein

rain	water falling to earth from clouds	The *rain* ended the drought.
reign	the time a king or queen rules	The *reign* of Queen Elizabeth II of England has been controversial.
rein	a strap attached to the bridle, used by the rider to control a horse	The young rider grabbed the *reins* in fear.

sight/site/cite

sight	ability to see; a view	Her *sight* was excellent. The pep assembly was a confusing *sight*.
site	a location	They visited the *site* of their new home.
cite	to quote as an expert in research	Always *cite* any outside sources used in your writing.

to/too/two

to (preposition)	toward a given direction	The students ran *to* class.
too (adverb)	very; also	The sale was *too* tempting. My friend bought a dress and shoes, *too*.
two	the number 2	He needs *two* cups of coffee in the morning.

waist/waste

waist	the middle of the body and the part of clothing that covers this area	The *waist* of the suit fits too snugly.

| waste (verb) | careless use | Don't *waste* your time in class. |
| waste (noun) | objects/concepts that are not used and discarded | Often, *waste* can be recycled. |

weather/whether

| weather (noun) | conditions of the atmosphere | The *weather* in the midwest changes hourly. |
| whether (conjunction) | if this were the case | He does not know *whether* or not he will pass. |

whole/hole

| whole | all; complete | She read the *whole* novel in one day. |
| hole | an opening | The mouse came through the *hole* in the wall. |

write/right/rite

write	to convey ideas using words; to create	The students will *write* several essays.
right	correct	She enjoys being *right!*
	conforming to morality, justice, or law	We all know the *right* thing to do.
	close to a conservative position	The president's position is shifting to the *right*.
rite	ritual; repeated ceremonial action	Getting a driver's license at age 16 is a *rite* of passage for teenagers in our society.

▼ **PRACTICE 1   Frequently Confused Words**

Underline the correct sound-alike word in the parentheses for the sentence's meaning.

1. The students were nervous because this was their first (aural/<u>oral</u>) exam.

2. The (<u>capital</u>/capitol) of Missouri is Jefferson City.

3. The school's (principle/<u>principal</u>) left for a week to attend an educational seminar.

4. The guests brought many (<u>presents</u>/presence) to the baby shower.

5. The dessert was rather (plane/<u>plain</u>) for such a fancy party.

6. The taxi drove (<u>past</u>/passed) the address where it was supposed to have stopped.

Copyright © 2004 by Pearson Education, Inc.

7. (To/<u>Too</u>) many travelers often cause congestion at airports over Thanksgiving.

8. The belt was too small for my (<u>waist</u>/waste).

9. The game would begin (<u>whether</u>/weather) or not all the team members arrived on time.

10. Because his mother was watching, Jeremy ate the (<u>whole</u>/hole) plate of spinach.

▼ **PRACTICE 2**   **Frequently Confused Words**

Underline the correct sound-alike words in the following sentences.

1. We should (<u>buy</u>/by) a new car before the old one falls completely apart.

2. His uncle cannot accept a (<u>compliment</u>/complement).

3. Students need to learn how to (site/<u>cite</u>) sources used in research.

4. Linda leads the horse while holding the (<u>reins</u>/reigns).

5. Natalie is a dramatic (presents/<u>presence</u>) when she enters a room.

6. Getting a driver's license is a (right/<u>rite</u>) of passage in the United States.

7. She jogs (<u>two</u>/to) miles before work every day.

8. James is the (<u>principal</u>/principle) cellist of the local symphony orchestra.

9. The young couple does not have much (<u>capital</u>/capitol) to invest.

10. The runner (<u>passed</u>/past) the walkers on the track.

▼ **PRACTICE 3**   **Frequently Confused Words**

Write a sentence using each of the following words correctly.

1. aural: **Answers will vary.** _____

2. oral: _____

3. compliment: _____

4. complement: _____

5. passed: _____

6. past: _____

7. plain: _____

8. plane: _____

9. rain: _____

10. reign: _____

11. rein: _____

12. too: _____

13. two: _____

14. to: _____

15. weather: _____

16. whether: _____

17. whole: _____

18. hole: _____

19. write: _____

20. right: _____

21. rite: _____

Contractions That Sound Like Other Words

Another category of words which sound alike but are spelled differently are **contractions**. The following words are frequently punctuated/spelled incorrectly.

Contraction it's/its	Definition	Example
it's	contraction: it is	*It's* going to rain.
its	belonging to it	*Its* wings were broken.
they're/their/there		
they're	contraction: they are	*They're* ready for any adventure.
their	belonging to them	*Their* pets run their home.
there	at that place	The library is over *there*, not here.
we're/were/where		
we're	contraction: we are	*We're* going to the beach for vacation.

Copyright © 2004 by Pearson Education, Inc.

were	verb/past tense of *are*	We *were* ready for a week.
where	in which location?	*Where* is the map?
who's/whose		
who's	contraction: who is	*Who's* going to the party?
whose	belonging to whom?	*Whose* socks are on the sofa?
you're/your		
you're	contraction: you are	*You're* in the way.
your	belonging to you	*Your* gift is in the mail.

 PRACTICE 1   Contractions That Sound Like Other Words

Underline the correct word in the parentheses for the meaning of the sentence.

1. (You're/<u>Your</u>) package was sent yesterday by overnight mail.

2. (<u>It's</u>/Its) in (they're/<u>their</u>/there) best interest to listen to the supervisor.

3. Do you know (<u>whose</u>/who's) socks these are?

4. I forgot where (were/<u>we're</u>) going this afternoon.

5. (Whose/<u>Who's</u>) going to the ice cream shop after dinner?

6. Are you certain that (<u>you're</u>/your) ready to take the driving test?

7. (Their/<u>There</u>/They're) is a trail that (their/there/<u>they're</u>) supposed to walk.

8. Exactly (we're/were/<u>where</u>) did you think the restaurant was located?

9. (It's/<u>Its</u>) engine overheated in the hot, arid Nevada desert.

10. The leaves (we're/<u>were</u>/where) turning colors as autumn approached.

 PRACTICE 2   Contractions

Underline the correct word in the parentheses.

1. (<u>Your</u>/You're) luck is about to change.

2. He isn't sure (<u>whose</u>/who's) book is under the desk.

3. (<u>Where</u>/Were) did you expect to find happiness?

4. Getting from here to (their/<u>there</u>) is not as easy as it seems.

5. The cat howled for (it's/<u>its</u>) dinner every night at five o'clock.

6. (<u>Were</u>/Where) (<u>your</u>/you're) notes on the computer?

7. (<u>Who's</u>/Whose) leaving early for the concert?

8. (<u>There</u>/They're) are no tickets left!

9. We (<u>were</u>/where) going to camp out overnight to get good seats.

10. (<u>It's</u>/Its) not a good idea to wait until the last minute to start an essay.

Words That Sound or Look Almost Alike

The following words may not be spelled exactly alike. However, they sound alike and are often confused.

Words	Definition	Example
accept/except		
accept (verb)	to acknowledge as true; to receive	She *accepted* his explanation. They *accepted* the wedding gifts.
except	other than	All of the assignments *except* one were easy.
advice/advise		
advice (noun)	wise suggestions about solutions to a problem	He never listens to *advice*.
advise (verb)	to make suggestions; to give advice	The counselor *advises* the confused freshmen.
affect/effect		
affect (verb)	to influence	The weather will *affect* your mood.
effect (noun)	end product; result	The *effect* of the accident was obvious for years.
breath/breathe		
breath (noun)	air inhaled or exhaled by living creatures	The swimmer held his *breath*.
breathe (verb)	to exhale or inhale	The cat *breathes* silently.
choose/chose		
choose (verb, present tense)	pick/select	They could not *choose* a restaurant.
chose (past tense)	picked/selected	They *chose* to order pizza.
conscience/conscious		
conscience	thought process acknowledging right and wrong	He has no *conscience*.
conscious	aware of being/ existence; thinking	The students were not *conscious* after lunch.

Copyright © 2004 by Pearson Education, Inc.

Words	Definition	Example
council/consul/counsel		
council (noun)	group which meets/ plans/governs	The city *council* meets each month.
consul (noun)	government official in foreign service	The German *consul* met with the President.
counsel (verb)	to advise	The department chair *counseled* the frustrated student.
desert/dessert		
desert (noun)	dry, barren land	The sunsets on the *desert* are spectacular.
desert (verb)	to leave alone/abandon	His friends *deserted* him.
dessert (noun)	last dish of a meal; often sweet	They decided to avoid sweet, fat *desserts.*
diner/dinner		
diner (noun)	a long narrow type of restaurant with counters and booths; a person who is eating	At the *diner,* they have an old juke box. The *diners* enjoy listening to oldies from the juke box.
dinner	the large, important meal of the day! (mid-day or evening)	The fried chicken is for *dinner.*
emigrate/immigrate		
emigrate	to leave a country	They *emigrated* from China.
immigrate	to enter a new country	*Immigration* is very complex.
farther/further		
farther (physically)	greater distance	The sprinter ran *farther* than he had to.
further	to advance an ideal/ goal/cause; greater distance (mentally)	The protesters *further* the cause of equality. Most arguments can be *further* developed.
loose/lose		
loose	not tight	*Loose* fitting clothing has been in style recently.
lose (verb)	to misplace; to be unable to find; to fail to win	I always *lose* my earrings. He *lost* the tennis match.
personal/personnel		
personal	pertaining to the individual; private concerns	*Personal* information should remain confidential.
personnel	employees	*Personnel* should be aware of their benefits.

Words	Definition	Example
quiet/quit/quite		
quiet	little noise; peaceful	The class is too *quiet*.
quit	to stop suddenly, to give up	The employee *quit* suddenly.
quite	definitely	You were *quite* right.
special/especially		
special (adjective)	unique	Their anniversary was a *special* event.
especially (adverb)	even more; very	Final exams can be *especially* difficult.
than/then		
than	word to make comparison	Sale prices are better *than* original prices.
then	at that time	First they studied; *then*, they took the exam.
thorough/though		
thorough	detailed, complete, accurate	Social attitudes changed after several *thorough* studies were made.
though (conjunction)	despite	*Though* the trees are changing colors, the temperature is warm.
through/threw		
through	in one side and out the other	The ball crashed *through* the window.
threw (verb)	to throw/past tense	The president *threw* the first pitch.

Copyright © 2004 by Pearson Education, Inc.

▼ **PRACTICE 1   Words That Sound or Look Almost Alike**

Underline the correct word in parentheses for the meaning of the sentence.

1. After the race, the swimmer was short of (breathe/breath).

2. The county (council/consul/counsel) met shortly after the disaster occurred.

3. The members of the symphony orchestra ate (diner/dinner) at the (diner/dinner).

4. I need to (loose/lose) weight before my next physical exam.

5. Shanika ran (further/farther) than her brother Latrelle.

6. The Surf Shop clerk didn't (except/accept) the shipment of dogsleds.

7. The library was (quiet/quit/quite) (quiet/quit/quite).

8. The officer's talk about drugs had quite an (affect/effect) on the seventh grade class.

9. The (personal/personnel) office's task was to evaluate all employees.

10. In the (desert/dessert), nuts and dates often are eaten for (desert/dessert).

▼

| PRACTICE 2 | Words That Sound or Look Almost Alike |

Write a sentence for each of the following words, demonstrating the difference in meaning from similar words.

1. accept: **Answers will vary.** _____

2. except: _____

3. advice: _____

4. advise: _____

5. conscience: _____

6. conscious: _____

7. loose: _____

8. lose: _____

9. thorough: _____

10. though: _____

Confusing Verbs That Sound Alike: Lie/Lay; Rise/Raise; Sit/Set

These six verbs are often confused. In order to understand how to use them correctly, it is important to understand the difference between *reflexive verbs* which *do not* take an object (the verb needs no noun to complete the meaning of the sentence), and *transitive verbs* which *do* take an object. *Lie, rise,* and *sit* are reflexive; *lay, raise,* and *set* are transitive.

Lie, Rise, Sit

Meaning	Present	Present Participle	Past	Past Participle
lie (to rest or recline)	lie	lying	lay	has/have lain
rise (to move upward)	rise	rising	rose	has/have risen

Meaning	Present	Present Participle	Past	Past Participle
sit (to move body into sitting position)	sit	sitting	sat	has/have sat

The family dog loves *to lie* by the front door.

The bread dough *rises* well on the warm kitchen counter.

She *sits* in front of a computer for eight hours every day.

Reflexive verbs are often followed by a prepositional phrase, not a stand-alone noun.

Lay, Raise, Set

Meaning	Present	Present Participle	Past	Past Participle
lay (to put an object down)	lay	laying	laid	has/have laid
raise (to lift or move something up)	raise	raising	raised	has/have raised
set (to carefully place something)	set	setting	set	has/have set

She *lay* the flowers carefully on the table.

Please *raise* the window shades.

She *sets* a lovely table.

The object (underlined) is necessary to complete the meaning of these sentences.

▼ **PRACTICE 1   Using Lie/Lay, Rise/Raise, Sit/Set**

Fill in the blanks with the correct form of the above verbs.

1. The book has __lain__ (lie/lay) out in the rain all day.

2. Steam is __rising__ (raise/rise) from the hot pavement.

3. He __laid__ (lie/lay) the knife carefully on the counter.

4. __Set__ (sit/set) the boxes down before you hurt yourself!

5. She is feeling ill suddenly, so she is __lying__ (lie/lay) down in the guest room.

6. He had to move because the landlord __raised__ (raise/rise) the rent.

7. Don't __sit__ (sit/set) on those chairs!

8. His clothes are __lying__ (lay/lie) all over the room.

Copyright © 2004 by Pearson Education, Inc.

9. <u>Rising</u> (Rise/Raise) in unison, the students left the classroom.

10. They are <u>**setting**</u> (sit/set) the chairs in the park for the picnic.

▼
PRACTICE 2   Using Lie/Lay, Rise/Raise, Sit/Set

Write your own sentences, using each verb correctly.

1. Lie/Lay

Answers will vary.

_____

2. Rise/Raise

_____

_____

3. Sit/Set

_____

_____

▼
PRACTICE 3   Using Lie/Lay, Rise/Raise, Sit/Set

Determine if the verbs are used correctly in the following sentences. Change those that are incorrect.

C 1. He is lying about his curfew.

           raise
2. You do not have to ~~rise~~ your hand at the dinner table!

         lying
3. She spent the day ~~laying~~ on the sand or sitting by the shore.

       sit
4. Set the table, and ~~set~~ up straight!

C 5. At the end of the paintball tournament, the losing team raised a white flag.

     sat
6. Tatyana has ~~set~~ in the front row all semester because she lost her glasses.

C 7. Her empty purse lay on the desk all day yesterday.

C 8. The moon is rising slowly this evening.

      sitting
9. The vase was ~~setting~~ on the table.

C 10. You have lain on your bed all afternoon!

Two- and Three-Word Verb Phrases

These phrases are often difficult for non-native speakers. Many of them are idiomatic expressions, and they need to be studied or memorized.

Phrasal Verbs (Two-Word and Three-Word Verbs)

The term *phrasal verb* refers to a verb and preposition which together have a special meaning. For example, ***put + off*** means "postpone." Sometimes a phrasal verb consists of three parts. For example, ***put + up + with*** means "tolerate." Phrasal verbs are also called *two-word verbs* or *three-word verbs*.

Separable Phrasal Verbs	A phrasal verb may be either *separable* or *nonseparable*.
(a) I ***handed*** my paper ***in*** yesterday.	
(b) I ***handed in*** my paper yesterday.	With a separable phrasal verb, a noun may come either between the verb and the preposition or after the preposition, as in (a) and (b).
(c) I ***handed it in*** yesterday. *(INCORRECT: I handed in it yesterday.)*	A pronoun comes between the verb and the preposition if the phrasal verb is separable, as in (c).
Nonseparable Phrasal Verbs	With a nonseparable phrasal verb, a noun or pronoun must follow the preposition, as in (d) and (e).
(d) I ***ran into*** an old friend yesterday. I ***ran into*** her yesterday. *(INCORRECT: I ran an old friend into.)*	
(e) *(INCORRECT: I ran her into yesterday.)*	

Phrasal verbs are especially common in information English. Below is a list of common phrasal verbs and their usual meanings. This list contains only those phrasal verbs used in the exercises in the text. The phrasal verbs marked with an asterisk (*) are nonseparable.

A	ask out	*ask someone to go on a date*
B	bring about, bring on.......	*cause*
	bring up	(1) *rear children;* (2) *mention or introduce a topic*
C	call back..........................	*return a telephone call*
	call in	*ask to come to an official place for a specific purpose*
	call off............................	*cancel*
	*call on	(1) *ask to speak in class;* (2) *visit*
	call up	*call on the telephone*
	*catch up (with)................	*reach the same position or level*

---

*Indicates a nonseparable phrasal verb.

Copyright © 2004 by Pearson Education, Inc.

	*check in, check into.........	*register at a hotel*
	*check into.......................	*investigate*
	check out........................	(1) *take a book from the library;* (2) *investigate*
	*check out (of).................	*leave a hotel*
	cheer up..........................	*make (someone) feel happier*
	clean up..........................	*make clean and orderly*
	*come across....................	*meet by chance*
	cross out.........................	*draw a line through*
	cut out...........................	*stop an annoying activity*
D	do over...........................	*do again*
	*drop by, drop in (on).......	*visit informally*
	drop off..........................	*leave something/someone at a place*
	drop out (of)...................	*stop going to school, to a class, to a club, etc.*
F	figure out.......................	*find the answer by reasoning*
	fill out...........................	*write the completions of a questionnaire or official form*
	find out..........................	*discover information*
G	*get along (with)..............	*exist satisfactorily*
	get back (from)...............	(1) *return from a place;* (2) *receive again*
	*get in, get into...............	(1) *enter a car;* (2) *arrive*
	*get off...........................	*leave an airplane, a bus, a train, a subway, a bicycle*
	*get on...........................	*enter an airplane, a bus, a train, a subway, a bicycle*
	*get out of.......................	(1) *leave a car;* (2) *avoid work or an unpleasant activity*
	*get over.........................	*recover from an illness*
	*get through....................	*finish*
	*get up...........................	*arise from bed, a chair*
	give back........................	*return an item to someone*
	give up..........................	*stop trying*
	*go over..........................	*review or check carefully*
	*grow up (in)..................	*become an adult*
H	hand in..........................	*submit an assignment*
	hang up..........................	(1) *conclude a telephone conversation;* (2) *put clothes on a hanger or a hook*
	have on..........................	*wear*
K	keep out (of)..................	*not enter*
	*keep up (with)................	*stay at the same position or level*
	kick out (of)..................	*force (someone) to leave*

*Indicates a nonseparable phrasal verb.

L   *look after .... *take care of*

    *look into .... *investigate*

    *look out (for).................. *be careful*

    look over .... *review or check carefully*

    look up .... *look for information in a reference book*

M   make up......................... (1) *invent;* (2) *do past work*

N   name after, name for....... *give a baby the name of someone else*

P   *pass away....................... *die*

    pass out.......................... (1) *distribute;* (2) *lose consciousness*

    pick out.......................... *select*

    pick up........................... (1) *go to get someone (e.g., in a car);* (2) *take in one's hand*

    point out........................ *call attention to*

    put away......................... *remove to a proper place*

    put back.......................... *return to original place*

    put off............................ *postpone*

    put on .... *put clothes on one's body*

    put out........................... *extinguish a cigarette or cigar*

    *put up with..................... *tolerate*

R   *run into, *run across .... *meet by chance*

    *run out (of) .... *finish a supply of something*

S   *show up.......................... *appear, come*

    shut off .... *stop a machine, light, faucet*

T   *take after .... *resemble*

    take off............................ (1) *remove clothing;* (2) *leave on a trip*

    take out .... (1) *take someone on a date;* (2) *remove*

    take over......................... *take control*

    take up........................... *begin a new activity or topic*

    tear down .... *demolish; reduce to nothing*

    tear up .... *tear into many little pieces*

    think over....................... *consider carefully*

    throw away, throw out ... *discard; get rid of*

    throw up......................... *vomit; regurgitate food*

    try on............................. *put on clothing to see if it fits*

    turn down .... *decrease volume or intensity*

    turn in .... (1) *submit an assignment;* (2) *go to bed*

    turn off .... *stop a machine, light, faucet*

    turn on .... *begin a machine, light, faucet*

    turn out .... *extinguish a light*

    turn up .... *increase volume or intensity*

Copyright © 2004 by Pearson Education, Inc.

*Indicates a nonseparable phrasal verb.

▼
PRACTICE 1   Using Two- and Three-Word Phrases

For each sentence, choose a verb phrase from the previous list. Write it correctly in the sentence.

1. I cannot _____**figure out**_____ the answer to the physics problem.

2. Don't _____**drop in on**_____ Grandmother without calling first.

3. _____**Check out**_____ the facts before you make accusations.

4. After Luis stopped attending classes, he was _____**kicked out of**_____ school.

5. James Rojas III was _____**named after**_____ his father and grandfather.

6. Don't forget to _____**pick up**_____ the kids from soccer practice.

7. He _____**tore up**_____ her note to destroy the evidence.

8. _____**Think over**_____ your plans to drop out of school; you may regret your decision.

9. _____**Turn down**_____ the volume on your television! I think the phone is ringing!

10. Please _____**turn in**_____ your homework on the assigned date!

Readings

Copyright © 2004 by Pearson Education, Inc.

DESCRIPTION

THE MUTE SENSE

Diane Ackerman

In the following essay, "The Mute Sense," Diane Ackerman creates strong, visual images by using very specific verbs, by modifying nouns with descriptive adjectives, and by making comparisons through the use of metaphor. The author also uses many specific examples to develop the picture being described and supports this development through the particular sensory device of smell.

Pre-reading exercise: Meaning comes primarily from words. Before reading the essay, look up the definitions of the following words that appear in the text. The numbers in parentheses refer to the paragraph number of the essay.

curd (1)	larder (2)
decipher (2)	paraphernalia (2)
detonate (1)	poignant (1)
etymology (3)	succulent (1)
exaltation (3)	vigilant (2)
inarticulate (3)	

1 Nothing is more memorable than a smell. One scent can be unexpected, momentary, and fleeting, yet conjure up a childhood summer beside a lake in the Poconos, when wild blueberry bushes teemed with succulent fruit and the opposite sex was as mysterious as space travel; another, hours of passion on a moonlit beach in Florida, while the night-blooming cereus drenched the air with thick curds of perfume and high sphinx moths visited the cereus in a loud purr of wings; a third, a family dinner of pot roast, noodle pudding, and sweet potatoes, during a myrtle-mad August in a midwestern town, when both of one's parents were alive. Smells detonate softly in our memory like poignant land mines, hidden under the weedy mass of many years and experiences. Hit a tripwire of smell, and memories explode all at once. A complex vision leaps out of the undergrowth.

2 People of all cultures have always been obsessed with smell, sometimes applying perfumes in Niagaras of extravagance. The Silk Road opened up the Orient to the western world, but the scent road opened up the heart of Nature. Our early ancestors strolled among the fruits of the earth with noses vigilant and precise, following the seasons smell by smell, at home in their brimming larder. We can detect over ten thousand different odors, so many, in fact, that our memories would fail us if we tried to jot down everything they represent. In "The Hound of the Baskervilles," Sherlock Holmes identifies a woman by the smell of her notepaper, pointing out that "There are seventy-five perfumes, which it is very necessary that a criminal expert should be able to distinguish from each other." A low number, surely. After all, anyone "with a nose for" crime should be able to sniff out culprits from

their tweed, Indian ink, talcum powder, Italian leather shoes, and countless other scented paraphernalia. Not to mention the odors, radiant and nameless, which we decipher without even knowing it. The grain is a good stagehand. It gets on with its work while we're busy acting out our scenes. Though most people will swear they couldn't possibly do such a thing, studies show that both children and adults, just by smelling, are able to determine whether a piece of clothing was worn by a male or a female.

3   Our sense of smell can be extraordinarily precise, yet it's almost impossible to describe how something smells to someone who hasn't smelled it. The smell of the glossy pages of a new book, for example, or the first solvent-damp sheets from a mimeograph machine, or a dead body, or the subtle differences in odors given off by flowers like bee balm, dogwood, or lilac. Smell is the mute sense, the one without words. Lacking a vocabulary, we are left tongue-tied, groping for words in a sea of inarticulate pleasure and exaltation. We see only when there is light enough, taste only when we put things into our mouths, touch only when we make contact with someone or something, hear only sounds that are loud enough. But we smell always and with every breath. Cover your eyes and you will stop seeing, cover your ears and you will stop hearing, but if you cover your nose and try to stop smelling, you will die. Etymologically speaking, a breath is not neutral or bland—it's *cooked air*; we live in a constant simmering. There is a furnace in our cells, and when we breathe we pass the world through our bodies, brew it lightly, and turn it loose again, gently altered for having known us.

Descriptive Technique Questions

1. What is the dominant sensory area that the author uses to develop the essay? Point out some examples.

2. Is the essay more subjective or objective? Point out examples to support your point of view.

3. Ackerman uses many active, vivid verbs to enhance the descriptive quality of the essay. Point out several, and explain how they help to make the description more effective.

Suggestions for Writing

1. Choose a sensory area (touch, smell, taste, sight, hearing), and write a paragraph describing it. To make the assignment more challenging, do not mention the name of the sense you are describing. See if your reader can guess what it is by the way you describe it.

2. Write a paragraph describing a particular sense area that you associate with a famous person, place, or thing.

Copyright © 2004 by Pearson Education, Inc.

THE ICE CREAM TRUCK

Luis J. Rodriguez

> In this essay taken from Rodriguez' *Always Running,* the author, a former Los Angeles gang member, describes people, places, and things, and paints an intimate and tactile portrait of an environment and its population in "ruin." Pay attention to how the random act of violence that occurs during the story doesn't seem shocking or unexpected; rather, it is an almost natural consequence of the poverty-stricken surroundings. Because of its liberal use of colloquial speech and slang, this essay is not a typical model for college essay writing. It is used here to emphasize the power of descriptive creativity and personal expression.

Pre-reading exercise: Meaning comes primarily from words. Before you start to read, use a dictionary to look up the definitions for the following words appearing in the essay.

burdensome (3)	hovered (37)
chimed (2)	litany (8)
cinder (1)	protruding (10)
clod (13)	rasp (3)
crevice (37)	ricocheted (32)
embankment (38)	spittle (15)

See the Glossary at the end of the essay for a translation of the words marked with an asterisk (*).

"You cholos* *have great stories about climbing fences."*

—a barrio boxing coach

1 The Hills blistered below a haze of sun and smog. Mothers with wet strands of hair across their foreheads flung wash up to dry on weathered lines. Sweat-drenched men lay on their backs in the gravel of alleys, beneath broken-down cars propped up on cinder blocks. *Charrangas** and *corridos** splashed out of open windows.

2 Suddenly from over a hill, an ice cream truck raced by with packs of children running beside it. A hurried version of "Old McDonald Had a Farm" chimed through a speaker bolted on the truck's roof. The truck stopped long enough for somebody to toss out dozens of sidewalk sundaes, tootie-fruities and half-and-half bars to the children who gathered around, thrusting up small, dirt-caked hands that blossomed open as their shrieks blended with laughter.

3 Then the truck's transmission gears growled as it continued up the slope, whipped around a corner and passed a few of us *vatos** assembled on a field off Toll Drive. We looked over toward the echoes of the burdensome chimes, the slip and boom of the clutch and rasp of gears as the ice cream truck entered the dead-end streets and curves of Las Lomas.

4 *"Orale, ése, ¿qué está pasando?"** a dude named Little Man asked while passing a bottle of Tokay wine to Clavo.

5   "It's Toots and the *gaba**, you know, Axel," Clavo replied. "They just stole an ice cream truck on Portrero Grande Drive."

6   "*¡Qué cábula!*" Little Man said. "They sure is crazy."

7   We continued to talk and drink until the day melted into night.

8   Little Man and one of the López brothers, Fernie, all Tribe, were there in the field with me and my *camaradas* Clavo, Chicharrón, and Wilo. The four of us were so often together that the list of our names became a litany. We spray-painted our *placas** on the walls, followed by *AT* for Animal Tribe or *SSG* for South San Gabriel.

9   Everyone called me Chin because of my protruding jawbone. I had it tattooed on my ankle.

10   We sat around a small roasting pit Chicharrón made from branches and newspaper. Around us were ruins, remains of a home which had been condemned and later ravaged by fire. We assembled inside the old cement foundation with its scattered sections of brick and concrete walls splattered with markings and soot with rusted re-enforcing bars protruding from stone blocks.

11   We furnished the lot with beat-up couches and discarded sofas. Somebody hung plastic from a remaining cinder-block wall to a low branch so homeboys could sleep there—and miss most of any rain—when there was nowhere else to go. It was really a vacant lot but we called all such lots "the fields."

12   Even as we talked, there was Noodles, a wino and old *tecato,** crashed out on the sofa.

13   "Get up Noodles, time for some *refin**," Chicharrón exclaimed as he placed stolen hot dogs and buns on the fire. Wilo threw a dirt clod at the sofa and Noodles mumbled some incoherent words.

14   "*Orale*, leave the *vato* alone, *ése**," Little Man said.

15   But Noodles got up, spittle dripping from his mouth.

16   "Hey *ése*, Noodles is awake, and man is he pissed," Wilo said.

17   "How can you tell?" Chicharrón asked.

18   "When he moves fast and you can't understand what he's saying, then he's pissed," Wilo answered. "When he moves slow and you still can't understand what he's saying, he's all right."

19   Noodles staggered toward us, his arms flailing, as if boxing—huffing, puffing, and dropping mucus from his nose.

20   "Get the hell out of here, *pinche**," Wilo said as he stood up and pushed the wino aside.

21   "You thinks youse are tuss dues . . . you ain't so tuss," Noodles said, throwing sloppy left hooks and uppercuts into the air.

22   Wilo placed his hand over Noodles' head, whose wiry body looked like a strand from a dirty mop. Wilo was also thin and slippery. The rest of us laughed and laughed at the two *flaquillos** goofing around.

23   "Ah leave the *vato* alone, homeboy," Clavo suggested. "Let's break out another bottle."

24   As we cooked, shared wine and told stories of *jainas** and the little conquests, of fights for honor, homeys and the 'hood, a gray Mercury sedan with its headlights turned off crept up the road. Wilo was the closest up the slope to the street. He looked over at the Mercury, then frowned.

25   "Anybody recognize the *ranfla**?"Wilo inquired.

26   "*Chalo*," Chicharrón responded. "It looks too funky to be gangbangers."

27   "Unless that's what they want it to look like."

28   Wilo moved up the slope from the field, followed by Clavo, Chicharrón, and Little Man. Fernie stayed back with Noodles and me. Wilo and Clavo were the first ones to hit the street as the Mercury delayed a turn around a curve.

Copyright © 2004 by Pearson Education, Inc.

29 Clavo moved to one side of the Mercury, its occupants covered in darkness. He stretched out his arms and yelled out: "Here stand The Animal Tribe—*¡y qué!*"*

30 The Mercury stopped. A shadow stepped out of a bashed-in side door, a sawed-off shotgun in his hands. Another shadow pushed an automatic rifle out the side window.

31 "Sangra Diablos! *¡Qué rifa!*"* the dude with the shotgun yelled out. Then a blast snapped at the night air.

32 Wilo and Chicharrón fell back down the slope. Automatic gunfire followed them as they rolled in the dirt. The bullets skimmed off tree branches, knocked over trash cans and ricocheted off walls, Wilo ended up face-down; Chicharrón landed on his butt. Noodles knelt behind the sofa, whimpering. The cracking sounds stopped. The Mercury sped off, its tires throwing up dirt and pebble behind it.

33 I could see the car speeding down another hill. I ran up the slope, slipping and sliding toward the road. On the street, Little Man kneeled over Clavo, who lay sprawled on the ground and trembling. Half of Clavo's face was shot full of pellets, countless black, streaming round holes; his eye dripping into the dirt.

34 Wilo and the others climbed up and rushed up to Little Man. Fernie began jumping up and down like he had been jolted with lightning, letting out *gritos**. I kept looking at Clavo's face, thinking something stupid like how he was such a dummy, always taking chances, all the time being "the dude." Then I squatted on the ground, closed my eyelid and let a tear stream down the side of my face.

35 Windows flung upwards. Doors were pushed aside. People bolted out of their homes. Mothers cursed in Spanish from behind weather-beaten picket fences.

36 As Clavo was taken to the hospital, Fernie talked about getting all the Tribe together, about meeting later that night, about guns and warfare and "*ya estuvo*"—that's it. A war, fought for generations between Lomas and Sangra, flared up again.

37 Later, as I walked down the hills on the way back home, sirens tore across the sky and a sheriff's helicopter hovered nearby, beaming a spotlight across shacks and brush, over every hole and crevice of the neighborhood.

38 I mounted a fence which wound around a dirt embankment, hoping to get out of the helicopter's sights. I looked over the other side and there overturned at the bottom of the gully, to be ravaged by scavengers for parts, to be another barrio monument, lay an ice cream truck.

Glossary

chale (expression) something akin to "Aww, man!"

charranga lively Latin music

cholos gangbangers; homeboys

corridos Mexican ballads usually accompanied by guitar

flaquillos skinny ones

gaba (gabacho) gringo

gritos shouts or yells

jainas young women; chicks

"Orale, ése, ¿qué . . ." "Hey, you, what's happening?"

pinche kitchen boy

placa graffiti: badge of honor; name or nickname (personal); gang name or symbol

¡Qué cábula! "They sure are crazy!"

ranfla car

refin unpaid for; stolen

"Sangra Diablos! . . ." "The Bloods are devils!"

tecato addict (usually heroin)

vato (bato) simpleton; hombre of low esteem

". . .—¡y qué!" "So there!"

Descriptive Technique Questions

1. Is the essay more objective or subjective? Point out examples to support your choice.

2. Rodriguez uses many Spanish words and phrases. How do they add to the descriptive quality of the essay?

3. How does the ice cream truck come to represent the barrio Rodriguez describes in the essay?

4. Point out some figurative language devices (simile, metaphor, personification) Rodriguez uses in the essay. How do they effectively support the author's description of the barrio and its inhabitants?

Suggestions for Writing

1. Write a paragraph about a group of people and their environment that is familiar to you. Use several figurative language devices to help describe them and their relationships.

2. Do the people you know use slang or other specialized language? Write a paragraph using slang or terms (even from a different language) that help describe the people and their culture.

▼ HALLOWEEN HAVOC

Erin Nelson (student)

In the following descriptive essay, student writer Erin Nelson creates a spooky night of Halloween fun, filled with all the traditional images of ghosts and goblins that have scared and excited children through the ages. Pay particular attention to the author's use of figurative language devices (e.g., personification and simile) to create vivid images and sensory emotion.

Pre-reading exercise: Meaning comes primarily from words. Before reading the essay, look up the definitions of the following words that appear in the text. The numbers in parentheses refer to the paragraph number of the essay.

Copyright © 2004 by Pearson Education, Inc.

briskly (1)   musty (4)
curdle (5)   prey (2)
grotesque (2)   vicious (3)
gruesome (2)

1   When the wind begins to howl like the wolves and the leaves begin to fall, the time is coming nearer to the creepiest night of the year. The silvery moon is full; the clouds briskly roll across the black sky. A chill is sent down spines, and the neck hairs stand on end. What could it be? Halloween? All Hallows Eve can be the spookiest night of the year because of the creepy decorations, the chilling weather, and the scary goblins.

2   The spooky old houses come to life at night with gruesome decorations. With grotesque carved faces, the jack-o-lanterns give off an eerie glow. The tombstones line the sidewalk; beware of the bloody hands, for they may grab intruders. Bats as black as the night sky fly around in the air, and a black cat with razor sharp fangs crosses the path of terrified prey. The ghosts and the goblins sneak around the monster-like trees, ready to grab the next victim with ease.

3   The wind begins to whip, and the branches of the trees begin to sway like the bones of a forgotten skeleton. The fallen dead leaves whirl around like a vicious tornado. When the fog rolls in, the eyes begin to play tricks. A monster! With the fog comes the mist that makes you chilled down to the bone.

4   Screams echo from all directions. A witch, a vampire, and a ghost fly by; consequently, they disappear down the dark, damp street. The hairy werewolf howls, and the musty old mummy moans. Look out! Here comes Freddy—with blood dripping from his razorblade fingers. He's going to get you!

5   One night of the year is all it takes to get the heart pounding and the blood flowing. To be out on this night is quite a fright, so beware of the boogie man. With all the scary sights and the blood curdling sounds on Halloween, a flashlight will come in handy. Happy Halloween!

Descriptive Technique Questions

1. Alliteration is the repetition of the same sounds (e.g., consonants: the willowy, whipping wind; or vowels: as loose as a goose or a moose) usually done to support or help create a particular mood. Point out examples of alliteration in the essay using both consonants and vowels and explain how they help support or create a mood.

2. Brief writing doesn't have to mean underdeveloped writing. All of the paragraphs in this essay are short. However, the author packs each paragraph with vivid descriptions. Point out single words, phrases, similes, metaphors, and sensory images that help create distinct moods quickly and fully.

3. The author refers to "Freddy" in paragraph 4 but does not explain who he is. Is an explanation necessary? Did you know to whom the author is referring? Explain how making such a reference might hurt an essay.

Suggestions for Writing

1. In her light-hearted essay, Erin Nelson describes Halloween as spooky. Write a paragraph describing a holiday that evokes one particular emotion for you.

2. Choose one of the body paragraphs in Nelson's essay, and rewrite it choosing a feeling other than spooky. Remember to use figurative language and sensory images to create and support the feeling you have chosen.

NARRATION

THE ROOMMATE'S DEATH

Jan Harold Brunvand

> In his essay, "The Roommate's Death," Jan Harold Brunvand relates one of a series of stories he calls "urban legends" because they have found their most popular and long-lived run in America and because, like all legends, they have been passed on from one person to another as having really occurred. The one telling the story usually states that he or she knew the person involved or that it was someone whom a close friend or family member had known. As Brunvand unveils the story and makes comments about it, see if you can recognize any larger contemporary fears held by society that might be captured by the specific incidents in the story.

Pre-reading exercise: Meaning comes primarily from words. Before reading the essay, look up the definitions of the following words that appear in the text. The numbers in parentheses refer to the paragraph number of the essay.

adornments (12)   plausible (3)
assailant (1)   refuge (1)
commission (1)   resolve (12)
elicit (7)   variants (10)
generalization (12)   venture (13)
motifs (4)

1   Another especially popular example of the American adolescent shocker story is the widely-known legend of "The Roommate's Death." It shares several themes with other urban legends. As in "The Killer in the Backseat" and "The Baby-sitter and the Man Upstairs," it is usually a lone woman in the story who is threatened—or thinks she is—by a strange man. As in "The Hook" and "The Boyfriend's Death," the assailant is often said to be an escaped criminal or a maniac. Finally, as in the latter legend, the actual commission of the crime is never described; only the resulting mutilated corpse is. The scratching sounds outside the girl's place of refuge are an additional element of suspense. Here is a version told by a University of Kansas student in 1965 set in Corbin Hall, a freshman women's dormitory there:

2   These two girls in Corbin had stayed late over Christmas vacation. One of them had to wait for a later train, and the other wanted to go to a fraternity party given that night of vacation. The dorm assistant was in her room—sacked out. They waited and waited for the intercom, and then they heard this knocking and knocking outside in front of the dorm. So the girl thought

Copyright © 2004 by Pearson Education, Inc.

it was her date and she went down. But she didn't come back and she didn't come back. So real late that night this other girl heard a scratching and gasping down the hall. She couldn't lock the door, so she locked herself in the closet. In the morning she let herself out and her roommate had had her throat cut, and if the other girl had opened the door earlier, she [the dead roommate] would have been saved.

3 At all the campuses where the story is told the reasons for the girls' remaining alone in the dorm vary, but they are always realistic and plausible. The girls' homes may be too for away for them to visit during vacation, such as in Hawaii or a foreign country. In some cases they wanted to avoid a campus meeting or other obligation. What separates the two roommates may be either that one goes out for food, or to answer the door, or to use the rest room. The girl who is left behind may hear the scratching noise either at her room door or at the closet door, if she hides there. Sometimes her hair turns white or gray overnight from the shock of the experience (an old folk motif). The implication in the story is that some maniac is after her (as is suspected about the pursuer in "The Killer in the Backseat"); but the truth is that her own roommate needs help, and she might have supplied it had she only acted more decisively when the noises were first heard. Usually some special emphasis is put on the victim's fingernails, scratched to bloody stumps by her desperate efforts to signal for help.

4 A story told by a California teenager, remembered from about 1964, seems to combine motifs of "The Baby-sitter and the Man Upstairs" with "The Roommate's Death." The text is unusually detailed with names and the circumstances of the crime:

5 Linda accepted a baby-sitting job for a wealthy family who lived in a two-story home up in the hills for whom she had never baby-sat before. Linda was rather hesitant as the house was rather isolated and so she asked a girlfriend, Sharon, to go along with her, promising Sharon half of the baby-sitting fee she would earn. Sharon accepted Linda's offer and the two girls went up to the big two-story house.

6 The night was an especially dark and windy one and rain was threatening. All went well for the girls as they read stories aloud to the three little boys they were sitting for and they had no problem putting the boys to bed in the upstairs part of the house. When this was done, the girls settled down to watching television.

7 It was not long before the telephone rang. Linda answered the telephone, only to hear the heavy breathing of the caller on the other end. She attempted to elicit a response from the caller but he merely hung up. Thinking little of it and not wanting to panic Sharon, Linda went back to watching her television program, remarking that the caller had dialed a wrong number. Upon receiving the second call at which time the caller first engaged in a bit of heavy breathing and then instructed them to check on the children, the two girls became frightened and decided to call the operator for assistance. The operator instructed the girls to keep the caller on the line as long as possible should he call again so that she might be able to trace the call. The operator would check back with them.

8 The two girls then decided between themselves that one should stay downstairs to answer the phone. It was Sharon who volunteered to go upstairs. Shortly, the telephone rang again and Linda did as the operator had instructed her. Within a few minutes, the operator called back telling Linda to leave the

house immediately with her friend because she had traced the calls to the upstairs phone.

9 Linda immediately hung up the telephone and proceeded to run to the stairway to call Sharon. She then heard a thumping sound coming from the stairway and when she approached the stairs she saw her friend dragging herself down the stairs by her chin, all of her limbs severed from her body. The three boys also lay dead upstairs in their beds.

10 Once again, the Indiana University Folklore Archive has provided the best published report on variants of "The Roommate's Death," Linda Dégh's summary of thirty-one texts and several subtypes and related plots collected since 1961. The most significant feature, according to her report, is the frequent appearance of a male rescuer at the end of the story. In one version, for example, two girls are left behind alone in the dorm by their roommate when she goes downstairs for food; they hear noises, and so stay in their room all night without opening the door. Finally the mailman comes around the next morning, and they call him from the window:

11 The mailman came in the front door and went up the stairs, and told the girls to stay in their room, that everything was all right but that they were to stay in their rooms [sic]. But the girls didn't listen to him cause he had said it was all right, so they came out into the hall. When they opened the door, they saw their girlfriend on the floor with a hatchet in her head.

In other Indiana texts the helpful male is a handyman, a milkman, or the brother of one of the roommates.

12 According to folklorist Beverly Crane, the male-female characters are only one pair of a series of significant opposites, which also includes home and away, intellectual versus emotional behavior, life and death, and several others. A male is needed to resolve the female's uncertainty—motivated by her emotional fear—about how to act in a new situation. Another male has mutilated and killed her roommate with a blow to her head, "the one part of the body with which women are not supposed to compete." The girls, Crane suggested, are doubly out of place in the beginning, having left the haven of home to engage in intellectual pursuits, and having remained alone in the campus dormitory instead of rejoining the family on a holiday. Ironically, the injured girl must use her fingernails, intended to be long, lovely, feminine adornments, in order to scratch for help. But because her roommate fails to investigate the sound, the victim dies, her once pretty nails now bloody stumps. Crane concluded this ingenious interpretation with these generalizations:

13 The points of value implicit in this narrative are then twofold. If women wish to depend on traditional attitudes and responses they had best stay in a place where these attitudes and responses are best able to protect them. If, however, women do choose to venture into the realm of equality with men, they must become less dependent, more self-sufficient, more confident in their own abilities, and, above all, more willing to assume responsibility for themselves and others.

14 One might not expect to find women's liberation messages embedded in the spooky stories told by teenagers, but Beverly Crane's case is plausible and well argued. Furthermore, it is not at all unusual to find up-to-date social commentary in other modern folklore—witness the many religious and sexual jokes and legends circulated by people who would not openly criticize a

Copyright © 2004 by Pearson Education, Inc.

church or the traditional social mores. Folklore does not just purvey the old codes of morality and behavior; it can also absorb newer ideas. What needs to be done to analyze this is to collect what Alan Dundes calls "oral-literary criticism," the informants' own comments about their lore. How clearly would the girls who tell these stories perceive—or even accept—the messages extrapolated by scholars? And a related question: Have any stories with clear liberationist themes replaced older ones cautioning young women to stay home, be good, and—next best—be careful, and call a man if they need help?

Narrative Technique Questions

1. Narrative storytelling is most effective when the tale appears realistic (that it really happened)—not made up or too fantastic to have actually happened. Pick one of the stories that Brunvald relates and point out elements that convinced you that the stories are based on real events.

2. What do you think of Beverly Crane's interpretation of the "Roommate's Death"? Are her ideas about feminist themes convincing?

Suggestions for Writing

1. Think of a horror story that scared you. Write a paragraph explaining what elements of the story had the greatest effect on you.

2. By yourself or in a group, create your own "urban legend." Write a narrative paragraph detailing the action.

▼

THE EYE OF THE BEHOLDER

Grace Suh

> In "The Eye of the Beholder" Grace Suh recounts a visit she made to a cosmetics counter for a facial makeover guaranteed by the "priestesses of beauty." However, after the process is complete, Suh does not like what she sees. Pay particular attention to the difference between "Estée's" idea of beauty and that eventually expressed by the author.

Pre-reading exercise: Meaning comes primarily from words. Before reading the essay, look up the definitions of the following words that appear in the text. The numbers in parentheses refer to the paragraph number of the essay.

astringent (9)	imperious (6)
bourgeoisie (3)	reclamation (5)
emulsifier (9)	renounce (3)
entropy (5)	reverie (11)
epiphanous (4)	scythe (5)
icons (5)	stark (2)

1 Several summers ago, on one of those endless August evenings when the sun hangs suspended just above the horizon, I made up my mind to become beautiful.

2 It happened as I walked by one of those mirrored glass-clad office towers, and caught a glimpse of my reflection out of the corner of my eye. The glass on this particular building was green, which might have accounted for the sickly tone of my complexion, but there was no explaining away the limp, ragged hair, the dark circles under my eyes, the facial blemishes, the shapeless, wrinkled clothes. The overall effect—the whole being greater than the sum of its parts—was one of stark ugliness.

3 I'd come home from college having renounced bourgeois suburban values, like hygiene and grooming. Now, home for the summer, I washed my hair and changed clothes only when I felt like it, and spent most of my time sitting on the lawn eating mini rice cakes and Snickers and reading dogeared back issues of *National Geographic.*

4 But that painfully epiphanous day, standing there on the hot sidewalk, I suddenly understood what my mother had been gently hinting these past months: I was no longer just plain, no longer merely unattractive. No, I had broken the Unsightliness Barrier. I was now UGLY, and aggressively so.

5 And so, in an unusual exertion of will, I resolved to fight back against the forces of entropy. I envisioned it as reclamation work, like scything down a lawn that has grown into meadow, or restoring a damaged fresco. For the first time in ages, I felt elated and hopeful. I nearly sprinted into the nearby Nieman Marcus. As I entered the cool, hushed, dimly lit first floor and saw the gleaming counters lined with vials of magical balm, the priestesses of beauty in their sacred smocks, and the glossy photographic icons of the goddesses themselves—Paulina, Linda, Cindy, Vendella—in a wild, reckless burst of inspiration I thought to myself, Heck, why just okay? Why not BEAUTIFUL?

6 At the Estée Lauder counter, I spied a polished, middle-aged woman whom I hoped might be less imperious than the aloof amazons at the Chanel counter.

7 "Could I help you?" the woman (I thought of her as "Estée") asked.

8 "Yes," I blurted. "I look terrible. I need a complete makeover—skin, face, everything."

9 After a wordless scrutiny of my face, she motioned me to sit down and began. She cleansed my skin with a bright blue mud masque and clear, tingling astringent and then applied a film of moisturizer, working extra amounts into the rough patches. Under the soft pressure of her fingers, I began to relax. From my perch, I happily took in the dizzying, colorful swirl of beautiful women and products all around me. I breathed in the billows of perfume that wafted through the air. I whispered the names of products under my breath like a healing mantra: cooling eye gel, gentle exfoliant, night time neck area reenergizer, moisture recharging intensifier, ultrahydrating complex, emulsifying immunage. I felt immersed in femininity, intoxicated by beauty.

10 I was flooded with gratitude at the patience and determination with which Estée toiled away at my face, painting on swaths of lip gloss, blush, and foundation. She was not working in vain, I vowed, as I sucked in my cheeks on her command. I would buy all these products. I would use them every day. I studied her gleaming, polished features—her lacquered nails, the glittering mosaic of her eyeshadow, the complex red shimmer of her mouth, her flawless, dewy skin—and tried to imagine myself as impeccably groomed as she.

11 Estée's voice interrupted my reverie, telling me to blot my lips. I stuck the tissue into my mouth and clamped down, watching myself in the mirror. My skin was a blankly even shade of pale, my cheeks and lips glaringly bright in

Copyright © 2004 by Pearson Education, Inc.

contrast. My face had a strange plastic sheen, like a mannequin's. I grimaced as Estée applied the second lipstick coat: Was this right? Didn't I look kind of—fake? But she smiled back at me, clearly pleased with her work. I was ashamed of myself: Well, what did I expect? It wasn't like she had anything great to start with.

12   "Now," she announced. "Time for the biggie—Eyes."

13   "Oh. Well, actually, I want to look good and everything, but, I mean, I'm sure you could tell, I'm not really into a complicated beauty routine . . . " My voice faded into a faint giggle.

14   "So?" Estée snapped.

15   "Sooo . . . " I tried again, "I've never really used eye makeup, except, you know, for a little mascara sometimes, and I don't really feel comfortable———"

16   Estée was firm. "Well, the fact is that the eyes are the windows of the face. They're the focal point. An eye routine doesn't have to be complicated, but it's important to emphasize the eyes with some color, or they'll look washed out."

17   I certainly didn't want that. I leaned back again in my chair and closed my eyes.

18   Estée explained as she went: "I'm covering your lids with this champagne color. It's a real versatile base, 'cause it goes with almost any other color you put on top of it." I felt the velvety pad of the applicator sweep over my lids in a soothing rhythm.

19   "Now, being an Oriental, you don't have a lid fold, so I'm going to draw one with this charcoal shadow. Then, I fill in below the line with a lighter charcoal color with a bit of blue in it—frosted midnight—and then above it, on the outsides of your lids, I'm going to apply this plum color. There. Hold on a minute . . . Okay. Open up."

20   I stared at the face in the mirror, at my eyes. The drawn-on fold and dark, heavy shadows distorted and reproportioned my whole face. Not one of the features in the mirror was recognizable, not the waxy white skin or the redrawn crimson lips or the sharp, deep cheekbones, and especially, not the eyes. I felt negated; I had been blotted out and another face drawn in my place. I looked up at Estée, and in that moment I hated her. "I look terrible," I said.

21   Her back stiffened. "What do you mean?" she demanded.

22   "Hideous. I don't even look human. Look at my eyes. You can't even see me!" My voice was hoarse.

23   She looked. After a moment, she straightened up again, "Well, I'll admit, the eye shadow doesn't look great." She began to put away the pencils and brushes, "But at least now you have an eyelid."

24   I told myself that she was a pathetic, middle-aged woman with a boring job and a meaningless life. I had my whole life ahead of me. All she had was the newest Richard Chamberlain miniseries.

25   But it didn't matter. The fact of the matter was that she was pretty, and I was not. Her blue eyes were recessed in an intricate pattern of folds and hollows. Mine bulged out.

26   I bought the skincare system and the foundation and the blush and the lip liner pencil and the lipstick and the primer and the eyeliner and the eyeshadows—all four colors. The stuff filled a bag the size of a shoebox. It cost a lot. Estée handed me my receipt with a flourish, and I told her, "Thank you."

27   In the mezzanine level washroom, I set my bag down on the counter and scrubbed my face with water and slimy pink soap from the dispenser. I splashed my face with cold water until it felt tight, and dried my raw skin with brown paper towels that scratched.

28   As the sun sank into the Chicago skyline, I boarded the Burlington Northern Commuter for home and found a seat in the corner. I set the shop-

ping bag down beside me, and heaped its gilt boxes and frosted glass bottles into my lap. Looking out the window, I saw that night had fallen. Instead of trees and backyard fences I saw my profile—the same reflection, I realized, that I'd seen hours ago in the side of the green glass office building. I did have eyelids, of course. Just not a fold. I wasn't pretty. But I was familiar and comforting. I was myself.

29   The next stop was mine. I arranged the things carefully back in the rectangular bag, large bottles of toner and moisturizer first, then the short cylinders of masque and scrub and powder, small bottles of foundation and primer, the little logs of pencils and lipstick, then the flat boxed compacts of blush and eyeshadow. The packages fit around each other cleverly, like pieces in a puzzle. The conductor called out, "Fairview Avenue," and I stood up. Hurrying down the aisle, I looked back once at the neatly packed bag on the seat behind me, and jumped out just as the doors were closing shut.

Narrative Technique Questions

1. What are the factors that influence Suh to seek out a facial "makeover"?

2. At what point in the story does Suh realize that what she is doing is not going to solve the problem she thought she was correcting?

3. What does Suh finally realize about herself, and how do her final thoughts relate to the essay's title?

Suggestions for Writing

1. Write a paragraph about some part of your looks that you would like to change, or a change that you had contemplated but decided not to complete.

2. Write a paragraph about how you think the culture influences people to want to change their appearance. Explore how this can be a negative or positive experience.

SHATTERED SANCTUARY

Stephanie K. Higgs (student)

> In the following narrative essay, student writer Stephanie Higgs recounts the frightening personal experience of being robbed at knifepoint in her own home. Pay particular attention to how the author builds drama and intensity by moving from internal thoughts and emotions to the external sounds, sights, and events taking place around her.

Pre-reading exercise: Meaning comes primarily from words. Before reading the essay, look up the definitions of the following words that appear in the text. The numbers in parentheses refer to the paragraph number of the essay.

Copyright © 2004 by Pearson Education, Inc.

bile (2)	predictable (2)
crescendo (2)	staccato (3)
incapacitated (2)	traumatic (1)
intimidate (1)	vacillate (9)
nook (1)	wielding (2)

1 Time stood still as I tried to reconcile in my mind what was happening in my cheery breakfast nook on that dreary Tuesday morning in September of 1998; a traumatic event happened there; consequently, my life has been changed forever. Before this event, I felt snug and secure in my roomy, comfortable two story home, peacefully nestled on three gently rolling acres where my loyal and intimidating German shepherds were on patrol, in a private neighborhood near suburban St. Louis. Two young men and their decision to invade my home took all of that away from me.

2 Thunderstorms the previous night had settled into a steady, rhythmic rainshower by daylight. After finally getting the last child out the door and onto the school bus around 7:00 A.M., I was alone in the house following my predictable routine. I had put the dogs in the garage by 7:45 A.M. because I was leaving the house for a college art history class. I heard the scraping of the vinyl floor trim on the French door against the ceramic floor tiles. Now, much like the sound of nails on a chalkboard, it is forever recorded in my memory to come back during waking and sleeping hours alike, to torture me. It makes no difference whether the door is actually opening or not because my mind will always believe that it is. Next, I remember calling out down the hallway to the kitchen, "What did you forget?" I guessed my husband had forgotten some important papers he needed for a meeting he had scheduled in Hazelwood that morning. As I rounded the corner, what I saw made fear rise in my throat like green bile forced up from the pit of my stomach. As soon as I saw them, panic increased my heart rate, bringing it to ear-shattering crescendos until I thought I would go deaf or explode. Incapacitating shock and disbelief bordering on denial paralyzed my entire body as I stared at two masked black men wielding knives standing in my kitchen breakfast room and heading straight toward me.

3 Walking past the wallphone, in one deft move they dropped the receiver to the floor and were right in front of me with a cold steel blade to my throat before I could comprehend what was happening. While looking into the cold dark, eyes of the one who seemed to be in charge, I heard someone who strangely sounded like me, but miles away asking "What are you here for?" I remember thinking he must be a rap singer because of the staccato style in which he answered, "We be axing the questions muthuh fuckin bitch! Don you scream bitch or we kill you!" He would kill me, I knew with a dull certainty, if I did not obey him. Gripped by the icy fingers of insanity, I heard myself laughing as I was pushed down onto my bedroom floor. I felt like a character in a Dean Koontz thriller. How did I get from the kitchen to here? Surely I made the movements to get there, but I could not recall them from the strange mind that didn't seem like mine anymore. Events were viewed, but from another place before this day unknown to me.

4 They grabbed my hands to tie them behind my back along with my feet. I realized, even though my mind was a tilt-a-whirl seriously out of control, this would more than likely be my last day to live on this earth; my thoughts began to organize as I focused on survival.

5 The men went through my bedroom like a tornado in a springtime storm, tossing my chest of drawers and all its contents, my private possessions, on the floor, crashing the crystal lamps off of night stands, also upending my

Copyright © 2004 by Pearson Education, Inc.

four poster bed. All the while my shepherds were howling and throwing themselves against the door to the mudroom located off the kitchen in a valiant, yet futile attempt to try and help me.

6   I was told to keep my face down and not to look at them. Even though they were both masked and wore latex gloves, there must have been some fear of discovery; this led me to believe they planned to leave me alive if things went well. At that point, I decided I would do everything in my power to make sure things went well, or I would quite literally die trying.

7   They discovered the gun shells in the nightstand and asked where the guns were. I told them, somewhat reluctantly, while wondering if I was crazy for giving them an even deadlier weapon. I asked what they were looking for. "We looking for money bitch! Where's the gold bitch?" What gold? I thought. Jewelry. A picture began to form in my mind from the things they were taking and asking about, things they could fence to get quick money. For what? Drugs?

8   Surely they were on drugs. How else would they ever work up the nerve to enter another person's house without invitation for the purpose they were carrying out? My mind began to dwell on what brought these young men to this end. I hated them for being the first vile, black people I had ever encountered, yet I pitied them as a mother of young men myself.

9   Suddenly, my mind was rudely snapped back to the present as they left the bedroom to go upstairs and ransack. Even though I couldn't see, I could hear the crashing and tearing; my rage swelled again. How dare they! This was my home, my property. What right did they have? I began to hope the loaded shotgun taken from under my bed would go off as they tried to leave, thereby blowing some part of their anatomy into the next county. I vacillated between hatred and gratitude within mere seconds of each other.

10   Lifting my face, I looked into the kitchen where they were stacking their bounty for a hasty exit. Taking in as many details as I could while I was free to look about, I started to allow myself the luxury of thinking about what I would do after they left. Also, what I could do to help catch them. Details, memorize details. I started to mentally catalog everything about their appearance and what they were taking.

11   Hitching the shotgun up over his shoulder, the leader said, "Let's get outta here." They loaded up and were gone. I lay where I was for what seemed an eternity, too scared to move, yet thrilled to be alive. Working frantically at freeing my hands and feet, I decided to run to the neighbor's house for help. I jumped up and ran like the devil himself was chasing me. What if they were waiting outside to see what I would do? I couldn't let myself think about that, or I would lose my nerve. Safely on my neighbor's porch, I began to heave; I didn't stop until well after the authorities showed up.

12   After taking my statement, it took only two hours for the detectives to take these criminals into custody. They were apprehended within one mile of my home along with all of the stolen property. Even though they are still in the St. Charles County jail, facing four first degree felony indictments, I have not forgotten their words of warning: "If you call the police bitch, we be back to kill you!"

13   My home is for sale; we are relocating for reasons of personal safety. The peace and comfort known before that day is gone—never to return. My sanctuary has been shattered, and I must try to find a new one.

Narrative Technique Questions

1. The author begins the narrative with a brief description of her home, the rain, and getting her children off to school. Why does the author open the story this way?

2. The author identifies her two assailants as young black men. Would it have made any difference if she had not mentioned their race? Discuss how cultural bias can influence people's perceptions of events.

3. At the end of the story, the author relates that she and her husband have put their house up for sale because they want to find a new sanctuary somewhere else. Point out some examples from the story to support the idea that simply moving will not create peace and serenity for the author.

Suggestions for Writing

1. From your own personal experience or knowledge, write a paragraph relating the events of a dramatic incident.

2. In her essay, Stephanie Higgs recounts how the burglary led her and her husband to put their house up for sale so they could move to another area. Write a paragraph recounting how an event made you or someone you know make a life-altering decision.

EXAMPLE

▼

HEROINE WORSHIP: THE AGE OF THE FEMALE ICON*

Holly Brubach

> In this essay, Brubach inspects women as role models in a culture that increasingly values the rich and famous. She concludes, however, that today's female has many more role models from which to choose. She begins the essay with an extended list of famous role models. As you read the remainder of the essay, pay attention to the number and variety of other famous females she uses as examples.

Pre-reading exercise: Meaning comes primarily from words. Before reading the essay, look up the definitions of the following words that appear in the text. The numbers in parentheses refer to the paragraph number of the essay.

apotheosized (1)	idiosyncrasies (13)	proliferation (11)
contemporaneous (1)	inculcated (6)	quotidian (8)
deployed (10)	modulate (14)	reproach (6)
enigma (2)	oblique (12)	synonymous (2)
genre (8)	pantheon (1)	ubiquitous (3)
icon (2)		

1 It's the 90's, and the pantheon we've built to house the women in our minds is getting crowded. Elizabeth Taylor, Eleanor Roosevelt, Oprah Winfrey, Alanis Morissette, Indira Gandhi, Claudia Schiffer, Coco Chanel, Doris

---

*"Heroine Worship: The Age of the Female Icon," by Holly Brubach as appeared in *The New York Times*, November 24, 1996. Copyright © 1996 by The New York Times Co. Reprinted by permission.

Day, Aretha Franklin, Jackie Onassis, Rosa Parks—they're all there, the dead and the living side by side, contemporaneous in our imaginations. On television and in the movies, in advertising and magazines, their images are scattered across the landscape of our everyday lives. Their presence is sometimes decorative, sometimes uplifting, occasionally infuriating. The criteria for appointment to this ad hoc hall of fame that takes up so much space in our thoughts and in our culture may at first glance appear to be utterly random. In fact, irrespective of their achievements, most of these women have been apotheosized primarily on the basis of their ability to appeal to our fantasies.

2   An icon is a human sound bite, an individual reduced to a name, a face and an idea: Dale Evans, the compassionate cowgirl. In some cases, just the name and an idea suffice. Few people would recognize Helen Keller in a photograph, but her name has become synonymous with being blind and deaf to such an extent that she has inspired an entire category of jokes. Greta Garbo has gone down in collective memory as an exalted enigma with a slogan about being alone. Asking a man if that's a gun in his pocket is all it takes to invoke Mae West. Catherine Deneuve's face, pictured on a stamp, is the emblem of France. Virginia Woolf has her own T-shirt. Naomi Campbell has her own doll. Celebrity being the engine that drives our culture, these women have been taken up by the media and made famous, packaged as commodities and marketed to a public eager for novelty and easily bored. . . .

3   Our icons are by no means exclusively female, but the male ones are perhaps less ubiquitous and more accessible. The pedestals we put them on are lower; the service they are called on to perform is somewhat different.

4   Like women, men presumably look to icons for tips that they can take away and apply to their lives. The men who are elevated to the status of icons are the ones who are eminently cool, whose moves the average guy can steal. They do not prompt a fit of introspection (much less of self-recrimination), as female icons often do in women. What a male icon inspires in other men is not so much the desire to *be* him as the desire to be accepted by him—to be buddies, to shoot pool together, to go drinking. I have all this on good authority from a man of my acquaintance who insists that, though regular guys may envy, say, Robert Redford for his ability to knock women dead, what they're thinking as they watch him in a movie is not "Hey, I wonder if I have what it takes to do that, too," but "I wonder if Redford would like to hang out with me."

5   Whereas women may look at an icon like Raquel Welch, whose appeal is clearly to the male half of humanity, and ask themselves, "If that's what's required to appeal to a man, have I got it, or can I get it?" (The thought of hanging out with Welch—going shopping together or talking about boyfriends—would, I think it's safe to say, never cross most women's minds.)

6   An entire industry, called fashion, has grown up around the business of convincing women that they need to remake themselves in someone else's image: makeup and clothes and other products are presented not as alterations but as improvements. The notion of appearance and personality as a project to be undertaken is inculcated early on. A man may choose to ignore certain male icons; a woman has no such luxury where the great majority of female icons are concerned. She must come to terms with them, defining herself in relation to them—emulating some, rejecting others. In certain cases, a single icon may exist for her as both an example and a reproach.

7   Our male icons are simply the latest entries in a tradition of long standing, broad enough in any given era to encompass any number of prominent men. But the current array of female icons is a rare phenomenon, the outgrowth of aspirations many of which date back no more than 100 years.

Copyright © 2004 by Pearson Education, Inc.

8   What were the images of women that informed the life of a girl growing up 200 years ago? It's hard to for us to imagine the world before it was wall-papered with ads, before it was inundated with all the visual "information" that comes our way in the course of an average day and competes with real people and events for our attention. There were no magazines, no photographs. In church, a girl would have seen renderings of the Virgin Mary and the saints. She may have encountered portraits of royalty, whose station, unless she'd been born an aristocrat, must have seemed even more unattainable than that of the saints. There were picturesque genre paintings depicting peasants and chambermaids, to be seen at the public salons, if anyone thought to bring a girl to them. But the most ambitious artists concentrated on pagan goddesses and mythological women, who, being Olympian, inhabited a plane so lofty that they were presumably immune to quotidian concerns. History and fiction, for the girl who had access to them, contained tales of women whose lives had been somewhat more enterprising and action-packed than those of the women she saw around her, but her knowledge of most women's exploits in her own time would have been limited to hearsay: a woman had written a novel, a woman had played hostess to one of the greatest philosophers of the age and discussed ideas with him, a woman had disguised herself as a man and gone to war. Most likely, a girl would have modeled herself on a female relative, or on a woman in her community. The great beauty who set the standard by which others were measured would have been the one in their midst—the prettiest girl in town, whose fame was local.

9   Nineteenth-century icons like Sarah Bernhardt and George Sand would have imparted no more in the way of inspiration; their careers were predicated on their talents, which had been bestowed by God. It was Florence Nightingale who finally provided an example that was practicable, one to which well-born girls could aspire, and hundreds of women followed her into nursing.

10   Today, the images of women confronting a girl growing up in our culture are far more diverse, though not all of them can be interpreted as signs of progress. A woman who in former times might have served as the model for some painter's rendering of one or another pagan goddess is now deployed to sell us cars and soap. The great beauty has been chosen from an international field of contenders. At the movies, we see the stories of fictional women brought to life by real actresses whose own lives have become the stuff of fiction. In the news, we read about women running countries, directing corporations and venturing into outer space.

11   The conditions that in our century have made possible this proliferation of female icons were of course brought on by the convergence of advances in women's rights and the growth of the media into an industry. As women accomplished the unprecedented, the press took them up and made them famous, trafficking in their accomplishments, their opinions, their fates. If, compared with the male icons of our time, our female icons seem to loom larger in our culture and to cast a longer shadow, perhaps it's because in so many cases their stories have had the urgency of history in the making.

12   When it comes to looking at women, we're all voyeurs, men and women alike. Does our urge to study the contours of their flesh and the changes in their faces stem from some primal longing to be reunited with the body that gave us life? Women have been the immemorial repository of male fantasies—a lonesome role that many are nonetheless loath to relinquish, given the power it confers and the oblique satisfaction it brings. The curiosity and desire inherent in the so-called male gaze, deplored for the way it has objectified women in art and in films, are matched on women's part by the need to

assess our own potential to be found beautiful and by the pleasure in putting themselves in the position of the woman being admired.

13   Our contemporary images of women are descended from a centuries-old tradition and, inevitably, they are seen in its light. Women have often been universalized, made allegorical. The figure who represents Liberty, or Justice, to say nothing of Lust or Wrath, is a woman, not a man—a tradition that persists: there is no Mr. America. The unidentified woman in innumerable paintings—landscapes, genre scenes, mythological scenes—transcends her circumstances and becomes Woman. It's the particular that is customarily celebrated in men, and the general in woman. Even our collective notions of beauty reflect this: a man's idiosyncracies enhance his looks; a woman's detract from hers.

14   "I'm every woman, it's all in me," Chaka Khan sings, and the chords in the bass modulate optimistically upward, in a surge of possibility. Not all that long ago, the notion that any woman could be every woman would have been dismissed as blatantly absurd, but to our minds it makes evident sense, in keeping with the logic that we can be anything we want to be—the cardinal rule of the human-potential movement and an assumption that in America today is so widely accepted and dearly held that it might as well be written into the Constitution. Our icons are at this point sufficiently plentiful that to model ourselves on only one of them would seem arbitrary and limiting, when in fact we can take charge in the manner of Katherine Hepburn, strut in the way we learned by watching Tina Turner, flirt in the tradition of Rita Hayworth, grow old with dignity in the style of Georgia O'Keeffe. In the spirit of post-modernism, we piece our selves together, assembling the examples of several women in a single personality—a process that makes for some unprecedented combinations, like Madonna: the siren who lifts weights and becomes a mother. We contemplate the women who have been singled out in our culture and the permutations of femininity they represent. About to move on to the next century, we call on various aspects of them as we reconfigure our lives, deciding which aspects of our selves we want to take with us and which aspects we want to leave behind.

Example Technique Questions

1. In paragraph 8, the author suggests that a girl several centuries ago would model herself after someone in her community or someone in her immediate family. How is this different than in today's society?

2. In paragraph 14, Brubach gives many examples of famous women. What is the point she is trying to make about how today's modern young woman can use these role models?

Suggestions for Writing

1. Write a paragraph about one of today's female icons. Discuss the qualities that make her famous and/or popular.

2. Write a paragraph about a woman you admire. Discuss the qualities that influence her appeal for you.

Copyright © 2004 by Pearson Education, Inc.

▼
THE CULTURE OF VIOLENCE

Myriam Miedzian

In "The Culture of Violence," Myriam Miedzian inspects the culture that is influencing our children. The essay creates a fictional situation in which a group of anthropologists from Australia examine contemporary America. Pay particular attention to the variety of examples the author makes available for the visitors to evaluate.

Pre-reading exercise: Meaning comes primarily from words. Before reading the essay, look up the definitions of the following words that appear in the text. The numbers in parentheses refer to the paragraph number of the essay.

acculturate (3)	exacerbated (23)
anthropology (10)	indignation (7)
chaste (3)	intricately (1)
collateral (5)	intuitively (3)
deleterious (4)	laissez-faire (34)
detrimental (4)	

1   Anyone who has ever taken a cultural anthropology course is aware that different societies weave different patterns of culture, and that the different threads—religion, music, sports, children's games, drama, work, relations between the sexes, communal values, and so on—that make up the cultural web of a society are usually intricately related.

2   If a tribe's songs and dramas are centered on violence and warfare, if its young boys play war games and violently competitive sports from the earliest age, if its paintings, sculptures, and potteries depict fights and scenes of battle, it is a pretty sure bet that this is not a peaceful, gentle tribe.

3   Every child in the world is born into a particular culture and "from the moment of his birth the customs into which he is born shape his experience and behaviour," we are told by anthropologist Ruth Benedict.[1] Throughout history people have known this intuitively and so they have been careful to acculturate their children from the youngest age into a pattern of behavior that is acceptable to the group. We have in our own society some very clear and simple examples: Christian groups like the Hutterites and the Amish, or Jewish groups like the Hasidim want their children to grow up to be devoted primarily to religious rather than material values, to be sexually modest and completely chaste before marriage. They share a strong sense of community and commitment to taking responsibility for the well-being of all their members. Among the Hutterites and Amish there is a strong emphasis on non-violence. None of these groups allows their children to participate in the mainstream culture.

4   Sometimes societies develop customs that become highly detrimental to their members. A cultural trait that may be of considerable value in a limited form or that was of value at an earlier point of history is elaborated and continued in a form that is socially deleterious. Ruth Benedict refers to this as the "asocial elaboration of a cultural trait."

5   A prime example is the incest taboos and marital customs of the Kurnai tribe of Australia. Many a student of anthropology has laughed or at least chuckled at Benedict's descriptions. Benedict explains that all human soci-

eties have incest taboos, "but the relatives to whom the prohibition refers differ utterly among different peoples."[2] The Kurnai, like many other tribes, do not differentiate "lineal from collateral kin." Fathers and uncles, brothers and cousins, are not distinguished, so that "all relatives of one's own generation are one's brothers and sisters."[3]

6   The Kurnai also have an extreme horror of "brother-sister" marriage. Add to this their strict rule with respect to locality in the choice of a mate and the right of old men to marry the attractive young girls, and a situation is created in which there are almost no mates for young people, especially young men. This does not lead the Kurnai to change their incest taboos or rules of marriage. Quite to the contrary, "they insist upon them with every show of violence."[4]

7   As a result, the usual way for tribe members to marry is to elope. As soon as the villagers get wind of this crime, they set out in pursuit of the newly-weds with the intent to kill them if they catch them. That probably all the pursuers were married in the same way does not bother anyone. Moral indignation runs high. However, if the couple can reach an island traditionally recognized as a safe haven, the tribe may eventually accept them as husband and wife.

8   Cultural webs and irrationalities are simpler and easier to see in small, isolated tribes or small communities than in large industrial societies, but they exist in both.

9   Industrialized societies are made up of different socioeconomic classes, and often different ethnic groups. In a large country like ours, differences in geography and climate affect people. Nevertheless, there are certain aspects of our culture, besides a common language, that are widely shared. Children and adolescents from coast to coast play with the same toys, see many of the same films and TV shows, listen to the same rock music, play many of the same sports.

10   I suspect that if the Kurnai were to send a few anthropologists over to study contemporary American society, they would be as amused by our irrationalities as we are by theirs.

11   On the one hand, they would find in our Declaration of Independence a deep commitment to life, liberty, and the pursuit of happiness. An examination of the Constitution would reveal that the goals of our government include "justice," "domestic tranquility," and "the general welfare." An examination of contemporary society would reveal that we deplore murder, assault, wife- and child-battering, sexual abuse of children, and rape.

12   On the other hand, our newspaper headlines, our TV news with its daily roundups of murders and rapes, our crime statistics, and the fact that over six hundred thousand of our citizens—mostly male—are in prison would inform them just how deeply these problems afflict us. Having established this strong contradiction between our professed goals and beliefs, and our reality, our Kurnai anthropologists would begin to wonder what we teach our boys that makes them become such violent men. They would ask, "Who are your young boys' heroes, who are their role models?"

13   Rambo, Chuck Norris, Arnold Schwarzenegger, would be high on the list.

14   "Do your boys watch only violent adventure films?"

15   No. They like comedies too, but when they reach adolescence many of them become particularly fond of "slasher" films in which they can watch people being skinned, decapitated, cut up into chunks. Wanting to experience all aspects of our culture, the Kurnai anthropologists would undoubtedly watch a few slasher films. They would find out that the perpetrators are practically all male, and the films frequently center on the victimization of females.

16   "What about the rest of their leisure time, what do your boys do with it?"

Copyright © 2004 by Pearson Education, Inc.

17   Our young boys spend about twenty-eight hours a week watching TV. By the time they are eighteen, they have seen an average of twenty-six thousand TV murders, a vast majority of them committed by men.

18   "Do they listen to much music?"

19   They certainly do. They spend billions of dollars a year on records and tapes, not to mention radio and MTV. The Kurnai anthropologists might be advised to turn on MTV to see what the young boys like. They would find that the programming often consists of very angry-looking young men singing lyrics that are hard to make out, but the music sounds as angry as the men look. Women on the shows are often scantily clad, and sometimes it looks as if they are about to be raped.

20   "Can we see the texts of some of these lyrics?"

21   Samples of popular hits might include an album by Poison that reached number three on the Billboard pop charts and has sold over two million copies. Its lyrics include, "I want action tonight . . . I need it hot and I need it fast/*If I can't have her, I'll take her and make her* [my emphasis]."

22   Switching channels from MTV, the Kurnai would find that a considerable amount of American television is devoted to sports. Brawls and fistfights are common at these events, particularly in hockey but also in baseball and basketball. The main tactics in football, tackling and blocking, look exactly like bodily assault.

23   The anthropologists would find out that our high rates of violent crime have been exacerbated by an ever-growing drug problem. In light of this they would note that drug and alcohol abuse are common among athletes and the heavy metal musicians that many young people admire and emulate.

24   "What about your sons' toys?" the Kurnai might ask next.

25   A trip to the playground or a look under Christmas trees—religious symbols used to commemorate the birth of the deified founder of the nation's leading religion who preached a gospel of love and nonviolence—would reveal that while little girls get dolls and carriages and dollhouses; little boys get guns, "action figures" like GI Joe, and violent space-age toys and games.

26   By now the Kurnai would no doubt have discovered that rates of violence in our society are highest among boys and men raised by single mothers. Being anthropologists they would not be surprised since they would be aware of cross-cultural data indicating that the presence of a caring, involved father decreases the chances of a son being violent.

27   Delving deeper, they would find out that many boys who start out with fathers lose them along the way through divorce. They would hear divorced women, [as well as] social workers, psychiatrists, and other professionals complain bitterly that a large percentage of divorced fathers never or rarely see their children, nor do they make child support payments.

28   Increasingly stunned by the irrationalities of our society, they might inquire of these professionals: In light of the lack of interest of so many of your men in nurturing and taking responsibility for their children, and the subsequent increases in rates of violence and other social problems, why don't you encourage your little boys to become good fathers by buying them dolls and baby carriages and dollhouses? Why don't you encourage them to play house instead of training them to become warriors?

29   "Parents would never stand for that," professionals and parents would explain. "They are much too afraid that their sons might grow up to be gay if they played with 'wimpy' girls' toys."

30   At this point the visiting anthropologist might emit a cry of disbelief. Is it not obvious to these strange people who deplore violence, yet do everything possible to encourage it in their sons, that gay men do not have children? They don't push baby carriages, change diapers, or give bottles to their babies.

Only heterosexual men become fathers and do these things. What could be more absurd than to think that little boys will become gay by rehearsing the quintessentially heterosexual role of being a father?[5]

31   Having established the deep contradictions and absurdities of our customs, the Kurnai would look for their origins. They would find that like many warrior societies, we have a long tradition of raising our boys to be tough, emotionally detached, deeply competitive, and concerned with dominance.

32   These traits, they would note, have gotten out of hand. The enormous escalation of violence that Americans are experiencing seems to coincide with the development of a vast system of communications technology that has led to the creation of a culture of violence of unprecedented dimensions, much of it directed toward or available to children. Instead of treasuring their children as a precious national resource to be handled with the utmost care, Americans have allowed them to be exploited as a commercial market.

33   How could they let this happen? the Kurnai would wonder. Surely they must understand that one of society's most important tasks, the socialization of the next generation, should not be left in the hands of people whose main concern is financial gain, people who will not hesitate to exploit the basest human tendencies for profit?

34   In their efforts to understand this puzzle they would be helped by their understanding of their own culture. The Kurnai would see that our "laissez-faire" attitude toward our children can be traced to the asocial elaboration of some of our most beneficial and admirable values, just as their absurd marital rules can be traced to originally useful taboos.

35   A system of largely unfettered free enterprise led to the extraordinary economic development of the nation. The subsequent commitment to free enterprise is so deep that the economic exploitation of children is taken for granted. Companies manufacture toys for six-year-olds that encourage reckless violence, sadism, and torture, and few people question their right to do so.

36   The Kurnai would turn next to the First Amendment, the embodiment of the national commitment to free speech.

37   It would not escape their attention that with respect to pornographic and "indecent" material, it has long been acknowledged that the First Amendment cannot apply equally to children and adults. Long-standing laws protect children from such material. That is why there are no Saturday morning pornographic TV programs.

38   For some strange reason, the Kurnai would conclude, these people have blinded themselves to the fact that what makes sense with respect to sex makes at least as much sense with respect to violence. And so they have allowed their children to be raised on tens of thousands of TV murders, detailed depictions of sadistic mutilations on the screen, and song lyrics that advocate rape.

39   What a perfect example of an asocial elaboration, they might exclaim! Everything is justified in terms of free enterprise and free speech, but this freedom as interpreted in present-day society contributes to the nation's enslavement!

40   Don't these Americans see that boys raised in a culture of violence are not free? Their basest, most destructive tendencies are reinforced from the youngest age to the detriment of their altruistic, pro-social tendencies. Then when they commit serious acts of violence they are sent to prison.

41   Don't they see that millions of Americans, especially women and elderly people, live in great fear of being mugged, raped, or murdered? Many are afraid to leave their homes after dark.

42   A survey of national crime statistics published by U.S. government agencies would inform the Kurnai that about twenty-thousand Americans a year

Copyright © 2004 by Pearson Education, Inc.

suffer the greatest loss of freedom. They are deprived of their lives through violent deaths. Their families and friends are permanently deprived of someone they love.

43   How long will it take these people, the exasperated anthropologists might wonder, until they realize that an interpretation of freedom that allows for no restraints with respect to the commercial exploitation of children is self-destructive?

44   The Kurnai would note that in other areas Americans acknowledge there is no such thing as absolute freedom. Ordinances prohibit people from playing loud music in the middle of the night if in doing so they deprive others of sleep. Laws restrict the freedom of chemical companies to dump pollutants into streams and rivers. But when it comes to producing a culture of violence that pollutes the minds of their young and encourages violence, these strange people act as if freedom were an absolute!

***

Notes

1. Ruth Benedict, *Patterns of Culture* [New York: Mentor Books, 1946 (1934)], p. 18.
2. Ibid., p. 42.
3. Ibid., p. 43.
4. Ibid.
5. I owe this point to Letty Cottin Pogrebin in *Growing Up Free: Raising Your Child in the 80's* (New York: Bantam Books, 1981).

Example Technique Questions

1. How does the culture influence young people's behavior? Point out some elements in the first three paragraphs that Miedzian identifies.

2. What is the single most important source that the author identifies as the cause for most violence (paragraphs 34 and 35)? Can you think of other reasons?

3. The essay focuses on male experiences, from boys to men. How do female experiences differ as girls grow into womanhood?

Suggestions for Writing

1. Write a paragraph describing how a group you are associated with influences your behavior. The group can be friends, an athletic team, your family, etc.

2. Write about a movie you have seen or a story you have read that deals with violence and young people. Are the reasons for the young people's behavior similar to or different from what Miedzian describes?

CLASSIFICATION

▼
THE PLOT AGAINST PEOPLE*

Russell Baker

> In "The Plot Against People," Russell Baker takes a humorous look at the frustrating relationship that often exists between people and inanimate objects. Pay particular attention to how Baker divides the various objects into distinct categories as he classifies them.

Pre-reading exercise: Meaning comes primarily from words. Before reading the essay, look up the definitions of the following words that appear in the text. The numbers in parentheses refer to the paragraph number of the essay.

conciliatory (12)	incapable (6)	plausible (7)
constitutes (11)	inanimate (1)	utterly (15)
cunning (3)	invariable (10)	virtually (9)
idle (3)	locomotion (7)	

1   Inanimate objects are classified into three major categories—those that don't work, those that break down and those that get lost.

2   The goal of all inanimate objects is to resist man and ultimately to defeat him, and the three major classifications are based on the method each object uses to achieve its purpose. As a general rule, any object capable of breaking down at the moment when it is most needed will do so. The automobile is typical of the category.

3   With the cunning typical of its breed, the automobile never breaks down while entering a filling station with a large staff of idle mechanics. It waits until it reaches a downtown intersection in the middle of the rush hour, or until it is fully loaded with family and luggage on the Ohio Turnpike.

4   Thus it creates maximum misery, inconvenience, frustration and irritability among its human cargo, thereby reducing its owner's life span.

5   Washing machines, garbage disposals, lawn mowers, light bulbs, automatic laundry dryers, water pipes, furnaces, electrical fuses, television tubes, hose nozzles, tape recorders, slide projectors—all are in league with the automobile to take their turn at breaking down whenever life threatens to flow smoothly for their human enemies.

6   Many inanimate objects, of course, find it extremely difficult to break down. Pliers, for example, and gloves and keys are almost totally incapable of breaking down. Therefore, they have had to evolve a different technique for resisting man.

7   They get lost. Science has still not solved the mystery of how they do it, and no man has ever caught one of them in the act of getting lost. The most plausible theory is that they have developed a secret method of locomotion which they are able to conceal the instant a human eye falls upon them.

8   It is not uncommon for a pair of pliers to climb all the way from the cellar to the attic in its single-minded determination to raise its owner's blood pressure. Keys have been known to burrow three feet under mattresses.

---

*"The Plot Against People," by Russell Baker as appeared in *The New York Times*, June 18, 1998. Copyright © 1996 by The New York Times Co. Reprinted by permission.

Copyright © 2004 by Pearson Education, Inc.

Women's purses, despite their great weight, frequently travel through six or seven rooms to find hiding space under a couch.

9   Scientists have been struck by the fact that things that break down virtually never get lost, while things that get lost hardly ever break down.

10   A furnace, for example, will invariably break down at the depth of the first winter cold wave, but it will never get lost. A woman's purse, which after all does have some inherent capacity for breaking down, hardly ever does; it almost invariably chooses to get lost.

11   Some persons believe this constitutes evidence that inanimate objects are not entirely hostile to man, and that a negotiated peace is possible. After all, they point out, a furnace could infuriate a man even more thoroughly by getting lost than by breaking down, just as a glove could upset him far more by breaking down than by getting lost.

12   Not everyone agrees, however, that this indicates a conciliatory attitude among inanimate objects. Many say it merely proves that furnaces, gloves and pliers are incredibly stupid.

13   The third class of object—those that don't work—is the most curious of all. These include such objects as barometers, car clocks, cigarette lighters, flashlights, and toy train locomotives. It is inaccurate, of course, to say that they never work. They work once, usually for the first few hours after being brought home, and then quit. Thereafter, they never work again.

14   In fact, it is widely assumed that they are built for the purpose of not working. Some people have reached advanced ages without ever seeing some of these objects—barometers, for example—in working order.

15   Science is utterly baffled by the entire category. There are many theories about it. The most interesting holds that the things that don't work have attained the highest state possible for an inanimate object, the state to which things that break down and things that get lost can still only aspire.

16   They have truly defeated man by conditioning him never to expect anything of them, and in return they have given man the only peace he receives from inanimate society. He does not expect his barometer to work, his electric locomotive to run, his cigarette lighter to light or his flashlight to illuminate, and when they don't, it does not raise his blood pressure.

17   He cannot attain that peace with furnaces and keys and cars and women's purses as long as he demands that they work for their keep.

Classification Technique Questions

1. According to the author, what is the goal of all inanimate objects?

2. What are Baker's classification categories? You can group them by paragraphs 3–6, 7–12, and 13–16.

3. In the concluding paragraphs, 15–17, Baker suggests that these inanimate objects have defeated both science and humanity. How does this add to the overall tone of the essay?

Suggestions for Writing

1. Write a paragraph about an inanimate object in your life that has caused you problems.

2. Select an inanimate object that "science" has touted as having the ability to save you time and effort in your life. Explain how it had the opposite effect.

Copyright © 2004 by Pearson Education, Inc.

▼ **MICHELANGELO MADNESS**

Martin Brink (student)

In the following essay by student writer Martin Brink, tools that are supposed to help humans are classified by their design and by how they actually frustrate us. Pay attention to the examples the author uses; for the most part, they are activities that most people have, unfortunately, experienced.

Pre-reading exercise: Meaning comes primarily from words. Before reading the essay, look up the definitions of the following words that appear in the text. The numbers in parentheses refer to the paragraph number of the essay.

averted (1)	evoke (1)
cloaks (4)	gizmo (1)
contraption (1)	indispensable (5)
cunning (4)	primal (5)
ensue (1)	tedious (3)

1   Since the dawn of man, humanity has striven to enhance the quality of life by inventing and employing gadgets and gizmos to reduce time and labor in everyday chores. Man, consequently, also created maintenance mayhem because of a dependency on machines, not only in the work place, but also at home. The contraptions are truly wonderful when fully functional, but when failing as a result of Murphy's law, frustration and anger ensue. Stress can be averted by avoiding the use of three types of home maintenance tools that are unreliable, counterproductive, and evoke health hazards to the operator.

2   A good rule of thumb (red and swollen by now) to follow is that any tools powered by fossil fuels—weed whackers, lawn mowers, edgers, and snow blowers—are temperamental by design. These helpful devices (a.k.a. "accidents waiting to happen") have starter cords to assist in starting the engine. According to the manual, the happy homeowner should pull the starter cord three or four times to prime the engine with gas. The manufacturer calls this activity "pre-ignition" because on the fifth pull, the engine is supposed to hum into full force. This activity should really be called "aerobic exercise" because the only thing demonstrating full force is the red-faced homeowner who is approaching unconsciousness after pulling on the starter cord fifty-seven times without so much as a puff of exhaust.

3   Believe it or not, science has created tools that are actually counterproductive. One such tool comes to mind: "The Wagner Power Roller Machine." This machine is supposed to save time when applying paint to walls; consequently, anything within ten feet of the operator is painted, too. Apart from dripping paint on everything, cleaning the machine is a tedious and time-consuming task, greater than the job of painting itself.

4   Basic instinct is all that is needed to realize the danger involved with chain saws and 35 foot extension ladders especially when used together. But none are more cunning and unsuspected as a hammer, the most widely used tool. Its simplistic design cloaks its true destructive force; anyone who is experienced in the application of this hand tool knows of the potential hazards or pain of a smashed thumb.

5   Over the years, man's tireless refinement of machines has only made life more complicated. Despite the frustration of mechanical failures and injuries

caused by these devices, mankind still finds them indispensable. Humans are enslaved by the notion that bigger is better, faster is fabulous; therefore, the smell of two-cycle exhaust in the morning is addicting. Satisfying primal instincts to mulch, cut, and conquer, machines are embedded in our minds.

Classification Technique Questions

1. The author does not define "Murphy's law." Why not? If you don't know what Murphy's law is, can you figure out what it might mean from the essay? Point out some examples that support your definition of Murphy's law.

2. What is the essay's tone: serious, humorous, sarcastic, or angry? Point out some examples to support your answer.

3. Personification is giving human qualities to inanimate objects. Can you find some examples in the essay? How do they support the tone of the essay you identified in question 2?

4. How many categories does the author use to classify tools? Can you think of some other tools that would fit into the categories in the essay?

Suggestions for Writing

1. Write a paragraph about an appliance or electronic device that was supposed to make your life easier, but, in reality, often had the opposite effect.

2. The computer is an amazing invention. There is hardly an aspect of life that it has not touched. Write a paragraph about how different types of computers or computer programs have helped or hurt life as we know it. Your tone can be serious, sarcastic, ironic, or humorous.

PROCESS

CONVERSATIONAL BALLGAMES

Nancy Masterson Sakamoto

Nancy Masterson Sakamoto lived in Japan with her artist/Buddhist priest husband for over twenty years. In this essay, the author discusses the processes involved in the conversational styles of Japanese and Americans. Notice that her specific comments about the two different styles also apply to the differences between the two cultures in general.

Pre-reading exercise: Meaning comes primarily from words. Before you start to read, use a dictionary to look up the definitions for the following words appearing in the essay.

belatedly (18)	instinctively (18)
converse (20)	murmuring (10)
customarily (19)	refer (15)
elaboration (4)	register (verb) (10)
etiquette (22)	unconsciously (3)
indispensable (20)	vigorous (6)

1   After I was married and had lived in Japan for a while, my Japanese gradually improved to the point where I could take part in simple conversations with my husband and his friends and family. And I began to notice that often, when I joined in, the others would look startled, and the conversational topic would come to a halt. After this happened several times, it became clear to me that I was doing something wrong. But for a long time, I didn't know what it was.

2   Finally, after listening carefully to many Japanese conversations, I discovered what my problem was. Even though I was speaking Japanese, I was handling the conversation in a western way.

3   Japanese-style conversations develop quite differently from western-style conversations. And the difference isn't only in the languages. I realized that just as I kept trying to hold western-style conversations even when I was speaking Japanese, so my English students kept trying to hold Japanese-style conversations even when they were speaking English. We were unconsciously playing entirely different conversational ballgames.

4   A western-style conversation between two people is like a game of tennis. If I introduce a topic, a conversational ball, I expect you to hit it back. If you agree with me, I don't expect you simply to agree and do nothing more. I expect you to add something, a reason for agreeing, another example, or an elaboration to carry the idea further. But I don't expect you always to agree. I am just as happy if you question me, or challenge me, or completely disagree with me. Whether you agree or disagree, your response will return the ball to me.

5   And then it is my turn again. I don't serve a new ball from my original starting line. I hit your ball back again from where it has bounced. I carry your idea further, or answer your questions or objections, or challenge or question you. And so the ball goes back and forth, with each of us doing our best to give it a new twist, and original spin, or a powerful smash.

6   And the more vigorous the action, the more interesting and exciting the game. Of course, if one of us gets angry, it spoils the conversation, just as it spoils a tennis game. But getting excited is not all the same as getting angry. After all, we are not trying to hit each other. We are trying to hit the ball. So long as we attack only each other's opinions, and do not attack each other personally, we don't expect anyone to get hurt. A good conversation is supposed to be interesting and exciting.

7   If there are more than two people in the conversation, then it is like doubles in tennis, or like volleyball. There's no waiting in line. Whoever is nearest and quickest hits the ball, and if you step back, someone else will hit it. No one stops the game to give you a turn. You're responsible for taking your own turn.

8   But whether it's two players or a group, everyone does his best to keep the ball going, and no one person has the ball for very long.

9   A Japanese-style conversation, however, is not at all like tennis or volleyball. It's like bowling. You wait for your turn. And you always know your place in line. It depends on such things as whether you are older or younger, a close friend or a relative stranger to the previous speaker, in a senior or junior position, and so on.

Copyright © 2004 by Pearson Education, Inc.

10 When your turn comes, you step up to the starting line with your bowling ball, and carefully bowl it. Everyone else stands back and watches politely, murmuring encouragement. Everyone waits until the ball has reached the end of the alley, and watches to see if it knocks down all the pins, or only some of them, or none of them. There is a pause, while everyone registers your score.

11 Then, after everyone is sure that you have completely finished your turn, the next person in line steps up to the same starting line, with a different ball. He doesn't return your ball, and he does not begin from where your ball stopped. There is no back and forth at all. All the balls run parallel. And there is always a suitable pause between turns. There is no rush, no excitement, no scramble for the ball.

12 No wonder everyone looked startled when I took part in Japanese conversations. I paid no attention to whose turn it was, and kept snatching the ball halfway down the alley and throwing it back to the bowler. Of course the conversation died. I was playing the wrong game.

13 This explains why it is almost impossible to get a western-style conversation or discussion going with English students in Japan. I used to think that the problem was their lack of English language ability. But I finally came to realize that the biggest problem is that they, too, are playing the wrong game.

14 Whenever I serve a volleyball, everyone just stands back and watches it fall, with occasional murmurs of encouragement. No one hits it back. Everyone waits until I call on someone to take a turn. And when that person speaks, he doesn't hit my ball back. He serves a new ball. Again, everyone just watches it fall.

15 So I call on someone else. This person does not refer to what the previous speaker has said. He also serves a new ball. Nobody seems to have paid any attention to what anyone else has said. Everyone begins again from the same starting line, and all the balls run parallel. There is never any back and forth. Everyone is trying to bowl with a volleyball.

16 And if I try a simpler conversation, with only two of us, then the other person tries to bowl with my tennis ball. No wonder foreign English teachers in Japan get discouraged.

17 Now that you know about the difference in the conversational ballgames, you may think that all your troubles are over. But if you have been trained all your life to play one game, it is no simple matter to switch to another, even if you know the rules. Knowing the rules is not at all the same thing as playing the game.

18 Even now, during a conversation in Japanese I will notice a startled reaction, and belatedly realize that once again I have rudely interrupted by instinctively trying to hit back the other person's bowling ball. It is no easier for me to "just listen" during a conversation, than it is for my Japanese students to "just relax" when speaking with foreigners. Now I can truly sympathize with how hard they must find it to try to carry on a Western-style conversation.

19 If I have not yet learned to do conversational bowling in Japanese, at least I have figured out one thing that puzzled me for a long time. After his first trip to America, my husband complained that Americans asked him so many questions and made him talk so much at the dinner table that he never had a chance to eat. When I asked him why he couldn't talk and eat at the same time, he said that Japanese do not customarily think that dinner, especially on fairly formal occasions, is a suitable time for extended conversation.

20 Since westerners think that conversation is an indispensable part of dining, and indeed would consider it impolite not to converse with one's dinner partner, I found this Japanese custom rather strange. Still, I could accept it as a cultural difference even though I didn't really understand it. But when my

husband added, in explanation, that Japanese consider it extremely rude to talk with one's mouth full, I got confused. Talking with one's mouth full is certainly not an American custom. We think it very rude, too. Yet we still manage to talk a lot and eat at the same time. How do we do it?

21   For a long time, I couldn't explain it, and it bothered me. But after I discovered the conversational ballgames, I finally found the answer. Of course! In a western-style conversation, you hit the ball, and while someone else is hitting it back, you take a bite, chew, and swallow. Then you hit the ball again, and then eat some more. The more people there are in the conversation, the more chances you have to eat. But even with only two of you talking, you still have plenty of chances to eat.

22   Maybe that's why polite conversation at the dinner table has never been a traditional part of Japanese etiquette. Your turn to talk would last so long without interruption that you'd never get a chance to eat.

Process Technique Questions

1. Is the essay intended to be informational or directional?

2. What sports does the author use to discuss the processes of western and Japanese conversation?

3. Do you think the comparisons make the process more understandable? Use supporting examples to support your answer.

4. Identify some transitional expressions that help connect the various steps in the processes the author discusses.

Suggestions for Writing

1. Write a paragraph about a process that is different for you than for someone else. This could involve a sport, a cultural event, or an everyday occurrence.

2. Write a paragraph discussing how processes can help or hinder how we get along with others, either as individuals or as groups.

HOW TO CRAM

Jill Young Miller

In this essay published in *Campus Voice,* a magazine distributed free at many colleges, the author gives advice on how to cram successfully, as the age-old but still widely used process most often fails. Pay attention not only to her advice about organization but also to how well her essay practices what she preaches.

Copyright © 2004 by Pearson Education, Inc.

Pre-reading exercise: Meaning comes primarily from words. Before you start to read, use a dictionary to look up the definitions for the following words appearing in the essay.

allusion (2)	impeding (16)	retrieve (10)
amble (23)	impose (23)	salvaged (30)
compose (17)	innumerable (2)	sequential (23)
chronic (1)	lulu (2)	threshold (27)
ditto (31)	mull (11)	transition (7)
elaborate (3)	quip (5)	

1   Frances Avila learned the hard way not to expect miracles overnight. A chronic crammer, the New York University senior did the usual for her midterm in "Major British Writers" last fall: she pulled an all-nighter. Fighting off fatigue and anxiety, Avila forced herself to concentrate on the novels and her notes through dawn, breaking only to splash cold water on her face. Near noon, she closed her books to head for the test.

2   The first question—"Expand on the gap between her front teeth"—was a lulu. Avila didn't recognize the allusion to Chaucer's Wife of Bath, even though she'd read the section only hours before. "Not only did I blank out, but I was also frightened," she recalls. "I didn't expect the test to be that elaborate." The bad situation only got worse. She fumbled through 14 more stray lines before plunging into part two, which wasn't any easier. Avila had studied innumerable facts for hours, but she knew only one thing for sure: she was in trouble.

3   "I failed the exam," she explains, "because I had to compare and contrast two poets from different time periods. In order to do that, I had to elaborate on all the details within the poetry. But I'd absorbed just enough information the night before to understand what I was reading and not enough to catch all the details."

4   Sound familiar? Almost all of us have stood (and sleepwalked) in Avila's shoes at one time or another. Sometimes push comes to shove, crunch comes to cram, and before you know it, you have to read 450 pages in six hours. Pour on the caffeine, you mumble.

5   About 90 percent of all students cram, estimates Don Dansereau, a psychology professor at Texas Christian University, who defines cramming as "intense studying the night before or the day of a test." Quips Ric Schank, a University of Florida senior, "Down here, it's the rule rather than the exception."

6   Despite its popularity, cramming gets low marks from educators and memory experts, who claim that the last-minute nature of the act kills your chances for payoff at test time.

7   A quick stroll down memory lane explains why. Most experts identify three types of memory: immediate, short-term, and long-term. You use your immediate memory as you read this, remembering each word just long enough to make the transition to the next.

8   Short-term memory is limited, too. For example, you use it when you look up a phone number, close the book, and dial. Short-term memory can supposedly hold a maximum of seven items for only a few seconds.

9   Long-term memory is the big daddy, the one that holds everything you know about the world. It's the memory that last-minute learners need to respect.

10   How well you organize information on its way into your long-term memory determines how quickly you can retrieve it later, or whether you retrieve

it at all. Think of a backpack you'd take on a hike, says Laird Cermak, a research psychologist at the Boston Veterans Administration Hospital and the author of *Improving Your Memory* (McGraw-Hill, 1975). "If your backpack is organized and you get bit by a snake, you can go right for the snakebite kit," he explains.

11   The magic lies in spacing your study over days, weeks, or even months. That gives you time to mull over the new stuff, relate it to what you already know, and organize it for exam-time recall. "The reason you forget the information is not because it was learned the night before," Cermak explains. "It's because when you crammed you didn't give yourself good ways to remember it in the future." In other words, last-minute studying limits the number of mental retrieval routes you can create.

12   But it doesn't take a psychologist to explain why cramming often fails. "You throw things into your mind, knowing that you're going to spit them out in a couple of hours and forget them. It's not a good way to learn at all," says NYU journalism senior David Reilly.

13   No quick-and-dirty detours to long-term retention and instant recall exist. But if you're forced into a late-night, last-minute study session, the results don't have to be disastrous. Here's some advice to help make the morning after less anxious than the night before:

14   **Find out what kind of test you're in for.** If you cram, you're likely to fare better on multiple-choice and fill-in-the-blank tests because they jog your memory with cues, Cermak says.

15   **Find a quiet place to study.** When Avila crams, she seeks out a small room at the library that's devoid of distractions. "I'm cornered," she says. "I have no choice but to look at the print."

16   If you like to study with music in the background, go for something without lyrics and keep the volume down low. Classical music such as Bach can have a soothing effect if your nerves are impeding your studies, says Danielle Lapp, a memory researcher at Stanford University and the author of *Don't Forget! Easy Exercises for a Better Memory at Any Age* (McGraw-Hill, 1987).

17   **Compose a scene that you can re-create during the exam.** If you can, study at the desk or in the room where you'll take the test, or do something while you study that you can do again when you take the test. For example, Dansereau suggests that you chew grape gum. "The flavor acts [as] a cuing [sic] device," he explains.

18   **Build your concentration.** Spend ten minutes warming up with a novel or magazine before you tackle a tough chapter. Says Cermak, "It helps you block out whatever else is going on."

19   **Watch what you eat and drink.** Avoid heavy meals and alcohol. Both could make you drowsy, cautions Lapp. If you need a cup of coffee to perk up, fine. But putting too much caffeine in your system can make you jittery and break your concentration.

20   **Mark your book.** Even if you only have time to read the chapter once, it helps to highlight important terms and sections. Identifying the key words and passages requires you to be mentally alert and forces you to be an active rather than a passive reader.

21   **Spend time repeating or discussing facts out loud.** Recitation promotes faster learning because it's more active than reading or listening. (Try it out when you study for your next foreign language vocabulary quiz.) Discussions groups are helpful for this reason.

22   **Take short breaks at least every few hours.** They'll help you beat fatigue, which takes a heavy toll on learning. Two hour-long sittings separated by a 15-minute break are more productive than one two-hour session in which you mind wanders throughout the second half. It doesn't matter what you do during those breaks; just take them.

Copyright © 2004 by Pearson Education, Inc.

23   **Experiment with memory techniques.** They impose structure on new information, making it easier to remember at test time. The "house" method is one of the oldest. Let's say you want to remember a list of sequential events for a history exam. Try to imagine the events taking place in separate but connected rooms of your house. When the test asks you to recall the events, take a mental amble through the rooms.

24   Another simple technique involves acronyms. You may have learned the names of the Great Lakes (Huron, Ontario, Michigan, Erie, and Superior) with this one: HOMES.

25   **Try some proven learning strategies.** Richard Yates, a counselor and time management expert at Cleveland State University, recommends the SQ3R method: survey, question, read, recite, review. Survey the material to formulate a general impression; rephrase titles and headings into questions; read through the material quickly to find the main points and the answers to your questions; recite those main ideas, taking brief notes; and review. Even when you're pressed for time, the strategy can help. "It may take a little longer," says Yates, "but it's worth the effort."

26   **Get some sleep.** UF's Schank quit all-nighters after his freshman year. "I'd go into a final and be so wired from staying up all night that I'd lose my concentration," he says. "I'd miss questions that I knew I wouldn't miss if I were in a good frame of mind." Now he crams until about 3 a.m., sleeps for about four hours, and hits the books again at 8 a.m.

27   Psychologists and memory researchers can't specify how much sleep you need—everyone has his or her own threshold—but they do stress its importance. Says Lapp, "You're better off getting some sleep so that your mind is rested for the exam than you are cramming the whole night." Just don't forget to set that alarm clock before you go to bed.

28   For an early-morning exam, it's best to do heavy-duty studying right before you go to sleep. In other words, unless you've got back-to-back exams, don't cram and then do something else for a few hours before a test. Freshly learned material is remembered much better after a period of sleep than after an equal period of daytime activity.

29   **Relax.** It may sound simplistic, but it's key to good test performance. "Anxiety is enemy number one of memory," Lapp explains. She compares a student taking a test to a singer performing onstage. "There's no way a completely anxious singer can utter a sound," she says.

30   Cramming is like going to the dentist; if you have to do it, you want it to be as painless and as productive as it can be. After all, no one goes to college to take a semester-long class and promptly forget all the new information that's been taught. At least Frances Avila didn't. After her disastrous midterm, she didn't dare risk cramming for her "Major British Writers" final exam. This time, she spaced her studying over a period of weeks, earned an A, and salvaged her grade for the semester.

31   That doesn'st mean she's quit cramming for good—in fact, she hasn't even tried to. Instead she's perfected her technique. Ditto for Reilly, who's tried unsuccessfully to break the habit. "Every semester I kick myself a million times and scream that I'm not going to cram next semester," he laments. "But it never seems to work."

Process Technique Questions

1. Is the essay intended to be informational or directional?

2. There are twelve steps in the process the author describes. How does she control describing the process so it does not seem too complex or complicated?

3. The steps of the process are described between paragraphs 14–29, and the conclusion takes just two paragraphs, 30–31. Why does the author spend thirteen paragraphs on the introduction? Give some examples to support your answer.

4. Identify some of the transitional expressions that help connect the various steps in the process the author discusses.

Suggestions for Writing

1. Write a directional paragraph describing the step-by-step process you use for studying.

2. Write an informational paragraph by discussing the environment you create for yourself to help you study. For example, do you have to have the television or stereo playing or do you study by yourself or with a friend? Explain why you think these steps help or hinder your performance on exams.

COMPARISON AND CONTRAST

GRANT AND LEE: A STUDY IN CONTRASTS

Bruce Catton

> In this essay, "Grant and Lee: A Study in Contrasts," Catton contrasts the two great American Civil War military leaders. However, while he recounts the basic differences between the two men, he also is making commentary on the significance the two men had in shaping the two sides embroiled in the conflict. By doing so, Catton makes understandable the reasons why the Union and the Confederacy came to war.

Pre-reading exercise: Meaning comes primarily from words. Before reading the essay, look up the definitions of the following words that appear in the text. The numbers in parentheses refer to the paragraph number of the essay.

aspiration (13)   indomitable (14)
burgeoning (12)   obeisance (7)
diametrically (12)   sinewy (7)
fidelity (14)   tenacity (11)
implicit (8)

1   When Ulysses S. Grant and Robert E. Lee met in the parlor of a modest house at Appomattox Court House, Virginia, on April 9, 1865, to work out the terms for the surrender of Lee's Army of Northern Virginia, a great chapter in American life came to a close, and a great new chapter began.

2   These men were bringing the Civil War to its virtual finish. To be sure, other armies had yet to surrender, and for a few days the fugitive Confederate

Copyright © 2004 by Pearson Education, Inc.

government would struggle desperately and vainly, trying to find some way to go on living now that its chief support was gone. But in effect it was all over when Grant and Lee signed the papers. And the little room where they wrote out the terms was the scene of one of the most poignant, dramatic contrasts in American history.

3   They were two strong men these oddly different generals, and they represented the strengths of two conflicting currents that, through them, had come into final collision.

4   Back of Robert E. Lee was the notion that the old aristocratic concept might somehow survive and be dominant in American life.

5   Lee was tidewater Virginia, and in his background were family, culture, and tradition . . . the age of chivalry transplanted to a New World which was making its own legends and its own myths. He embodied a way of life that had come down through the age of knighthood and the English country squire. America was a land that was beginning all over again, dedicated to nothing much more complicated than the rather hazy belief that all men had equal rights and should have an equal chance in the world. In such a land Lee stood for the feeling that it was somehow of advantage to human society to have a pronounced inequality in the social structure. There should be a leisure class, backed by ownership of land; in turn, society itself should be keyed to the land as the chief source of wealth and influence. It would bring forth (according to this ideal) a class of men with a strong sense of obligation to the community; men who lived not to gain advantage for themselves, but to meet the solemn obligations which had been laid on them by the very fact that they were privileged. From them the country would get its leadership; to them it could look for the higher values—of thought, of conduct, or personal deportment—to give it strength and virtue.

6   Lee embodied the noblest element of this aristocratic ideal. Through him, the landed nobility justified itself. For four years, the Southern states had fought a desperate war to uphold the ideals for which Lee stood. In the end, it almost seemed as if the Confederacy fought for Lee; as if he himself was the Confederacy . . . the best thing that the way of life for which the Confederacy stood could ever have to offer. He had passed into legend before Appomattox. Thousands of tired, underfed, poorly clothed Confederate soldiers, long since past the simple enthusiasm of the early days of the struggle, somehow considered Lee the symbol of everything for which they had been willing to die. But they could not quite put this feeling into words. If the Lost Cause, sanctified by so much heroism and so many deaths, had a living justification, its justification was General Lee.

7   Grant, the son of a tanner on the Western frontier, was everything Lee was not. He had come up the hard way and embodied nothing in particular except the eternal toughness and sinewy fiber of the men who grew up beyond the mountains. He was one of a body of men who owned reverence and obeisance to no one, who were self-reliant to a fault, who cared hardly anything for the past but who had a sharp eye for the future.

8   These frontier men were the precise opposites of the tidewater aristocrats. Back of them, in the great surge that had taken people over the Alleghenies and into the opening Western country, there was a deep, implicit dissatisfaction with a past that had settled into grooves. They stood for democracy, not from any reasoned conclusion about the proper ordering of human society, but simply because they had grown up in the middle of democracy and knew how it worked. Their society might have privileges, but they would be privileges each man had won for himself. Forms and patterns meant nothing. No man was born to anything, except perhaps to a chance to show how far he could rise. Life was competition.

9   Yet along with this feeling had come a deep sense of belonging to a national community. The Westerner who developed a farm, opened a shop, or set up in business as a trader could hope to prosper only as his own community prospered—and his community ran from the Atlantic to the Pacific and from Canada down to Mexico. If the land was settled, with towns and highways and accessible markets, he could better himself. He saw his fate in terms of the nation's own destiny. As its horizons expanded, so did his. He had, in other words, an acute dollars-and-cents stake in the continued growth and development of his country.

10   And that, perhaps, is where the contrast between Grant and Lee becomes most striking. The Virginia aristocrat, inevitably, saw himself in relation to his own region. He lived in a static society which could endure almost anything except change. Instinctively, his first loyalty would go to the locality in which that society existed. He would fight to the limit of endurance to defend it, because in defending it he was defending everything that gave his own life its deepest meaning.

11   The Westerner, on the other hand, would fight with an equal tenacity for the broader concept of society. He fought so because everything he lived by was tied to growth, expansion, and a constantly widening horizon. What he lived by would survive or fall with the nation itself. He could not possibly stand by unmoved in the face of an attempt to destroy the Union. He would combat it with everything he had, because he could only see it as an effort to cut the ground out from under his feet.

12   So Grant and Lee were in complete contrast, representing two diametrically opposed elements in American life. Grant was the modern man emerging; beyond him, ready to come on the stage, was the great age of steel and machinery, of crowded cities and a restless burgeoning vitality. Lee might have ridden down from the old age of chivalry, lance in hand, silken banner fluttering over his head. Each man was the perfect champion of his cause, drawing both his strengths and his weaknesses from the people he led.

13   Yet it was not all contrast, after all. Different as they were—in background, in personality, in underlying aspiration—these two great soldiers had much in common. Under everything else, they were marvelous fighters. Furthermore, their fighting qualities were really very much alike.

14   Each man had, to begin with, the great virtue of utter tenacity and fidelity. Grant fought his way down the Mississippi Valley in spite of acute personal discouragement and profound military handicaps. Lee hung on in the trenches at Petersburg after hope itself had died. In each man there was an indomitable quality . . . the born fighter's refusal to give up as long as he can still remain on his feet and lift his two fists.

15   Daring and resourcefulness they had, too: the ability to think faster and move faster than the enemy. These were the qualities which gave Lee the dazzling campaigns of Second Manassas and Chancellorsville and won Vicksburg for Grant.

16   Lastly, and perhaps greatest of all, there was the ability, at the end, to turn quickly from war to peace once the fighting was over. Out of the way these two men behaved at Appomattox came the possibility of a peace of reconciliation. It was a possibility not wholly realized, in the years to come, but which did, in the end, help the two sections to become one nation again . . . after a war whose bitterness might have seemed to make such a reunion wholly impossible. No part of either man's life became him more than the part he played in their brief meeting in the McLean house at Appomattox. Their behavior there put all succeeding generations of Americans in their debt. Two great Americans, Grant and Lee—very different, yet under everything very much alike. Their encounter at Appomattox was one of the great moments of American history.

Copyright © 2004 by Pearson Education, Inc.

Comparison and Contrast Technique Questions

1. Catton calls both Grant and Lee symbols of their respective sides. Point out some of the differences between the two men.

2. Beginning with paragraph 13, Catton changes his mode of development of Grant and Lee. Point out the similarities the two leaders share.

3. Catton has two paragraphs (paragraphs 3 and 4) consisting of only one sentence each. Do you find these effective or not? Explain.

Suggestions for Writing

1. Select two of today's world leaders, and write a paragraph either comparing or contrasting them.

2. Using yourself and someone you know or two other people you know, write a paragraph describing how the differences between these people actually make their relationship better, not worse.

▼

HASTA LA VISTA, ARNOLD

Margaret Talbot

> In this essay, "Hasta la Vista, Arnold," Talbot compares familiar male action heroes, like Stallone, Schwarzenegger, and Willis, with the new emerging female action hero. Notice that while her main interest is the difference between male and female movie heroes, she is also comparing whether cultural attitudes are changing or whether old cultural stereotypes are being reinforced.

Pre-reading exercise: Meaning comes primarily from words. Before reading the essay, look up the definitions of the following words that appear in the text. The numbers in parentheses refer to the paragraph number of the essay.

forged (3)	prowess (2)
ineffable (10)	rapacious (6)
mantle (10)	tensile (5)
marauding (13)	uncanny (14)

1 When I was eight or nine, I'd sometimes fantasize about single-handedly saving my classmates—all 32 of them—from some impending doom. Say we had a fire drill or a bomb scare at school, but this time the fire or the bomb was real. And only I knew about it.

2 Unlike my other girlhood fantasies of omnicompetence, though, this one was always a little fuzzy at the center, where the various feats of physical prowess should have been. How, exactly, was I to save them? I'd seen a few

Copyright © 2004 by Pearson Education, Inc.

action-hero movies, but they never had women or girls in the action-hero roles. Could a woman wield fists of fury if she had to? Or bolt through a wall of flame, grateful classmates in tow? What if she were wearing platform shoes? I wanted to be brave—spiritually, I was pretty sure I could be—but the physicality of bravery eluded me.

3   That was 1970 or so, and not even Charlie's ultra-coiffed Angels had been set in motion yet. Whatever the song said, not everybody was kung-fu fighting. Maybe now it's easier for girls to imagine themselves in postures of defiance. Maybe their fantasies of derring-do aren't quite so likely to sputter out. They've seen movies, like *Terminator 2* and *Speed* and the *Alien* series in which women—tough, buff, inexhaustibly resourceful women—play the central roles. They've seen *Xena: Warrior Princess,* the syndicated TV show that brings the Amazon virtues to *Baywatch* territory. ("In a time of ancient gods, warlords, and kings," the voice-over intones each week, "a land in turmoil cried out for a hero. She was Xena, a mighty princess forged in the heat of battle.") If they're nerdy-cool types, they may have seen some Hong Kong action movies—dizzy, kinetic kick-fests that have long made room for actresses trained in the martial arts to give as good as they get.

4   And as it happens, they are about to see many more female icons like these. For this, you might say, is the year of the action heroine, the year when women steer the blockbusters—the blow-hard, die-hard behemoths, the intergalactic star vehicles, the box-office bonanzas. This summer's *Speed 2: Cruise Control* has Sandra Bullock, as the plucky-by-nature Annie, fending off terrorists who have hijacked a cruise ship. The fourth *Alien* movie, due this fall, has Sigourney Weaver and Winona Ryder in the starring roles. The new *Batman* movie features Alicia Silverstone as (the perhaps inevitable) Batgirl. Actresses who seem to have been genetically engineered to play grimly determined action leads are playing them (Demi Moore as a Navy SEAL), and so are actresses who don't (Mira Sorvino in *Replacement Killers,* Minnie Driver in *The Flood*). There's even a spoofy send-up of the action genre, *Austin Powers: International Man of Mystery,* that costars Elizabeth Hurley as a trained fighter in Emma Peel rig-out.

5   Among other things, the new gender-bent action movie will bring us unprecedented displays of female grit. The wondrous Michelle Yeoh, a veteran of Hong Kong movies who upends her opponents with the tensile grace of the dancer she once was, will be starring as "a good guy" (her words) in the next James Bond movie. And though she's small (five foot four inches and 103 pounds) and beautiful (she's a former Miss Malaysia), Yeoh has a wicked roundhouse kick and a charming "Oh, do I have to save his sorry ass again?" expression. (See the Jackie Chan vehicle *Police Story III: Supercop,* in which she hops around like a Mexican jumping bean, hurling grenades and sucker-punching various mainland Chinese baddies—all the while trussed up in a bulletproof vest strapped with explosives.) Yeoh describes herself, simply, as "an actress who likes to do her own stunts. I like to be challenged. What can I say? I like strong women. I don't like wimps—of either sex."

6   Several of the actresses starring in the upcoming action movies said they relished the chance to show their stamina. "You really have to be in pretty great shape to do this part," says Sigourney Weaver, whose latest incarnation of Ripley has her swimming out of the flooded kitchen of a spaceship while battling ever-rapacious aliens. By all accounts, Weaver, at 47, *is* in great shape and does most of her own stunts.

7   Not so long ago, women hovered at the edges of action movies. They were the sacrificial lambs whose rapes or murders set our hero on his quest. Or they were the decorative gewgaws who offered proof of his heterosexuality. If they had power, it was the nefarious power of the spider woman, the vagina dentata, the comically wicked Bond villainess. (My favorite sub-B-grade version of this is the fifties sci-fi classic *Attack of the 50-Ft. Woman,* in which a neu-

rotic housewife gets irradiated, grows to colossal proportions, and handily pulverizes the puny blond who stole her husband. "No, no, Mrs. Archer!" the sheriff keeps shouting into the wind created by her Brobdingnagian crop top.)

8   Good women in action movies were never powerful, and powerful women were never good enough. Now, though, all that has begun to shift. Women are occupying the center of the story, almost as likely to play the avengers as the avenged. If an actress is strong—physically strong, especially—it's likely to be a sign of her character's integrity. Or as Iris Grossman, senior vice president of talent and casting at Turner Broadcasting, puts it, "The studios have finally woken up to the fact that women are as capable of running and jumping and slamming cars around as anyone else."

9   Not that this is exactly a feminist awakening. Conscience is nice, but money comes through a lot clearer on a cell phone. And the fact is that women have more power to make or break a film than ever before—or at least that's how the studios see it these days. Like soccer moms in last year's political campaigns, women moviegoers, especially those over 25, are the new swing constituency, sought after, fought over, and patronized. Women have been going to movies somewhat more often recently, according to figures from the Motion Picture Association of America. Female audiences were crucial to the success of several of this past year's most profitable films— including *The First Wives Club* and *Jerry Maguire.*

10   Besides, in this era of girl power and "work-life issues" and fashionable breast cancer fund-raisers, there is a kind of ineffable sense that catering to women, or being seen to do so, will earn you a mantle of virtue. Women are a "minority," but they are the biggest minority around; speaking feelingly of their special needs can be an easy way for politicians or companies or moviemakers to broadcast their compassion and rack up cultural brownie points for what George Bush memorably called "the vision thing."

11   When it comes to the new crop of action movies, the thinking goes something like this. On the one hand, big loud blockbusters with lots of things exploding in them are what Hollywood mostly does these days; the studios are in thrall to their money-making potential. On the other hand, women seem to like more character-driven movies and have turned some of those into big hits. So why not glom the two together? Put women in action movies, rejigger the genre slightly to accommodate the tastes of female audiences and voilà— you've got what you hope is a new sure-fire formula. "The aim is to do action films that are more women-friendly; that is, having strong women in top roles and taking out a lot of the violence," William Mechanic, chairman and CEO of Fox Filmed Entertainment, told *The New York Times* recently. "Women are not only driving the box office but also video-cassette rentals and sales and TV watching. Not respecting their taste level is silly." (And probably a lot harder to do now that so many more women executives are making green-light decisions at the major studios. At Paramount Pictures for example, close to half the top creative executives are women; at 20th Century Fox, about a third are, and many more women are making production deals.)

12   Maybe, too, we're at a cultural moment when we're willing, even eager to see women in strong roles—but we'd just as soon they be strong in space, or the future, or at least some pretty outlandish, exceptional circumstances in the here and now. Let them be queens for a day, just not every day. "I know that Ripley has become a feminist icon," says Sigourney Weaver when I ask her if she conceives of her *Alien* character that way. "But I've always thought that was kind of strange because everywhere I go, I see women doing everything, all kinds of physically demanding jobs. The fact that in general movies don't reflect that day-to-day reality is a measure of how out of it Hollywood is."

13   For actresses, the new availability of action roles is a boon, but not an unmitigated one. Action movies propel a few of them into the salary strato-

Copyright © 2004 by Pearson Education, Inc.

sphere as nothing else can. They still don't occupy the same gilded bracket as, say, Schwarzenegger, Stallone, or—God help us—Jim Carrey, all of whom make $20 million a film. But Sandra Bullock did take home $12.5 million for *Speed 2: Cruise Control,* and Sigourney Weaver got $11 million for *Alien Resurrection.* On the other hand, the roles can be, well, a bit robotic. Elizabeth Hurley had fun playing a jokey action heroine in silver lamé boots but says she's not especially eager to sign up for a lot of rock-'em-sock-'em blockbusters. "I really prefer to do a scene that you can get your teeth into, rather than just waiting around for things to blow up. Action films can be a little tedious." Minnie Driver agrees. In *The Flood,* she plays, of all things, a church restorer who manages to save her work and her town from rising waters and marauding robbers. She says she liked playing a character who was "definitely not a damsel in distress," and she's encouraged by the prospect of more parts for "women who can be strong across the board without being bitches." Still, Driver says she "wouldn't necessarily do another action thriller," because she's "interested in movies that are more about character. Though I have to say that if it involved somebody more like Sigourney Weaver's character in the *Alien* movies, I'd make an exception. That role, and Sigourney in it, has such grace and passion. It's never cheesy." Weaver herself worries that action movies may not embrace women who, like Ripley, project a sinewy tenacity rather than something more traditionally feminine. "The important thing in introducing new female action heroes," Weaver says, "is that they don't try to make us too glamorous, put us all in see-through uniforms or something."

14   The great strength of the *Alien* movies is their relative psychological complexity—above all, their ability to evoke a Freudian sense of the uncanny. All three of the previous *Alien* movies, with their dominant metaphor of violent birth, muck about in that mire. The next one, directed by Jean-Pierre Jeunet (*Delicatessen, City of Lost Children*), takes cloning as its dominant metaphor. The plot has Ripley, who plunged to a self-sacrificing death in the last installment, brought to life by the usual nefarious military-industrial complexers, who aim only to get at the alien inside her and to clone it for their own uses. That notion, too, has a primal pull. "I found the idea of being brought back to life against your will quite seductive," Weaver says. (The producers and publicists on *Alien Resurrection* may be among the few people who are positively cheerful about the recent cloning of a sheep and its implications for human experimentation. Everybody on the set is talking about it. Morally troubling, sure, but good box office.) Still, none of this would move us or scare us if we didn't have a central character—a woman pressing hard against her bodily limitations, not escaping her femaleness but letting her heroism transcend it—whose fate we care about and whose strength we trusted.

15   On a recent visit to the *Alien Resurrection* set, I thumbed through a stack of stills from the movie. There she was again, the nearly six-foot-tall Weaver as the larger-than-life Ripley. In the last movie, *Alien 3,* the bleakest and least successful of the series, poor Ripley was more beaten down than she'd been before. Still, even with her head shaved and her options spooled out, she at least had the charisma of her exhaustion—hollowed-eyed, sallow, a bruise blooming like a rose tattoo at her temple. She won't rest until it is vanquished. This time Ripley has hair, and her costume for most of the movie, a tunic and pants of dark, glistening leather, hugs her like a second skin. (Winona Ryder as a mechanic on a raging spaceship gets the somewhat humbler outfit—a blue-gray jumpsuit.) But even slightly glamorized, Weaver manages to look austere and haunted, her face an irreducible sliver of recognizable emotion in a technoslimed wasteland.

16   How important is it, I asked Bill Badalato, the producer of *Alien Resurrection,* to have a woman in the central role? Does it ensure greater audience appeal, bigger box office? Badalato, who produced *Broken Arrow,* among other noisy

action films, steepled his fingers and thought for a bit. "Well, the *right* woman in the role is very appealing to an audience," he said at last. "Sigourney manages to convey this steely persona that is feminine at the same time. It's a delicate balance: If a woman acts too tough and macho, an audience isn't going to buy it. If she acts too girly and gushy, they aren't going to buy it."

17   He's right, too. The best women action heroes aren't doing comic-book turns as girls with brawn *and* breasts. And they aren't doing Steven Seagal in drag, either. What you like about them is the sense that they are playing women, just women who might be a little—OK, a lot—stronger than you and me. Or, as Badalato put it of the ideal women's action role, "If men admire it and don't giggle at it and women admire it and aspire to it, then you've got it right." That's all I wanted when I was eight, after all. Is it too much to ask?

Comparison and Contrast Technique Questions

1. Point out some of the elements of contrast that Talbot makes in her discussion of female and male action heroes.

2. While some of the discussion in paragraph 13 has to do with the characteristics of female versus male action heroes, what other topic is being contrasted?

3. According to Talbot, how do the *Alien* movies, starring Sigourney Weaver, exemplify the best opportunity for women to establish a heroic identity as acceptable to audiences as are the traditional male heroes?

Suggestions for Writing

1. Select a female and a male "action hero" from recent movies and discuss how they compare or contrast to those in the essay.

2. Compare or contrast a female and male action hero of today with ones from 20 or 30 years ago.

DEFINITION

DISCRIMINATION IS A VIRTUE

Robert Keith Miller

In this essay, "Discrimination Is a Virtue," Miller defines "discrimination" in a very unconventional manner. Miller states that the term's true meaning is often misused and misunderstood. Pay particular attention to his use of *denotative* meaning (the conventional, literal meaning) and *connotative* meaning (the meanings evoked or suggested beyond a word's essential meaning).

Pre-reading exercise: Meaning comes primarily from words. Before reading the essay, look up the definitions of the following words that appear in the text. The numbers in parentheses refer to the paragraph number of the essay.

arbitrary (14)   irony (9)   radically (11)
euphemistically (12) notion (7)   realm (2)
hypocrites (3)   obsessed (7)

1 When I was a child, my grandmother used to tell me a story about a king who had three daughters and decided to test their love. He asked each of them "How much do you love me?" The first replied that she loved him as much as all the diamonds and pearls in the world. The second said that she loved him more than life itself. The third replied "I love you as fresh meat loves salt."

2 This answer enraged the king; he was convinced that his youngest daughter was making fun of him. So he banished her from his realm and left all of his property to her elder sisters.

3 As the story unfolded it became clear, even to a 6-year-old, that the king had made a terrible mistake. The two older girls were hypocrites, and as soon as they had profited from their father's generosity, they began to treat him very badly. A wiser man would have realized that the youngest daughter was the truest. Without attempting to flatter, she said, in effect, "We go together naturally; we are a perfect team."

4 Years later, when I came to read Shakespeare, I realized that my grandmother's story was loosely based upon the story of King Lear, who put his daughters to a similar test and did not know how to judge the results. Attempting to save the king from the consequences of his foolishness, a loyal friend pleads, "Come sir, arise, away! I'll teach you differences." Unfortunately, the lesson comes too late. Because Lear could not tell the difference between true love and false, he loses his kingdom and eventually his life.

5 We have a word in English which means "the ability to tell differences." That word is *discrimination*. But within the last 30 years, this word has been so frequently misused that an entire generation has grown up believing that "discrimination" means "racism." People are always proclaiming that "discrimination" is something that should be done away with. Should that ever happen, it would prove to be our undoing.

6 Discrimination means discernment; it means the ability to perceive the truth, to use good judgment and to profit accordingly. The *Oxford English Dictionary* traces this understanding of the word back to 1648 and demonstrates that for the next 300 years, "discrimination" was a virtue, not a vice. Thus, when a character in a nineteenth-century novel makes a happy marriage, Dickens has another character remark, "It does credit to your discrimination that you should have found such a very excellent young woman."

7 Of course, "the ability to tell differences" assumes that differences exist, and this is unsettling for a culture obsessed with the notion of equality. The contemporary belief that discrimination is a vice stems from the compound *discriminate against*. What we need to remember, however, is that some things deserve to be judged harshly: we should not leave our kingdoms to the selfish and the wicked.

8 Discrimination is wrong only when someone or something is discriminated against because of prejudice. But to use the word in this sense, as so many people do, is to destroy its true meaning. If you discriminate against something because of general preconceptions rather than particular insights, then you are not discriminating—bias has clouded the clarity of vision which discrimination demands.

9 One of the great ironies of American life is that we manage to discriminate in the practical decisions of daily life, but usually fail to discriminate when we make public policies. Most people are very discriminating when it comes to buying a car, for example, because they realize that cars have

Copyright © 2004 by Pearson Education, Inc.

differences. Similarly, an increasing number of people have learned to discriminate in what they eat. Some foods are better than others—and indiscriminate eating can undermine one's health.

10   Yet in public affairs, good judgment is depressingly rare. In many areas which involve the common good, we see a failure to tell differences.

11   Consider, for example, some of the thinking behind modern education. On the one hand, there is a refreshing realization that there are differences among children, and some children—be they gifted or handicapped—require special education. On the other hand, we are politically unable to accept the consequences of this perception. The trend in recent years has been to group together students of radically different ability. We call this process "mainstreaming," and it strikes me as a characteristically American response to the discovery of differences: we try to pretend that differences do not matter.

12   Similarly, we try to pretend that there is little difference between the sane and the insane. A fashionable line of argument has it that "everybody is a little mad" and that few mental patients deserve long-term hospitalization. As a consequence of such reasoning, thousands of seriously ill men and women have been evicted from their hospital beds and returned to what is euphemistically called "the community"—which often means being left to sleep on city streets, where confused and helpless people now live out of paper bags as the direct result of our refusal to discriminate.

13   Or to choose a final example from a different area: how many recent elections reflect thoughtful consideration of the genuine differences among candidates? Benumbed by television commercials that market aspiring officeholders as if they were a new brand of toothpaste or hair spray, too many Americans vote with only a fuzzy understanding of the issues in question. Like Lear, we seem too eager to leave the responsibility of government to others and too ready to trust those who tell us whatever we want to hear.

14   So as we look around us, we should recognize that "discrimination" is a virtue which we desperately need. We must try to avoid making unfair and arbitrary distinctions, but we must not go to the other extreme and pretend that there are no distinctions to be made. The ability to make intelligent judgments is essential both for the success of one's personal life and for the functioning of society as a whole. Let us be open-minded by all means, but not so open-minded that our brains fall out.

Definition Technique Questions

1. How does Miller define "discrimination"? How does he say most other people define it? What problems does this cause in various areas of society?

2. How does the personal story at the beginning of the essay help you understand what Miller is saying about the problems that misunderstanding terms can cause?

3. What is "one of the great ironies of American life" (paragraphs 9–13)? How does this affect American culture?

Suggestions for Writing

1. Select two words that you commonly confuse, and write a paragraph clarifying their definitions. Has confusing the words ever caused you any problems?

2. Write a paragraph about words you and your friends use that could be misunderstood by adults. Would most of the misunderstandings be innocent, or might some of the misunderstandings cause problems?

▼
THE HANDICAP OF DEFINITION

William Raspberry

In this essay, syndicated columnist William Raspberry discusses the many definitions of the word *black* and how those definitions negatively affect young black children. Pay attention to how the author extends and broadens the definition through a variety of examples that distinguish between "positive" and "negative" meanings.

Pre-reading exercise: Meaning comes primarily from words. Before you start to read, use a dictionary to look up the definitions of the following words appearing in the essay.

academia (6)	elocution (10)	perverted (13)
array (6)	inculcated (13)	prowess (13)
concede (12)	innate (11)	quintessentially (9)
deprivation (1)	myth (9)	scrimping (5)

1   I know all about bad schools, mean politicians, economic deprivation and racism. Still, it occurs to me that one of the heaviest burdens black Americans—and black children in particular—have to bear is the handicap of definition: the question of what it means to be black.

2   Let me explain quickly what I mean. If a basketball fan says that the Boston Celtics' Larry Bird [3-time NBA MVP and 12-time NBA All-Star] plays "black," the fan intends it—and Bird probably accepts it—as a compliment. Tell pop singer Tom Jones [still a fixture in Las Vegas] he moves "black" and he might grin in appreciation. Say to Teena Marie [for over two decades she recorded for Motown] or the Average White Band that they sound "black" and they'll thank you.

3   But name one pursuit, aside from athletics, entertainment or sexual performance in which a white practitioner will feel complimented to be told he does it "black." Tell a white broadcaster he talks "black," and he'll sign up for diction lessons. Tell a white reporter he writes "black" and he'll take a writing course. Tell a white lawyer he reasons "black" and he might sue you for slander.

4   What we have here is a tragically limited definition of blackness, and it isn't only white people who buy it.

5   Think of all the ways black children can put one another down with charges of "whiteness." For many of these children, hard study and hard work are "white." Trying to please a teacher might be criticized as acting "white." Speaking correct English is "white." Scrimping today in the interest of tomorrow's goals is "white." Educational toys and games are "white."

6   An incredible array of habits and attitudes that are conducive to success in business, in academia, in the nonentertainment professions are likely to be thought of as somehow "white." Even economic success, unless it involves such "black" undertakings as numbers banking, is defined as "white."

Copyright © 2004 by Pearson Education, Inc.

7 And the results are devastating. I wouldn't deny that blacks often are better entertainers and athletes. My point is the harm that comes from too narrow a definition of what is black.

8 One reason black youngsters tend to do better at basketball, for instance, is that they assume they can learn to do it well, and so they practice constantly to prove themselves right.

9 Wouldn't it be wonderful if we could infect black children with the notion that excellence in math is "black" rather than white, or possibly Chinese? Wouldn't it be of enormous value if we could create the myth that morality, strong families, determination, courage and love of learning are traits brought by slaves from Mother Africa and therefore quintessentially black?

10 There is no doubt in my mind that most black youngsters could develop their mathematical reasoning, their elocution and their attitudes the way they develop their jump shots and their dance steps: by the combination of sustained, enthusiastic practice and the unquestioned belief that they can do it.

11 In one sense, what I am talking about is the importance of developing positive ethnic traditions. Maybe Jews have an innate talent for communication; maybe the Chinese are born with a gift for mathematical reasoning; maybe blacks are naturally blessed with athletic grace. I doubt it. What is at work, I suspect, is assumption, inculcated early in their lives, that this is a thing our people do well.

12 Unfortunately, many of the things about which blacks make this assumption are things that do not contribute to their career success—except for that handful of the truly gifted who can make it as entertainers and athletes. And many of the things we concede to whites are the things that are essential to economic security.

13 So it is with a number of assumptions black youngsters make about what it is to be a "man": physical aggressiveness, sexual prowess, the refusal to submit to authority. The prisons are full of people who, by this perverted definition, are unmistakably men.

14 But the real problem is not so much that the things defined as "black" are negative. The problem is that the definition is much too narrow.

15 Somehow, we have to make our children understand that they are intelligent, competent people, capable of doing whatever they put their minds to and making it in the American mainstream, not just in a black subculture.

16 What we seem to be doing, instead, is raising up yet another generation of young blacks who will be failures—by definition.

Definition Technique Questions

1. Some of the examples in the essay might seem out-of-date, but what about Raspberry's thesis? Do you agree with it or not? Is it still a valid topic for discussion?

2. How would you define the term "black"? Try and develop a definition in one or two sentences.

3. Does it make any difference that Raspberry is a black man? What if he were white? How would that affect your perception of the article?

Suggestions for Writing

1. What label is attached to you or your peer group? Are you labeled a soccer mom; a slacker; a generation x-er, y-er, z-er; a suit; a rocker; a geek;

or a homeboy? Write a paragraph defining the label most associated with you or your peer group. Comment on whether you think the definition is accurate.

2. What ethnic heritage do you claim? Are you Hispanic-American, Ukrainian-American, Thai-American, African-American or some other "-American"? Write a paragraph defining your cultural label. You can develop your definition by including such elements as food, music, dance, art, rituals, religion, etc.

PERSUASION

THE REVOLT OF THE BLACK BOURGEOISIE*

Leonce Gaiter

In "The Revolt of the Black Bourgeoisie," Gaiter argues that the black middle class has to fight negative stereotyping caused mainly by its being associated with the black underclass. He maintains that the black middle class is professionally competent, educated, and culturally talented. Pay attention to the number and variety of examples that the author uses to convince the reader that his point of view is a valid one.

Pre-reading exercise: Meaning comes primarily from words. Before reading the essay, look up the definitions of the following words that appear in the text. The numbers in parentheses refer to the paragraph number of the essay.

authenticity (3)	intelligentsia (11)	psyche (9)
bourgeoisie (11)	misogyny (5)	stereotype (4)
depicted (3)	monolith (17)	superficial (6)
idiosyncrasies (17)		

1   At a television network where I once worked, one of my bosses told me I almost didn't get hired because his superior had "reservations" about me. The job had been offered under the network's Minority Advancement Program. I applied for the position because I knew I was exceptionally qualified. I would have applied for the position regardless of how it was advertised.

2   After my interview, the head of the department told my boss I wasn't really what he had in mind for a Minority Advancement Program job. To the department head, hiring a minority applicant meant hiring someone unqualified. He wanted to hire some semiliterate, hoop-shooting former prison inmate. That, in his view, was a "real" black person. That was someone worthy of the program.

3   I had previously been confronted by questions of black authenticity. At Harvard, where I graduated in 1980, a white classmate once said to me, "Oh, you're not really a black person." I asked her to explain. She could not. She

---

Copyright © 2004 by Pearson Education, Inc.

*"The Revolt of the Black Bourgeoisie," by Leonce Gaiter as appeared in *The New York Times,* June 26, 1994. Copyright © 1995 by The New York Times Co. Reprinted by permission.

had known few black people before college, but a lifetime of seeing black people depicted in the American media had taught her that real black people talked a certain way and were raised in certain places. In her world, black people did not attend elite colleges. They could not stand as her intellectual equals or superiors. Any African-American who shared her knowledge of Austen and Balzac—while having to explain to her who Douglass and DuBois were—had to be *willed* away for her to salvage her sense of superiority as a white person. Hence the accusation that I was "not really black."

4   But worse than the white majority harboring a one-dimensional vision of blackness are the many blacks who embrace this stereotype as our true nature. At the junior high school I attended in the mostly white Washington suburb of Silver Spring, Md., a black girl once stopped me in the hallway and asked belligerently, "How come you talk so proper?" Astonished, I could only reply, "It's proper*ly*," and walk on. This girl was asking why I spoke without the so-called black accent pervasive in the lower socioeconomic strata of black society, where exposure to mainstream society is limited. This girl was asking, Why wasn't I impoverished and alienated? In her world view, a black male like me couldn't exist.

5   Within the past year, however, there have been signs that blacks are openly beginning to acknowledge the complex nature of our culture. Cornel West, a professor of religion and the director of Afro-American Studies at Harvard University, discusses the growing gulf between the black underclass and the rest of black society in his book "Race Matters"; black voices have finally been raised against the violence, misogyny and vulgarity marketed to black youth in the form of gangsta rap; Ellis Cose's book "The Rage of a Privileged Class," which concentrates on the problems of middle- and upper-income blacks, was excerpted as part of a Newsweek magazine cover story; Bill Cosby has become a vocal crusader against the insulting depiction of African-Americans in "hip-hop generation" TV shows.

6   Yes, there are the beginnings of a new candor about our culture, but the question remains, How did one segment of the African-American community come to represent the whole? First, black society itself placed emphasis on that lower caste. This made sense because historically that's where the vast majority of us were placed; it's where American society and its laws were designed to keep us. Yet although doors have opened to us over the past 20 years, it is still commonplace for black leaders to insist on our community's uniform need for social welfare programs, inner-city services, job skills training, etc. Through such calls, what has passed for a black political agenda has been furthered only superficially; while affirmative action measures have forced an otherwise unwilling majority to open some doors for the black middle class, social welfare and Great Society-style programs aimed at the black lower class have shown few positive results.

7   According to 1990 census figures, between 1970 and 1990 the number of black families with incomes under $15,000 rose from 34.6 percent of the black population to 37 percent, while the number of black families with incomes of $35,000 to $50,000 rose from 13.9 percent to 15 percent of the population, and those with incomes of more than $50,000 rose from 9.9 percent to 14.5 percent of the black population.

8   Another reason the myth of an all-encompassing black underclass survives—despite the higher number of upper-income black families—is that it fits with a prevalent form of white liberalism, which is just as informed by racism as white conservatism. Since the early 70's, good guilt-liberal journalists and others warmed to the picture of black downtrodden masses in need of their help. Through the agency of good white people, blacks would rise. This image of African-Americans maintained the lifeline of white superiority that whites in this culture cling to, and therefore this image of blacks stuck. A strange tango was begun. Blacks seeing advancement opportunities allied

themselves with whites eager to "help" them. However, those whites continued to see blacks as inferior, victims, cases, and not as equals, individuals or, heaven forbid, competitors.

9   It was hammered into the African-American psyche by media-appointed black leaders and the white media that it was essential to our political progress to stay economically and socially deprived. To be recognized and recognize oneself as middle or upper class was to threaten the political progress of black people. That girl who asked why I spoke so "proper" was accusing me of political sins—of thwarting the progress of our race.

10   Despite progress toward a more balanced picture of black America, the image of black society as an underclass remains strong. Look at local news coverage of the trial of Damian Williams and Henry Watson, charged with beating the white truck driver Reginald Denny during the 1992 South-Central L.A. riots. The press showed us an African-print-wearing cadre of Williams and Watson supporters trailing Edi M. O. Faal, William's defense attorney, like a Greek chorus. This chorus made a point of standing in the camera's range. They presented themselves as the voice of South-Central L.A., the voice of the oppressed, the voice of the downtrodden, the voice of the city's black people.

11   To anyone watching TV coverage of the trial, all blacks agreed with Faal's contention that his clients were prosecuted so aggressively because they are black. Period. Reporters made no effort to show opposing black viewpoints. (In fact, the media portrait of the Los Angeles riot as blacks vs. whites and Koreans was a misrepresentation. According to the Rand Corporation, a research institute in Santa Monica, blacks made up 36 percent of those arrested during the riot; Latinos made up 51 percent). The black bourgeoisie and intelligentsia remained largely silent. We had too long believed that to express disagreement with the "official line" was to be a traitor.

12   TV networks and cable companies gain media raves for programs like "Laurel Avenue," an HBO melodrama about a working-class black family lauded for its realism, a real black family complete with drug dealers, drug users, gun toters and basketball players. It is akin to the media presenting "Valley of the Dolls" as a realistic portrayal of the ways of white women.

13   The Fox network offers a differing but equally misleading portrait of black Americans, with "Martin." While blue humor has long been a staple of black audiences, it was relegated to clubs and records for *mature* black audiences. It was not peddled to kids or to the masses.

14   Now the blue humor tradition is piped to principally white audiences. If TV was as black as it is white—if there was a fair share of black love stories, black dramas, black detective heroes—these blue humor images would not be a problem. Right now, however, they stand as images to which whites can condescend.

15   Imagine being told by your peers, the records you hear, the programs you watch, the "leaders" you see on TV, classmates, prospective employers—imagine being told by virtually everyone that in order to be your true self you must be ignorant and poor, or at least seem so.

16   Blacks must now see to it that our children face no such burden. We must see to it that the white majority, along with vocal minorities within the black community (generally those with a self-serving political agenda), do not perpetuate the notion that African-Americans are invariably doomed to the underclass.

17   African-Americans are moving toward seeing themselves—and demanding that others see us—as individuals, not as shards of a degraded monolith. The American ideal places primacy on the rights of the individual, yet historically African-Americans have been denied those rights. We blacks can effectively demand those rights, effectively demand justice only when each of us sees him or herself as an individual with the right to any of the opinions, idiosyncracies and talents accorded any other American.

Copyright © 2004 by Pearson Education, Inc.

Persuasion Technique Questions

1. How does Gaiter's personal story in the opening paragraphs support his argument about how the black underclass is holding the black middle class back?

2. Paragraph 7 uses statistics as the method of persuasion. How effective are the statistics in convincing you that the author's point of view is valid?

3. In paragraph 5, the author mentions several well-known black men who have spoken out about how successful blacks are treated unfairly. Is this effective support for his argument? How could quoting such successful blacks actually work against his argument?

Suggestions for Writing

1. Gaiter's essay was written more than a decade ago. Write a paragraph arguing for or against the idea that the black middle class is still being identified as having the same goals, attitudes, and abilities as the members of the black underclass.

2. From your own personal experience or knowledge about how successful blacks are accepted into your community, write a paragraph supporting or rejecting Gaiter's contention that attitudes concerning the black underclass affect white society's treatment of the black middle class.

▼ CYBERSPACE: IF YOU DON'T LOVE IT, LEAVE IT*

Esther Dyson

In "Cyberspace: If You Don't Love It, Leave It," Dyson argues for freedom from regulation of the Internet by the government, even in the face of growing problems, such as child pornography and racial hate group sites. Pay attention to how Dyson uses transitional devices ("The first order of business," "First," "Second," "Third," and so on) to help organize her points and to keep the momentum of her argument going.

Pre-reading exercise: Meaning comes primarily from words. Before reading the essay, look up the definitions of the following words that appear in the text. The numbers in parentheses refer to the paragraph number of the essay.

affluent (13)	metaphor (3)	terrestrial (15)
alluring (8)	oriented (19)	tyranny (15)
consensual (9)	provoke (2)	unsavory (6)
hanker (1)	psyche (1)	

---

*"Cyberspace: If You Don't Love It, Leave It," by Esther Dyson as appeared in *The New York Times,* July 17, 1995. Copyright © 1995 by The New York Times Co. Reprinted by permission.

Copyright © 2004 by Pearson Education, Inc.

1 Something in the American psyche loves new frontiers. We hanker after wide-open spaces; we like to explore; we like to make rules instead of follow them. But in this age of political correctness and other intrusions on our national cult of independence, it's hard to find a place where you can go and be yourself without worrying about the neighbors.

2 There is such a place: cyberspace. Lost in the furor over porn on the Net is the exhilarating sense of freedom that this new frontier once promised—and still does in some quarters. Formerly a playground for computer nerds and techies, cyberspace now embraces every conceivable constituency: schoolchildren, flirtatious singles, Hungarian-Americans, accountants—along with pederasts and porn fans. Can they all get along? Or will fear of kids surfing for cyberspace behind their bedroom doors provoke a crackdown?

3 The first order of business is to grasp what cyberspace *is*. It might help to leave behind metaphors of highways and frontiers and to think instead of real estate. Real estate, remember, is an intellectual, legal, artificial environment constructed *on top of* land. Real estate recognizes the difference between parkland and shopping mall, between red-light zone and school district, between church, state and drugstore.

4 In the same way, you could think of cyberspace as a giant and unbounded world of virtual real estate. Some property is privately owned and rented out; other property is common land; some places are suitable for children, and others are best avoided by all but the kinkiest citizens. Unfortunately, it's those places that are now capturing the popular imagination: places that offer bomb-making instructions, pornography, advice on how to procure stolen credit cards. They make cyberspace sound like a nasty place. Good citizens jump to a conclusion: better regulate it. . . .

5 Regardless of how many laws or lawsuits are launched, regulation won't work.

6 Aside from being unconstitutional, using censorship to counter indecency and other troubling "speech" fundamentally misinterprets the nature of cyberspace. Cyberspace isn't a frontier where wicked people can grab unsuspecting children, nor is it a giant television system that can beam offensive messages at unwilling viewers. In this kind of real estate, users have to *choose* where they visit, what they see, what they do. It's optional, and it's much easier to bypass a place on the Net than it is to avoid walking past an unsavory block of stores on the way to your local 7-11.

7 Put plainly, cyberspace is a voluntary destination—in reality, many destinations. You don't just get "onto the Net"; you have to go someplace in particular. That means that people can choose where to go and what to see. Yes, community standards should be enforced, but those standards should be set by cyberspace communities themselves, not by the courts or by politicians in Washington. What we need isn't Government control over all these electronic communities: We need self-rule.

8 What makes cyberspace so alluring is precisely the way in which it's *different* from shopping malls, television, highways and other terrestrial jurisdictions. But let's define the territory:

9 First, there are private e-mail conversations, akin to the conversations you have over the telephone or voice mail. These are private and consensual and require no regulation at all.

10 Second, there are information and entertainment services, where people can download anything from legal texts and lists of "great new restaurants" to game software or dirty pictures. These places are like bookstores, malls and movie houses—places where you go to buy something. The customer needs to request an item or sign up for a subscription; stuff (especially pornography) is not sent out to people who don't ask for it. Some of these services are free or included as part of a broad service like Compuserve or America Online; others charge and may bill their customers directly.

11   Third, there are "real" communities—groups of people who communicate among themselves. In real-estate terms, they're like bars or restaurants or bathhouses. Each active participant contributes to a general conversation, generally through posted messages. Other participants may simply listen or watch. Some are supervised by a moderator; others are more like bulletin boards—anyone is free to post anything. Many of these services started out unmoderated but are now imposing rules to keep out unwanted advertising, extraneous discussions or increasingly rude participants. Without a moderator, the decibel level often gets too high.

12   Ultimately, it's the rules that determine the success of such places. Some of the rules are determined by the supplier of content; some of the rules concern prices and membership fees. The rules may be simple: "Only high-quality content about oil-industry liability and pollution legislation: $120 an hour." Or: "This forum is unmoderated, and restricted to information about copyright issues. People who insist on posting advertising or unrelated material will be asked to desist (and may eventually be barred)." Or: "Only children 8 to 12, on school-related topics and only clean words. The moderator will decide what's acceptable."

13   Cyberspace communities evolve just the way terrestrial communities do: People with like-minded interests band together. Every cyberspace community has its own character. Overall, the communities on Compuserve tend to be more techy or professional; those on America Online, affluent young singles; Prodigy, family oriented. Then there are independents like Echo, a hip, downtown New York service, or Women's Wire, targeted to women who want to avoid the male culture prevalent elsewhere on the Net. There's Surf-Watch, a new program allowing access only to locations deemed suitable for children. On the Internet itself, there are lots of passionate noncommercial discussion groups on topics ranging from Hungarian politics (Hungary-Online) to copyright law.

14   And yes, there are also porn-oriented services, where people share dirty pictures and communicate with one another about all kinds of practices, often anonymously. Whether these services encourage the fantasies they depict is subject to debate—the same debate that has raged about pornography in other media. But the point is that no one is forcing this stuff on anybody.

15   What's unique about cyberspace is that it liberates us from the tyranny of government, where everyone lives by the rule of the majority. In a democracy, minority groups and minority preferences tend to get squeezed out, whether they are minorities of race and culture or minorities of individual taste. Cyberspace allows communities of any size and kind to flourish; in cyberspace, communities are chosen by the users, not forced on them by accidents of geography. This freedom gives the rules that preside in cyberspace a moral authority that rules in terrestrial environments don't have. Most people are stuck in the country of their birth, but if you don't like the rules of a cyberspace community, you can just sign off. Love it or leave it. Likewise, if parents don't like the rules of a given cyberspace community, they can restrict their children's access to it.

16   What's likely to happen in cyberspace is the formation of new communities, free of the constraints that cause conflict on earth. Instead of a global village, which is a nice dream but impossible to manage, we'll have invented another world of self-contained communities that cater to their own members' inclinations without interfering with anyone else's. The possibility of a real market-style evolution of governance is at hand. In cyberspace, we'll be able to test and evolve rules governing what needs to be governed—intellectual property, content and access control, rules about privacy and free speech. Some communities will allow anyone in; others will restrict access to members who qualify on one basis or another. Those communities that prove self-

sustaining will prosper (and perhaps grow and split into subsets with ever-more-particular interests and identities). Those that can't survive—either because people lose interest or get scared off—will simply wither away.

17   In the near future, explorers in cyberspace will need to get better at defining and identifying their communities. They will need to put in place—and accept—their own local governments, just as the owners of expensive real estate often prefer to have their own security guards rather than call in the police. But they will rarely need help from any terrestrial government.

18   Of course, terrestrial governments may not agree. What to do, for instance, about pornography? The answer is labeling—not banning—questionable material. In order to avoid censorship and lower the political temperature, it makes sense for cyberspace participants themselves to agree on a scheme for questionable items, so that people or automatic filters can avoid them. In other words, posting pornography in "alt.sex.bestiality" would be O.K.; it's easy enough for software manufacturers to build an automatic filter that would prevent you—or your child—from ever seeing that item on a menu. (It's as if all the items were wrapped, with labels on the wrapper.) Someone who posted the same material under the title "Kid-Fun" could be sued for mislabeling.

19   Without a lot of fanfare, private enterprises and local groups are already producing a variety of labeling and ranking services, along with kid-oriented sites like Kidlink, EdWeb and Kids' Space. People differ in their tastes and values and can find services or reviewers on the Net that suit them in the same way they select books and magazines. Or they can wander freely if they prefer, making up their own itinerary.

20   In the end, our society needs to grow up. Growing up means understanding that there are no perfect answers, no all-purpose solutions, no government-sanctioned safe havens. We haven't created a perfect society on earth and we won't have one in cyberspace either. But at least we can have individual choice—and individual responsibility.

Persuasion Technique Questions

1. Government regulation of the Internet is an important issue. Does Dyson's argument support or reject this idea?

2. Dyson compares the Internet to real estate, even though it is not a tangible piece of property. Does this comparison help support her point of view?

3. How does Dyson's argument in paragraph 18 support or reject her stated opinion about freedom of speech and freedom of choice? Does this help or hurt her overall argument?

Suggestions for Writing

1. Write a paragraph agreeing or disagreeing with Dyson's contention that parents should be responsible for what their children access on the Internet.

2. Write a paragraph agreeing with Dyson's point of view about whether the government should regulate the Internet. Then, write a paragraph that takes the opposite point of view.

Copyright © 2004 by Pearson Education, Inc.

LIMITED ANSWER KEY

Note: Answers are not included for practice materials in which answers will vary.

Chapter 3

PRACTICE 1
1. airliner
3. lights
5. air traffic controller
7. Passengers
9. Signs

PRACTICE 2
2. It
4. Adler and Sullivan Company
6. philosophy
8. carport
10. Frank Lloyd Wright

PRACTICE 3
1. Yukon Territory
3. wealth; vistas
5. plateaus
7. Forests
9. climate

PRACTICE 6
2. The carton ~~of oranges~~ floated ~~in the water.~~
4. ~~Between the two hills,~~ the houses are made ~~from cedar logs.~~
6. ~~During the week~~ and ~~on the weekend,~~ homework is a constant activity.
8. ~~Over the river~~ and ~~through the woods,~~ the wolf raced ~~to Grandmother's house.~~
10. Three ~~of the guitarists~~ are alternative musicians.

PRACTICE 7
1. ~~In a presidential election,~~ the challenger has to choose a running mate.
3. ~~At the beginning of the process,~~ many candidates are considered.
5. ~~After the elimination of some candidates,~~ a short list is assembled.
7. ~~Without the interview process,~~ the final choice cannot be made.
9. ~~By the end of the process,~~ the challenger can make a clear choice ~~for the party.~~

PRACTICE 8
2. The rocking motion ~~of the plane~~ was somewhat disturbing.
4. ~~Outside the cabin,~~ the stars shone like small fireflies ~~in the dark.~~
6. ~~In most cases,~~ smaller children slept ~~on their parents' laps.~~

8. ~~After the flight landed,~~ the passengers walked ~~to the baggage carousel.~~
10. ~~During the trip to the hotel,~~ their bags were carried ~~on the top of the bus.~~

PRACTICE 9
1. ~~As a young child,~~ (he) learned the proper mechanics ~~of the swing.~~
3. The (youngster) progressed rapidly ~~as a golfer.~~
5. ~~Without hesitation,~~ (Woods) won three straight Amateur championships.
7. (He) regularly launched 300-yard drives ~~on the longer holes.~~
9. (Tiger) stunned the golfing world ~~with his outstanding and exciting play.~~

PRACTICE 10
2. (She) opened the letter ~~on the kitchen table.~~
4. (She) unfolded the piece ~~of paper.~~
6. (Tears) ~~of happiness~~ flowed ~~from her eyes.~~
8. ~~After calming down,~~ (Marjorie) called her mother and father ~~on the phone.~~
10. (She) had won round trip tickets ~~for four to London.~~

PRACTICE 11
1. Most (people) participate ~~in outdoor activities.~~
3. (Another) skis ~~in the mountains of Colorado.~~
5. A (group) ~~from Vermont~~ searches ~~for rare birds in the deep forests.~~
7. (Missourians) ride bikes ~~on the scenic Katy Trail.~~
9. (Others) leap ~~from bridges with bungee cords~~ attached ~~to their ankles.~~

PRACTICE 13
2. The (foyer) looked (buffed and polished) from floor to ceiling.
4. (People) in the audience seemed (nervous)
6. The symphony (orchestra) sounded (confident and well-rehearsed).
8. The (music) remained (controlled) throughout the evening.
10. At the concert's end, the (applause) became (louder) with each bow.

PRACTICE 14
1. My (life) was not (wonderful.)
3. My family said (I) looked (depressed)
5. Even (food) smelled (dull and tasteless.)
7. (I) felt (disassociated) from my true self.
9. (I) turned to a counselor (for help)

PRACTICE 16

2. However, (exercising) must be done ~~on a regular basis~~.
4. ~~On the other hand~~, (exercising) too much <u>may be</u> detrimental ~~to your health~~.
6. (Lifting weights) should be accompanied ~~by an aerobic exercise~~.
8. (Mental health) also <u>will be stimulated</u> ~~by physical exercise~~.
10. Regular (exercising) <u>would lower</u> health-related costs nationally.

PRACTICE 17

1. How <u>do</u> (you) <u>start</u> a hobby?
3. Then, (you) <u>should ask</u> your friends and neighbors what hobbies they have.
5. (Budgeting) <u>may help</u> you narrow your choices.
7. (This) <u>could put</u> you ~~in touch with other enthusiasts~~ interested ~~in the same hobby as you~~.
9. (Being a member) ~~of a club~~ also <u>might get</u> you discounts ~~on materials and publications~~.

PRACTICE 19

2. danced
   dances
   will dance
4. played
   plays
   will play

PRACTICE 20

1. cornered
   corners
   will corner
3. consumed
   consumes
   will consume
5. camped
   camps
   will camp

PRACTICE 21

2. coordinated
   coordinates
   will coordinate
4. juggled
   juggles
   will juggle

PRACTICE 24

1. The child's <u>ears and nose</u> (looked) just like its mother's.
3. <u>Jupiter, Mars, and Venus</u> (are) planets ~~in our solar system~~.
5. The <u>antique sofa, the art deco clock, and the abstract painting</u> (were sold) ~~at auction~~.
7. The <u>slithery snake, the prickly hedgehog, and the colorful parrot</u> (are) the most popular animals ~~at the children's zoo~~.
9. *Hamlet and Macbeth* (are) two ~~of Shakespeare's~~ most famous plays.

PRACTICE 25

2. <u>Brad Pitt, Harrison Ford, and Tom Cruise</u> (are) popular movie stars.
4. <u>The lawn mower, the edger, and the cultivator</u> (sat) unused ~~in the garage~~.
6. Either <u>you or I</u> (will have to make) dinner ~~for the cub scouts~~.
8. ~~In the middle of the night~~, <u>snoring, cat calls, and crying infants</u> (can reduce) sleep.
10. <u>Nike, Adidas, and Reebok</u> (are) best-selling athletic shoes.

PRACTICE 26

1. The horse <u>trotted and galloped</u> around the track.
3. The audience <u>laughed and cried</u> at the actor's performance.
5. The motel room <u>was clean and smelled</u> of lilacs and roses.
7. In New York City, skateboarders <u>ride</u> on subways and <u>skate</u> in parking garages.
9. The legislature <u>argued and voted</u> on fifty-three bills this current session.

PRACTICE 27

2. In the auditorium, students <u>clapped</u> their hands and <u>stomped</u> their feet.
4. The old fire engine <u>jiggled and rattled</u> down the cobblestone street.
6. After the huge meal, the diners <u>moaned and groaned</u>.
8. Seabirds <u>fly, dive, swim, and float</u> while searching for food.
10. The dancers <u>twirled and leaped</u> in time with the music.

Chapter 4

PRACTICE 1

1. Jawan hit the ball, but Christie caught the ball.
3. Pang ran quickly to third base, yet Chinua tagged him out.
5. Tom singled four times, and Angie hit two home runs.
7. Joe caused three errors, so the other team scored five runs.

PRACTICE 2

2. , so
4. , for
6. , yet

PRACTICE 6

Sentence corrections will vary.
1. CS
3. C
5. RO
7. C
9. CS

Copyright © 2004 by Pearson Education, Inc.

PRACTICE 7

Sentence corrections will vary.

2. RO
4. C
6. CS
8. CS
10. RO

Chapter 5

PRACTICE 1

The surgical team prepared the operating room for the procedure. The surgeon dressed in a green surgical gown; she wore a protective cap covering her hair. Bach's *Toccata and Fugue in D Minor* was piped into the operating room during the operation; it helped to maintain a relaxed atmosphere during the delicate procedure. The operation was a success. The patient experienced a quick recovery; he was back at work in less than two weeks. His insurance paid for the operation. His family was happy to have him healthy again.

Chapter 7

PRACTICE 1

1. They ordered <u>steak, potatoes, and asparagus</u> at dinner.
3. C
5. The garden consisted of <u>tulips, crocuses, and jonquils</u> during the three months of spring.
7. The fog blanketed the fields <u>in the morning, during the afternoon, and after dark</u>.
9. The orchestra's <u>violins, cellos, and violas</u> answered the woodwinds during the second movement.

Chapter 8

PRACTICE 1

2. Jerry enjoyed many activities while vacationing: boating, fishing, and hiking.
4. The librarian reshelved the book left on her desk: *Retire Early: How to Make Money in Real Estate Foreclosures.*
6. The office workers ate lunch in a variety of places: in the employee lounge, on the roof, and out by the lake.
8. Joaquin used three types of peppers to add color to his special salsa: red, yellow, and green.
10. The children enjoyed the party because of the food: hot dogs, hamburgers, and chips.

PRACTICE 2

1. The two falcons found a tree, gathered twigs, and built a nest.
3. The surgical team had a good reputation because they were up on the latest techniques and had worked together for four years.
5. The movie was titled *Strangers: The Story of a Mother and a Daughter.*
7. The plane could not take off; the engine wasn't powerful enough to handle the load.

9. Amelia was in a hurry because her date was at 7:00 P.M. and it was already 6:45 P.M.

PRACTICE 4

Movies are popular because of two factors: actors and genres. Star-power can almost guarantee that a movie will make money. There are a handful of stars in this category: Denzel Washington, Julia Roberts, and Tom Hanks. If tickets for movies starring one of these actors go on sale at 2:00 P.M., the "Sold Out" sign usually lights up by 4:00 P.M. Fantasy-action movies are some of the most popular movies currently running. Some of the largest grossing movies in history belong to this genre: *Star Wars: The Return of the Jedi, Lord of the Rings: The Fellowship of the Ring,* and *Harry Potter: The Sorceror's Stone,* to name a few. If movie producers can combine a popular star with a popular genre, a box-office bonanza is almost a sure thing.

PRACTICE 5

Dear Ms. Morgan:

Thank you for your recent inquiry concerning what to expect here at Middletown University during your first year as a student. As you know, there are certain personal traits that will stand you in good order both at school and your future place of employment: financial responsibility, time management, and cooperation. Working to help with expenses teaches the value of money and what it represents in terms of goods and services. Time management is an important skill to learn. For instance, in her best selling business book, *Time Management: Workplace Wizardry,* author Meghan Brooks suggests that you should never get out of bed later than 6:00 A.M. By 7:00 A.M. you should have your daily schedule complete. Doing this will keep you organized and focused on each task. Cooperation, of course, will help you enormously while you are attending Middletown. You will be working and interacting with a wide array of individuals: administrators, staff, faculty, and other students. I hope this letter helps answer your concerns. Please do not hesitate to contact me during my office hours: 3:00 P.M., Wednesdays, and 10:00 A.M. Thursdays.

Sincerely yours,
Ronald Blevins, Dean
Arts & Humanities Division

Chapter 9

PRACTICE 1

1. <u>Gas prices increase during the summer (because) many people drive on their vacations.</u>
3. <u>Golfers can play all day and night in Finland (since) the sun never sets.</u>
5. <u>(Before) an earthquake sends tremors through the ground, some scientists believe animals can somehow sense it is going to happen.</u>
7. <u>(Until) their economy failed, the Russians were considered a world power.</u>

9. The students had a study session every Sunday evening (unless) there was a good concert at the student center.

Chapter 10

PRACTICE 1

2. At first, I did not see the need to know CPR for my job as a lifeguard.
4. More often, the traffic is heavier in the evening than in the morning.
6. All in all, it was a very profitable day selling pennants outside the stadium.
8. Being thin and tall, the model easily fit into all the designer's latest gowns.
10. Whether guilty or not, the defendant seemed believable when testifying.

PRACTICE 2

1. After the matinee showing, the tour bus left Las Vegas and headed for Reno.
3. On most sunny days, the students gathered in the quadrangle to read and visit.
5. Over the mountains, the highway trailed away like a giant black snake.
7. Under the viaduct, a homeless person had established a camp.
9. As lava eventually cools, more living space is realized.

PRACTICE 4

2. description
4. comparison
6. definition

Chapter 11

PRACTICE 1

1. No, taking the driver's exam is not possible until Monday morning.
3. Nevertheless, we are spending a full week in Toronto.
5. Yes, the mechanic says he can fix the radiator.
7. Hmmm, I can't decide on sausage or pepperoni on my pizza.
9. Well, I might go hang gliding if the weather conditions are good.

PRACTICE 2

2. Nevertheless, (express a contrast)
4. Ah, (express surprise or wonderment)
6. However, (express a contrast)
8. Well, (express a contemplative pause)
10. Leonardo, (address by name)

Chapter 12

PRACTICE 1

1. World War II, naturally, is an event discussed to this day.

3. Poor relations, meanwhile, developed between the two powers.
5. The Empire of Japan, therefore, attacked Pearl Harbor.
7. The United States, consequently, entered World War II on December 8, 1941.
9. The United States, eventually, would fight a war on two fronts: Asia and Europe.
11. Today, the United States and Japan, however, are considered allies.

PRACTICE 2

2. Frost, in fact, was from New England.
4. His poetry, on the other hand, often dealt with death and alienation.
6. Frost, as a matter of fact, achieved his first success while living in England.
8. Robert Frost, at last, had attained the status of a major poet worldwide.

PRACTICE 3

1. Our solar system, the only planetary system in this part of the galaxy, consists of nine major planets.
3. The inner planets, Mercury, Venus, Earth, and Mars, are composed primarily of rock and iron.
5. Mercury not only is nearest the sun but also orbits the sun most quickly.
7. The earth, with a myriad of life forms, is the only planet known to have abundant liquid water and oxygen.
9. Jupiter's mass of 317 times that of earth makes it the largest of the planets.

Chapter 13

PRACTICE 1

1. (Mud-slinging and personal attacks) turn off some people when it comes to politics.
3. (Families can help children) by being a support system for all their activities.
5. (The movie was a success) because of the script, the acting, and the special effects.
7. (The depletion of the ozone layer) might cause global warming and an increase in skin cancers.
9. (Helping others) can make almost any profession a rewarding experience.

PRACTICE 2

2. The (fence) was built to keep the coyotes away from the livestock.
4. Great teamwork has made the (United States') (women's soccer team) an international success.
6. Versatility and size make the (laptop computer) a good business tool for travelers.
8. (The Spanish Inquisition) impaired scientific thought for decades.
10. (A quiet place) with good lighting can help students study more effectively.

Copyright © 2004 by Pearson Education, Inc.

PRACTICE 14

soothing
deserted
rushing
crash
warped
tables
leading
replaced
boards
scene
beautiful

PRACTICE 15

to
broaden
can
mellow
story
elevators
classical
or
western
your

Chapter 14

PRACTICE 4

1. Halloween—stated in the title, not in the paragraph.
3. Similes add descriptive images that support the "scary" dominant impression. The trees are also personified as they can "snatch their next victim."

PRACTICE 5

2. Excitement

PRACTICE 6

1. Smells
3. "The opposite sex was as mysterious as space travel," and "smells detonate softly in our memory like poignant land mines."
5. These verbs are very dramatic, and they combine to stimulate visual memory because of their ability to elicit memories from sensory stimulation.

PRACTICE 7

1. The ice cream truck.
3. In ¶ 3, "Then the truck's transmission gears growled," and "the echoes of the burdensome chimes."

Chapter 15

PRACTICE 7

1. The writer uses telephone calls to order the events. There are two phone calls and a third is inferred. The first call is introduced in the first sentence: "It was not long before the telephone rang." The second call is introduced in sentence five: "Upon receiving the second call. . . ." And the third call is inferred by the operator in the last sentence: "The operator would check back with them."

PRACTICE 8

1. The writer orders the events chronologically as they occur: first, the writer resolves to do something about her looks; second, how she feels about the project; third, she sprints to the department store; fourth, she goes to the cosmetics counter; and lastly, her decision to broaden her original desire to go for BEAUTIFUL, rather than just attractive.

Chapter 16

PRACTICE 6

2. The desire is to acculturate children with the values of their own group.

PRACTICE 7

1. Dale Evans (the wife of cowboy star Roy Rogers), Helen Keller (the famous woman who was blind and deaf), Greta Garbo (a famous movie star who shunned the limelight), Mae West (one of the first movie "sex goddesses"), Catherine Deneuve (the famous French actress), and Naomi Campbell (the famous super model).
3. Only a few: "In some cases," in the second sentence, is used to introduce the listing of famous female examples; and, in the third sentence, the coordinating conjunction "but" to combine ideas. The writer probably could have used more. Other answers will vary.

Chapter 17

PRACTICE 1

2. b
4. b
6. b

PRACTICE 2

1. d
3. b
5. b

PRACTICE 3

2. "The second category" (sentence 4)

PRACTICE 7

1. They all have "starter cords."
3. Weed whackers, lawn mowers, edgers, and snow-blowers. Yes, because most people probably own at least one of the machines, so they have personal knowledge of and experience with them.
5. No, the writer does not use transitional expressions. Other answers will vary.

PRACTICE 8

2. Pile drivers, carpenters, and millwrights. All their jobs are dangerous.
4. "The first type" (sentence 2); "The second kind" (sentence 4); "The last category" (sentence 7). They organize the three types of workers chronologically.

This organization helps the reader remain focused on the categories.

PRACTICE 9

1. "Pliers . . . climbing" with "single-minded determination"; "Keys . . . burrow"; "Women's purses . . . travel . . . to find hiding space." The tone is humorous. It's as if the objects are planning to do these things to annoy us.
3. Answers will vary.
5. To entertain by giving us humorous situations that we can identify with because we have all most likely experienced such exasperating activities.

PRACTICE 10

2. Disciplining, rulesetting, and visitation.
4. Many readers will come from split families, and they will have their own experiences in similar situations.

Chapter 18

PRACTICE 1

1. D
3. D
5. I
7. D
9. I

PRACTICE 2

2. I
4. D
6. D
8. I
10. I

PRACTICE 3

1. 4, 5, 3, 2, 1

PRACTICE 4

2. X, 5, 2, 4, 1, 7, 6, 3

PRACTICE 5

1. How to make a pizza.
3. Three steps: making the dough, making the sauce, assembling the pizza and toppings.

PRACTICE 6

2. Informational
4. "first . . . step" (sentence 2); "while" (sentence 6); "now" (sentence 7)

PRACTICE 8

1. Producing a photograph from a negative.
3. Three: setting the scene, developing the negative, and enlarging the print.
5. Answers will vary.

PRACTICE 10

2. Five
4. Answers will vary.

PRACTICE 11

1. Conversation
3. Tennis and bowling

Chapter 19

PRACTICE 1

Answers may vary, but the following are the most popular approaches.
2. Contrast
4. Contrast
6. Compare
8. Contrast
10. Contrast

PRACTICE 2

1. Compare
3. Compare
5. Contrast
7. Contrast
9. Compare

PRACTICE 7

2. Point-by-point
4. While the author talks about "character," in general terms, no specific characters are offered as examples.

PRACTICE 8

1. Who pays for the commercial and residential real estate marketing costs—the company or the agent. Yes, the first sentence.
3. By using transitional expressions: "similarly" (sentence 1); "like" (sentence 2).

PRACTICE 9

2. Block
4. Yes, the author mentions activities when she was a girl, such as sports and driving with her father to Wal-Mart, and she mentions the things she did on her own as an adolescent, such as deciding when to go to bed, what to wear, and what to eat.

PRACTICE 10

1. Ulysses S. Grant and Robert E. Lee, the two military commanders for the North and South during the Civil War. Yes, although Grant and Lee are not specifically mentioned. It might have been a more effective topic sentence had the author done so.
3. "again" (sentence 3); "very different" (sentence 5); "very much alike" (sentence 5). Yes. Answers will vary.

PRACTICE 11

1. Yes, new (stated) versus traditional (inferred) action roles for women.
3. Yes. "On the other hand" (sentence 4); "like" (sentence 15).

Copyright © 2004 by Pearson Education, Inc.

Chapter 20

PRACTICE 1

2. To blunder is to make a mistake.
4. Rustic means relating to the rural or country life or people.

PRACTICE 2

1. A robin is a bird having a red breast and gray and black upper plummage.
3. A shark is a marine carnivorous fish having a cartilage skeleton and scratchy skin.
5. A prude is a person who is excessively concerned with appearing proper, modest, or righteous.

PRACTICE 5

2. Informational process: World War II soldiers returning home. Description: the engine was cheap, plentiful, a popular choice, easy to customize, and a winning combination when coupled to a light-bodied chassis.
4. It was cheap, plentiful, easy to customize, and powerful.

PRACTICE 6

1. Yes, the perfect store. Process—how the customer is sold merchandise and how the customer can evaluate merchandise by price.
3. Sentence 5. It not only honors its own coupons and advertised prices, but it does so for its competitors' coupons and advertised prices as well.

Chapter 21

PRACTICE 2

2. The writer uses the first sentences to state the opposition's point of view. Then, he uses the next two sentences to refute the opposition's position by introducing the negative aspects of nuclear waste material.

PRACTICE 3

1. An idea many have about a thing, another person, or a group that is often untrue or partially untrue.
3. Black political leaders, whose agenda seems to be limited to Great Society-style programs aimed at the lower class.

PRACTICE 5

2. F
4. O
6. O
8. O
10. F

Chapter 22

PRACTICE 1

1. Not a good thesis because it is in the form of a question.
3. Not a good thesis because the writer's position is not clear.

5. Not a good thesis because it asserts two main ideas.
7. Not a good thesis because it is a statement of fact.
9. Not a good thesis because it does not clearly define the topic.

PRACTICE 2

2. are more successful
4. should not be installed
6. was not any better
8. promotes
10. helps

PRACTICE 3

1. Salt and water retention may be related as unhealthy aspects of eating meat versus vegetables, but temperature is not a viable reason supporting a vegetarian diet.
3. These three essay map items do not support why household chores help children in any way.
5. Correct.

PRACTICE 4

2. Playmaking, speed, and bench-clearing brawls make ice hockey an exciting sport.
4. College students go to class, study, and write papers. (No attitude.)
6. Solar power should be a governmental priority because of diminishing fossil fuels, environmental pollution, and skyrocketing costs.
8. The St. Louis Rams, Green Bay Packers, and Pittsburgh Steelers are football teams. (No attitude.)
10. Humor, social satire, and musicality made the Beatles popular long after their breakup as a rock group.

PRACTICE 8

1. A shocking statistic: over six million people were exterminated.
3. The Holocaust.
5. Horrendous policies; numbers of victims, and the terrible effects it continues to have on the survivors.
7. Body Paragraph #1: What the horrendous policies led to.
   Body Paragraph #2: Who was affected by the Holocaust.
   Body Paragraph #3: How the liberators and survivors were affected.

PRACTICE 9

2. Exercising the upper body, abdominal muscles, and leg muscles correctly is important for proper functioning.
4. Is important
6. The most important muscles to exercise in the upper body are the triceps, biceps, and pectorals. The abdominal muscles are significant because they support the entire body. The three major muscles in the legs give you the ability to stand, walk, run and jump.
8. Call to action: it is important to exercise. Prediction: If you exercise properly, you will lose weight, have more energy, and feel younger.

GLOSSARY

Absolute phrase: A group of words consisting of a noun or pronoun and a **participle** (not the regular verb form), plus any other completing words. Absolute phrases modify the entire sentence and cannot be punctuated as a complete sentence.

Action verb: A verb that states what a subject does (in the past, present, or future tense).

Active voice: A verb form in which the subject of the sentence does the acting (using action verb/transitive verb).

Adjective: A word that modifies (or describes) a noun or pronoun. Adjectives come before the nouns they describe; they can also follow the noun. Adjectives can be objective (describing nouns with sensory details) or subjective (describing concepts, feelings, or ideas in more general terms). Both are useful in good writing and enhance meaning, especially in combination.

Adverb: A word that modifies (describes) a verb, or an adjective. Often adverbs end in –ly. Another test to identify adverbs is to ask if it answers one of the questions *where, how,* or *when.* Adverbs describe the action of a passage; in some cases they refer to other adverbs to intensify meaning.

Adverbial conjunction: A word that often follows a semicolon to explain how or in what way the two clauses joined by the semicolon are logically related; often called a *transitional word.*

Antecedent: The noun (or words) to which a pronoun refers in a sentence. (See *Pronoun.*)

Apostrophe: The apostrophe is used to indicate contractions or possession/ownership.

Appositive: A word or phrase which renames the word or phrase preceding it. Appositive words or phrases are often called noun phrases.

Article: A type of word that introduces a noun and indicates whether the noun is specific or countable. Frequently used articles are *a, an, the.*

Body: The central section of a paragraph or essay that explains the topic sentence of the paragraph or the thesis statement of the essay.

Brackets: Punctuation marks [ ] used in quoted material to set apart editorial explanations.

Brainstorming: A form of freewriting in which the writer lists thoughts freely, at random.

Chronological order: An organization system for events according to how they occur in order of time. This order is used most often in narratives, process analysis, and cause-effect essays.

Classification: An organization system that divides the subject matter into categories determined by one criterion or basis for grouping.

Clause: A group of related words containing both a subject and a verb. There are two types of clauses: *independent clauses* and *dependent clauses.* **Independent clauses** can stand alone as a complete sentence. A **dependent clause** (or subordinate clause) begins with subordinating words/conjunctions and cannot stand alone as a sentence (see Chapter 9 for more information on dependent clauses).

Clustering: A type of pre-writing in which the writer explores and organizes thoughts in a chart that begins with putting the main topic in a circle in the center of the page, then connecting related ideas (in smaller circles) with lines (branches).

Coherence: A quality in which the relationship between ideas is clear throughout a paragraph or essay.

Colon: A punctuation mark [:] that is most often used to show that a list is following a complete introductory sentence.

Comma: A punctuation mark [,] used for separating ideas, independent clauses, items in a list, and enclosing descriptive phrases.

Comma splice: A sentence containing two independent clauses incorrectly joined by a comma.

Comparison-contrast: An organization system showing similarities and differences between two or more subjects/topics. The organization can be blocked by topic, or point by point by criteria.

Complex sentence: A sentence that contains an independent clause and a dependent clause.

Compound verb (predicate): A predicate (the part of the sentence containing the verb) containing two or more verbs.

Compound sentence: A sentence consisting of two or more independent clauses.

Compound subject: A subject consisting of two or more nouns and/or pronouns joined by a coordinating conjunction.

Conclusion: The last sentence of a paragraph or the last paragraph of an essay, which ties together the preceding ideas and smoothly ends the work.

Conjunction: A joining word or phrase. (See *Coordinating conjunction, Adverbial conjunction* and *Subordinating conjunction.*)

Coordinating conjunction: A word that joins grammatically equal structures. There are seven of these conjunctions: *but, or, yet, for, and, nor, so (BOYFANS).*

Coordination: Joining of two or more grammatically equal structures, most often with a coordinating conjunction or a semicolon.

Countable nouns: Nouns that can be either singular or plural.

Criterion: The method used to classify things (basis for grouping, evaluating, comparing, and contrasting).

Dangling modifier: A descriptive phrase or clause that does not modify (describe) any word or phrase in a sentence.

Dash: Punctuation mark [—] used to set apart parenthetical information that needs more emphasis than would be indicated by parentheses.

Copyright © 2004 by Pearson Education, Inc.

Definition: An organization system that explains the meaning of a term or concept using a variety of strategies (examples, contrast, description, etc.).

Demonstrative pronouns: The demonstrative pronouns (*this, that, these,* and *those*) are used to point out or specify certain people, places, or things.

Dependent clause: A group of words with a subject and verb but which cannot stand alone and must be joined to an independent clause to complete its meaning. Most dependent clauses begin with subordinating conjunctions or relative pronouns.

Direct object: The word or words (usually nouns or pronouns) following and receiving the action of an action verb, or following a preposition.

Editing: One of the final steps in the writing process during which the writer checks over the draft of the essay for misspelled words, grammatical errors, missing words, and other errors.

Essay: An organized written work on a topic in a series of paragraphs, including an *introduction*, which attracts the reader's attention and states the *thesis* of the essay; *body* paragraphs, which present the supporting points of the thesis and develop them with facts, details, and examples; and a *conclusion*, which summarizes the ideas and coherently ends the work.

Exemplification: The use of examples to clarify or illustrate a topic.

Expository writing (exposition): Informative writing, the primary purpose of which is to explain a concept.

Fact: A statement that can be proven to be true.

Fragment: An incomplete sentence because it (1) is missing a subject, a verb, or both; (2) the verb is incomplete; or (3) it is a dependent clause that is not attached to an independent clause.

Freewriting: Writing that is used to explore the author's ideas without concern for grammar, spelling, or organization.

Gerund: The *-ing* form of a verb that functions as a noun in the sentence.

Gerund phrase: A gerund phrase includes a gerund and its completing words.

Helping verb: The part of the verb before the main verb, conveying the most important information about tense or

mood of the verb (examples are forms of *have, be, do, will,* etc.).

Hyphen: A punctuation mark [-] used to join descriptive adjectives before a noun, to join compound words and prefixes, or to separate syllables at the end of a line.

Indefinite pronouns: These pronouns do not refer to a specific person; they refer to general or indeterminate people, places, or things. Examples are *everyone, everybody, someone, somebody, everything, something, nothing, anyone,* etc.

Independent clause: A clause that can stand alone as a sentence, containing a complete subject and verb.

Indirect object: A noun or pronoun following a verb that receives a direct object.

Infinitive phrase: A group of words consisting of *to* plus a verb and its completing words. An infinitive phrase can function as a noun, adjective, or adverb.

Interrupters: Sentences may be interrupted by clauses or phrases that clarify or provide additional meaning. These clauses usually begin with the relative pronouns *who, whom, which,* or *that.* See also *Restrictive clause* and *Nonrestrictive clause.*

Irregular verbs: Many irregular verbs (more than 100 in English) do not form the past tense by adding *-ed* or *-d.* Some verbs do not change form at all, or they form the past tense by changing the spelling of the entire word ("stem-changing verbs").

Linking verb: A verb that does not express action, but links the subject to the word or words that describe the subject. The most common linking verbs are forms of the verb *to be.*

Main verb: The last word in a verb phrase, usually conveying the action of the sentence.

Metaphor: A way to describe a topic in terms of another concept (e.g., love is *a rose*).

Modifier: A word or group of words that functions as an adjective or adverb (providing description).

Narration: A story, usually told in chronological order, that usually builds to a climax and then resolves.

Nonrestrictive clause: A clause that is not essential to complete the meaning of the sentence. If a nonrestrictive

clause is removed from the sentence, the basic meaning of the sentence will remain clear. Because it is nonessential, commas always set off this type of clause.

Noun clause: A clause functioning as a noun, usually beginning with *a, the, what, where why,* or *when.*

Nouns: Words that stand for people, places, or things. They can be singular or plural.

Object: A word or words (usually nouns or pronouns) following action verbs, or following words formed from verbs (*-ing* words, past participles, and infinitives); prepositions; or direct objects/indirect objects.

Paragraph: A group of sentences that discuss/develop a topic.

Parallel construction (parallelism): The repetition of the same grammatical structure for coherence or emphasis.

Paraphrase: The writer restating ideas in his or her own words and sentence structure (not directly quoting another author's words).

Parentheses: A mark of punctuation [( )] used to set off specific details giving additional information, explanations, or qualifications of the main idea in a sentence. This would include words, dates, or statements.

Participle: A verb form ending in *-ed* or *-ing,* used as an adjective or used with helping verbs to form present perfect or past perfect forms.

Participial phrase: A group of words (verb phrase) consisting of a participle and its completing words which can function as an adjective or adjective phrase. Participles also are used with helping verbs to clarify tense or voice. All verbs have present participle and past participle forms.

Passive voice: A verb form chosen when the actor of the sentence is not important or when the writer wishes to avoid naming the subject. In the passive voice, the object of an active verb becomes the subject of the passive verb. The form of the verb becomes *be* + past participle.

Past continuous (progressive) tense: A verb tense showing an action in progress in the past, formed from helping verbs *was/were* and adding *-ing* to the verb form.

Past perfect tense: A verb tense used to describe a past action or event occurring prior to a later time in the past.

The past perfect is formed from *had* + the verb's past participle form.

Past tense: A verb tense used to discuss completed past actions. All *regular* past tense verbs end in *–ed*. However, there are more than 100 *irregular* verbs (see The Writer's Resources).

Period: A punctuation mark [.] that is used to end a complete statement or is included in an abbreviation.

Personal pronouns: Those pronouns which refer to a person (*I/me, you, he/him, she/her, it, we/us,* and *they/them*). They are divided into three forms, depending on how they are used in a sentence. These forms are *subjective* (pronoun used as a subject), *objective* (pronoun used as an object), or *possessive* (pronoun indicates possession/ownership).

Personification: Giving human characteristics to non-human or inanimate objects (e.g., *The wind howled all through the night.*).

Phrasal verb: A two-word or three-word expression that combines a verb with another word, changing the meaning (e.g., *pick it up*).

Phrase: A group of related words missing a subject, verb, or both subject and verb. Phrases are used in sentences to complete thoughts or add descriptive detail; they may be restrictive or non-restrictive (see Additional Punctuation Rules, Interrupters in The Writer's Resources). There are several types of phrases used as modifiers in sentences: *prepositional phrases, participial phrases, gerund phrases, infinitive phrases,* and *absolute phrases.*

Predicate: The part of the sentence containing the verb, making a statement or asking a question about the subject.

Prepositional phrase: A **preposition** connects a noun or pronoun to the rest of the sentence, often showing location or time. A **prepositional phrase** contains a preposition (e.g., *in, on, over, before, after,* etc.) and its object.

Present continuous (progressive) tense: A verb tense that discusses actions that are happening now or are planned for the future. This tense is formed by adding a form of the verb *to be* (*is, am, are*) with the verb + *ing.*

Present perfect tense: A verb tense used to describe an action or condition in the past that continues up to the present. The tense is formed by combining *has/have* + the past participle.

Present tense: A verb tense used to discuss habitual actions, facts, or conditions that are true of the present.

Pre-writing: The step in the writing process in which the writer thinks about the topic, purpose, and audience, and explores ideas for development through **brainstorming, clustering,** or **freewriting.**

Process analysis: An organizational structure that explains how to do something or how something works.

Pronoun: A word that takes the place of, or refers to, nouns. The word or words that the pronoun refers to are known as the **antecedent(s)** of the pronoun. Pronouns can be divided into several categories. The most common categories are *personal pronouns, relative pronouns, demonstrative pronouns, indefinite pronouns,* and *reflexive pronouns.*

Question mark: A punctuation mark [?] that ends direct questions.

Reflexive pronouns: The reflexive form adds *–self* or *–selves* to the pronoun and is used to indicate action performed to or on the antecedent.

Regular verb: A verb ending in *–ed* in the past tense or past participle, or forming its third person singular form by adding *–s* or *–es.*

Relative clause: A clause that functions like an adjective, beginning with a **relative pronoun** (*who, whom, which, that*).

Relative pronouns: Those pronouns used to introduce a qualifying or explanatory clause (*who, whom, which, that, whoever, whichever*).

Restrictive clause: Clause that is essential to identify a noun or to complete the meaning. This type of clause simply follows the noun or idea it is modifying. No commas are used to set off restrictive clauses.

Run-on sentence: A sentence containing two independent clauses with nothing that joins them together (a serious grammatical error).

Semicolon: A mark of punctuation [;] that usually joins two independent clauses, or occasionally separates items in a series containing internal commas.

Sentence: A complete statement or question containing a subject, a verb, and expressing a complete thought.

Simile: A comparison using *like* or *as* (e.g., my love is *like a rose*).

Simple sentence: A group of words with a subject and verb, expressing complete meaning.

Subject: The topic (who or what) about which a clause makes a statement or asks a question. Usually the subject is a noun or pronoun, and usually the subject precedes the verb.

Subject-verb agreement: Subjects and verbs in the present tense (as well as in the past and future tenses) should agree in number. Thus, singular subjects require verbs with singular endings, and plural subjects require verbs with plural endings.

Subordinating conjunction: A word that joins two clauses by making one clause less in importance and dependent on the second (independent) clause. (Examples: *although, after, because, while,* etc.) See The Writer's Resources for more information.

Subordination: Joining a dependent clause to an independent clause.

Synonym: A word with the same, or close to the same, meaning as another word.

Tense: The form of the verb that shows when in time an action occurred (present, past, future). See The Writer's Resources for more information.

Thesis statement: The sentence, usually included in the introduction, which states the main idea of the essay, and often outlines the subtopics of the essay **(essay map).**

Topic sentence: A sentence stating the main idea of a paragraph.

Transitional word: A word explaining how or in what way two ideas are related. These are often *adverbial conjunctions* (see *Adverbial conjunctions*).

Uncountable nouns: Nouns that represent an idea or concept that cannot be counted (e.g., water, air, fruit), and cannot be made plural.

Verb: A word indicating action, feeling, or being; verbs can be divided into three classes: *action verbs, linking verbs,* and *helping verbs* (see Chapter 3). Additionally the form of the verb can indicate the time of the action: **present, past,** or **future** (also known as **tense**).

Copyright © 2004 by Pearson Education, Inc.

CREDITS

Text Credits

Basic Article Usage, from Betty Schrampfer Azar, *Understanding and Using English Grammar, 2/e*. Reprinted by permission of Pearson Education.

"Conversational Ballgames" by Nancy Masterson Sakamoto from Kinsiedo, Ltd., 1982. Reprinted by permission of the author.

"The Culture of Violence," from *Boys Will Be Boys* by Myriam Miedzian. Copyright © 1991 by Myriam Miedzian. Used by permission of Doubleday, a division of Random House, Inc.

"Cyberspace: If You Don't Love It, Leave It," by Esther Dyson as appeared in *The New York Times*, July 17, 1995. Copyright © 1995 by The New York Times Co. Reprinted by permission.

"Discrimination is a Virtue," by Robert Keith Miller. *Newsweek*, 1980.

"The Eye of the Beholder" by Grace Suh. Copyright © 1992. Reprinted by permission of the author. First appeared in *A Magazine*, 1992.

Forms of Yes/No & Information Questions, from Betty Schrampfer Azar, *Understanding and Using English Grammar, 2/e*. Reprinted by permission of Pearson Education.

"Grant and Lee: A Study in Contrasts" by Bruce Catton from *The American Story*, Earl Schneck Miers, editor. Capitol Historical Society. Reprinted by permission of the United States Capitol Historical Society.

"The Handicap of Definition" by William Raspberry. Copyright © 1982, The Washington Post Writers Group. Reprinted by permission.

"Hasta La Vista, Arnold" by Margaret Talbot. *Vogue*, May 1997.

"Heroine Worship: The Age of the Female Icon" by Holly Brubach as appeared in *The New York Times*, November, 24, 1996. Copyright © 1996 by The New York Times Co. Reprinted by permission.

"The Ice Cream Truck" from *Always Running-La Vida Loca, Gang Days in L.A.* by Luis J. Rodriquez. (Curbstone Press, 1993) Reprinted by permission of Curbstone Press. Distributed by Consortium.

Irregular Verbs, from Betty Schrampfer Azar, *Understanding and Using English Grammar, 2/e*. Reprinted by permission of Pearson Education.

"Making the Grades: How to Cram" by Jill Young Miller, *Campus Voice*, Fall 1987. Copyright © 1987 by Jill Young Miller. Reprinted by permission of the author.

"The Mute Sense," from *A Natural History of the Senses* by Diane Ackerman. Copyright © 1990 by Diane Ackerman. Reprinted by permission of Random House, Inc.

Phrasal Verbs, from Betty Schrampfer Azar, *Understanding and Using English Grammar, 2/e*. Reprinted by permission of Pearson Education.

"The Plot Against People," by Russell Baker as appeared in *The New York Times,* June 18, 1998. Copyright © 2000 by The New York Times Co. Reprinted by permission.

Preposition Combinations with Adjectives and Verbs from Betty Schrampfer Azar, *Understanding and Using English Grammar, 2/e.* Reprinted by permission of Pearson Education.

Prepositions and Prepositional Phrases, from Betty Schrampfer Azar, *Understanding and Using English Grammar, 2/e.* Reprinted by permission of Pearson Education.

Question Words, from Betty Schrampfer Azar, *Understanding and Using English Grammar, 2/e.* Reprinted by permission of Pearson Education.

"Relatively Speaking" by Jan Borst from *Newsweek,* July 22, 1996. Copyright © 1996 Newsweek, Inc. All rights reserved. Reprinted by permission.

"The Revolt of the Black Bourgeoisie," by Leonce Gaiter as appeared in *The New York Times,* June 26, 1994. Copyright © 1995 by The New York Times Co. Reprinted by permission.

From *The Vanishing Hitchhiker: American Urban Legends and Their Meanings* by Jan Harold Brunvand. Copyright © 1981 by Jan Harold Brunvand. Used by permission of W.W. Norton & Company, Inc.

Photo Credits

P. 3, Kevin Radford/SuperStock; p. 4, Chris Minerva/Index Stock Imagery; p. 4, Jerry S. Mendoza/AP/Wide World Photos; p. 4, Paula Lerner/Index Stock Imagery; p. 4, Ed Lallo/Index Stock Imagery; p. 24, Mark J. Terrill/AP/Wide World Photos; p. 51, Tom Rosenthal/SuperStock; p. 83, William H. Mullins/Photo Researchers, Inc.; p. 118, Hulton/Archive/Getty Images; p. 133, Michael Dwyer/AP/Wide World Photos; p. 152, Jeff Greenberg/Photo Researchers, Inc.; p. 154, J. Pat Carter/AP/Wide World Photos; p. 171, Jeff Vanuga/Corbis; p. 173, Don Ryan/AP/Wide World Photos; p. 186, Sandy King/The Image Bank/Getty Images; p. 188, Jim Mone/AP/Wide World Photos; p. 200, Bob Kramer/Index Stock Imagery; p. 202, Ed Betz/AP/Wide World Photos; p. 215, Harry Cabluck/AP/Wide World Photos; p. 215, Paul Warner/AP/Wide World Photos; p. 216, Monika Graff/The Image Works; p. 228, A. Ramey/PhotoEdit, Inc.; p. 230, Corbis; p. 245, SuperStock; p. 247, Justin Sullivan/Getty Images; p. 257, National Gallery of Art, Washington, D.C./ © Photothèque R. Magritte-ADAGP/Art Resource, NY; p. 259, Ulrike Welsch/Photo Researchers, Inc.; p. 280, Walter Bibikow/Index Stock Imagery; p. 285, Stock Image/SuperStock; p. 306, Laura Rauch/AP/Wide World Photos.

Copyright © 2004 by Pearson Education, Inc.

INDEX

Copyright © 2004 by Pearson Education, Inc.